MW00962659

TIPTOE THROUGH THE SNOWDROPS

BY

BOB CRAVEN

1663 LIBERTY DRIVE, SUITE 200
BLOOMINGTON, INDIANA 47403
(800) 839-8640
WWW.AUTHORHOUSE.COM

© *2004 BOB CRAVEN.*
All Rights Reserved.

No part of this book may be reproduced, stored in a retrieval system, or transmitted by any means without the written permission of the author.

First published by AuthorHouse 10/07/04

ISBN: 1-4184-8023-1 (e)
ISBN: 1-4184-8022-3 (sc)

Printed in the United States of America
Bloomington, Indiana

This book is printed on acid-free paper.

TABLE OF CONTENTS

ACKNOWLEDGMENT

To Dorothy

My life, my love, my best friend, nurse and counsellor.

You have given so much and received so little.

I can never thank you enough.

Greatest of thanks to:

my many friends for their patience and understanding,

Neil Gosling for the Images,

Andy Pond for the Cover Graphics

and

Judy's Snowdrops of Rugby for the Cover Photo

INTRODUCTION

Countless Police Officers have told their story but "Tiptoe" is the first that takes the reader through a career, so full of promise and fulfilment of a dream, but is eventually and totally destroyed by the catastrophic physical effects and mental anguish of post-traumatic stress disorder.

PTSD, as it is commonly known, is a disability where the brain and associated bodily functions of a victim re-visit the memory of a traumatic incident in all its horrific detail.

This is my story from 1967 when I joined the "Snowdrops", The Southend on Sea Borough Constabulary as an enthusiastic, happy-go-lucky young Police Constable with high expectations and noble intentions, to the trendy 70's detective and the CID.

Through the disjointed and uncoordinated efforts of the Regional Crime Squad and other Law Enforcement Agencies, to politically sensitive duties as one of the first Detective Inspectors in the newly formed National Criminal Intelligence Service, the UK FBI, in the 1990's.

In between, attacked by a gang of skinheads after a shop raid, kicked to a pulp by a shoplifter, carried on the bonnet of a stolen car having a leg broken by passing vehicles whilst being shot at by my own side and being hung by a rope round the neck from the balustrade of a fifth floor landing whilst on a drugs operation.

It describes how it feels to be a victim of crime, suffering the inadequacies of the then Police Welfare system and the demeaning taunts and jibes of the bigoted with little knowledge of the complaint.

Being ignominiously retired early from the Police Service, disabled without any official support, forced to grab any work capable of providing much needed income, to alleviate the financial ruin that premature, forced, early and unplanned retirement brings.

More importantly it explains to those, less informed, what it really means to suffer from post-traumatic stress, and hopefully assists them to understand the disorder and perhaps help others to avoid its debilitating effects.

Writing Tiptoe has been a painfully slow and difficult passage lasting over 8 years. It could not have been completed without the help and caring support of my loving wife, Dorothy, our daughters, Clare and Karen, and their husbands, Simon and Mike.

My best friend, David Westoby has been at my side throughout this difficult time and with the help of many of my close friends has given some semblance of order to the book. Therapeutic it also closes a cherished chapter of my life.

This is not a literary masterpiece, it is my story told by me in the only way I know how, as I speak it and emotionally suffer it. In that light I make no apology for its content and minor mistakes.

It will leave a legacy for future generations to learn from my experience.

PICTURES

A Snowdrop - 1969

Daily Sketch Front Page - May 1970

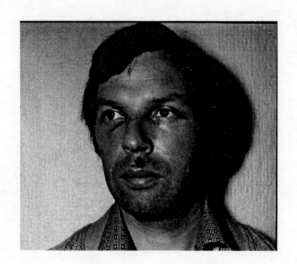

Facial Injuries - 1978

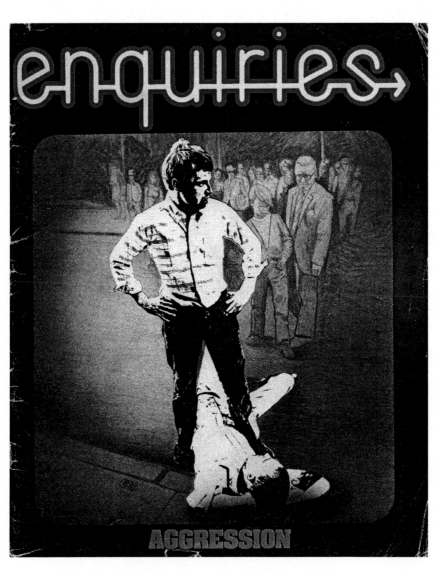

Enquiries Book Front Page - 1984

research

- What do you think of these views?

- What are the alternatives?

- What is the Christian point of view on this matter? What did Jesus Christ say about non-violence? If you don't know, refer to Matthew chapter 5, verses 5, 7, 9, 10–12, and 38–48. Which part of the Lord's Prayer is relevant here?

  You could invite a Christian minister to talk to you on these questions.

43

Enquiries Book Page 43 – 1984

Children, Police, Business and Sport in Unison

Dressed for the Occasion

LETTER FROM A FRIEND

Bob, now 57, sits with his head bowed sobbing uncontrollably, why, he can't tell me. He is ill, diagnosed as suffering from Post Traumatic Stress Disorder some eleven years ago. It may be hard to believe but in fact he's a lot better these days.

I've known Bob Craven since he joined the Police in 1967, we served together as young constables and I'd describe him then and now as my best mate. As a detective Bob had the sort of police career of which TV series are made. However this brought with it an unusual number of traumatic experiences, viciously beaten on five occasions, carried on the bonnet of a getaway car his leg smashing into a passing truck, shot at by his own side and hung over a fifth floor balcony with a noose around his neck, not your every day copper.

Initially Bob cleverly hid the symptoms but slowly they took their effect, changing his life from a dedicated family man, charity fundraiser and first class detective to what was to become a living hell. After 26 dedicated years, having clawed his way to the rank of Detective Inspector, he was forced to leave the job he loved, left to try and understand and deal with his illness.

This remarkable story details the fascinating career and the slow destruction of Bob's life, but it also demonstrates Bob's desire to ensure others do not go through the hell he still experiences.

You will not be able to read this book without thinking 'BLOODY HELL'.

David B Westoby

Retired Detective Chief Inspector - Essex Police

LETTER FROM KAREN AND CLARE

This is our Dad's story. The story in itself astounds … being about our very own dad pushes it to the limit.

Stories in the book conjure up memories that have long faded. Now it seems strange to think of those and how they affected my Dad's life. Perhaps comparable to being on holiday when you expect life at home to stand still, I never really thought of his work. It seemed so far away. I just ploughed on with my own very important existence as a teenager and young adult. My sister and I were never made aware of the extreme situations he dealt with. Only now I reflect on what I thought was a comfortable suburban lifestyle in a very different way. My Mum's question at the dinner table "had a nice day at the office dear?" seems quite ridiculous.

Since reading the book, I look at people differently - passengers on my train journey to work, diners in restaurants, families' at the park. Most are oblivious, as my sister and I were, to the input and consequences caused by police officers' duties. Many people complain of the errors made or lack of efficiency by the police forces, rarely taking time to evaluate how the very same people improve the quality of the community and protect families from harm, directly or indirectly. All are away on their own little holidays until, of course, they become targets of crime themselves and are in need of police assistance. Somewhat comparable to peoples' ignorance in the film Men in Black of Will Smith's and Tommy Lee Jones's dedication to protect citizens from villainous aliens!! Hopefully this book will go someway in closing that gap.

Yes this is my Dad's story but I am sure so many other service men have similar stories of dedication. The other extreme, of course, are those who pushed paper all their careers and those who were carried on the wake of other's hard work. My Dad's shear dedication to uphold the law in order to provide a safer place for families is astounding. His story brings to light the commitment of police officers and the consequences they, and their families, suffer as a result of them.

Dad through his devotion is, some would say, only part of the man he used to be. Only now do I understand how much the role has shaped his character and personality. But after everything, all of his good qualities remain – loving, determined, damn right entertaining to the extent of being, well, a bit mad. To the latter Dad would remark "…in all ways really"!!

Most of our lives, my sister and I have placed Dad on a pedestal only to realize now that both he and Mum (due to her unremitting support) are worthy of the very one Nelson stands on in Trafalgar Square.

Upon that pedestal though they both cling to each other. Carefully they balance the disappointment of broken dreams with their need to achieve some normality. Somehow dealing with the constant dread of teetering off ……

Karen and Clare

XXXXXXXXXXXX

Chapter One
DID IT HAVE TO END LIKE THIS

November 2001 once again I am at the doctor's surgery mind going wild, shaking and shivering, sweating, weeping and snivelling, having vomited and crapped seemingly continuously for several days. Life is like living in a box, not being able to get out. With a head full of cotton wool, surrounded by people with muffled voices. Always distorted. Frustratingly never clear, never making sense. Desperately hoping for some respite but always so far from it.

Crying also and clinging to me was my dearest friend, nurse, comforter and love of my life, Dorothy, my wife. Gently reassuring me "It will pass as it always does Bob. Just hang on". She has been there for me so many times. For years before when things were not so bad she washed my blood stained clothes and supported me after I had broke bones or was going through the pain from other injuries. She never moaned or complained and was always there to mop up after the each incident.

Even though her personal hopes had been dashed so many times. Here she was providing her undoubting comfort and support to her miserable weak snivelling wreck of a husband.

My GP sympathetically and in a reassuring tone said, "You know that it is permanent, the surge of enzymes in your brain is telling you to slow down. You are obviously at the stage where you need help to control your problem. Take it from me you have to be selfish and think of yourself. Pills can help". The GP was the seventh in a long line of Doctors and specialists who I had seen since 1993 when I was first diagnosed as suffering from PTSD. This debilitating illness had only been recognised in the Police Service and Armed Forces in recent years and many GP's still did not have first hand knowledge of the problem. This softly spoken middle-aged Asian lady Doctor gave me that confidence that at this stage I desperately needed to get me out of the mess I was in.

"I do not want pills", I retorted angrily. "They make me worse. When I took them before I was like a zombie. I lost more of my life. I have been able to control this myself without them. The flashbacks are still there and I never know when they are going to happen. They leave me so drained".

"Yes", she replied firmly, "But you can only continue like that for a short time. You are putting your brain and body under extreme pressure. It could have far serious consequences. According to your notes, more qualified Consultants have told you about the problems that this can cause. Haven't they? The drugs that are now available help to balance your mind and relax your anxiety. I think you should give them a try and perhaps some sleeping pills to help you get a good nights' sleep"

I reluctantly agreed nodding. I was so exhausted. I had had great difficulty keeping control of myself and concentrating at work. Even simple tasks were impossible.

"A complete rest and slowing down will help to recharge your batteries", said the doctor, "But take one day at a time to get the balance right first, then see what you can do".

It did not take much time for me to realise that we were back where we were in 1993.

We came away from the surgery, in a stunned silence with the realisation that our lives and all the aspirations we had of getting ourselves back on our feet were dashed yet again.

I knew that stopping all work would have a devastating affect on our finances but I had to admit that this was the only course I could take to stop me from going completely insane. All the stuffing had been knocked out of me and I had to run the white flag up.

I could feel that Dorothy knew and even wanted for me to say this. Without talking we cried all the way back home.

Our two daughters, Clare and Karen, came round that night, determined to give their opinions that they had obviously sorted out before coming round. I felt a sincere and deeply worried tone to their voices when asked, "What are you going to do now?"

I answered, "I don't think I have any alternative but to pack up work completely".

"And all the other stuff like NARPO?" they questioned. "You've got to Dad. We are very worried about you both. You are worn out. You will be all right. We are here to help in what way we can. It's just as well you decided to pack up work as we were going to be very insistent that you did", they fired at me in quick succession.

Then a broadside, "You've got the garden, the seafront, your bike and you could write that book you have always gone on about!"

Over the following days and weeks I started to put together the personal notes I had written in self counselling therapy. Also trying to put some sense in my own mind to what had happened to me, why it had happened and perhaps identifying whether I could have prevented it.

Chapter Two
THE FIRST DAYS

It did not seem that long ago in October 1967 when I left home to report for my first day as a fully fledged officer of the law, probationer constable of course.

MARCHING INTO THE UNKNOWN

I was cruise-marching with the swaggering step acquired at Eynsham Hall, the police training school near Witney in the heart of Oxfordshire. Momentarily I was back on the parade ground swinging along to the many marching songs that echoed off the old brown grey stonewalls of that magnificent country house that was my prison for the previous thirteen weeks. The Guards marching pace was the excepted style because the drill pig was ex-Guards. Thankfully he was not an ex-Green Jacket soldiers who used to march on the run. We made a big enough cock up of it at the slower rate. Hell only knows what mess we would have been in at the passing out parade.

It did not help that we had been on the booze until 5.00 am that morning. I had woken up at that time still lying under the beer barrel in the main dining room with tap immediately above my open mouth which by then had a dried up with a foamy crust around it.

Immediately in front of me in our marching Class of 1967 was "Gunsight" Graham of the Mid Anglia Constabulary. A ginger six foot four inch thin bloke who got the name after the first time we all had a communal shower after the torturous physical training we had to endure. The drill pig who was also the PE and Defence Training Instructor took great delight in destroying every bone and muscle of ones body, even the fittest sportsman like me until you dropped to crawling on hands and knees with every bodily extremity and nerve ending shook uncontrollably in a tensed fit of expended energy.

In the shower, a short Essex Constabulary man, had dropped to his knees and came face to face with Grahams penis. "What the f… is that?" he shouted with eyes widened in both total awe and disbelief. "Ohh Arr". Graham replied in his Norfolk droll, "Haven't you seen a large prick before?"

"It's bleeding large but what's that on it?" gasped Andy. "Its what I call my gunsight. It's only a wart. I was going to have it cut off at one time. But a few girlfriends have said it tickles the parts that other pricks don't and they have been very delighted. The size and no doubt the design of his appendage convinced us of the truth to his claim. So he got the label "Gunsight".

He had proved his qualities with Ruby, one of the youngest cleaners at the school. She had gratefully received his attentions throughout the course term and behind the curtain to the rear of my resting place under the barrel the night before the parade. I remembered the sounds of what I thought was the barrel emptying but realised that the beer had stopped flowing and the it was the noise of a Mid Anglia man making a pig of himself with Ruby who occasionally gurgled with delight and sighing with contentment.

On the parade I noticed that Gunsight was walking as if he was dragging his crutch on the ground and that Ruby was standing very bandily legged and rosy cheeked in the crowd of parents and well wishers.

He had a job keeping step and his pole like legs were all over the place like a rampant spider. It did not take long for him to trip up the stupoured Andy in front who was worse the wear for drink.

It did not help that I was in charge of the School Bar for the last week of the Course. It was supposed to be a punishment for getting dust on my trousers. The bastard of a Deputy Commandant gave me jankers as they called it. My boot had rubbed down my trousers when I had come to attention on the morning inspection parade. The trousers that had been issued to me on my joining date, Friday the 13th July 1967, would you believe it, were so full they went with the area known for its 1930's Oxford bags.

Any way, he gave me extra duties but fortunately my course instructor who was duty Sergeant that week took pity on me and gave me the Bar Duties. Basically I had to serve the drinks to all students every night. So many insisted on buying me a drink that I rarely remembered going to bed. Except, one night, when I got the wrong room. In the nick of time I heard snoring coming from the bed and to my dismay saw the drill pig in the bed. He obviously heard someone come and suddenly go out. I heard him whining "Trubshaw just one more blow-job. Pleeease? Trubshaw was one the training course before me. A burly bloke built like a brick shithouse rugby scrum half from the Bucks Constabulary. Obviously a Madam, he put me off rugby for life.

I did stay awake that night for fear of a visitation from the scrum half or the drill pig. And I kept my tightly belted trousers on in bed in case I slipped into a foolhardy sleep.

Although I felt jaded at the start of the parade. The sudden movement out of the ordinary in front caused me to fall over Gunsight, on top of Andy and then in my efforts to carry on marching veered to the right and took out the column on that side which just happened to be in front of the dignitaries' platform.

In true disciplined fashion we picked ourselves up immediately except Humphrey, the weight lifter, from the City of London, who round shaped like a weeble was like a little man from a budgies cage who had great difficulty converting to the upright position.

All ended peacefully, the Deputy Commandant couldn't find any of us to shout his disgust and the drill pig had found out that I knew his secret. So I got a glowing end of course report on that Friday.

It was now the Monday after and I am strutting my stuff towards my first days of duty.

My brain continued to blast out as I came back to concentrate on my march.

"We must have safety on the Queens highway
Look left, look right, and look left again".

Out of my parents high rise flat at Porters Grange, down the new road, Queensway, in the County Borough of Southend-on-Sea towards Victoria Circus, being developed into a shopping centre, in the full uniform of the Southend on Sea Borough Constabulary. This is it I thought, with immense anticipation, my first day as that shining knight who would save Southend from all harm and make it a safer place for all the wonderful people who live in this glorious seaside town.

"It's a long way to Tipperary
It's a long way to go"

20 years of age, highly trained and fighting fit. I felt like the cats whiskers as I strode into Victoria Avenue in the direction of the Police Station. At 9.00 am in the morning the tree-lined road was thronging with office workers, college students and others scurrying to their various destinations. Holding my large sports bag in my left hand, swinging my right arm in pace with my left foot to the regulation shoulder level of the imaginary marcher in front and leaving it free to salute senior officers, civic dignitaries, royalty, funeral hearses out of respect to the deceased and in the training sergeants words, "anyone else you want to suck up to if you're into career development but never ever an acting Inspector, Salute the uniform not the pratt in it". I was ready and confidently tuned to take command and deal with any emergency or incident that presented itself.

"Hitler he only had one Ball
Hitler he only had one ball"

The early autumn air was cool and clean, just as me. I was ten feet tall and could take on the world.

Like magic the crowds would part to allow me free passage. Whereas normally individuals would have to tussle and weave to make headway through, a uniformed Police Officer was given the courtesy of his own road. It was as if nobody dared touch him or brush against him for fear of being accused of assaulting him. Or could it be just sheer respect?

"All of a sudden a dirty great puddin' came flying through the air
Oh what a pity she only had one titty to feed the baby on"

A few comments passed between people as I passed, "Don't coppers look so young these days" and "He is only a kid" and then suddenly "Here they come. The bloody snowdrops!"

"All the nice boys love a sailor
All the nice boys love a tar
All the nice boys love a candle
Well you know what sailors are
Slips' in easy…………….."

It seemed only for a split second that I looked down to my bulled-up boots when the crowd parted as usual and I hit a blue serge chest festooned with medal ribbons against which my nose was now pressing. The massive frame towered above me forcing me to step backwards to take in the whole view of the obstruction.

As I did so the extremely white large stripes appeared to blind my vision like two lasers from either side of the body. A bloody Sergeant, a God, oh shit!

"And who the hell are you" the wall retorted. "What you doing prancing along like a fairy?" I must have forgot myself and put a bit too much into my swagger. Christ! I hope it doesn't know the drill pig or play rugby.

"Where is your white helmet? Dark helmets are only worn at night till after illuminations are stopped", he irritated waiting for a reply.

I had removed my right nostril from his metal war medal ribbon by this time and risked a reply. The trouble was that at training school you had to shout any response to a Senior Officer, especially a very big Sergeant. I shouted reply at the top of my voice, "**APOLOGIES SERGEANT BUT IT IS MY FIRST DAY FROM TRAINING SCHOOL AND I HAVE NOT GOT A WHITE HELMET**".

I did get a little bit annoyed when an old lady standing nearby said to her friend, "Shame he's probably only got a pink one being a young lad".

9

BOB CRAVEN

The Sergeant pulled me to him by the lapel. It did cross my mind that he may know the drill pig and he was going to kiss me but this was scotched as he whispered abruptly, "Are you taking the piss, son or just trying to make me look a fool. Either way you could be in fucking trouble! Get on with you and always wear civvies to and from the station when off duty." I replied loudly, "**YES.**" He pulled me shutting me up, "There is no need to shout anymore. You are in the real world now. We all have normal hearing".

ENTER THE SNOWDROPS

I then saw behind him a line of uniformed bobbies all in the whitest helmets, smart pressed uniforms, shining chrome silver buttons, belt buckles, whistle chains and the Borough crest, the Monk and the Fisherman, on their lapels.

The Monk signified the close proximity of the Priory that was situated in the north of the town until it was demolished by Henry the VIII's lot. The Fisherman for the age old profession that continued to work from a jetty near our Pier, the longest in the world, and the cocklers at Old Leigh just up river.

Historically these were the beginnings of Southend that probably started with the Priory and St Mary's Church. But spread southwards to the Thames Estuary, east to the fringes of Foulness Island, west to Hadleigh and Rayleigh and north to Rochford. Now a slither of town about three miles wide by 8 miles long accommodating 150,000 people and on average the same number of day trippers to the "Golden Mile" pleasure seafront and nearby beaches. There were countless pubs, dance halls and the centre for entertainment for the county of Essex and the East End of London. Potentially loads of fun for the young copper who was born and bred here.

Marching on to the Police Station, with a less exaggerated swagger I left the clatter of the public domain to retreat into the tranquillity of the Front Office. The front door was opened to reveal at first a beautiful display of flowers in the stairwell opposite.

To the right, at a counter, the Station Sergeant was engaged in a meaningful conversation with a young man, "I haven't got time to listen to you. If you haven't left this station by the time I have rolled my sleeves up. I will throw you out".

"But Sergeant. I have been subjected to police brutality. I wish to complain". Cried the very posh talking youth.

"You were creating a disturbance in the High Street", accused the Sergeant.

"Yes I know, but I do not think that deserved me being transported to the far end of Foulness Island and made to walk back!" pleaded the youth.

"Why not?" the Sergeant queried with eyebrows curled.

"It is over 15 bloody miles! It is totally wrong. My father is a Councillor and he would not like it " blurted the youth.

"Would your father prefer that you went to Court for Breach of The Peace and have your name plastered all over the papers?" scoffed the Sergeant.

The youth stepped back as his mini skirted girlfriend, with blond "Mary Quant" style hair, thick black eyeliner, highline boots and floppy hat, exclaimed, "Would he have his picture in the paper as well?"

The Sergeant, realising he had an unwitting ally, gave them a parental look saying, " Really think about the consequences of making a complaint. Sir and (acknowledging the young lady) Madam?" The pair gave him the shortest nod and the Sergeant softly continued, "I think you have made a wise decision. Take this booklet should you want to complain. We are always at your service"

The hunched dissatisfied couple dragged themselves out of the station and the Sergeants gaze turned to me. "Have you lost something Constable?" Stopping myself at the last moment from shouting I replied, "I am supposed to report to the Divisional Sergeants office". "Through the double doors and first on your right.

It seemed so different from when I was last here before training school and on interview days. The double doors led into a corridor that from the cool calm of the front office just buzzed with excitement and anticipation. Typewriters clattered, telephones rang loud and continuous, voices everywhere shouting, advising, and ordering, uniformed officers scurrying from office to office with clutched papers.

I had arrived at the inner sanctum, the temple of crime fighters and defenders of the law, the round table of the Borough Knights.

"New recruit? What's your name then lad?" came a voice from the left. "Craven.........Sir" as I then realised it was an Inspector. Still in momentary shock I went to salute but before I could raise my hand he grabbed hold of it and shook it firmly. "Heard about you, good footballer. Come back and see me to sign for our team. Report upstairs to training. They will sort you out." Yes sir. Thank you", I shakily replied.

I left the hive of industry corridor and went through the next set of double doors into a stairwell that led to the upper floors.

My mind went back to the very first time I had climbed these stairs. I had successfully gained an interview to become a Police Cadet and had come with a number of other young teenage candidates. We were all dressed smartly in differing items of fashionable attire for the sixties. There was one boy, portly built, slicked back black curly hair, taller than the rest who inspected the rest of us. Looking us up and down he said to one boy "You won't get in your hair is too long", to another, " Your ties too loud", and to me, " You haven't got turn-ups mate". I am sure we all thought the same, "I hope you don't get the job!" Guess what, the bastard did get it!

A few months later I was at Victor Sylvester's' Dance hall above the Odeon in the High Street when a fight took place and this same boy drew a knife on another. I went up too him after the situation had cooled down and told him that that behaviour was not expected from a bloke in his profession. A short time later I found out that he had been sacked from the Police and was driving a train on the Pier.

TRAINING AND SALUTES

Up the stairs I climbed to the second floor and the training department, going through another set of double doors I passed the Sports Club and Welfare Department. I glanced through the open door and was stunned to see a rotund gentleman with a handle moustache and dressed in an impeccably smart grey suit. He was standing to attention in front of a full-length mirror and in one movement putting his left arm forward in a pulling motion and saluting at the same time with his right arm. I heard the words "Welcome your Majesty. Please be careful of the step" coming from his stiffened lips.

"Don't worry about him. He's not gone mad", a voice said from the training room. I turned to see the Training Sergeant who had seen me through the first days of joining. "He's practising opening the car door for the Queen Mum when she comes to open the Civic Centre in a few weeks", he continued. "Craven isn't it?"

"Yes. Sergeant?" I replied a little suspiciously as he had taken my details of height, weight and so on when I joined. The height measurement stick on the wall had been inadvertently pushed upwards above the qualifying 5 foot 10 inch requirement for the Borough Force. I was only 5 foot 91/2 inches at the time and about to become the shortest copper in the Borough Force. He had asked at the time if I was sure that I had been accepted and checked my job offer letter accordingly. I still don't think he was convinced!

"You are the last to arrive. Go in and sit with the others", he said pointing towards the training classroom from where the clatter of familiar banter was coming.

My five "wet behind the ears" probationer constable mates who all joined on the same day were seated and engaged in excited conversation about the future days. Left behind were the memories of the training course at Eynsham although much of the banter was due to the experiences we had suffered at the hands of the drill pig and PE Instructor.

There was the ex-Guardsman and greatest singer (so he thought) on the course. He spent a lot of his time standing on a bar stall singing his songs from the musicals. We spent most of our time buying him drinks to make him drunk and stop singing.

Next to him sat the up right, very well spoken and Old Westcliffian High School boy, ex-Boys Brigade member like me and ex Police Cadet. Thoroughly decent chap!

Behind him was our articulate but a bit serious fellow who was excellent company and some years later left the force to become a priest.

Next to him sat another ex-army bloke who was the son of a serving police constable who was always meticulously smart. By coincidence, some years before I had gone out with a girl who he considered to be his. Never did tell him, irrelevant detail, besides he was much bigger than me. He later left to become a security officer for a large tobacco firm.

Beside him was the ex-Fords worker, very quiet but a smashing bloke and good friend like all the others. He left the Force to return to Fords but rejoined and worked through to be a Superintendent.

The Training Sergeant breezed into the room holding a clipboard with numerous papers attached", right, this week is your local procedure course and settling in time to equip you for your role as constables in the Southend-on-Sea Constabulary. You will all know the definition of "A Constable" and all the other ones for the offences in the Larceny Act and all other legislation". Beckoning his hands at us he said, "Come on then let me hear the definition of this auspicious office you are to are about to perform. All together, "A constable is…"

In parrot fashion we took up the challenge, virtually singing, "A Constable is a citizen, locally appointed, having authority under the Crown for the protection of life and property, the maintenance of order and the prosecution of offenders against the peace".

I drifted as endless hours, came back to me, of pounding round the beautiful gardens and grounds of Eynsham Hall with all the others mumbling to ourselves the stream of verbatim definitions on every conceivable Act of Parliament we were expected to implement on duty.

"Well the good news is that as you have all completed your initial course, I am sure you all know your definitions", announced the Sgt. "Yes sarge", we all echoed back. He paused and then continued with a frown, "But the bad news is that the Larceny Act is being repealed and a new Theft Act comes into force in January so you have got to learn a whole load of new definitions for that!" he retorted with a self amused smile.

Bloody hell what terrific planning, I thought. All that flaming work over the last 13 weeks and now we have got to do it all again and work our normal hours duty as well!

After order was restored the Sgt continued with his announcements, "Here are your postings. Two of you are posted to Southend Eastern Division (me and the ex-police cadet), The remainder to Southend Western Division, Leigh and Westcliff. I was delighted. Posted within walking distance of home. A real bonus! Especially when you haven't got a car. Well hardly anybody did have one then.

"Everyone happy with that?" We all nodded in approval. "Just as well cos there is bugger all you can do about it anyway!" he snapped.

The Sgt placed his thumbs in behind the silver buttons of the breast pockets of his tunic jacket and in a stance of pride stated, "You have joined the Borough at a historical time". He paused to inspect the awe on our faces. "A time when Policing as we know it is to be changed forever. We are to be more mobile, quicker off the mark and in front of the villain. This wonder of ingenuity from the Home Office is called Unit Beat Policing. We are going to have Panda Cars, little zippy cars to whisk you to emergencies and enable you to cover your beats with speed and efficiency. The Eastern Division are going to have Mini's and the Western Ford Anglia's. Aren't you lucky?"

A buzz of excitement sprang from us. "Brilliant! Marvellous!" exclaimed most except the ex-guardsman. "How the hell am I going to fit in one of those bloody things?" he complained. "You're on Western. They have the Anglia's. If that doesn't work we can take the front seat out and you can drive from the back", replied the smirking ex-cadet.

The ex-guardsman squirmed uncomfortably on his chair, "Look I am 6 foot 7 and I am not the smallest in the Borough. You saw the traffic blokes squeezing into that Mini Cooper and TR4. They were so packed in they could only change gear with their pricks!"

"That as may be", controlled the Sgt, "it will be sorted and it's not happening till next April. In the meantime you have much to get to grips with this week. You will need to learn Local Orders and By-Laws, forms, procedures and other important issues you will require to know before you are let loose on the streets.

Over the next days we attended the "Local Procedure Course" and were treated to the delights of "How to fill out a Process Card" for traffic offences. These were little post card size in various colours. Orange for parking offences and green for more serious matters like speeding. You would issue these after reporting a person for committing an offence and submit them to the supervisor for a decision whether the person should be prosecuted. Probationer constables such as us would be measured as to our capabilities by the number of process cards we put out and some senior officers would have competitions as to whose officers in their charge could put out the most.

This back fired on one newly promoted Inspector who entered into such a laugh with his counterpart on another shift. He instructed us to swamp the area with tickets, process cards on all vehicles that did not display a parking light during the night. "All motor vehicles parked on the public highway were required to have a light illuminated, red to the rear and white to the front". Quite a good idea really especially as the street lights at that time went out at midnight and cars running into an unlit vehicle and also particularly dangerous caused many an accident to cyclists who used to hit them with regularity. On this occasion we managed to put out over two hundred tickets on unlit cars.

A pity that most of them were placed on vehicles parked down the street where the Inspector lived and he had to write some most embarrassing letters to his neighbours. We were not asked to enter into any further competitions after that.

Other issues on the course were explained including the purpose of making points. We were given a small booklet containing the beats within the Borough and times and locations where we had to be during our shift.

Radios were a luxury and the only form of communication we had were our whistles, blue police posts or boxes inside which was a telephone and the larger ones a dry place for a smoke and warm up or the normal post office telephone or "TK" as we called them.

It was the only time that we could be contacted whilst out on the beat. If the police station control room wanted to contact you for any reason you had to be at that point at the designated time to receive a call, meet the Sergeant who would then check your pocket book and sign it as having met you. The Sarge would be in a vehicle of some sort either a Velocette motorcycle ("Noddy bike") or a duty vehicle such as an Austin Cambridge. It was guaranteed that he would be more comfortable than you. Some of them were really harsh and would force you to make a point every half hour. Bearing in mind that these locations were designed for the mode of transport you were required to have on a particular beat. If you did not have that transport you were still expected to make the point at every designated time. Even if were on foot or cycle when you should have been on a motorcycle beat.

FIRST BLOOD

On one occasion I was designated "Motorcycle North beat" that stretched from the whole of the north side of the railway lines that cut Southend in two. The points to be made were every hour "thank goodness" at North Shoebury Corner TK to the east and the Police Post outside the Cricketers Pub on the border with Westcliff to the west. Some four miles apart!

I had cycled out of Southend Police Station at 10.00pm on night duty. I made the first point at Shoebury at 11.00pm easily and the next at midnight at the Cricketers just as comfortably. Although I was having difficulty with the height of the saddle to the pedals I was managing to slide my backside across the leather seat to more than compensate for my small legs on this oversized bike designed for nine-foot police officers.

I had a refreshment break at the police station at 1.00am and then went back out to make the point at 2.00am at the Cricketers. I had just had one of Mary the cooks wonder night duty meals of fried eggs, sausages and bubble and squeak with two rounds of thick white buttered bread out of which I made this enormous bubble butty and a huge mug of tea. Needless to say I was feeling the pinch around the trouser belt and suffering a bit of flatulence as I pushed the pedals up the London road towards the point.

As I sweated passed Nazareth House, a large orphanage, about two hundred yards from the pub a grey mini van careered passed at an extremely high speed with youths hanging out of the front windows shouting, screaming out obscenities and gesticulating "v" signs from the back.

I think the driver was so busy taking the piss out of me that he failed to notice that at the pub corner the road took a sharp turn to the right. The car hit the horizontal railings straight on. There was a grinding thud. Sparks, glass, metal, steam and debris burst in all directions striking the pub walls and hurtling across the road in all directions. The front body and engine of the car sliced through the lower railing snapping it off its mounting on the pavement but the top railing slice the upper part of the van, just like a knife through the top of a boiled egg, peeling the roof back in a concertina shape and smashing its way through the harder van sides. As it did a football shot up from inside the thudded on the road nearby.

I got to the wreck as the last of the debris fell to the ground. I abandoned the bike and slid on the black sludge that was by now coming from the wreckage. The mini had lost its identity and I tried to make out where the front seats would have been. I saw the glinting of some silver on a torn black leather jacket. I could see one arm but the other side of the body was hidden by mangled metal.

Liquid spurted from the top of the jacket. I then realised that there was no head on the body. I searched what was the back compartment of the van and could hear some moaning coming from underneath a pile of debris. I pulled away at the pile and saw an arm and then a hand. The hand had a ring with a skull and cross bones on one of its fingers and the letters H A T E tattooed on each of its fingers. It moved. I pulled some more twisted metal away and saw a bare stomach with a huge gash in it with part of an intestine hanging out.

Lights were coming on in windows above and I shouted to people above to phone for ambulances and the Fire Brigade. I repeated the shout several times telling them that I believed there could be four injured people. In my mind I thought that perhaps only one was still alive.

Suddenly a voice shakily came from beside the wreck, "Officer have you seen this?" A man in a Railway Uniform was standing there ashen faced and with shaking hand pointing in the direction of the football. The shape glinted and the ghastly sight of nearly a whole head revealed itself. I asked the rail man to help me pull the debris off the moaning body so that I could assess and do some first aid for the injuries hoping that someone would have the presence of mind to cover the severed head up.

I shouted to the body in the wreckage, "I am a first-aider do not worry. I will get you out". That was what we were instructed to say by our St John's Ambulance First Aid instructors when I was in the Boys Brigade. It gave confidence to the victim they said. Somehow I don't think the body in the wreckage cared. It sent a warm wave of confidence through me and an assertive strength pushed my chest out and straightened my back.

Taking complete control and the lead I urged the railwayman to help me bend and pull at the torn metal and other debris revealing the now very quiet body. I could feel no pulse on his neck and we removed the muck over his face and I gave him the kiss of life. There was no taste of rubber like you got from the practice dummies. Even though I had wiped around its lips and removed a lot of gunk from its mouth I still felt grit and tasted oil, beer and blood as I worked through the procedure we had practiced. When I pumped the chest it oozed blood. I wondered if I was pumping the blood out of its heart. The thought of it being a man did cross my mind. Sub-consciously I had impressed on myself that it was a woman just to keep the record straight. The mouth suddenly coughed spewing blood and snot just as a convoy of rescue vehicles arrived. Ambulances, fire engines and the elite traffic department in their Jaguar patrol cars. Flashing blue lights, powerful floodlights and the shouts of officers leaping into their trained professional action now illuminated the quiet and dark scene.

The methodical way they went about their business, caring to the injured but carrying out the necessary legal duty left me aghast and ineffective.

BOB CRAVEN

It was time for me to step back and let the experienced ones take over. I noticed the blue light flashing on the Police Box and sloped over to it. I picked up the receiver and the Sergeants voice barked down, "Where the fuck have you been Craven. I have been waiting for ten minutes for you. There's been an accident at The Cricketers. Get there and see what you can do to help". "Yes sarge," I replied wearily. "It's sergeant not sarge. Report to me when you get back in", he came back. "Yes Sergeant", you bastard I thought.

Later I was told that three lads had been killed in the mini but one had survived. They had stolen the van form the seafront and were driving home to Dagenham.

When I returned to the station as ordered, the sergeant had obviously been told that I had been first on the scene and told me not to bother to report to him.

Funny but I was more pleased that I did not get a bollocking for failing to keep a point than being upset for not receiving some acknowledgement for the work I had done at the accident scene.

I would like to think that the Sergeant was worried about me as that was one of the main reasons for having points in those days when the security of a personal radio was not available.

OATHS AND EQUIPMENT

The week of local procedure training continued.

We went to the Magistrates Court to take our oath as Constables. Proudly, smartly and in true training school fashion we rattled off the oath

"I Robert George Craven do solemnly and sincerely declare and affirm that I

will well and truly serve Our Sovereign Lady the Queen in the office of

constable, without favour or affection, malice or ill will and that I will to the best of my power cause the peace to be kept and preserved, and prevent

all offences against the persons and properties of Her Majesties subjects;

and that while I continue to hold the said office I will to the best of my

skill and knowledge discharge all the duties thereof faithfully according to

law".

After that we were whisked off to the Mortuary at Southend General Hospital to be shown an autopsy. A memorable occasion as all of us were violently sick, smoked several packs of cigarettes and smelt like death when we got back for our dinner. Complaints flew from all directions in the police station canteen as the stench from the morgue had somehow impregnated our uniforms and was contaminating the food and the air around the diners. Those of us that could did not take much time to eat the morsels we had chosen.

The issue of equipment and measuring and fitting of uniforms was an event in itself. We were taken along to Horne Brothers, the bespoke high-class menswear shop in London Road. After a warning about the effeminate tailor who lingered on the inside measurement, we were then kitted out with our prestigious "Borough" uniforms. Southend Police was renowned for their high-class uniforms. The quality and cut of material outshone most massed produced outfits worn by the other forces.

Smartness and good grooming promoted respect and confidence within us and towards us from our public, we were told. Looking respectable and clean cut makes for efficient and effective policing. Look like a sack of shit and you'll get treated like one. That was the name of the game.

The White Helmet that gave us the tag of "snowdrops" was worn to make us conspicuous during the daytime and the height requirement of the Borough Force of five feet ten inches put us head and shoulders above the average crowd. Dominating the town's streets and providing a commanding sight for individuals.

White gloves we carried, woollen in winter and cotton in summer, and used for traffic point duty accessorised and further complimented the look of confidence.

The other issue items included:

Whistle (continuous blows for emergencies – Morse code dots and dashes for non-urgent contact).

Truncheon (various shades of ebony – useful for cracking nuts at Christmas and breaking windows – never used on any heads only about the body)

Handcuffs (Victorian type – snap shut with key the size of a door knocker – not be used as an aid to better sex)

Police cape (not Batman type – used in bad weather and never whilst on traffic duty – useful on pedal cycle)

Great-coat (heavy wool – only worn by the fittest as it weighed a ton)

Inner-jacket waistcoat – (for even worse weather and fitter officers)

Waterproof leggings - (like cowboy chaps with tags that were secured to your trouser belt and only worn with braces on the trousers that would fall down without support).

Keys to Police Stations, posts and boxes, traffic light junction boxes, the sports field gates and clubhouse.

The combined weight of all these items should you have the misfortune to require to wear and carry them all at the same time gave you the ability to be used as a heavy duty battering ram at any incident. In a fight you always survived, got spun round a lot, could not move or use your arms and sometimes were able to sit on a prisoner to quell his wrath.

The local procedure-training week completed and armed with the most up to date tools and knowledge we were now finely tuned for action

Chapter Three
THE SHIFT

The Divisions' police officers were split into shifts or relief. Each relief or shift was made up of about fifteen to twenty officers divided into three types of beat either foot, cycle or mobile patrols totalling twenty beats in and around Southend town centre and busy seafront and to its east towards Shoeburyness.

PRETTY TOUGH

We also had the usual specialist departments dealing with crime, traffic, vice, juveniles and a separate police women's section. The ladies were led by a very astute and strict Woman Chief Inspector who would stand for no nonsense from her girls or from the male officers who she thought continuously lechered after her younger charges.

She was not far wrong from that though, as many of the ladies were pretty and a natural attraction to any self-respecting virile young officer. In addition these were the days of suspenders and stockings that added to the attraction of girls in various uniforms. Women Constables found themselves looking after lost children, women prisoners and female aggrieved parties in sexual offences as part of their normal duties. However most were eager to be involved in all aspects of police duties and yearned for equality in responsibility and salary that was below that earned by male officers.

We were not allowed to patrol together or fraternise however circumstances always presented themselves where we did police together.

Although sometimes physically weaker than most male officers the ladies were more prone to use guile and ingenuity than just brute force when dealing with situations.

I was having difficulty with a large and strong man who was drunk and disorderly in the High Street one afternoon. With no radio to summon assistance I was struggling to place handcuffs on his wrists to the delight of the watching crowd that always gathered to gawp on such occasions. We were rolling around on the pavement to the cheers and clapping of the onlookers when this female voice said, "Can I help Bob?" I looked up and there was immaculate WPC complete with white-topped cap and white gloves standing above me braced for action. The drunk continued to struggle violently as I sat on his stomach and tried to hold onto his arms. Quite suddenly he froze as the WPC dropped to her knees and sat on his upturned face.

Whether it was calculated shock treatment or an accident did not matter but the shock of being hit in the face by a set of suspenders and stocking tops momentarily silenced him enough to enable me to clip the handcuffs on him and detain him without further problems. The WPC stood up, regained her composure and said, "There. That was easier than we thought. Wasn't it?"

I could not decide if the drunk was naturally boss-eyed or still in a state of deep satisfaction from the experience but he went quietly to the waiting paddy wagon like a lamb.

In another incident a number of us male officers were having a problem with a gang of drunks who were finishing off their day out with a fight with the locals. We were all in various states of boxing, wrestling and other methods of self-defence to make arrests when two of our women police officers came to help.

They were like chalk and cheese in appearance one young small pretty slightly built and eloquently spoken. The other an older WPC, craggy weathered face, stocky with a gruff voice, which could expertly roll her own cigarettes in one hand.

Their approach to the situation was very different. The younger one walked up to the nearest drunk, a sweating thickset thug a good foot taller than her, who was wringing the neck of another equally ugly opponent. Both were shouting abuse at each other and were oblivious to her when she tapped the larger of the two on the shoulder She quietly but sternly warned him that if he persisted in this disorderly manner she would be forced to arrest him and put him before the court, "And you would like that would you?" she added with her fists stuffed firmly into her shapely hips and head raised with eyes transfixed as if they would cut him in half.

The drunk shouted, without turning to see who it was and said, "Oh fuck off!" She showed a slight increase in her stern qualities and tapped him even harder on the shoulder once more saying, "If you do not desist from this behaviour I will have no alternative but to arrest you Sir".

The drunk let go his victim and turned round to face the young WPC, raising his clenched fist as he did so to punch the now cowering, winced face girl. In surprise at what was facing him he momentarily stopped himself from hitting the young figure in front him. His hesitation gave the youngster the opportunity to place her handcuffs on his huge wrists before he came out of the shock of her slight stature and strong character.

He then realised he was in a "no win" situation and the shred of chivalry that he possessed would not allow him to attack such a pretty young thing.

The older WPC's approach was very different. Upon entering the melee she saw that I was trying to separate two fighting, spitting punching drunks. They had suddenly turned their joint attentions onto me when she dragged one off my back and spun him round to face her. As he did he took a swing at her with his fist. She parried the punch with her left forearm and masterfully punched the astounded assailant squarely on his nose. He hit the pavement with a thud as if pole axed, out for the count and going nowhere.

The second drunk was still attacking me when the WPC stepped between us and said, "Stop farting about trying to get hold of him.

Sort the bastard out." She then struck him so hard that he fell backwards grabbing her lapels as he did so. Behind him was a shop window selling fishing tackle, camping equipment and accessories. The drunk hit the window first following instantly by the WPC. Their combined weight shattered the glass and they fell head long into the display of fishing rods and tackle inside.

There they rolled amongst the debris of cane rods, line, hooks, outdoor clothing, sheath knives and broken jagged glass oblivious to the danger. It was hard to distinguish who was attacking whom or if in their own individual way they were trying to get out of the mess that had been created. Such was the confusion and tangle they found themselves in.

Hauling herself out of the shop window was far easier than expected for the WPC who did not rely on the grace and dignity required by most ladies. She stepped out of the shattered remains with a confident leap unabashed that her skirt and stockings had been ripped to shreds and her uniform caps had been dented beyond recognition leaving her hair wrapped in "Ena Sharples" hairnet exposed to the open air.

Almost in the same movement she took hold of the dazed drunk, who had likewise removed himself from the display and was plunking fishhooks from his straggly hair, by the arm with one hand and led him to the waiting police van and with the other hand she drew a roll up fag from her skirt pocket, slipped it between her lips, place her hand back into her pocket produced a lighter, lit the cigarette, drew a satisfying drag on it, picked a small piece of tobacco from her tongue and then placed the drunk into the van beside the other WPCs' prisoner.

She closed the door of the van with gusto, pulled her skirt into some semblance of order, brushed it down and said to her younger officer, "Come on girl. Time to do the reports and it's tea break time". Off they then strode in the direction of the Police Station.

The pretty one looked quite unsteady with the elder striding strongly as they walked in step away. Unfortunately the pretty ones ordeal continued at the Court Case that followed when she was asked by the Prosecuting Solicitor to state exactly what the defendant had said to her. Finding it difficult to say, "Fuck" with a eloquent "plum in the mouth" voice was perhaps the deciding factor in the young WPC changing her vocation from the Police to the work of the Probation Service some weeks later.

PANDAS AND HOT AIR

The advent of Policing with Panda Cars and the issue of personal radios were eagerly awaited but we had to make do with footslogging, bicycles, Velocette motorcycles (Noddy bikes) and the odd Austin Cambridge estate car if the Inspector or Sergeant was not using it. We also had the use of Austin J4 Personnel Carrier (the fighting group wagon or Team Policing Unit) and an Austin J4 Van that was used as a carrier for drunks (unfortunately nearly all were Irish hence it was called - Paddy wagon), stray dogs and general undesirables who did not deserve the luxury of transportation in our luxury patrol cars.

These included sedate Austin Westminster's, Ford Zephyr Sixes with the long bonnet commonly and affectionately nicknamed "Dagenham Dustbins" and very occasionally elegant Jaguars. These would have an advanced driver from the Traffic department and an observer from Division foot patrols. They were known as area patrol cars

These vehicles would respond to all incidents other than Major Road Accidents requiring the skills the elite Traffic Department. Always considered a plum job in the winter months as these cars had tremendously warm heaters.

I found the Dagenham Dustbins heater too efficient at one time after I had attended to a lovely old lady in Westcliff. She was very disabled and fell out of bed regularly. She had a telephone by her bed and when this happened was able to ring the Police to get her back into bed. We attended her this particular night at about 2.00am. When we arrived she announced that she was hoping to get to the toilet before we put her back into bed. I bravely worked it out that if she stood on my toes, facing me like a dancing partner, I could walk her there. My driver lifted her from the back and I put my arms around her middle lifting her onto my feet. She was a rather round lady and about a foot shorter than me. With my arms under hers I had my head on her shoulder and felt her whiskered face on my cheek.

All went well until we were just about to get her to back into the loo when after a breaking of wind I felt this wet warm feeling down my lower trouser leg. I was not sure if the wind had come from my police colleague but it definitely was not one of mine. Did not like to embarrass her so kept quiet until we had put her back into bed and out of earshot. We tucked her up into bed with her exalting how wonderful policemen were, said our goodbyes, closed the outside door, locked it and placed the key in the usual hiding place.

Outside I told my illustrious traffic driver that I think she had wet my leg. "The Dustbin super heater will soon sort that out", he confidently replied. We got back into the Ford Patrol car. He turned the ignition key. The engine roared into life. The heater switch was turned to full blast and belched a wave of warm to hot air straight in our faces. I could feel my legs warming up and a damp atmosphere filling the car. Within seconds the whole car was consumed by the most pungent smell of bodily fluids similar to that suffered at the mortuary. The car doors burst open as if a bomb had exploded inside and we both ran for the cover of enough distance to inhale fresh clean air.

Unfortunately the lady suffered from a loose bowel and my trousers had received a significant quantity of its contents. "You are not getting back in the car in that state", shouted the driver. "You can walk back to the nick and spray yourself down with the car wash hose before I'm taking you out again tonight".

My protests were useless, so I walked back as he instructed. I had to convince him most definitely that the entire grievous problem had to be removed before he would let me back into "his" car. I sprayed the trousers as instructed. All ended well, the heater eventually dried them out completely. I can guarantee that it is the best car heater I have ever experienced.

Our shifts were 6.00am to 2.00pm, 2.00pm to 10.00pm, 10.00pm to 6.00am, earlies, lates and nights respectively. Half nights were 6.00pm to 2.00am and day shifts of 8.00am to 4.00pm and 10.00am to 6.00pm.

TIPTOE THROUGH THE SNOWDROPS

A Sergeant and Constable in the Admin Office dealt with the day to day running of the division ensuring that it was managed efficiently and effectively. Two men to keep on the right side of if you wanted your holidays and days off at desired times. The Constable had a very useful welfare responsibility. "Joes Specials" condoms were on sale from his desk drawer. Coming in packets of three for a price equivalent to 10p these days saved many officers from too early fatherhood and the embarrassment of having to buy them over the counter in a Chemists.

The Admin Office also contained the Force Standing Orders and Force Orders that were the bibles in which could be found any plan, instruction or advice on any incident that an officer could face. These would set out the legal requirements and responsibilities, internal and external law, local mandates and Police Regulations. If you had a problem then the answer was in these.

Next to the Admin Office was the Parade Room. Set out with black and grey metal tables and steel framed chairs. Notice Boards behind with bull dog clips holding the latest Force Orders – announcing anything from the transfer / appointment of officers and other force changes to new and recent legislation updates, Police Gazettes (circulated nationally by Scotland Yard details of Wanted / Missing Persons. Stolen Property, Escaped Prisoners and other important information), wanted posters and circulations from other forces, sports club news and memorandums from senior officers.

Force Orders were very mundane but on one occasion the first one to read the burst into laughter exclaiming, "This has got to be a wind-up! The DCI is coming off CID and being put in charge of the Information Room, Dogs and Mounted Section. The new Woman Inspector is taking over the diving section and sea rescue squad." Disbelief echoed throughout but there it was in black and white on Force Order 355/67.

HORSE SHIT

The DCI had only just completed an internal investigation into the theft of horse manure from the police horse stables. Being a trifle bombastic and a keen gardener it would seem.

He had gone to the stables to collect his usual few bags of the stuff for his roses and in boiling fury had come out shouting, "Someone's stolen my shit. It was here half an hour ago! Who took it?" He remonstrated at the Mounted Section Sergeant. "I haven't got a clue guv", replied the wily Sergeant.

He shouted to one of the civilian drivers, who cleaned cars and other mundane tasks for the Police Garage Manager, "Close that gate. Nobody is leaving here till I get to the bottom (in his fury not realising his pun) of this". The driver muttered, "Don't you mean horses bottom, arsehole", as he did as ordered and closed the gates stopping everyone from leaving the Police Compound.

Even though it was 6.00pm and the busiest time for staff and officers to be leaving the police station yard in their cars, it did not deter the man from his quest to solve the heinous theft of two bags of horse-shit.

The DCI recruited his most trusted Detective Sergeant to assist him.

Every car was searched until finally not two bags but three bags were found in the boot of a car owned by the biggest motorcyclist the Traffic Department had.

"Got the bastard", the DCI exclaimed gleefully rubbing his hands together. The DCI and his dutiful but regretting Detective Sergeant, who had accompanied him on so many ridiculous investigations, took the motorcyclist to an interview room situated in the haven of their Criminal Investigation Department. Usually avoided by all Traffic Officers in case they were tainted with being bent.

"You have got three bags of stolen horseshit in your car"; the DCI said started the accusation. "No I haven't", replied the motorcyclist confidently.

"Where did you get it then?" retorted the DCI. "I'm not telling you", the big man said folding his arms defiantly, "And you can't make me".

The DCI continued, "Like that is it? All you traffic blokes are bent. You get your hook money from the crashed cars you put the way of those criminal car repairers. I know all about that. Don't you worry!" The huge frame of the motorcyclist was rising from his seat and starting to fill the small interview room. The DCI seemed unaware of the threat but his Detective Sergeant, with the tiniest rolled up cigarette hanging stuck to the bottom lip of his gaping mouth saw the problem. The DCI had the habit of looking out of the window when speaking to people and was oblivious to the big mans reaction and said, "I am seizing those three bags as evidence".

"I am leaving, sir, "snarled the motorcyclist. "The manure needs to be well rotted before I put it on my allotment. Make sure it has not been tampered with and spoilt when you give it back". In one stride he left the room. The DCI ordered the DS, "Nick him Sergeant". The DS turned to his boss and said, "Lets not be too hasty guv". He then realised he had to go and book the three bags into the Property Store as evidence. The Property Officer would need to be convinced that it was necessary. Internal Investigations always took priority and were treated for more importantly so the DCI always got his way in such cases.

The end result went to the motorcyclist as he had bought the manure from a local farmer earlier that day. The DS said he had the Scene's of Crime Officers take samples from all the police horses and had it compared with that from the bags.

To this day it is suspected that he had more common sense than the DCI and had a spoof "Result of Analysis Form" typed out stating it was a negative result and the alleged stolen poo did not come from the police horses. The Borough was saved from a very embarrassing and damaging Court Case.

The Women Inspector also mentioned in the Force Order was a short brunette in her mid twenties, good looking with a particularly curvaceous figure that was very noticeable in a swimsuit when attending swimming instruction and life saving procedures at the local open air swimming pool on Westcliff Esplanade. She had just returned from the Police College as an articulate graduate entrant with a well-spoken soft voice that many found attractive. The author of the Force Order was obviously a fan of hers or a member of the marine section. Giving a number of likely suspects.

The secret admirer and comedian author was never caught.

"Prior to every shift it was the duty of all officers to read each and every notice displayed on this board", the Training Sergeant had told us. "To go out on your beat without doing so is like a carpenter turning up to do a job without his tools!"

Reporting time for duty was 10 minutes before each shift. Not many arrived before 15 minutes to the hour so there was then a mad clamouring of 14 / 18 officers wanting to equip themselves with all the info they could before parading for duty.

The Shift Sergeant would parade us for duty. The officers would be seated at the desks around the perimeter of the parade room. The Sergeant would enter and all would stand. My very first shift was a night duty. After reading every bit of paper on the notice board I was informed by my new colleagues that when the sergeant came in it was courteous to stand and to make sure he was convinced that we had all our equipment we banged the desks with our truncheons, blew our whistles, shone our torches (after all we did get a light and boot allowance) in the sergeants eyes and had our pocket books had to be shown sticking out of our top pockets.

All the officers sat down at 10 minutes to the hour, helmets on, whistles in mouth, torch in one hand, truncheon in the other and pocket book just protruding out of their top tunic pockets. The door banged open, the sergeant whisked in clipboard clutched under his arm and one of the senior constables snapped "Shun". I shot up from my seat, stood to training school attention, blew my whistle to highest pitch having to close my eyes slightly to do so, slammed my truncheon down on the desk and shone the torch at the sergeants eyes.

The whistling stopped. I opened my eyes. I was the only one standing. All the others were still seated with heads buried in their arms on the tables and shook, some violently, with muffled laughter. The sergeant holding back a snigger calmly holding his head to one side in a semi-comforting tone said", It is a bit early for attention seeking Constable unless you say different I will proceed with the parade". "Yes Sergeant", I meekly replied.

As he waited for the banter in the room to calm down the sergeant placed the large book, clipboard and bundle of papers, he was carrying under his arm, over his desk and sat down. He swayed his head around the room in a silent gesture to gain our undivided attention.

He then called out our names and beats we were appointed to cover that night. I was placed under the wing of a seven-year experienced Constable to walk the, "Top-end fronts of the High Street", Beat One.

The Sergeant then read out the passages from the very large book called the "Occurrence Book". Officers entered all incidents they had attended and also process (offences they had reported persons for) carried out during their tour of duty.

The other papers were circulations and teleprinter messages containing details of stolen cars, wanted persons and local items of interest that we dutifully recorded in the back of our pocket books.

Now fully armed with the necessary information and equipment I was ready to be let lose on the lawbreakers of the Borough, with the assistance of my senior Constable, of course.

"Have you got everything?" he asked before we left the Station. "I reckon so", I confidently replied. "Well we don't come back here until grub time at 1.00am. If we get any problems we can always telephone in for help". He reassured. "It's not like training school in real life. You can take things more casually but be ready to put everything you have learnt into action at the drop of a hat", he added.

"Thanks", I faltered and panic built up inside me as I realised I was part of this very thin blue line between violent anarchy and democratic peace. In my case the line was so thin it was almost transparent. What would I do if I were asked a question I did not know the answer. How would I cope? How big a Pratt am I going to be? How big a cock up can I make? Will the bosses be kind to me?

I comforted myself when I remembered how previous employers had been when I crashed a brand new VW Beetle at a nasty bend in Battlesbridge. I had picked the car up from Colchester to bring it back to the showrooms in Leigh. The car did have fifty miles on the clock so it wasn't exactly new. The showroom was closed when I drove the sorrowful front dented but rear sparkling car onto the forecourt. I did leave a very large "Sorry" note on the windscreen for the boss when he got in first thing the following day. Funny though he did not say a thing but he knew I was joining the police force and I suppose you could say that he and the other staff may have been a little wary of me being as they had shown me how to turn a speedo clock back and get two crashed vehicles made into one!

Another occasion was when I was doing a job as a "Setter Out" for a local joinery firm. My job was to set out the exact measurements and positions of component parts for mass-produced timber window frames. The machinists would drill or bore out timber framing in accord with my blue print.

Fifteen thousand of our window frames were fitted to ten high-rise flats at a large building project in the London East End. These were the answer to the severe housing shortage and our firm were honoured to be part of this groundbreaking initiative. Unfortunately I delayed the project for six months, as the glass, pre-cut and ready to fix into our frames, did not fit. One piece of clear could be cut down to size but the more expensive, Georgian wired plate, was too short and totally useless.

I tried to explain to the boss that I was very upset because a girl I loved had chucked me. Also I think I had been inadvertently going out with her identical sister that had left me very confused.

Actually what had happened was that one night we were kissing goodnight when she said, "You never guess what my sisters boyfriend did to her?" I said, "I don't know. What?" "He put his hand up inside her bra", she exclaimed. In true Boys Brigade fashion I promised, "I would never do anything like that. That's terrible". She looked up into the sky and said, "There's a wishing star. Make a wish". Romantically I did so and she said she did as well. The next day I got a message to say she did not want to see me again. In my naivety it took many years to appreciate why she had chucked me.

I didn't bore the boss with all these details as I thought they would not have been well received at that time. He changed my job to working in the timber yard loading and unloading lorries. He obviously thought my physique lent towards the manual side of employment.

I left the police station with my senior constable. Although I was the shortest copper in the Borough at that time he was not much taller than me and had an enormous stride. I tried to keep pace but as he strode out I had the devil of a job to keep in step (to ensure our "military precision and effective bearing" on our public as insisted on by our training school instructors).

I found myself concentrating on this aspect of beat patrol for the first 100 yards or so and clean forgot about my thoughts of failure and its consequences. Just as well really, because I was fast getting to the stage of reaching for the comforting senior constables' hand to lead me through the forthcoming perils.

By the time I had got to grips with the step we had reached Southend Victoria Railway Station and the northern edge of a huge building site that was due to become "The" shopping centre of East Anglia. A gantry footbridge took you over this construction site and the new dual carriageway also being laid out below. The noise of traffic and other hub-bub left us as we looked down on the roundabout known as Victoria Circus the traffic mostly consisting of buses entering the roundabout from all directions. From this vantage point I could feel a sense of confidence engulfing me. This was my destiny! For years I had waited for this to happen. All the disappointments of being turned down to be a cadet in the Metropolitan Police and the Borough disappeared into insignificance. I had arrived. My stride lengthened, my shoulders pulled back and head held high. We were also going down hill as the gantry bridge inclined to the normal footpath onto the Circus.

The Blue Bird Café and a shop called Heaths that sold records and cycles were situated where the gantry bridge ended. This was also a large bus stopping area and regular meeting place for people going to the town shops and cinemas. I looked out for people who would know me. Hoping for someone to see me and pass me a compliment or two.

No such luck, although the old newspaper seller who was always outside the Blue Bird, even at ten past ten at night, approached us. "I'm glad I've seen you two", he said.

He was well known in the town and had perhaps the pole position for newspaper sellers in that his pitch occupied arguably the busiest in the High Street. In my school days I remembered classmates saying how they had sorted out "Mole the news" by taking the mickey out of him. He had the droll of a news seller when he shouted out what obviously was "Paper". This had become distorted by time, and possibly a stroke or two, to sound like "Mole". Hence the nickname.

He was very short, slightly built, had a pot marked weather lined face, large nose, greasy unwashed matted curly brown hair and always wore a filthy dirty grey overcoat. His left shoulder stooped outwards and he dragged his left foot along the floor half stumbling as he walked.

"Those bloody kids are getting on my wick", he spitted. He aimed his anger at me and continued, "They've been throwing bangers at me and one has burnt my coat. I only got it yesterday from the Salvation Army. I want compensation". Before I could open my mouth to clarify that he meant fireworks and not sausages when he said bangers. Using my training school acquired skills of being specific at all times. My senior Constable said, "Look, Sir, you tried this last week. Don't go bothering our new recruits to get some money that is not due. This is the same coat you have been wearing since the court case when you got compensation from the two boys who did it". Mole replied disappointedly, "Can't blame me for trying". He slinked away as the constable continued, "You could be done for wasting police time. So be careful".

We left Mole sulking by the café and crossed the road to the central reservation and then onto the roundabout in the middle of the Circus. I was amazed how we managed to do that through traffic that gave no quarter to ordinary pedestrians. Just by the casual raising of his arm and the thank you wave in acknowledgement for the vehicles that gave us passage we were able to cross the road unimpeded. The respect we were shown was uncanny, a first for me and a boost to my confidence putting another six inches on my height.

TRAMPS AND MISPLACED TRUNCHEON

Having negotiated the traffic my senior constable went to go down into the underground ladies toilets situated on the roundabout. I took his arm and said, "Hang on mate you've got the wrong one. The Gents is there." Pointing to the entrance next door. "I know what I'm doing", he replied. I thought, just my luck to get a pervert as a senior constable.

"Come on", he said impatiently. "Bloody hell", I muttered. Giving him the benefit of the doubt I thought that perhaps he has got super hearing and has heard some scream from a maiden in distress. That has got to be worth a risk. I had never been in a ladies toilet but duty calls. My senior was right inside the bowels (sorry) of the toilet and shouting, "Police Officers. Just checking to ensure everything is okay". He was pushing the cubicle doors open. Fortunately no females were embarrassed by the manoeuvre.

One door, however, moved slightly and was stopped from opening by an obstruction inside. My senior gave it a mighty kick with his huge boot. I thought if some old dear is just pulling her draws back then she is going to have the fright of her life and possibly a broken skull. The door thudded against the obstruction and a male voice slurred loudly, "Alright you bastards, fucking wait a minute". There was a shuffling of feet and clothing then the door burst open. A burly long black haired and bearded bloke came out fighting an imaginary adversary. We instantaneously stepped back although he was some distance from us. His eyes opened as he got nearer and realising who were said, "Thank fuck you have arrived. I radioed for help when those bastards chased me in here". "Who?" I said.

"They're always after me", he pulled me towards him as my senior introduced me to him by name. I smelt the harrowing mixture of the stench of alcohol and unwashed substances coming from as he continued, "I am one of your original fucking war heroes. The war is going on now and am fighting it on your behalf son". "That's enough now Kenny. Time to go. You are in the ladies. I'll check up on you later", my senior said.

Kenny climbed the stairs with the greatest of difficulty and then weaved his way through the traffic and away out of sight. The senior constable explained that the town had a few down and outs but they were tolerated as long as they did not make a nuisance of themselves. There were a few out of Towner's who came down for the summer and the regulars who slept in the public toilets after everyone had gone home. He said it was sadly the only thing they could do, as there was no lodgings or shelters available for them.

The regulars included, "Popeye", who entertained the drunks and trippers with his tap dance act. Wearing his distinctive sailor's cap looked like the comic character complete with twirling pipe, baggy trousers and anchors tattooed on his forearms. His sleep pitch was usually the public toilet at the other end of the High Street where it met Pier Hill, which led down to the seafront.

Another one was a bit of a mystery. He may have been a down and out but it was rumoured that a chauffeur driven Rolls Royce quite often picked him up.

He was locally known as "The Reverend Happy Harry". He would stand on a wooden box on the crowded Marine Parade opposite the amusement arcades and the Ship Hotel on the tripper crowded seafront. He would engage in speaking on any subject, the more contentious the better, whether it was religion, politics, and price of beer or bread, just anything to gain the crowds interest. He drew substantially more people into his audience than the Salvation Army and the Elim Church group that also had their speakers on that little stretch of seafront. He used to wind the people up sometimes to an unhealthy level but was a craftsman at bringing the situation under control for his finale of the song, "It's rolling in, it's rolling in. The sea of love keeps rolling in". This was a cue for the crowd to throw him coins in appreciation for his entertainment. His beady eye always kept a close watch for silver coins especially half a crowns (two shillings and sixpence). Some kids were known to cover one-penny pieces wrapped in silver paper, making them about the same size as a half crown, hold the penny over a cigarette lighter and throw it onto the ground to Happy Harry. Being potential silver he would immediately go to it and then the whole crowd would rock with laughter as he juggled with the hot coin. It never deterred him from his pitch and his preaching.

I then noticed a blue flashing light coming from the corner of the Municipal College that stood on the north west side of the Circus. "There's a call for us. Come on hurry", ordered my senior. He stopped a bus from running us down. Thanked the driver with a wave and walked positively towards the blue flashing light on the top of the small hut next to the College.

This was twenty-four "box", our police post. I used my issue key and we went in. A constable was already inside and writing in his pocket book. He said to us, "Sorry but I've got to write this RTA up. There is some trouble down outside the Sutton Arms. Some old bird giving a taxi driver some trouble!" With this my senior spun round and was out of the door without even stopping or altering his pace.

We crossed the roundabout again and marched at record pace into Southchurch Road eastwards away from the Circus. I kept pace and was about to break into a trot when my senior touched my arm and said, "Don't run. You will be knackered before you get there. If there is a fight that will make you useless and there is a chance that if you take your time the opposing sides would have exhausted themselves and all we have got to do is pick up the pieces". I was just about to argue that I was fit enough to fight after running a mile let alone a few hundred yards and the possibility of arriving too late to stop a major crime when I heard this high pitched scream and the words, "You bit me you fucking cow. Get out of my taxi!"

The taxi was parked right beside a large crowd at several bus stops outside the pub. Leaning inside the rear compartment of the Ford Consul saloon taxi was a man in his fifties who was holding his bleeding nose. "Look. She has bitten my fucking nose. I can feel it moving", he screamed. He took his hand away and you could see the teeth marks indented in the flesh at the end of his nose.

A husky female voice came from within the taxi shouting, "You should keep your filthy hands to yourself. I am going to report you for failing to take me home". I then saw the woman. She was spread legs open wide across the back seat. She wore a furry short jacket, a micro mini leopard skin patterned skirt (designed for girls at least thirty years younger and a third of her weight) and her laughing line (known commonly by us blokes as once you got there you were laughing) was quite obvious above her torn stockings. She left nothing to be desired, her face was heavily made up with thick mascara (Dusty Springfield thick), her lipstick was smeared covering half her face and its was debateable whether her facial appearance was uglier than her private part which was open for all to see as she was wearing no knickers.

My senior said to her, "Come on Daisy. You have had your say the taxi driver will not take you anywhere, as he has been booked by someone else. I will help you out. Cover yourself up." She fluttered her enormous black eyelashes like a sixteen year old and said, "Your young officer can help me". I shuddered and hesitated somewhat and my senior said, "I know it's rough mate but if you don't we are going to be a long time and the pub will be chucking out soon. That could cause us some hassle. Get in there and get her out".

I still hesitated and thinking duty was duty and I was wearing gloves leant into the taxi. As I did she caught me off balance and pulled me on top of her. The crowd cheered as I struggled to free myself from her embrace. Her legs locked around my waist. I was afraid that I was in the grip of a black widow and about to be devoured. I said, "Stop playing around". She said, "Stop playing around. I am deadly serious. Go on get your Willy out and give me one. No one will notice. Go on give us a kiss".

A large crowd had gathered to watch the "fun" and some were shouting, "Go on give her one", and other comedians, "She's paid her taxes. She's entitled to a service". Very witty!

The frightening sight of her huge red smeared pouting lips spurred me into a brainwave. I put my arms around her legs pulling her tightly towards me. I couldn't make out if she was going to be sick or she was groaning with anticipation. Dug my knees into the seat to get a better grip. With this she tightened her legs, pushing her crutch towards me and in the direction of the open door and my freedom. She cavorted her hips and with eyes closed and smiling expectantly she seemed to be enjoying herself.

At the threshold of the door I let go of her and pushing my arms onto the roof I hauled us both out of the taxi. She then spilled out on to the pavement in a heap of lace stockings, tatty fur coat, matted black hair and creased up red smeared face.

"You fucking bastard", she squirmed out of her contorted mouth. "I was enjoying that. You had to go and spoil it", she added pulling her skirt down over her crumpled legs. "Sorry madam but I was only doing my job", I replied hating the fact that I had to say that.

"I felt you're hard on. You were having a good time as well. You were as solid as a rock!" she nodded knowingly.

It wasn't worth telling her that the trousers I was wearing were my old baggy ones with a long pocket for my truncheon that seemed to have a mind of its own. When I had knelt down in the taxi it had drifted across my front and what she had felt was my large unused shiny truncheon. The thought that I a young 20 year old, would get a hard on, and fancy an old bag like that was not worth thinking about.

Having sorted the incident out and sent the rejected woman and her man on their way and allowed the taxi driver to pick up his client. Part of me still wanted to convince the gathered crowd that I did not have hard on and that it was my truncheon that she felt. Fortunately the sensible part realised that this would be a lost cause. So after checking that my raincoat did not contain any unsightly stains from the woman's sexual advances and that the truncheon had returned from between my legs to its proper place down the side of my trousers, we returned to our beat duties at "the top end " of the High Street.

The remainder of the night was uneventful and I was taught the beat craft of checking all doors and windows of all the premises on our beat. This meant shaking every door handle of every shop, office and other premises but being careful not to disturb those entry alarms by over doing the shake.

No real surprises to that except when my senior constable smartly entered a secluded shop doorway and bowled over a courting couple in the advanced stages of passion. Amid all three giving their apologies he was still able to affect his duty and shake the door handle before continuing the beat responsibilities.

At the end of the shift the whole of "D" Relief would stand to attention in the corridor outside the parade room in the Police Station. The Shift Sergeant would read off our names from the Duty Roster on his clipboard. After each name he would ask, "Anything to report?" Those who did, tried to create a balance between their desire to promote their own ego, efficiency and professionalism by describing in painful detail the incidents they had so bravely dealt with during their tour of duty and the awareness that the rest wanted to bugger off duty and could not care a less what he had done or how he had done. "Let's get home and wrap ourselves around the warm bums of our wives", was the only thought of most. I was still single then and had not experienced that pleasure but when I did there was no other feeling of warmth and satisfaction that could ever compare with it. Well there is but this is not that sort of book!

For the next six days I was escorted around Southend by a procession of senior constables and shown the ropes into being a fully-fledged police constable. Each night I would return to my parents flat totally exhilarated and pleasurably satisfied that there could be no better job in the world.

I had found my niche in life and was on the threshold of fulfilling my life's ambition of saving the world from thugs, criminals and all other nasties. At the end of the week we were given two days off before returning to duty and I was being let out on my own. Brilliant!

Chapter Four
DUTY TO PERFORM

The first few hours of being on my own were perhaps the worst. What will happen if I cock up? But with every conceivable aide memoir and précised notes on how to deal with every subject from sheep pox to murder tucked away in aide memoirs, books and scraps of paper in the breast pocket of my uniform jacket I was bound to succeed and be a credit to the Force.

In hindsight I don't think the High Street has ever suffered either of these offences but the bulk of paper in my pocket would have stopped any bullet from hitting my vital organs. That's positive thinking for you!

I CAN HANDLE IT

Time to think am I man for this job or is this a dream that is going to back fire on me. Yes I had got the butterflies in my stomach and I was nervous about the possibility of being over whelmed by the unknown but I could handle it.

I had survived beatings at school. The time when a fifth former, twice my size, had beaten me, a very slightly built first year, to pulp and when bruised and battered with my blazer ripped and my smart grey trousers torn and scuffed with the gravel from the school

43

playground my Dad had said, "Don't worry mate! You'll be that size one day and knock shit out of blokes like that".

AND there was the time when all hell let lose at Southend Youth Centre after I had bumped into this hard nut, a hod carrier with shoulders as wide as a doorway. Decided to teach me a lesson and knocked me cold with one tremendous punch. When I came to, my best mates were knocking seven bells of shit out of the hod carrier's gang. One was being pulverised on the stairs in front of me by my large friend and screaming for him to stop kicking him in the nuts. Another was leaning precariously against a wooden bar that stretched across a large plate glass window to the street two floors below. My shorter mate, a four-foot six-inch boxing powerhouse, was punching him incessantly. Every time he bounced back from the wooden bar he would be hit again and spring back against the bar. Although he was a good foot taller than the powerhouse and a lot heavier he had no chance. The powerhouse was using him as a punch bag but as there was a danger that he would go through the window onto the street below we saw fit to ask the powerhouse to break from his concentration and leave him in a heap at the foot of the window.

I had survived this ordeal, although nursing a beautiful shiner of a left eye was also able to balance the incident and quieten things down. The powerhouse was in the Boys Brigade with me and we had been taught such discipline and even temperament.

With the exception of the time when the ministers wife first came to a church parade! They were newly married and she was very attractive which in the days of mini skirts and suspender belts was not a good idea to be shown to so many eager and easily corrupted teenager boys.

The Minister was taking the salute with his good lady and as we marched past all our juices must have rushed to our heads. Our magnificent meticulous band music gathered sudden pace. I was the drum major then, unwittingly I increased the pace and the beat from the bass drum followed suit. All eyes were turned right instead of just mine. The well known dare I say, rousing, tune of "Sure and Steadfast" reached an untimely climax and then disintegrated into a shambles of muffled limp bugle blasts and drumming clatter. After another hundred or so paces we managed to revive ourselves and attained a swagger never to be repeated again.

Some of the boys remarked that when they woke up the following morning they found that the strange phenomena of hard and starch stiff pyjamas had hit them during the night.

For some weeks later there was a sudden increase in the boys who wanted to find God and attend biblical instruction at the Ministers' house with his lovely wife serving us with tea and her own home made buns. Others, I understand, found salvation in an alternative way by using a lot of imagination.

The Ministers wife did not come on the annual camp. Not surprising really as I suspect her husband twigged something was "up" with the increase in volunteers to help him in his garden. The skimpy shorts, not his – hers, did it with a large number of small boys being able to pull the strongest of weeds out with their strong and now well practised hand and wrist action. If she had have joined us at camp all the ropes to the archaic World War 2 bell tents would have had to be reinforced. We joked that eight boys in one tent, all dirty dreaming would have blown them away

I was worldly wise, brought up on the Temple Sutton council estate, no silver spoon job, where you were kept on your toes by the opposition from the Bournemouth Park lot at football in Cluny Square Park. Changing ends when the first side reached twenty goals. Not quite in the realms of West Side Story gang warfare but the same passion dominated. All brought up by parents who had lived and served through the World War and saw the area as the stepping stone for a more peaceful and stable environment. The residents ranging from the well educated to the unfortunate but all with the same hopes of a better future for their offspring.

All types of people with problems of their own but prepared to work for each other for a common community purpose. What I had the pleasure to experience there stood me in good stead for my role as a police officer and how valuable and essential it was for him to be a part of that community.

I had seen the wild side. I had been a mod. Back combed my hair, got all the right fashion gear at the time it was out. Bounced along in my bumpers, ankle swinging green pastel jeans and zipped cycle shirt and could do the "walk" like a cockerel on heat with all its nuts and bolts gone at its joints. I was able to reason as to what was right and wrong, what was legal and what was not. Some of the wild bunch I was part of had fallen on the wrong side of the life tight rope but I was always able to steady myself and either stay straight or step off at the right time.

EX-BOYS BRIGADE ESCAPE

Only once was I nearly succumbed and that was when I was at a coffee bar named the Capri in Weston Road one summers evening. It was in a cellar opposite the Post Office and my large mate and me had settled down to drink our lemon tea (all the rage then). The Walker Brothers were booming out "The Sun Ain't Gonna Shine Anymore" when there was a shout at the bar near the entrance stairs. I heard a police whistle and a loud voice shout, "Everyone stand still!" Not a hard task as by this time there were what seemed like a hundred coppers cramming into the small low ceiling cellar, cricking their necks to make room for their helmets and pushing all the brightly coloured clothed customers towards us in the rear of the bar. In the melee my large mate nodded towards the fire exit above us.

This was an old coal delivery manhole that formed a cavity in the ceiling. We were too far away to be noticed by the Bobbies' pushing from the other side of the coffee bar so we jumped up onto our seats and pushed the trap door to the open the fire escape. Feeling the fresh air burst in to the by now stifling heat of the crush below we clambered out onto the pavement above. My large mate went first and I scrambled out after him and straight through the legs of one enormous towering copper who had been standing over the manhole.

"What the f…" he exclaimed as I nearly toppled him over. "I know you, you're Bob Craven from the 11th Southend". Afraid to agree, I nodded and saw that it was the burly discus thrower from the 1st Southend Boys Brigade Company. Built like a brick shit house, his enormous body had developed even more from the days only a short few years earlier. I waited for the words, "You're nicked" or similar as I kept my position on all fours on the pavement. To my relief he just gave me a kick up the backside and said, "I haven't seen you. Bugger off and fast". "Cheers mate", I shouted gratefully and my large friend and I ran off like rabbits. "I never thought I would be able to praise the Boys Brigade", my mate gasped. He was a Boy Scout and was probably not used to such camaraderie.

I was not a person who was politically motivated. I still really did not understand what politics were about. It wasn't something that was ever discussed at home. I knew Mum and Dad leaned towards the Labour Party because they had their poster in our window at election time. Alderman Trevitt, who was the Mayor of Southend and Labour councillor kindly, gave me a reference for the Police. He was regular churchgoer where I went to Boys Brigade. Also I suppose you could say that the experience I got in the timber yard when the foreman insisted that before the start of work each morning we stood around an imaginary flag pole while he sung a rendition of the "Red Flag". The only words of which I could remember was those my Dad used to sing which I think was the end lines, "The working class can kiss my arse I've got the foreman's' job at last".

I could honestly say that by default, of not knowing anything political, I was non-politically motivated.

I was mature. I knew when I had reached that maturity the first time I went to Boys Brigade Camp. The bus had arrived and we had loaded all our bags onto the baggage lorry. I kissed my Mum goodbye and was just about to kiss my Dad when she pulled me back and said, "No. You don't do that now Bobby. You're grown up now". From that day on Dad and I always shook hands like men.

I was the descendant of an extremely large family. Dad was the youngest of a family of fourteen all London East Enders with the odd villain and Mum the middle one of eight nearly half of whom were Dorset Salvation Army and one who was a Detective Sergeant in Manchester, all honourable people with heaps of respect and dignity. I had gone through the gruelling tests of the Duke of Edinburgh's' award scheme and been to Buckingham Palace to receive the gold medal from the Duke himself. I never saw my Dads chest so stuck out as he and Mum stood with all the other proud parents.

I had seen the extreme of someone overcoming adversity and possessing such inner strength at its ultimate whilst doing the Award part of "Service to the Community" when I went to help a disabled elderly lady who had been abandoned by her family. She had no legs, both having been amputated some years previous, had lost the use of one arm and she crawled around the house finding no job too difficult to do.

She sang all the time. All the old music hall songs and was forever laughing. She would go out on her own in her wheelchair and before doing so would take meticulous care to her hair and makeup, "Just in case that Mr Right", turned up.

She was an inspiration, bright as a button and put all of us to shame for her enthusiasm for life.

She was the type of person above all others that I wanted to protect and serve as a police officer and the one of many who gave me the confidence to do that job effectively.

I could not hope to achieve her high degree of strength and determination but I was going to give it my best shot.

Could I have been more prepared for the experience of being a Copper? Only time would tell.

I was to be tested to the extreme throughout my career and none more so than dealing with death and its horrendous aftermath for the bereaved. However, in the beginning a felt none other than a need to do my duty and get on with what was expected of me.

AGONY MESSAGE

Reverence in such situations was a natural instinct but how to deliver an "agony" message to the very elderly required tact and understanding that "could only be gained from actually doing the job" explained the Sergeant when he gave such a message to deliver to an old chap whose brother had died suddenly.

Not many people possessed a telephone and telegrams could only be delivered during the day so the Police were asked quite often to deliver the "nasty". Even the BBC gave out messages to relatives who were urgently required to attend the bedside of an ailing relative near to death.

The Sergeant said, "We are told by the relatives in London that the chap is very frail and the death has been very sudden. Think about what you are going to say very carefully. We don't want another hospital job. Do we, son?" In a way I was pleased that I was now considered mature enough to be passing such a message. I had been back from training school two weeks so it was a time to be hard to the cause.

I borrowed the Sergeants bicycle and rode resolutely round to the leafy suburb of Southend to the small shrub surrounded bungalow where the agony had to be delivered. Agonising somewhat as to what to say to help the old man over the shock I marched up to the front door through a maze of overgrown bushes and perennials that seemed to tug at my raincoat almost trying to persuade me not to make the call. The smell of autumn leaves hung in the air just like it did at the local cemetery on those traditional dark rainy days that funerals always seem to take place. It was spooky!

The un-kept garden, slightly slippery wet path and dim yellowy light in the hall at the door impressed me more that this was not a good situation. I dusted the pollen and leaf debris of my uniform to make me at least presentable and lightly pressed the large white button on the bell in the centre of the door.

The ringing that came from within filled the whole garden and most of the road outside. Its' high pitched sound echoed on for a lifetime before receding into the distance. I heard the faint sound of a faraway voice, "Be with you in a minute", followed by a soft dragging of feet. The sound got slowly louder as a figure reached the front door. I felt sick by now and seriously thought about running away and returning with a note later. How do you tell a frail person that a loved one has passed away? There's no book to tell you how!

Numerous bolts slid and locks clicked open and the door creaked to allow the old man to appear before I could decide what best to do. "Mr Billings?" I asked. "Yes. Who are you?" he replied. "Police Constable Craven, sir", he's blind I thought.

"Sorry mate. Couldn't see you standing in the dark. Come in. It's bleeding cold out there", he replied and turned to shuffle back down the hall. I couldn't say to him that his brother was dead with his back turned to me so had to patiently follow him to the sitting room at the far end of the bungalow. Again this took ages until finally we got into the room where he lounged back into a huge armchair that seemed to envelope him.

"Would you like a cup of tea?" I said hoping to get the comforting off to a nice start. "Yea. 'Course mate never say no to a cuppa. But what exactly have you come round for. It ain't a social visit is it?" he replied.

Shit, I thought, I am going to have to come right out with it. Taking a deep breath I said, "I am afraid I have got some sudden bad news for you. Are you okay?" reassuring myself that he was as prepared as he could be. He nodded and I continued," I am afraid you brother Albert has passed away earlier this evening in London".

There was a gasp from his lowered face, "Fucking hell. I didn't expect that mate. That is a shock". "Yes it must be when someone dies so sudden like that", I agreed. He said, "No. Nothing to do with that mate, I thought Albert had died fucking years ago. I hated the bastard anyway. Bloody conchie during the war! Couldn't stand him. Here officer you look as if you could do with a cuppa. You ain't half white". I nodded with relaxed humour and several cups of tea, with snorts of whisky topping it up, later left with all intact and message satisfactorily delivered.

Actual dead bodies were something I had not experienced. My first was a "sudden death" as it was said when I received the telephone call from the Station Information Room. The landlady of a guesthouse in Heygate Avenue had said that one of her lodgers had been found dead when she had taken him his morning cup of tea. I was on a High Street foot patrol on early turn and sauntered to the house just off my beat. The call was given to me to get me some experience so I was aware that the rest of the shift was waiting in anticipation of my sickly return.

By the time I got to the house the funeral directors were already in attendance, the doctor had signed the certificate enabling them to remove the body and they awaited the arrival of officialdom, me, to give my verdict and then (the real reason) to assist them to carry the body to the hearse.

Eager to please and enthusiastic to help I naturally agreed to put my youthful strength to good use. I took command of the situation as per training school instructions and stated that as the youngest I would take the lower stairs of the narrow landing and hallway whilst the older ones took the top half of the body and carrying position. "If you are sure Constable", said one of the Funeral Directors, not so confident in my decision.

I then entered the deceased's bedroom and to my horror saw the most enormous trunk of a body laying on a weight sagged bed. The landlady said remorsefully, " Mr Lawton was renowned for his drinking. It must have got the better of him. He seemed okay to me last night and ate several helpings of his favourite sausage and onion pie and rhubarb crumble". I didn't fail to notice the anguish displayed on the smaller funeral director's face but revived my anxiety by clapping my hands together and revving myself into action saying, " Let's get on with it. Duty calls!"

All went well. We negotiated the upper landing and then turned to go down the stairs. The two directors had worked well by holding the deceased under his arms and I had positioned myself between the top parts of his legs. They had tried a box (coffin) but could not get it up the stairs and round the corners.

We got down four steps when the deceased farted. Before the landlady could finish her habit, of saying "Pardon" on his behalf, the stairwell filled with the most grotesque smell. The shock of such an immediate affect almost put me off balance. The small director quickly brought back to my senses when he shouted with screwed-up nose, "For fuck sake! Sorry madam for swearing. Get him down the bloody stairs before he shits all over you!"

It took no more encouragement to get me floating down the stairs in two long strides. Frantically pulling the two directors men with me through the hall, out the front door, across the small front garden path and onto the road and onto the collection tray that protruded from the hearse. "Jesus. That was close", the relieved directors agreed.

I waved them off and then closely inspected my uniform for any tell tale signs of body fluids. I had six more hours on duty yet. I am sure some people smelt that strange smell on me as they past me on my beat on the High Street.

It became quite common for bodies to be part of our duties. All were treated with dignity and care for the bereaved but in some cases it was impractical and basic handling had to take over.

SLIPPERY FRIED EGGS AND LIQUOR

A body had been found floating out at sea by local fishermen. They had managed to catch it in their net and were unable to get it on board their boat so they brought to the Lifeboat jetty at the far end of our pier. Southend Pier is purported to be the longest pleasure pier, at one mile and a third long, in the world and you get to the end by using a train.

When I got to the jetty the fishermen were very anxious to get back to work as they were losing the tide. The water was still coming in and about to take the body back out to sea very soon. They had disentangled it from their net and it lay at the waters edge. Just as I arrived a large wave, caused by some large vessel passing down the Thames, crashed onto the jetty displacing the body and floating it back towards the edge and deep water.

I instinctively leapt forward and grabbed hold of its arm at the elbow. As its weight pulled away from me I tightened my grip and the rotting flesh started to strip from the bone and a slimy cold translucent yellowy jelly oozed through my fingers. A watch on its wrist seemed to congeal the sludge enabling me to pull the body a little further up the jetty. I was determined not to use my other hand that I dearly wanted to keep clean but this soon changed as I lost my footing on the slippery seaweed that covered the jetty. I was suddenly aware that the fishermen had left me, obviously not realising my predicament, and I was on my own fighting to save the corpse from a burial at sea, again, and it was taking me with it.

I grabbed hold of the remnants of a shirt collar that covered the body and then heard a voice, "Okay officer I've got the legs". The coxswain from the Lifeboat station stood there. An imposing character with grey beard and smart uniform and the brightest of yellow waders stood there. He tightly gripped the clothing of the body at its waist and with one haul swung it back onto the jetty. "Thanks mate ", I sighed to which he replied, "Years of experience went into that Constable. I've got a carrier for these up top. I'll go and get it if you want". I acknowledged him and then washed the slime from my hands in the seawater.

The body was blackened and small creatures crawled over every part. I was tempted to search it to identify the deceased but decided to wait for some hand covering that I hoped would turn up with the funeral directors or doctor. The coxswain returned to his lifeboat station and the body was soon taken away.

We later identified him as a seaman who fallen overboard three days earlier from a Swedish cargo ship en-route to Tilbury. He had had a drink or two too many and stumbled over the railings during the night. The ship was still moored in the estuary and arrangements were made for myself, and a Detective Sergeant to go out to the ship and interview the crew and any likely witnesses to the incident.

We went out on a small boat the following day. Quite a swell was kicking up on the sea and waves were crashing over the top of the craft. We were sheltered by a front open backed cabin from the spray but still got soaking wet. I was not badly protected by my uniform raincoat but the DS wore a blazer and grey slacks with a white shirt and ex-army association tie, the accepted attire worn by CID officers.

A blue pair of overalls was handed to him to change into from his wet outfit that was taken away by the steward fro drying.

The overalls did not show off degree of officialdom that the suit was supposed to display.

Quick interviews were the order of the day to accommodate the DS's predicament and all the crew were soon seen and their accounts of the incident were recorded in my pocket book. Most were able to speak good English but I was concerned when the DS told me that I would have to take notes in Swedish if some did not speak our language. He very quickly comforted my fear realising that he needed to get the job done so he could get dressed normally.

Two crewmen who were on duty and sober at the time and assuring us said that the deceased, who was drunk, fell overboard quite accidentally as he leant over the railing being sick. The job seemed to be wrapped up and we were just about to pack up and leave when the Captain announced that they had just been warned that a bad squall was expected and it would very dangerous for us to sail in a small craft back to the Pier Head.

The trip out to the ship was bad enough but climbing up the side of it from the small boat on a one-foot wide rope ladder was one of the scariest moments I have ever experienced. Climbing up a six storey high dead flat metal wall with no hold places rocking in a swelling sea and gusting wind. Even though we had a safety rope tied to our waists and held by the crew above my knuckles, arms and shoulders were grazed and bruised as I was swung and crashed against the ships hull.

We could very well appreciate that the going down the rope ladder would not be any easier and a lot more dangerous that was be before we got onto the small boat, if we did, and made our way to dry land.

The DS obviously had something else more important on his mind and exclaimed, "Well that's fucking great! DS. "The DCI will go berserk".

The Captain replied in impeccable English with a soft calming Swedish lilt. "Do not worry Detective Sergeant. I will explain to your superiors how serious the situation is. We have to leave the mooring and sail to Tilbury. (Pity it wasn't somewhere more exciting like the Caribbean – I thought) You will be able to get off there tomorrow.

We were shown to a cabin where we could shower and get some sleep. But what could we do until then. It was only 8 pm.

The Captains steward soon set the scene saying, "You will have dinner with the Captain and his officers and they have invited you to their lounge for drinks and perhaps a game of cards or pool. Sounded okay to me but the DS was still sulking in his overalls".

"Have you got any other clothing more suitable that I can use?" he pleaded with the steward. "You're clothes have been dried and are being pressed now", said the steward reassuringly.

I showered and changed and smartened myself up for the dinner. Assuming it was going to is a formal event like you see on the films. All sparkling medals, slick haircuts, razor sharp creases in the uniforms and mirror shiny shoes. My uniform tunic was presentable, the trousers had been wet but had ironed out to a stiff crease but in my haste to button up my collar I had broken the front collar stud. Our uniform shirts still had separate collars. Very handy when you were single as you could wear a shirt for a few days, subject to sweat etc, and have a clean collar everyday.

You could always recognise an off duty police officer when he had an open neck shirt or similar on, as he would have a red coin sized mark in the area of his Adams' apple on the front of his neck which is where the stud was forced against the skin. Some traders in the town used to recognise this mark and give you 10% off the bill. So it did come in handy even though it was very sore when you first joined the Police.

If the front stud could not be secured to attach the collar to the shirt the loose collar could spring out. I did not want to let the side down at the dinner so I struggled for ages to secure the collar. I tried a paper clip, cello tape and chewing gum but none would work so when the steward called us for dinner I had to work out how I could eat with one hand and hang onto the wayward collar with the other without drawing attention to myself.

I got to the officers mess first, not knowing whether it was appropriate or bad manners to do so before the hosts, and the steward, now smartly dressed in short white jacket, black trousers, white winged collared shirt and black bow tie, welcomed me asking if everything was in order in my cabin. Then from an implement that resembled a wooden log he poured a clear liquid into a small glass, which he then placed on a small silver napkin covered tray.

The glass looked very lonely on the tray and somewhat threatening as I thought. "Am I being compromised by a villainous opponent with evil intent using some lethal high octane drug or is it an mildly alcoholic drink from a genuinely innocent and friendly host?"

I examined the look on the steward's face to establish the truth of the situation. Thought should I be drinking on duty? But was I actually on duty? Then bollocks to it! He seems okay. The drink looks okay. So I took it and sipped delicately from the rim of the tiny glass. My lips set fire and the tip of my tongue numbed instantly.

The steward studied for a response and advised me, "You will find that it is better to drink pine schnapps down in one so it hits the centre of the body in a solid mass. The reindeer nomads in the north of our country find this the best way to counter the freezing elements they suffer". My instant reaction was to decide that this man was a liar and just trying to get one over me.

My indecision was soon overcome as the door opened and the ships officers entered one by one. Gripping the glass in one hand and shaking theirs with the other I waited for them to take the potion from the glasses that now filled the tray.

To my relief they all took one swig of their glasses without any adverse reactions. Some straightened their backs and others rubbed their hands together in a natural acceptance of the feelings their bodies were going through and said various Swedish words of appreciation. None fell around in pain or shock so I felt comfortable to take my turn.

I took one swig. A cool icy feeling flowed down my throat and into the centre of my chest. It reached just below my rib cage and then suddenly burnt its way back up to my throat, flew into my ears and down my nose. My eyes burst into tears and my mouth gaped open to release a body load of overbearing heat. I gasped that well known sexual expletive, "F.......... sake!" Hunched back and holding onto the table I was struggling to regain my composure when the door opened and the captain entered. Dressed resplendent in full evening uniform he looked at me then glared at the steward and said, "I suppose you have given our guest a full tot of the schnapps and not a half measure as a first timer should have. One day Stefan you will give someone a heart attack. Get on with the dinner". "Are you okay, Officer?

I must apologise for the behaviour". He patted my back and obviously did not expect an answer as he turned the tray, drank two glasses in quick succession of the schnapps and as if to reinforce the fact that I would get my voice back shortly, turned to one of the other officers who were doing their best not to laugh and said, "Have we sorted out dinner. What have we got?"

One officer approached him and whispered in his ear. The captain showed a sense of displeasure at what he heard and stormed into the galley next door. The two way door crashed against a table on the other side so much that it returned crashing against the book case in the mess and then repeated itself several times before resting to a halt. I monstrous row then took place beyond the door. The captain's voice could be heard shouting and screaming. Even to the non-Swedish speaking layman there was no doubt the intention of the tirade and the meaning behind the fury that included a lot of table thumping, utensil usage and what was suspiciously like face slapping. My mind had regained a bit of stability to question if we were in international waters and if there was a murder how we would be able to deal with it when the Detective Sergeant came into the mess. "What the fuck is happening? I thought we had been boarded by pirates!" he exclaimed.

The sight of the DS standing in the doorway stunned us all into to silence in total contrast to the din that was still coming from the galley. Our gaping mouths and shocked expressions triggered a response from the DS who could only stand with arms outstretched and a look of "Give me some sympathy" on his face.

His smart blazer sleeves now only reached to about half way down his forearm and showed about twelve inches of shirt and his trousers resembled a pair of pedal pushers worn by teenage girls then. The legs were so short that a length of hairy bare skin could be seen above the top each sock. It did not help that the wind outside had blown his hair so that it stood on end and his tie was dishevelled and on the skew either. To the ships officers the circus had come to town.

"I know," he retorted, "That stupid bastard steward put my trousers and blazer in the boiler room. They were so close to the boiler and got so bloody hot that I had to hang them outside on the deck to cool them down before I could put them on. Then they got wet again so I had to wait for them to dry. They of course are wool aren't they? So they've fucking shrunk. Haven't they?"

None of us had realised that the Captain had rejoined us in the mess and had heard the best part of what the DS had said. The door to the galley flew open as the Captain launched himself in at the steward again.

A second round of verbal violence followed with this time yells of pain. Shortly the captain reappeared. Pulling his uniform straight, brushing himself off to remove some dust from his tunic and then raising his chest to gather composure he announced, "Gentlemen. It would appear that Stefan has created a high degree of embarrassment to us and he will not be able to serve the first class type of cuisine that we are usually able to honour our guests with. He gives his sincere apologies and promises to create an "extravaganza of eggs" as that is all he has in the kitchen. Apparently he did not check the grocery delivery in Zeebrugge and appears that instead of the usual foodstuffs of meat, vegetables etc he had ordered we only received three very large boxes of goose eggs that should have been transported to a local restaurant. Please accept my sincerest apologies."

We all settled down at the table and formal chat descended into the room. What seemed to be an age passed before Stefan the steward announced at the galley doorway, "Dinner. It is to be served". Napkins were placed upon laps and cutlery handled in expectation as Stefan entered carrying a large stainless steel platter aloft in one hand looked proud enough to please any experienced silver service waiter.

He placed the platter in the centre of the table avoiding touching any of those seated and especially avoiding any eye contact with the Captain. Silence and open mouths greeted the sight of the huge slimy piled mass of half cooked fried eggs that filled the platter.

Holding his hand outstretched in the direction of the head of the table the First Officer said with some gall, "Captain would you do the honours and cut the joint?" A moments' thought by the Captain and uncertainty paused the remainder and then with a shrug the Captain replied, "Oh what the fuck. I am pissed at it is and so fucking hungry. It could be oysters as far as I could taste. Lets' get on with it".

My sentiments entirely I thought and we all set in to devour the imaginary oysters and copious quantities of pine schnapps. Stefan even felt secure enough to ask if we required a sweet after the main course. A drunken response from us all resulted in a further mountain of slime. This time I could not focus very well and I was not sure whether the ship was rolling or the eggs were swimming around naturally in the platter.

I remember a number of those present collapsing in a variety of positions in the room but little else of that evening. I woke up in the cosy cabin, fully dressed and body aching from end to end. A sharp knock on the door and the sudden gust of salty air mixed with oil fumes gathered my senses sufficient enough to remind me that I was still on the ship and "on duty".

A large mug of hot liquid that resembled tea and Stefan's answer to an English wake up beverage was thrust under my nose. One sip from the foul substance enabled me to gather my senses and rush to join the DS and captain in the Officers Mess. An egg breakfast was offered and immediately turned down. To our rescue came the dockside at Tilbury and DS and I floated ashore down the stairway attached to the side of the ship. Fortunately the height from dry land was fairly short as the fully laden vessel settled against the dockside. We waved to the crewmembers who maybe waving us farewell but unable to raise our chins above our chests did not see anyone.

We drifted through the bustling docks gaining the occasional glance from forklift drivers and stevedores when we were aware of a police car at our side. The Port of London Officer in the drivers seat said sympathetically, "I heard about your demise and thought you may need a lift to the station. Can't have the cream of the county coming to any harm in this den of iniquity. Can we?" He laughed and en route to Tilbury Dock Station he comforted us that we were not the only people to fall foul of the pine schnapps. Some had even ended up in hospital suffering from alcoholic poisoning. The level of pure alcoholic in the stuff is apparently well over the safety level for human consumption.

A very grateful snowdrop and detective sergeant dressed like a clown caught the train back to the safety of home turf and the Borough. After a short nap and a wash and brush up in the train toilet (or what passed as a toilet) I was prepared for the walk from Southend Central Railway Station to the nick.

"Take a deep breath son", Said the DS as left the station and walked into the High Street. "Just keep your head up and eyes straight ahead", he nodded forwarded and we both marched in step up the High Street. We were totally unaware of what our public was seeing as our sole concentration was fixed on keeping awake and purposefully marching straight, erect and in step. This was the only way we could guarantee that we reached our goal without embarrassing the "cloth" or ourselves.

We coasted through the crowds, negotiated the gantry temporary bridge at the Victoria Circus development site that worryingly took us to the dizzy height of the ship once again and onto Victoria Avenue and into the rear entrance of the police station.

We crashed through the door leading to the stairs up into the CID office. Turned right still in marching automatic and into the detective sergeants office. The sergeant collapsed into a chair and I fell against a filing cabinet holding onto the shoulder height handle for support.

There was not time to catch our breath when the Detective Chief Inspector screamed at us, " Where the fuck have you two been. You've been missing for three days"! The DS looked questioningly at me, looked at his watch, tapping it and then shrugging his shoulders with a questioning frown asked me, "Is there a dateline between here and Tilbury"? "I don't bloody know", I answered silently by shaking my head. Even though I had got an 'o' level in geography my brain could not take that level of thought at that time.

"I'll soon sort you two out. Think you can have me over. Suppose you've got pocketfuls of duty free. In my office now", blasted the DCI. We sloped off into his office that looked out over the fountains of the Town Square with the Civic Centre on one side and the Court House on the other.

As we went in the DCI was standing facing out of the window with his hands behind his back, cigarette dangling from his pouting lips and singing a little song. We went in further and heard the tune of the Rolf Harris song "Two Little Boys" but with the words, "Do you think I'll believe you lying when there's room over there for you". Looking straight at the Court House at the time it was obvious what his intentions were and what followed was a tirade of accusations that we had been malingering on a cruise ship in the sunny Thames Estuary when the whole Force, Coastguards, Lifeboats and international agencies were searching for us believing that we were lost at sea.

It was a hopeless task trying to explain although as a lowly Constable I had no desire to gain an opportunity. The DS tried in vain to explain that there was a severe storm and the captain had advised us to stay aboard but even he did not attempt to try and say why we were away for three days. He did suggest that it was only two days but the DCI retorted that this was the third day and went into another tirade suggesting that we everything but pirates on the high seas. Realising the hopelessness of the situation the DS settled back in his chair and just let the DCI continue. As he relaxed he caught sight of the DCI's cigarette box on his desk. It was open and a handful of cigarettes found there way via the DS and into my the large pocket of my raincoat that had fallen at the foot of the bosses desk.

I froze and in fear of disturbing the DCI in full flow was only able to silently mouth my disapproval to the DS. He reassured me in kind by closing the lid of the cigarette box, in sign language told me not to worry and "It's okay" with a circle of his thumb and finger, "thumbs up" sign and then settled back in his chair to listen intently to the DCI.

A nervous age of half consciousness went by when the DCI startled us into full attention, turned to look in our direction and said, "Make a full duty report and cover all the points I have raised. I want it on my desk in two days, right"? "Yes Sir. Can it be a joint report", asked the DS. I was out the door, straight into the toilets opposite and puked for England. As I recovered to my horror I realised that I had left my raincoat on the floor in the DCI's office.

In a blind panic I hurtled through the swing doors of the CID office, scattering everyone in my wake to spill the bad news to the DS. With a broad grin on his face he held the raincoat in my direction and gave a satisfying nod that all was well. He said, "Don't worry about anything mate. I'll sort this lot out. Go home and sleep it off. I am". I grasped the raincoat and scooted out of the office, only stopping to get my breath when I had reached the sanctity of uniform cloakrooms where I checked the pockets of my raincoat. There were no cigarettes in the pockets. Was it something I had dreamed in my stupor?

A quick visit to the Admin Office satisfied me that we had only been gone for two days not three and I didn't hear any more about the incident again.

DEALING WITH DEATH

As time passed I became hardened to dealing with the dead and dying although the hard exterior could never prepare you for the "kiss of life" of an elderly male who had suffered a heart attack after consuming a large portion of cod and chips accompanied by a pickled onion and wally washed down by three pints and Watneys Red barrel bitter after a starter of jellied eels.

Such a situation does call for an extremely high level of dedication, resolve and persuasion by the victims begging relatives. Without the help of the aids now available to first aiders to cover over distasteful areas I had to help such a chap outside the Peter Pans Playground next to the Pier one sunny summers day. Following instructions to check for a pulse and remove all obstacles like false teeth from the airway it suddenly struck me that nobody had told me the dangers of someone having false teeth, as I did, giving mouth to mouth. Was there a chance that you blow your false teeth down the casualties' throat?

As a safeguard I delicately removed my teeth and having ascertained that he had no pulse and no teeth commenced to blow into his open mouth. The thought did cross my mind that I had put his teeth in the same pocket as mine and to make sure that when the time come not to mix the sets up.

He did not show any signs of pulse so I started to do heart massage and place timed pressure on his chest. As I pumped a second time, one, two, three a sudden whooshing sound and a large piece of cod hit the left side of my face followed by chips, eels and beer. The old boy had started to breath again!

The ambulance arrived and took him and his relative to hospital. As I went to find the nearest washrooms I felt something hard in my pocket. Realising it was my teeth I took them and placed them in my mouth only to discover that they did not fit and it was the old boys. Spluttering somewhat I retrieved my own and had a good wash out and wash over. Then I had to find a volunteer patrol car to take the forgotten teeth to be joined up with their owner.

A messy business, but humour of a kind that helps you to do the job. I gave such assistance to other probationer constables at times when I would hide on the tray of the mortuary fridge until younger probationers were brought in by other officers to see "a corpse". The probationer would be left in the mortuary on their own and told to open a drawer number and prepare the body (Me) for autopsy (undress and clean).

He would pull the drawer out to reveal a sheet-covered corpse. As he pulled the sheet back I would just say, "Boo!" It was quite unbelievable the different reactions you got. Nobody fainted or was affected in any serious way until one day I was lying in the fridge awaiting my next victim. All prepared and waiting patiently in the chill air, at first I was not too concerned about the length of time it was taking for the probationer to come and be surprised.

I could get out if there was a problem by just releasing the catch to the drawer from the inside but the time seemed to tick by and I was starting to feel a cold chill entering my body. I do not know why but I looked for some reassurance along the line of drawers inside the fridge. It was dark but you could make out other bodies lying there as light shone from outside through tiny cracks between the drawers.

I started to feel for the release catch above my head and had difficulty in getting the appropriate pressure to get me out. I slight wave of panic came over me but a gigantic wave of terror stuck me when the corpse beside me in a broad Scots accent said, "Fucking cold in here mate. Isn't it"? My whole body exploded into a frenzy of the need to escape but before I could do so my drawer and the one of the talking corpse were opened to roar of laughter from a mortuary full of policemen. The probationer, a mature Scots ex-army, constable had heard about my trick and turned the tables.

I did manage to repay the compliment to the Scotsman some months later when he was asked to investigate some noises coming from a freshly dug grave in a local cemetery.

As he gingerly approached and peered into the grave he was confronted by a skeleton (loaned from a local second hand shop) and wired hand and foot so that one pull in four directions made it leap upwards out of the grave. He did not catch any of us who carried the job out but he knew who it was we are sure.

SPRATS AND BESTIALITY

The first arrest is not to be forgotten by any officer but mine came at a very inopportune moment. Still living at home with my parents it was not unusual to be asked by my Mum to pick up something on my tour of duty. If I could carry it!

At Southend we have the delight of having our own fishing fleet that every Friday would sell their catch from one of the jetties next to the Pier. Our family loved sprats, the very small fish that taste delicious covered in flour and just fried. Eaten with bread and butter and large mug of tea, beautiful!

I was on the beat that covered the south end of the High Street and therefore well placed to nip down to the jetty and pick up the fish. No problem with that, but as I walked back up Pier Hill and into the High Street the police post blue light at that point was flashing. "Constable 169 reporting in. What's up?" I responded. "Get up to the traffic lights at Heygate and the High Street. There're up the creek for some reason", was the ordered reply from the Information Room Controller.

Great! What do I do with the sprats? Put them in my helmet. It is just big enough!

My first opportunity to take control of a set of traffic lights! The traffic was grid locked at the junction. Tempers were fraying, fists raised, hooters sounding and a lot of shouting as I took up my position of total command. I raised my right arm to all those vehicles that had not entered the middle of the junction and stopped them from driving any further.

I then meticulously signalled by hand commands all vehicles on the junction to proceed with caution away from the area. Some seemed angry that I had ordered them away in a direction that they did not wish to go but went the same anyway. I was all-powerful and made the drivers know that I was in charge.

Then, having cleared the junction of all vehicles I smartly marched to the traffic light junction box. I placed my official traffic light switch key into the switch and turned the key onto red at all entrances to the junction then systematically manually operated the lights to clear the backlog of traffic. As motorists passed you could sense that their answer to the hold up was some stupid copper was operating the lights and causing the problem. I did not really care I had so much control. One nasty look and I could quite easily stop them at the junction for hours.

As I revelled in the esteemed dominance I heard this little voice crying at me from the opposite side of the road. It seemed like a cry but was actually a little woman in her late twenties shouting and waving at me, "Officer, Store detective - Marks and Spencer. That man has just stolen things. Chase after him "! I looked in the direction she was pointing and saw this man, middle aged carrying a large holdall, running with a woman of similar age.

I took off my helmet and placed it securely under my arm to safeguard the sprats, having taking pride in my fitness and being ready to leap into action I took up the chase of a runaway thief at last. Oh! How I had been waiting for this opportunity.

I did not have to run very far. The old chap seemed to accept his destiny and slowed down however the woman carried on. I caught up with the man and took his wrist. The store detective soon joined us and explained that she had seen him take a number of items from the store without paying for them.

My mind had to get back to training school and the scenario of an arrest and how the procedure went. Holding his arm firmly I led him back to the store There I got the store detective to explain the allegation in the presence and hearing of the accused. I then had to caution the accused and ask him if he has anything to say. I arrested him, cautioned him and take him to the police station.

Done job! Although during our time in the store office a number of people present kept looking at each other as if there was a nasty smell somewhere. In the patrol car taking the thief and me to the station one the crew asked the thief if the shock of the arrest had made his bowels loose. I did not like to say it was coming from my now sweaty helmet.

I noticed as we drove down the High Street to the Police Station that the traffic was particularly heavy but had not got a clue until I was called into the Inspectors office after taking my prisoner in.

I thought he was going to pat me on the back for carrying out my first arrest and showing the Force in good light by running after the thief but, no! "You stupid bastard. Do you know the problems you caused today?" I silently shook my head. "The mayor was held up getting to a funeral because you broke your key off in the lock of the traffic light box. The bottom end of the High Street and town has been a nightmare. We could not get the box to operate so I have had to supply an officer on permanent point duty until we can get an engineer to sort it out and guess who that is going to be. Get your paperwork sorted out with the prisoner and get down to the traffic lights and stay there until you are relieved.

Good job he did not know about the sprats. I managed to put them in the canteen fridge until I went off duty but my hair smelt of fish for weeks.

A footnote to this arrest was another eye opener to the job. After an arrest an officer has to check the identity of the accused and ensure that there are no warrants for his arrest elsewhere or likely matters that could be relevant such as "is on bail already for other offences, has he any previous convictions, has he a fixed address etc".

This shoplifter had quite a few convictions for theft and unusually one for bestiality (Having sexual intercourse with an animal). Being young in service and open to any form of education I asked the man to tell me about the incident. He said, in a deep East Anglia brogue, that it was with a cow in a milking shed on a farm where he was working.

He casually explained the finer details of raising the cows' tail and being drawn into its body. I said disgustedly, "Surely that must have hurt you?" He replied, "Only when the fucking stool fell over and I was left hanging there. Bloody farmer heard me screaming and had to call the vet to get me out!"

I didn't really want to know any more of the sordid details and really wished I hadn't asked in the first place. Such is the learning curve us probationers have to tread.

The fact that I had inadvertently left the traffic lights and chased the shoplifter, without regard for the plight of the motorists, was probably an omen for things to come. My enthusiasm for dealing with criminal offences was to be far greater in later years than that of motor vehicle misdemeanours.

Many officers of my young years of service had aspirations to be a detective in the CID or a Traffic Officer in the elite department driving fast cars. Both departments had a degree of suspicion of the other. CID officers were thought to be drunks who spent most of their time hanging around licensed premises mixing with loose women supposedly seeking out criminals and informants whereas the Traffic Officer was deemed to be earning a nice bonus by sending accident damaged cars to the favourite garage who paid for a "golden hook" job which meant being paid to send crashed cars to particular garages.

This always caused harmless banter between the fine officers of both.

HEART PUMPING AND KARMA SUTRA

My first experience of a real live criminal investigation operation was to be one of the most heart stopping occasions that I can remember in my police service.

I was placed on permanent duty with a large number of other uniform and CID officers to work from 6.00pm to 6.00am every night for the next seven nights. We paraded for duty at 5.50pm on the designated night in the CID office. The office was packed with detectives, in suits, puffing on cigarettes who kept their distance from the lower uniform officers noticeable for their trendy late sixties casual attire like polo neck sweaters, Fred Perry shirts and corduroy trousers. The age difference between the two was quite significant, as it was well known that you did not stand a chance of getting into the CID until you had ten years service.

There were all these old boys; some even had trilby hats, and all these young, wet behind the ears upstarts making up the investigation team.

The Detective Inspector outlined the work to be done. We were all to split up in pairs of one CID Officer with one Divisional Officer, like me, and each pair was to take up an observation point in either a Hairdressing Salon or Opticians. All premises of that type were to be occupied by us in the Borough. I had no idea how many there were in the Borough but by the huge number of officers gathered there must have been enough men to cover in excess of sixty odd shops.

The DI explained that we had suffered twenty break-ins at such premises and we had no idea who was doing it. Fingerprints had been found but they did not match anyone who had been convicted in the past. Small amounts of cash had been taken and other odd items of value. The last one to have been done was the salon where the wife of one of the "scrambled egg lot" (reference to Chief Officers whose lapels and caps bore an insignia that resembled scrambled egg) got her hair done. It sent the "teasy weezy" into such turmoil that he was not able to concentrate on any blue or pink rinses for sometime to come.

The DI continued, "As you are no doubt aware we cannot have that. Now can we men"?

A wave of muffled laughter rippled round the room. The DI then read out the pairings and the premises we all designated to observe from.

I was partnered with a very experienced Detective Sergeant who recognising my inexperience put his arm over my shoulder and said, "When we get to the hairdressers just keep your mouth shut. Let me do the talking. Just be there to back me up.

We arrived at our salon. A very upmarket "Salon de Coiffeur", not hairdressers, in a Westcliff on Sea. We were met by the owner, a lady about the same age as the DS, immaculately turned out with a superb figure, glossy magazine make up, manicured nails and exquisite jet black hair. She thanked the DS for his protection, acknowledged me, turned the lights off and cruised out of the shop locking the front door as she went.

"Stop gaping you stupid bastard", the DS snapped as he lit yet another cigarette. "Let's have a look round the place. Must be some tea making stuff here somewhere", he added. "Shit", I suddenly remembered that I had left my neat box of sandwiches and flask of tea back at the nick. My Mum will be mad! "Just like you being back at school this is", she had said as she tucked the Tupperware box full of goodies and flask under my arm.

Now I had left all of it back at the nick I had to survive somehow until six in the morning. Another eleven hours or so! The DS's idea of tea making might mean a tin of biscuits or other emergency rations. We were okay of sorts and found some coffee, no milk and three stale Crawford Cream Cracker biscuits. Although the DS hadn't told me I gathered that he had not provided himself with some refreshments. I got the impression that he thought he may have been sharing mine. Black coffee it was. There weren't any weevils in the biscuits either to provide us with some protein.

We checked the premises and ensured all doors and windows were secured and settled down for a long night. We took up positions on the soft salon chairs and unable to read or carry out any conversation drifted off into our own thoughts. The DS lit yet another cigarette and threw his head back and blew the smoke silently upwards into the air. My mind floated and took me back into the Mickey Spillane detective novels I used to read but this time I was on a real life stake out.

I must have drifted off a lot further as what seemed like hours later I was suddenly hauled out of my chair by a massive explosion of breaking glass coming, from the rear of the salon. I could almost see my heart pounding against the inside of my chest and its' thumping filled my head. I was suddenly struck with the fear that the burglar could actually hear my heart beating.

A hand gently calmed me back down into the chair, the thumping receded slowly and the DS's face came into focus with his finger over his lips to further console me.

Reassuring me to stay in my chair with an open hand he went and stood by a dividing wall that separated the kitchen where the smashing sound had come from and the main salon area. I full expected the burglar to come through and braced myself with one hand on my truncheon and the other on firmly grasping heavy rubber torch. I was steady and ready now.

My eyes had adjusted to the yellow light from the street outside I saw the DS beckon me up to his side then over to the opposite side of the door to the kitchen. He passed me a cigarette. It was already lit. How he did that without me knowing is still a mystery. I didn't smoke but it seemed rude to refuse. After a dizzy shaking of the head and the huge battle not to cough the fag seemed to calm me down. I finished it and was then left with what to do about the butt. Its first burn of my finger made me drop it on the kitchen floor. I trod it out with my foot. The DS said nothing and handed me another fag. I refused and signalled to him by placing my hand with small finger and thumb at my ear asking silently, "Shall I telephone?"

He nodded in approval. I crawled to the reception desk carefully lifted the receiver and suddenly thought, "What the hell is the Police Station number?" I crawled back to the DS and mimed, "Don't know number". He mouthed an obscene word (part of a ladies anatomy) and crawled to the phone. He came back a short time later and mimed with the finger and thumb to his ear and then a slash of the outstretched hand across his throat that I took to mean the phone was dead.

As we stood in the dark either side of the smashed window, unable to move in case we trod on the broken glass strew across the tiled floor of the kitchen, the DS was like a cigarette machine, producing a never ending stream of already lit cigarettes from his pocket. He would do this by dipping his lower part of his head, with the cigarette in his mouth, into his raincoat, holding his lapel outwards with one hand. A quick flick of the lighter in his other hand would successfully light the cigarette without so much of a glimmer of light to be seen around to him.

I marvelled at this professional expertise and thought that this could only have been achieved from hours of standing in the dark undercover.

What seemed like even more hours passed until we heard the sound of glass being picked out of the smashed window. Anticipating that a leg and then the full body of the burglar was about to come through the window I tensed myself up to grab whatever I could of the person as he hit the kitchen floor. The picking stopped after a couple of seconds and all went very quiet.

The stony silence continued until eight o'clock the following morning when the lovely salon owner returned to unlock. Momentarily startled by our presence in the shop, she apologised and said it had slipped her mind that we were there, and then the DS explained what had happened. Obviously annoyed that we had not protected her property as expected she agreed to leave the window until the scenes of crime officers had inspected the window. He warned her that they would leave a lot of black dust in their search for fingerprints. A lowering of the thick black lined eyes and faint "tut" from tightened lips showed further irritation as her busy day had not even started.

When we returned to the police station the DS dismissed me back to the uniform offices saying he will sort things out from here. I headed for the lunch box and flask that I left the previous night and gorged on the now soggy sandwiches and luke warm tea from the flask. I just could not waste my Mums' efforts and sheer hunger dictated that they be gone before I left to go home to bed.

These night observations continued at various other premises with different partners for the rest of week without any more excitement except at one salon a found a copy of the Karma Sutra. A very interesting and very satisfying read in torch light under a raincoat in a perfumed ladies hairdressing salon. Fortunately I was assigned these same premises for four nights so I was able to complete the whole educating volume.

Some weeks later the burglar was arrested after attempting to break into an opticians in Southchurch. I never found out why he did not continue his break in at the posh salon. Something spooked him or I suspect that he saw or smelt the cigarette smoke pouring through the smashed window.

This first prestigious selection of working with CID gave me a small incite into the work of investigating criminals and sowed the seed to get into that department. My work edged towards that goal and I found a natural leaning and interest in criminal affairs rather than traffic concerns.

My eye was always on the lookout for the unusual and the villains that lived in the town. Every one of them was known for his full Christian name, middle names and second name followed by his nickname, alias address and vehicle. Submitting information on them became an obsession for all of us young officers who wanted to "get on" and get noticed by those senior officers who could place us on the path to transfer upwards. Such was the competition for this elevation that one particular officer even stole information that he over heard others conferring on and would rush up to the senior CID officers and tell them before it could be told by those who had received it in the first instance. A type of nepotism we had to get used to in later years.

I was one of a large number of officers who had been born and grown up in the town. Information on criminal activity was easy to come by from old school mates, football teams and the many guys I knew from the pubs, coffee bars and clubs I used to frequent.

Southend did not have the level of very serious crime at that time. Whether it was because we were in the far corner of Essex and easily closed off, the tough stance by the Police or the natural good citizens who lived here, I do not know. But violence, burglary and vehicle crime was on the same level as other major towns in the southeast.

ICE COOL SAFE BREAKERS

Sometimes you would wonder how some of these villains made crime a worthwhile occupation. Such persons were two brothers who I met whilst working in an ice cream factory when I was at school.

The owner was a kindly Italian whose father had come to this country during the two world wars and set up his business making ice products and selling them during the summer months and then during the winter selling toffee apples and other home made sweets from his van around the streets of Southend. He had built up his business to a total of five vans and leased these to anyone with a driving licence and able to cope with the limited income that seasonal work would produce.

The two brothers' main aim was to work as little time for as much money they could purloin out of the Italian. The term "ducking and diving, swooping and probing" was used quite often by them when you asked about the "capers" they were currently up to.

When the vans were loaded you had to be extra vigilant that no other stock would disappear in their direction. The Italian always took pity on them after some misdemeanour especially when their elderly mother would come to see him and plead for him to give them regular work, "to keep them out of trouble".

One day on Early Turn the Sergeant gave me an anonymous telephone message addressed to me at the police station to the ice cream factory.

It said there was something funny about the van that the two brothers were driving last evening and that I should go and have a look at it. It wasn't unusual to have the occasional cup of tea with the Italian whilst I was on duty.

In those days "tea stops" were encouraged as a means of keeping your "ear to the ground" for local information and intelligence. The line was drawn with relatives and friends though as one of my colleagues found out when he was disciplined for neglect of duty (drinking tea) at a friends' house and received a fine of £5.

You had to be aware of your position being compromised though by some of the people you had tea stops with. One chef would insist you took his money to the local betting shop and place it for the noon horse races. It was very hard not to as his dripping toast and crusty rolls with fresh cut hot roast beef and horse radish sauce or home sausage and mustard fillings were a dream.

I followed up the anonymous information and went to the Ice Cream Factory.

The Italian greeted me in the usual way, a smiling face but a small frown of "what the bloody hell does he want"?

In a way I felt that he was proud that one of his boys had made it in the world so when he said, "Cup of tea Officer?" I took it as him relaying a bit of pride. As he greeted me he lead the way through the clutter of vans in the yard. All of the vans were at least 20 years old, in various states of disrepair and some probably un-roadworthy. Several skeletons of older vans stood to the back having been bastardised to supply parts for the aging fleet. Best that I did not see them close up.

One van however was quite distinguishable from the others. It settled extremely low on its axle, so much so that the tyres were barely off the main bodywork. I could see a small red fluffy mouse on the dashboard that was the trade toy belonging to the brothers. They were both reckoned to have mousy facial features and slightly buck teeth and warmed to being thought of as cuddly friendly people. Vermin never came into the equation.

Having exchanged pleasantries and drank the cup of tea I wished the Italian farewell and left, taking the details mentally of the low lying van on the way out.

Having no radio, I went to the public telephone opposite the factory entrance and using my issue account card arranged for the area car with two other officers on board to rendezvous with me to wait the departure of the two brothers.

Before the area car could make the meeting the van containing the two brothers came out of the yard. I sprinted across the road and waved it down to stop. The brothers one driving and the other standing in the serving area of the van looked startled but on seeing me relaxed a little. The driver leant out of the window and shouted, "For fuck sake Bob! Don't do that you frightened the shit out of me". I said, "Don't be daft. Thought I would have a chat. Haven't seen you for some time".

The van pulled over to the side with tremendous lurch. The passenger side door was opened so I could get in and sit on the dashboard inside the vehicle. That way I could eat an ice cream with my head above the windows and counter with nobody outside able to see my mouth devouring it.

As I got in I noticed the apprehension on the brothers' faces but when I said, "Ninety nine please mister". "Anything to oblige officer", replied the younger of the two as he went to the large cooler container. These were large insulated aluminium fridge boxes that filled the width of the van and went back about three feet. They had double lids at the top that gave access to ice cream and other products cooled by large flat solid ice packs inside.

As he took a cornet in one hand and serving spoon in the other I said, "You've got quite a load on here. You're almost down on your axles!" "Yea, I know we are expecting a good day today", said the older driver.

"What flavour do you want", said the younger. "I don't know. What have you got?" I replied and went to look in the fridge.

"You fucking dipstick. There is only one flavour!" shouted the driver to his brother. But by this time I was looking into the open fridge and saw the front of a green bank safe inside. There was the gold coloured embossed manufacturers insignia plate and large brass keyhole plate and heavy handle.

The Italians lack of mechanical expertise came in handy as the driver tried to vacate the vehicle only to have the door handle come off in his hand and as I was just about level with his younger brother any escape for both of them had to be made past me. I whispered the immortal words of arrest to them just to see the area car, my back up, arrive in support.

The area car took the brothers to the police station and I drove the ice cream van. As I entered the rear yard to the nick I couldn't resist playing the van chimes to signify my arrival. In July the sound of

"Rudolph the Red Nose Reindeer" always guaranteed an audience. The Italian wrote off the ice cream and those officers that devoured it, made a nice contribution to the Police Dependants Benevolent Fund.

When I interviewed them later they explained that they had stolen the safe from a factory in Benfleet the previous night. As the older brother said, " That fucking stupid brother of mine had a brain wave. Infallible he said. We'll drop it into the fridge then if we are stopped it's hidden from the old bill. Course, we did not reckon on the fact that we would not be able to lift it out again. It was stuck and so fucking heavy we needed a block and tackle to get it out. Fucking brilliant! What was in it?"

I asked, "What were you expecting?" "A few quid. It was payday at the factory today", he replied.

"You were right there. But everyone gets paid by cheque and that's all that was in there", I answered. "Shit doesn't anyone deal in cash these days. What chance have us blokes got", he laughingly shrugged.

Once again the brothers went to prison. When they came out the Italian took pity on them "one more time".

THE QUEEN MUMS VISIT

The new 18 story towering Civic Centre, pride of the County Borough Council, a tall imposing glass, steel and concrete bland monstrosity stood blotting the skyline of the local authority town centre enclave with the Courthouse and Police Station at its feet.

Imposingly towering over its servants and public with a courtyard below yet to be filled with a controversial work of art statue and fountain, that would be filled regularly with soap powder and multi-coloured dyes to the delight of local technical college students, the structure patiently waited for its' grand opening by the Queens Mum.

Council Officials and Police Commanders had worked forever to ensure the occasion would run without a hitch of any type. The routes of the Royal Party's cavalcade of vehicles, security men and hangers on and the programme of the visit had been set with precision and such continuity of planning that every possible eventuality had been accounted for.

It was rumoured that even toilet facilities had been earmarked, cleaned spotless and completely refurbished where necessary on the route to ensure her utmost comfort should she be caught short.

The tree-lined boulevard of the Victoria Avenue nearest to the Civic Centre was closed to traffic and every officer and civilian member of staff of the Southend on Sea Borough Constabulary was on parade outside the favoured building.

Ranks three deep of white helmeted officers with barrel chests proudly showing medals for acts of bravery and service in the world wars. Our Horne Brothers uniforms pressed crisp and brushed speckles, boots with mirrored toe caps and brilliant white gloves pristine like torches we stood at ease awaiting the arrival of the royal person.

I then saw the Sergeant who I had seen, when I had arrived on my first day, practising saluting in the office near to the training department. He was looking hugely smart and standing next to a chalk mark on the pavement that signified where the royal lady was to step out of her car. The Sergeant was looking quite nervous and would occasionally pull his chest upwards in an obvious effort to calm his nerves by breathing in deeply. His right arm would move slightly upwards and his left simultaneously outward as he went through the mental motions of saluting and opening the car door for the lady to alight.

As the shout "Attention" went up the hairs on the back of my neck stood up with such a feeling of pride that I was part of this spectacle and so highly honoured to be an officer of this elite force. So far this was one of the proudest moments of my life.

A funny thought did cross my mind that she might recognise me as the lad that had shook hands with her son in law at the garden party in Buckingham Palace during the presentation of the gold Duke of Edinburgh awards some years earlier but how could she do so amongst four hundred other smart officers.

We drew ourselves upwards chests out, stomachs in and slammed our boots downwards bringing our legs together to attention. The military experienced would have noticed that the slamming of the boots was not as synchronised as it should have been but the effect was there and the pomp of the ceremony was not diminished.

We stood in suspense for what seemed ages, breathing gently and glancing to our right occasionally to see the line of black limousines crawling to the drop off point where the now erect Sergeant was standing facing the road. To his left also at attention was the Lord Lieutenant of Essex in full military uniform complete with sword, The Mayor of Southend in fur-trimmed gown of Office and heavy mayoral chain shining from his neck, the Acting Chief Constable of the Southend on Sea Borough Constabulary and in a line to their rear stood other dignitaries and ladies in the most feathery and flowery hats that waved in the slight breeze.

As the car drew closer to its appointed spot the Sergeant saluted impeccably and raised his left hand to take hold of the car door handle. He was looking straight ahead and waited for the handle to enter his hand. Held as practised at the right level it should just float into his grip.

Whether the Queen Mum had had enough of the starched programme by this time or if she thought she was being helpful we will never know but she decided not to wait for the door to be opened by her underlings and before the car had completely stopped she threw the car door open.

The Sergeant still looking forward and not expecting such behaviour was taken totally by surprise. The car door hit his left leg sideways, destroyed his balance, poise and dignity and reduced him to a heap on the pavement. His left arm stretched out and his right arm still undecided if it should be still saluting he crumpled to the floor as the car drew to a halt and this tiny pink shoe on a stocking leg appeared from the limos rear door.

A ripple of sniggered muffled laughter went down our ranks as the sergeant unabashed regained his composure and still saluting held onto the door to right himself and show his responsibility to his duty making sure that the door stayed open whilst the royal lady was greeted by her hosts.

As the lady and her entourage disappeared into the Civic Suite prepared for a buffet lunch in her honour we were dismissed and ordered to return to normal duties. This meant that those of us who were on nights could at long last go home to bed and those on days could revert to their beats. I did not think or appreciate the connotations of overtime payment in those days, which was very rare received and complicated to work out. But there is no doubt that in the present climate of paid overtime no such huge mustering of four hundred officers would be financially possible.

The Sergeant was slightly ruffled by the experience but later said that he did have some recompense when he used the loo specially constructed in the Civic Suite for the sole use of Her Majesty. He described how he had dumped "by Royal Appointment" to test the system on her behalf and she had to wait for him. We seriously doubted his audacity but still enjoyed the banter of the whole incident.

KEEPING THE QUEENS PEACE

Learning the craft of balancing authority with tenderness and fair play was difficult and always fraught with danger and caught between neglect of duty and being over zealous. What ever way you went or indeed meant at the time of an incident, no matter how honest your intentions, you were sure that someone somewhere would find fault and either criticise or worse make a formal complaint against you.

So early on in your service you became hardened to the fact that you were always in the shit and it was only the level that varied. The rest was down to you!

I took a great deal of pride in my ability to listen to each side of an argument and was even thank officially for sorting out a domestic dispute between a local councillor and his wife after she had found out about his small indiscretion with his secretary. I was wise enough to listen and advise them but a bit naive to realise that they were buying my silence to hide the public shame he would endure if the word got out to the media if I should officially report that she had stabbed him and he had run over her leg as he reversed his Rolls Royce out of their seafront mansion.

The letter they sent, applauding my action or as it was inaction, was handed to me, unopened, in person by a very senior officer who I was told some years later was in the same Lodge as the councillor. From that day I felt confident to handle any domestic dispute and I did not realise that the letter was written for self-preservation and not for praising my actions. I am sure my silver tongue saved many marriages and evened out many disputes with this falsely laid confidence. So what?

Some disputes were just too past it for reconciliation, no matter how silver tongued you were. These were mostly drink related and where husband and wife were both pissed, there was no hope of ever getting either party to see common sense let alone see things clearly.

Many officers used the silver tongue to iron out disputes, resolve arguments and quieten down noisy drunks and boisterous revellers. No better was it used than with the drunks that rolled out of the pubs at closing time.

The Irishmen were the most convivial characters in drink and required the gentle persuasion of the silver tongued officer to make his way home peacefully with as little noise or disturbance as possible.

The town had quite a large Irish population. Why I do not know. The amount of building work being carried out was no different to anywhere else. One older officer reckoned that they had got on trains from London, wishing to get as far away from Ireland as they could without emigrating to America or Europe and hit a dead end in our most south easterly spot of the country. They could not go any further so decided to stay.

The town centre pubs had their regular Irish clientele who apart from singing harmless patriotic songs, most of which could not be deciphered as either southern or northern Irish, in a drunken drawl left the premises at the designated closing time, shook your hand, sometimes saluted or doffed their caps and then went off home to their suffering wives.

The odd individual would stop to piss in a shop doorway. One in particular caused several complaints so positive action had to be taken. It was not in the best interests of the Force to arrest these drunks or in fact any drunk as the Station Sergeant would not thank you for bringing anyone in who was likely to upset the other prisoners with constant singing or was in danger of fouling the cells with the stench of alcoholic piss and vomit that would have to cleared up by his over run staff.

In the case of the shop door pisser we decided to frighten him off so that he would not contemplate doing his dirty deed again. At evening closing time he came out of the Middleton Pub in the High Street and walked under the railway bridge. One of the shops, the complainants one, had a very convenient corridor forming a square around a central display window. He fell into the corridor and waddled up and out of sight of anyone on the pavement and reached for his fly. As he did so a thunderous voice boomed from above him from the direction of a darkened small alcove. He looked up to see towering above him the tallest copper he had ever seen. He was all of ten foot tall with huge cape wrapped round a heavy barrelled chest. "What the hell do you think you are doing? You disgusting little cretin! Pissing in public is a felony carrying a very heavy sentence and will not be tolerated!

The Irishman stuttered, "But. But. I haven't done anything your worship!" He shivered as he realised that he had done something and a warm wet patch was starting to form on his trousers.

"You're not going to let that touch the floor are you?" the voice boomed once more. Realising his dilemma the Irish took hold of his crutch and ran like a bat out of hell out of the shop corridor and up the High Street. As he disappeared you could just about hear a feint whimpering of a prayer, "Heavens be praised. What a fucking monster!" coming form his breathless voice.

I got down off the shoulders of my partner officer for the night and took the station megaphone out from under my cape. It was a ten-foot copper made up of two officers five foot and something. The Irish pisser did get a fright but he was back drinking again as right as rain, telling all in the pub of his escape from the great big bastard of a copper who was now on patrol. He noticeably went to the toilet inside the pub before making his way home, never passing the shop with the corridor again.

The silver tongue even with the help of the station megaphone was never able to solve the problems caused by another Irish drunk who was the scourge of the town centre public houses. Fury by name and fury by nature, this character was of enormous strength, six feet five inches tall, jet-black long curly, always tussled, hair with fire red eyes, bloodshot to some people he would take any place or person who happened to cross his path after the miniscule amount of alcohol.

It seemed that the small amount of alcohol was the match that set the blue touch paper alight of the most incredible bomb inside him. When it exploded everything around him was blown away and anyone who had the bravery to try and calm him fell victim to his anger.

As a result Tommy Fury had been banned from entering all pubs in the town centre. Somehow he had managed to get into the Bottom Alex pub and purchased a pint of Guinness and a Cherry Brandy chaser without being noticed.

The frantic telephone call to the police station by the terrified barmaid who was enduring her first meeting with Tommy was enough to convince us that every available man would be required to arrest him. It usually took ten officers to over power him and the paddy wagon was the best means of transporting him away.

We all arrived at the pub and seeing the devastation and the other customers cowering in the far end of the bar, pulled our gloves on (the leather seemed to give the extra grip to restrain effectively) and entered en masse. Immediately Tommy took up the challenge, singing at the top of his voice mostly inaudible but with some decipherable individual words of a Republican song referring to "the boys against the black and tans" he stood with clenched fists held up surrounded by a wall of blue serge. Before he could make one swing the Sergeant, realising any attempt at persuasion would be futile, gave the order to attack. We, unfortunately, all went for the top half of his body and forgot about the size twelve working boots that he also used to mete out injury.

I took a heavy blow to my left shin and fell to the floor. Swinging wildly Tommy tried to throw his captors off in all directions but the weight of all of us defeated him and he fell to the ground pinned down. I another officer had grabbed hold of a leg apiece and were hanging on for dear life as he flailed about trying to shake us off.

We managed to stagger to our feet with this threshing mass of Irishman and pushed our way through the doors. Even the bash on his head that was inadvertently used as a battering ram to open the double doors onto the street had no effect on him as the violent struggle continued. The top half officers were having great difficulty holding onto the blazed eyed, flared nostrilled monster. His legs were flying around like tree trunks in a hurricane and a couple of times I lost grip and managed to regain my grasp pulling it against my body but still it maintained its kicking.

We tumbled thought he open doors of the paddy wagon and the writhing mass of bodies fell into a heap onto the cold metal floor of the van. It darkened as the doors closed and the tumultuous struggle continued unabated.

Inflicted pain was the answer, I thought, like a slap around the face to calm a hysterical person, a shock to overtake all the emotions and bring the person to his senses.

The bare leg above his ankle sock revealed the fat calf muscle of the flapping leg. I bit deeply and hard into the fleshy part and heard this scream of pain as the leg moved suddenly away from my mouth. I held on holding the leg tightly against my chest as the leg continued to try to throw me off.

An angry eloquent English accent shouted painfully to me, "Robert. Stop biting my bloody leg and get hold of Toms', will you. You idiot!"

How long I had been holding onto my posh fellow officers leg, I had no idea but it was the last time I used such a tactic. The posh officer was very forgiving and one not to hold a grudge. Although the bite caused him to limp for some days after he never complained.

BOB CRAVEN

Tommy? Well he appeared before the Court and was given his usual fine, which he paid there and then. He disappeared from Southend soon after. There was a rumour that he had become a monk and taken holy orders. I just hope he kept away from the communion wine!

Booze was not the only cause of the problems our public found themselves in. Those suffering from mental illness were not only a danger to themselves but to others also. Places for the care of these unfortunate people were very limited so many times we had to do our best to help the individual and protect those around them.

MENTAL ANGUISH

My first experience with mental illness was long before I joined the police service. Even at the young age of my junior school days I saw a family in turmoil when our next-door neighbour started to throw a wobbly as Dad would explain it. She was a middle-aged lady with two daughters much older than me, probably in their teens. I had no idea or inkling that they had a problem until one day when I was playing out on the front lawn of our semi-detached council house. Suddenly a milk bottle came smashing through the bay windows of the adjoining house and this woman's voice could be heard screaming and swearing from inside.

As kids we were just inquisitive and not frightened at all although a girls voice was calmly saying, "Mum please don't do this. Sit down. Calm down. You are all right. No one is going to hurt you". The shouting turned to sobs and distraught mumblings and shortly after the curtains, to the smashed window, was drawn and we went back to our play.

On several nights after that we were woken by shouting and screaming from next door and on some occasions the daughters of the lady would take refuge in our house as the sound of smashing glass and breaking wood could be heard on the other side of the walls.

Even now I have the lasting memory of the despair on the faces of the two daughters as they sat with my Mum and Dad sipping tea and trying to blot out the sound of their home being destroyed by their out of control loved one. Wanting to go and see her but knowing and being reassured by my parents that their, "father would sort it out" and "its best if you stay here where you will not be harmed.

Their Mum was "taken away" on many occasions returning after a while but slipping back into a mental turmoil soon after. The family moved away and lost touch with us but a few years later I saw the youngest daughter. She was in her late thirties / early forties but still recognisable with jet-black hair, always reminding me of the dishevelled, untidy but pretty girl in the book Wuthering Heights.

I was in uniform and not wanting to be too intrusive asked how things were. She said, "Dad and her sister had gone" (I did not like to ask her to clarify "gone" any further through fear of upsetting her). She looked so frail, tired and strained as she said, "Mum and I are living in a little flat. She still has her moments. But we're okay. She doesn't know anyone but we cope". I asked her if she worked or was married, "No. I haven't had time for that".

She had given her whole life to her Mum, as there was no help or support that could provide the type of care she required.

Arresting "nutters", as they were so ignominiously called, was never a pleasant or rewarding task. Unlike that of what we would consider an adversary or career criminal where the challenge and eventual result of a conviction could be satisfying and worthwhile, the arrest of a mental illness sufferer was always done with the knowledge that the wheels of justice for all was never fair or conclusive.

This person would be sent for treatment that very rarely found the target and when the space occupied in a treatment centre or institution was required for more pressing cases the unfortunate was released to fend for themselves unaided and eventually fall into trouble all over again.

The old lady that for some reason only known to her hated taxis who would throw stones at the cars as they passed. Around the developing Victoria Circus provided huge chunks of concrete for her to throw that nearly ended in a fatality when one rock completely smashed a windscreen causing the taxi to career off the road and crash into the window of Times Furnishing. Causing fortunately only minor cuts and bruises to the driver and passengers the whole incident was witnessed by a colleague and me.

The lady, a semi vagrant who lived between a meagre bed-sit and the High Street toilets had carried out such offences before but not with such gusto or near disastrous consequences.

Whether it was as a result of the shock of seeing the damage and injury caused could not be said but she collapsed in a heap on the pavement beside the demolished car. She sobbed uncontrollably and then went very quiet as she slipped into a coma.

My mate continued to deal with the wreck and its occupants who were now standing nearby to wait for an ambulance as I went to the old lady's aid.

She had almost stopped breathing. I put her into the recovery position just as the ambulance arrived and the crew took over. The occupants of the taxi and our old lady were taken away and we got on with the job of clearing up the mess.

An hour or so later we heard that the medical efforts could not save her from the hearty attack she had suffered and she had died. I went to the hospital to sort out identification and attempt to locate relatives. The mortuary attendant was very helpful, sympathetic to the lady's condition and was starting to prepare her for eventual post mortem. Her clothing was being cut away. Several layers, eleven in fact, of male overcoat, woollen jumpers and cardigans were far easier to remove than the newspaper that was wrapped to her legs.

Stuck fast to her legs were copies of papers dated some two years previous by a substance so close in texture to evo-stick. The attendant said it was a bodily puss of some sort, the like he had never seen before.

Layer after layer was removed to reveal maggots feasting on her flesh. Quite common for a body having laid dead for some time but this lady had only died three or four hours before. The attendant said that maggots take sometime to form like this and she must have had these for some weeks.

This lady had been arrested only four days ago and been sent to the local mental hospital surely, I thought, someone must have seen this and been in a position to help her. Society had let her down completely. She had no relatives, no support at a time in her life when it was needed most.

In her meagre possessions was a telephone number of a hostel in the east end of London and no other papers. In her bed-sit there were only piles of newspapers and bags of rubbish, discarded food cartons and little else to lead us to identify her. Social Services and other agencies were unable to help.

When I telephoned the hostel they were able to say her name was Lilly and the only thing they knew about her was that she was bombed out in the war in Hackney somewhere and had no other information. She had been a wanderer ever since.

This was a lady who society had let down whereas the majority of cases the situation was slightly different.

Throughout my career it was to come up so many times that lack of support and monitoring of persons suffering from mental illness would result in travesty and destruction for too many families on both sides of the fence.

The writing could be seen on the wall that the young boy who insisted on wanking himself off in amongst the tie display racks at the bottom of the escalators in Marks and Spencer Store in the High Street, needed help.

The racks gave him a direct unobstructed view of the young ladies in their fashionable very short mini-skirts as they went up the stairs to the ladies sales floor.

Once was forgivable, twice a problem but seven separate occasions should have rang some alarm bells. When he started to rake the streets at night seeking out windows through which he could peep at undressing ladies, something should have been done to stop him from doing what he progressed to.

His mother rang us up repeatedly when he went on his night walkabouts and pleaded with us to lock him up. She was terrified that he may do something horrible.

The woman he raped and beat senseless, after climbing in through her open window, kept on asking me and eventually demanding to know from me why we had not stopped her attacker in the very early days of his problems and prevented him from destroying her life.

Although a passionate supporter of the system under which we live and serve my reasons to her were futile and had no hope of achieving her understanding.

Even in those early days it became clearer to me that, all too often, we were only just about able to clear up the debris caused by breakers of the Queens peace and very rarely, if at all, were we in any position to prevent it happening.

Along the way we were to receive many knocks and kicks in the balls. Having just helped the old lady out the previous day and being very frustrated with not being able to help her I was quickly brought back down to ground when my mate and me turned a corner of the High Street to investigate some noisy singing and clapping. At just after midnight this was not acceptable and had to be stopped. As we approached nearer the words being sung became clearer, "We love Harry Roberts cos he kills coppers", followed by a chant and unison clapping from others. The words echoed around the hollow pedestrian precinct.

Harry Roberts was a London criminal who had shot dead three plain-clothes detectives in Shepherds Bush some years previous and the singer was obviously taking full advantage of his right to free speech and perhaps hoping that it would create some action by us.

I thought at the time, "How can someone hate the police so much to have no regard for the feelings of the family, friends and colleagues of those poor officers. We were just trying to perform a job and help people?" Yet here was the young man for reasons best known to him singing a song of hatred with such gusto.

After trying to get him to stop and he continuing to sing we arrested him much to the delight and approval of the many onlookers who had gathered.

This contradiction in attitudes toward the police was to create huge differences and levels of approach to our work. Receiving commendations for our endeavours at one moment only to be spat at and assaulted on another.

Chapter Five
NIGHT SHIFT

Night shifts could be very quiet as the late night discos and longer licensing hours were the things of the future. The town died after midnight so the Sergeant would be able to say before we set out on our beats, "Tip up anything that moves after midnight".

After the usual punch ups with drunks and yobs at pub closing time the town could become our playground and as long as we kept our guard up and did not lose sight of the reasons for being on duty.

Snowball fights and frightening the life out of each other. Dropping fluorescent tubes from the highest buildings so they exploded behind a patrolling officer or being targeted with rotten fruit as you turned a corner, made you sharpen up your senses for the eventual arrest of the villains you were there to catch.

Those who had the privilege of driving a patrol car or latterly a panda car were most likely to fool the beat officers but occasionally you could get your own back.

Putting a stink bomb under the seat frame, so when it was sat upon the steel bar would crush the glass casing. It would fill the car with the most pungent smell that lasted for hours and penetrated, uncomfortably deep into clothing and nasal passages. Or stealing the police car left unattended, by using the spare keys kept on a hook in the admin office. Then waiting for the driver to report it missing and leaving it in its original position for him to find hours later.

TRAMPS AND ICE CREAM

Apart from the occasional car the only persons who raked around the town centre at night would be two or three tramps. They were tolerated and allowed to sleep anywhere that gave them comfort without being a nuisance.

No shelters existed and the bed and breakfast accommodation supplied by the Social Services was too demanding and lacking in the freedom they desired.

Two dressed as "Popeye" look-a-likes earned pennies to buy their daily intake of cheap scrumpy cider by entertaining the day-trippers with twirling pipes and sea shanty dances. Another spent most of his time trying to chat up an elderly lady newspaper seller who took him under her wing when she was lonely. She would take him to her small basement flat for the odd night of joint comfort but most of the time they would sleep in the various public toilets that were dotted around the town.

The cleanliness of these toilets was always suspect but the tramps would have a code, of not, "shitting in their own back yard" and keeping their sleeping area as clean as when they entered.

All was not well when a visiting tramp threw all into disarray. A local down and out had actually made a formal complaint at the front office of the Police Station that this "reprobate", using his words, was responsible for fouling the floor in the toilets and "making life unpleasant for the others that used it".

The Station Sergeant told the complainant that we would look into it and sent me and another officer to investigate the matter.

The particular public toilets were near to the railway bridge in the High Street. Somewhat archaic Victorian with tiles loosened by years of damp and neglect they were not the best accommodation for any self respecting down and out but to the complainant they were home.

We were met by the foulest of smells that even by public urinal standards was massive for its strength and heaviest of odours. The producer of the stench was asleep in a cubicle in the well-practised position of, against the door so that the possibility of forced entry to remove or harm him was at its worst.

He had an obvious diarrhoeal problem, as the floor was drenched in an ugly substance coming from his trousers.

Covering our mouths, trying to stop ourselves from vomiting yet doing our duty we woke the sleeping bundle and roused him sufficiently to tell him to get out of the toilets before it was hosed down by the council attendants, "Who were about to come in".

We hastily left the enclosed underground stench for the bliss of the fresh air above and waited for the offending body to appear. We were in two minds to stop him from coming out. We did not know if sending him somewhere else would result in another desecration by poo.

We approached the figure that appeared at the toilet entrance to be met by a grunt of disapproval. The filthy dirt engrained raincoat that covered him fell in tatters around the concertinaed trousers at his ankles. He stooped badly after probably years of sleeping crumpled against toilet doors. Neither of us wanted to be near him but independently thought that he needed help of some sort.

We asked his name but he refused. We suggested some medical help via the Social Services but he refused and just told us to, "Fuck off and leave me alone".

Difficult to know if we should have arrested him, but we were not convinced that he was a mental case, very angry, yes. But then wouldn't you be angry if you had been woken up from a deep sleep and found that you had shit yourself!

Our powers were limited and was it worth reaping the Station Sergeants wrath by taking this slimy clothed, stench ridden member of the public into custody when he appeared to be more than capable of living his own life independently without our interference. We let him go on his way and kept our fingers crossed.

A month went by before we were on nights again and we had heard that an elderly lady who cleaned the ice-cream parlour at the lower end of High Street had been bothered by this tramp.

He kept on thumping his fist on the window of the shop that she had so meticulously cleaned for over forty years. He demanded tea and food from this kind lady of eighty plus years, "not violently", she said but, "just a nuisance".

At 4.00am in the morning six nights a week she had cleaned the same shop and never had any trouble.

She had a right to our protection especially as she had supplied the policeman on that beat, and some others who took the opportunity, with knickerbocker-glories, banana splits and as much cream, nuts and toppings, on every single one of those nights.

The odd Inspector was even known to partake of her hospitality by sitting in her parlour and enjoying a complete cream tea with scones, jam and clotted cream whilst his men hid in the back of the premises waiting for him to finish.

A lady as special as she deserved to be looked after and we were determined that she would not have to suffer this type of disturbance again.

He was sought, found and given the opportunity of a train ride to London where he was assured he would receive a welcome from the inhabitants, and be offered a bed in the only hostel in this part of the country. He went on the next goods train that left the sidings at Southend Central Station.

We thought that was the end of the saga but the following night at about 3.00am the High Street was shaken by a deafening explosion.

The toilets under the railway bridge were consumed by smoke, a dust cloud smelling of disinfectant and a huge flash of flame shot out from the entrance. The roar shattered the eerie night silence and echoed off the buildings.

Running to the scene we passed one of the Popeye's chuckling to himself, "That'll sort the bastard out!"

Staggering up the stairs, clinging unsteadily onto the rail and out of the billowing smoke came this hunched-back apparition, usually only seen in horror movies. Puffs of smoke hung to his coat and dragged after him as he stumbled onto the pavement,

Coughing long and hard to retrieve debris deep in his lungs, he held his arm upwards and said, "I only came back for my cap". He then waded through the now settling atmosphere back in the direction of the goods yard waving his arm and saying, "London's a lot more friendly than down here".

We saw the Popeye later and asked him what that was about and it turned out that the cleaner used to give him his breakfast every morning and he was incensed when he saw the "dirty bastard" back again. He took a "banger" down to frighten him. "Well a big one actually", he admitted and then added, "I did explosives in the war but I never thought there would be such a big bang as that. It must have been the methane from his fucking arse. Still, teach the bastard a lesson. Won't see him back here again. I reckon!"

We did not see that tramp again and the toilets were closed indefinitely. The Fire Brigade put the explosion down to a probable cause of "faulty wiring in the light switches igniting methane from a fractured sewer pipe". There was no other explanation!

BACKS, FRONTS AND PICKLED EGGS

Each night the shift would take turns to patrol the fronts and the backs of the shopping and business areas, rattling every doorknob and checking each window. Once when coming on duty and once before going off duty to make sure all properties in our charge were all present and correct.

Sometimes our efficient shaking was a trifle over zealous and this would set the alarm off to the annoyance of the owners who had to attend to turn it off. Our punishment was then to have that bell ringing incessantly in our ears for hours after it had been reset.

BOB CRAVEN

Patrolling the backs in the pitch black away from the daylight lighting of the fronts was only scary once to me. I had entered a narrow alleyway that cut through the oldest part of town. High walled Victorian houses containing offices and the occasional small flat towered above with a dirty brick wall about my height on one side.

As I walked through the darkness I sensed this movement to my right. I felt a sense of warmth and comforting softness coming form my right. Whatever it was did not seem to be harmful until I felt something touching my shoulder.

I don't know who was more frightened me, or the cat, that had been going along the wall beside me and suddenly turned left and stepped onto my shoulder. I thought cats were supposed to be able to see in the dark but this one obviously took me to be part of the wall, until it realised it was stepping onto blue serge and not brick. We both leapt up in the air and went to run for cover, before calming down and going our separate ways when we had realised the true situation.

The uniform night patrols were broken by the odd times carrying out observations with the CID in premises likely to be attacked. The hairdresser saga you have already heard about, but one other saga sticks in my mind, purely for the food we were allowed to eat by the owner of a large warehouse that we were asked to protect.

The warehouse was the only one of a chain throughout the country that had not been attacked. The CID Officer in charge said so it was a prime target. Armed with large staves, instead of our smaller truncheons, five of us, a dog handler and his mutt, set about making ourselves comfortable for the night, and the next, and the next night, until we had been there for over a month.

The would-be burglars had for some reason decided not to take on the warehouse.

This was so boring and led to me sleeping with the police dog snuggled up against me. Strange at first for me, as we did not have animals at home, but very warm and cosy on a cold winters night in a dark, draughty, stark warehouse.

All except, the dog had a tendency to fart the most horrid of smells, snore loudly and continuously jitter through the night dreaming.

As compensation for our labours the owners had told us to help ourselves to any sweets, cakes or snacks during our stay. Some of us took a liking to the numerous cakes on offer and could not help repeating that stock phrase, "Mr Kipling Makes Exceedingly Good Cakes!" and rubbing their bellies at the time.

I had a more unusual pallet and devoured a large jar of pickled eggs. The odd one I took as a laugh and said it was to get my own back on the farting dog but as the days progressed it became an obsession, perhaps to break the monotony, to have a couple each night. I was so embarrassed at having eaten the whole 5-pound jar that I insisted on paying for it much to the proprietors' surprise.

SMASHED AND GRABBED

Never knowing what to expect and the variety of characters you met during a tour of duty was what kept the interest going. On the way to an alarm call at a jewellers shop I stumbled across a middle aged man lying in a pool of blood at Victoria Circus, a large roundabout road junction at the top end of the High Street.

The half conscious man had a huge gash to his forehead and mumbled that he had been hit by a group of yobs as he was going home. My quickness to the scene had stopped them from robbing him he said. The wound was bleeding profusely so I radioed for an ambulance to take him to hospital.

Other officers were attending to the alarm call so I saw the injured man onto the ambulance, making sure to take his name and other personal details for my report.

The jewellery shop window had some superficial damage to its front window and all appeared to be in order when the officers checked the premises with the owners.

I telephoned the hospital later and was told that the injured man had been treated and then left. The CID apparently got no reply from the house when they called the following morning to take his statement of complaint and get a description of his attackers.

The following night another alarm went off at a jewellers shop further down the High Street. This time the window had been completely smashed and several trays of distinctive rings were missing. Although the smash and grab took place in the evening when many people were walking the High Street there was a lack of witnesses or persons willing to help us.

Later on in that night I went into a restaurant named "The What You Want". A local friendly proprietor would give us a cup of tea or bowl of hot soup to take off the night chill. It also gave the owner a little unpaid protection from the frequent undesirables that came to his late opening establishment.

As I was to about to take my second mouthful of the delicious soup I noticed the man with the head injury sitting in the corner. I said a friendly, "Hello". This obviously startled him as he flew out of his chair and pelted toward the glass doors. It was bad luck really, but the owner had locked the doors, as he usually does to enable him to vet incoming customers.

The man with head heavily bandaged smacked into the dead weight of the door and bounced back onto the tiles floor in a heap of ragged coat, tangled bandage and wound spitting blood. As he fell diamond rings, gold cuff links and bracelets dropped to the floor from his pockets.

I immediately recognised the rings as like the ones stolen from the jewellers earlier. I called for an ambulance again and also whispered the words of arrest to him. Thinking that he was not alone, and that he had a disagreement with some accomplices the night before, I asked how he had got his injuries.

"The fucking window threw back the brick. Didn't it? You Pratt!" he replied. The first jeweller's window was made of two layers of glass between which there was a layer of plastic. The brick had been bounced back by the window and knocked the thief for a six but he managed to get away from the scene before the police arrived. Great when the premises can actually fight back and wreak retribution on the opposition.

THE RESCUE

Unbelievably smoking can save lives and it was proved so on one February night when a Sergeant and his driver, a Constable from Westcliff were driving along Western Esplanade.

Even though it was well below freezing and flurries of snow were falling onto the icy road, the sergeant was polite and considerate to have the window on his side of the police car open to suck the cigarette fumes away from his non-smoking companion.

There was a lull in the nights' activities and the pair had decided to take a leisurely drive along the now tranquil quiet of the Esplanade to take the sea air and have an undisturbed fag. Fortuitous for someone, for as they drove along with only the car engine and the gentle lapping of the waves to disturb the peace, they heard the feint voice of a man in distress coming from the sea to the left.

As they got out of the vehicle they had to strain to identify the precise direction from where the voice was coming from. Alarmingly it seemed to be getting weaker with every sound. They called for assistance to locate the distraught male and I with other officers descended onto the seafront.

The freezing cold easterly wind blowing straight off the North Sea unsympathetically chilled our faces as we held clasped hands up to our mouths to amplify our voices as we shouted for him to keep calling out to help us locate his position and for him to hold on, encouraging him that help was on its way.

The still weaker voice said something about ice and then that he was slipping deeper. The word "blue" came across the water and our torches shone trying to seek out what blue boat we could find.

The foreshore along the Southend seafront is dotted with countless small craft, yachts, fishing boats and pleasure craft. All moored to tiny buoys and bobbing about on the incoming tide casting shadows over the gentle waves and creating confusing flashes of reflection from the street lights onshore.

Southend experiences a high tide twice a day and its mud flats, renowned for its medicinal properties and the subject of many an idyllic photograph or oil painting, are dangerous with too many people being caught by an incoming tide or swept out to sea by its fast flowing currents.

The weary waving arm of a man could be just about made out coming from the sea at the back of a small fishing vessel about 200 yards out.

We had a specialist sea rescue patrol boat during the summer months but in the thick of winter the craft was laid up and any attempt to launch it would likely be futile in the time we had available. The Lifeboat Crew had been called out but time was not on the distressed mans side.

Frantic efforts were then transferred to find a boat of some sort that we could use to get to this man. Survival in such an icy sea would be limited.

I and another officer tried out luck at wading out, until the water had reached a level just above our waists and we had only got 10 yards out. The Sergeant ordered us out as a shout went up, "I've got one".

The non-smoking Constable appeared from behind the storage shed of a small yacht club with the tiniest dinghy imaginable and as luck would have it a set of oars that were perhaps too big for the boat but would suffice to do the job.

The Sergeant, Constable and me got in as two other officers pushed us off from the stone and concrete sea defence wall. The sea was moderately calm but still choppy enough to make us wonder if the small dinghy would stay afloat. None of us thought that the reason it was not secure was that it was rubbish and not sea worthy. Hardier vessels of any value would be well locked to prevent them being stolen.

We reached the fishing boat where the man had last been sighted. The voice had stopped calling and we cracked the silence by shouting for him to tell us where he was. We clambered over tarpaulins and other junk that lay in its bowels to reach the stern. His arm could just be seen, hooked over the large wooden rudder. His head was just above the water that lapped at his mouth. Scattered beads of ice sparkled from his wet hair in the veiled moonlight.

The Sergeant being the tallest and longest of the three of us reached over to grab the man's arm. As he went to pull him up his hands slid the full length of the arm. "He's iced up! I can't get a grip", the Sergeant gasped as we all three leant further over the edge of the boat to get a better grip.

Being the shortest I had to lean over a little further and lost my footing, falling head first toward the water. Just as my hands flailed out in a panicked but vain attempt to stop myself I felt the strong hand of the constable grip my belt and stop me. Only my hands struck the water. "Stop fucking about Bob," he joked.

Spray forced up by the wind that always picked up as the tide ebbed, soaked all of us as we tried to gain a useful grip on the iced up male.

The other two were much stronger than me and strained to make headway. I was somewhat more nimble and lighter and thought the wet wooden rudder glinting from below would take my weight. I could supplement the huge strength that the other two had to use to pull the man into safety, by pushing him from behind.

As they held onto to him I climbed over the side and placed my foot on the top of the rudder. A couple of times my wet foot slipped off the wooden surface and the strong men grunted and swore in disappointment as they had to restore their tenuous hold.

I finally managed to manoeuvre both myself and the rescued man around so the other two could take hold of both his arms. As we manhandled him onboard we saw that the man was powerfully built and very stocky but what made him even heavier was the thick lambs wool sailors pullover he was wearing. It was hanging below his knees soaked heavily with seawater that had frozen solid with dripping icicles at its hem.

The man was blue with cold and chattered with steam drifting off of the top of his head. All together the three of us rubbed him hard and seemingly, violently to get or keep his circulation going. He went to lie down but we were keen to get him into the small boat and back to shore where the ambulance was now waiting.

Slowly and carefully we lowered him into the dinghy with the constable standing precariously in the unsteady floor. There was only room for three so I waited for them to deposit the man on shore then return.

Tranquillity returned to the boat as I waited. As the mass of adrenalin pumping round me abated peace returned to the shore. The muffled voices of the officers and ambulance men on the shore blended into the soft whisper of the breeze. The flashing blue lights mingled with the reflections of the streetlights and the moon shining on the white horse waves.

We had just rescued a man from near death. The feeling was one of the most satisfying I had ever experienced. What a brilliant job!

I was brought round by the feel of the cold water seeping through my uniform and it seemed like an age before the boat returned and I reached terra firma.

I was driven straight back to the station shivering and shaking with the unbelievable cold. My Sergeant insisted I went home but before I could I just had to get somewhere warm and get out of these icy clothes.

My shift mates had the showers running hot in the station changing rooms by the time I got there and one of them even had to help me unbutton my shirt as the buttons were too small for my now shaking uncontrollably cold hands to cope with.

I stayed under the shower for a lifetime until I could gradually sense my legs then arms and body getting the feeling of normality back. For a few days after I had chilblains, pins and needles and tingling over parts of me but nothing worse.

The man we found out later had been working on the engine of his boat that he had removed and winched to the shore. He had worked on it there while the tide went out and then winched it back before it came back in again. He had been out in the freezing open air for over 20 hours.

As he was doing so the water crept around the boat and he appeared to running out of time. He then slipped over board and into the icy incoming sea. It took him some considerable time to remove his thigh high waders that had filled with water and weighed an absolute ton.

By the time he had done this he was out of his depth and the incoming tide was taking its toll on all his strength. He said he was lucky that we had come along.

I wonder if he knew it was all down to the bad habit of one of our Sergeants that brought about his rescue.

The headlines in the local paper of the rescue and the gratitude of the man rescued were pleasing to see and the commendation we all got from the Chief Constable was a great finale to the incident.

The accolades did not really matter to me and it was not until sometime later that it came to me that we had all worked together, as one natural unit to rescue this man. Being part of that team, united and focused on one objective to save him made me feel more pride than receiving any award.

THE REGIMENTAL TROPHY

Saturday night and patrolling the backs of the High Street with my best mate, the one that all too often seemed to partner me, and find trouble at the same time.

I had just said foolishly, "Do you know? I really feel like a good punch up tonight!" Full of energy even though I had played football that afternoon I was on some sort of unhealthy high as far as my mate was concerned.

It could have been an omen, because as we rounded the corner and entered the High Street the commotion of breaking glass, shouts and screams hit us as a riot of bodies with flying fists and feet came into view.

Automatically we reached for our whistles, without any radios this was our only form of communication and only hope of alerting our colleagues on adjoining beats, with the added intention of drawing the assailants attention to stop the fighting.

Although our brother officers joined us quite quickly the fighting mass took no notice of our presence. Oblivious of our office and our efforts to stop damage and injury, the two sides of the conflict dealt with us in the same way they were dealing with each other. Trying to break up this melee between the two sides was nigh on impossible.

Both worse the wear for alcohol the members of the Heavy Air Defence Regiment from Shoebury Barracks were making a conscious effort to beat hell out of the stag night party of locals who had also seen fit to blind themselves with drink.

The glass doors to the shop where the bulk of the action was taking place had long since been demolished and bodies rolled around inside the premises scattering rails of ladies wear, hats and coats. Concerned that more serious injury would occur amongst the broken glass we hurled ourselves into the major area of conflict.

Attempting to restrain and suppress the violence in the way we had been taught at training school was just not an option. We had to make our presence felt quickly and effectively so the Queensbury rules went out of the window. Kicking, scratching, biting into whatever area of the body presented itself was the name of the game. Only when you had your back to the wall would you take out your feeble truncheon to protect yourself and this would be the absolute last resort.

Fighting was not my best forte but the training school had taught me some useful self-defence techniques and when given the opportunity came in handy. Placing two fingers under the nose or bending a thumb back was a quick and effective method of temporarily disabling an assailant. Our first efforts were aimed at stopping the fight.

Allowing for the odd fighter wanting to take a swing at us, most of them started to disperse before our back up arrived but a hard core of those less aware of our presence carried on fighting to the end.

Amongst them was an enormous ginger haired soldier, recognisable as were his mates, by the short back and sides hair cuts they all had. The opposition all had "Beatle type" or hippie flower power long hair so it was easy to distinguish between the two groups.

Ginger had taken on four of the other side, two of whom had sunk to their knees and the other two were still trying to get at him through his long reaching arms with the sledge hammer size fists on the end of them.

Realising that I was liable to receive the same treatment from this man mountain I shouted to them to, "Stop. Police!" No response! After ignoring two further shouts our only course was to use force.

A quick measure up of the consequences of doing so and his long reach identified that my short arms, in no way the long arm of the law, would not have to right effect. I pole axed Ginger with the best right boot kick I could muster and used regularly on the football pitch, especially when administering my favourite sliding tackle.

He hit the hard pavement and stunned slightly, rolled onto his stomach giving me the opportunity to take hold of his right thumb and bend it back against his wrist as far as I could. The pain of this hold reduced him to my size and after a few expletives and realizing who had floored him he shouted out, "Truce!"

By this time the officers in support had arrived and similar arrests of both sides were being made. All were thrown into the back of various police vehicles. One or two who continued to fight were handcuffed. None appeared to have any serious injuries other than dented pride. The groom from the stag night protested and begged that he was getting married the next day and he loved his future bride and did not want to miss it.

The squaddies from the Regiment were revelling in the proceedings and recounting their part in the fight and checking to ensure each other were okay.

I then realised that my helmet was missing. Seeing Ginger was placed into the paddy wagon, I went in search of my precious headgear. Into the devastated shop, pulling apart the displaced and scattered clothing, down the street in both directions revealed nothing. The helmet had been spirited away and I had a good suspicion who by!

The paper work for dealing with the culprits took the rest of the night. Most were charged with breach of the peace as no evidence could be attuned to who did what injury. As the Regiment was due to go back to Germany in the near future and injuries if at all were minor, lengthy trials were not in the public interest.

Those who were charged appeared before the court on the following Monday. Fortunately the bridegroom was not amongst these so his wedding went by without a hitch except some of his guests had arm slings and crutches to support injured limbs.

Regiment prisoners released without charge were placed in the custody of the Military Police, the red caps, who placed them on charges of bringing the Regiment into Disrepute.

A few weeks later out Police football team played the Regiment in the local Wednesday League. In the hope that the man would realise I was just doing my job I approached ginger who was the centre half. He recognised me and to my surprise, whilst shaking my hand with his powerful grip, apologised for his behaviour.

I saw that he had the remnants of a very bruised and blackened eye and upon seeing me noticing it, he explained, "Oh that. I didn't get that at the fight. I just got lippy with the red caps and one of them smacked me". "How big was he?" I asked.

"Not big", he replied, "But he is the Army District boxing champion and is representing GB in the next Olympics. So I was a bit thick and of course pissed as well".

Now friends, I realised that I may be able to appeal to his softer side and said, "Do you know who could have my helmet. It went missing at the time of the punch up and it looks like I might have to pay for a new one?" He said he would see what he could do and then ran off for the pre-match warm up.

The game went well although they thrashed us five nil, their fitness showing far more superior qualities. After the match ginger came into our dressing room and gave me a bag of coins and said, "We had a whip round to pay for your helmet. Hope it covers any loss". I found this quite touching but thought that it might be because they knew more about it than they were letting on".

My suspicions were compounded a few months later when I received an envelope containing a photograph from Germany. There was no note accompanying it but the picture was of a group of twenty soldiers in a bar and in the middle of them was ginger holding a police helmet aloft in the pose of a trophy.

I, at last, knew where it had gone and it was all the more comfortable for the fact that I did not have to pay for the loss and the whip round they collected had paid for a very nice evening out.

THE SET UPS

From time to time the opportunity would arise when the quiet of the night would allow for fun and games, with a junior member of the shift who for what ever reason needed to be shown up, brought down to size or merely be the brunt of older officers sense of humour.

THE APPLE TREE TRIST

A favourite, as in many trades, was to send the new boy on a false errand. This was very hard in the police service as there was always the danger of involving a member of the public and no one wished to embarrass a third party. Not so on one occasion when a young probationer was sent to a rear alleyway behind a row of shops.

He was told that a couple had complained about a man dressed in a top hat and Dracula cape, who had been seen in the alleyway, late at night peering into the lounge at the back of their shop.

The Constable went out, keen to catch this man red handed but, not twigging that he was dressed in full uniform, wearing his helmet and police issue, cape and that his shadow was not dissimilar to that of the alleged offender.

Soon after 11.00pm he made his way down into the darkened alleyway, through the gate into the rear garden of the aggrieved parties house and stood at the foot of a large apple tree. He turned so the tree hid him from the alleyway and waited. There was no sign of his suspect but his attention was drawn to noises coming from the lounge of the house.

The room was dimly lit and he could make out the shape of two naked bodies cavorting around the room. A woman was giggling and squealing with laughter and a man was chasing her around with what looked like a feather duster.

The woman stopped as if exhausted and lay on her stomach across the back of the settee. To the woman's expressed delight he mounted her from behind waving the duster in the air like a riding crop.

The officer did not know what to do. If he left his spot they might see him and he may bump into the Dracula man but if he stayed where he was, he had to endure the sight before him and he still might be seen.

Before he could come to any decision the pair had uncoupled and were now chasing around the lounge again with even more gusto and excitement. The woman was leading the male, stopping momentarily for him to catch up within touching distance. The feather duster was being brushed and caressed over the whole of her body and his.

The officer could not believe that he had to endure this but worse was to come. The French doors, leading onto the garden, burst open with the woman gleefully shouting, "He's here. Come on!"

The woman, with breasts bobbing and the man with genitals swinging, made straight for the officer who by now was trying to melt into the tree, the fingers of both hands trying to claw into the bark and drag him out of sight. She leapt at the officer wrapping both arms around his neck and both legs round his middle.

Stunned the officer was too late to stop the feather duster from being shoved directly under his nose. He recognised the ugly smell of fish. His hands were now gripping the cheeks of her backside, he was caught between embarrassment not wishing to offend or hurt her if he let go, confusion as whether he had got the wrong place and why the hell is this happening.

The woman groaned in semi-orgasm at his neck as the man clung on to her buttocks. The officer removed his hands and hoped to God that the man was not going to enter her from behind whilst he was in her grip.

The moment passed as quick as it started. They both left the officer shocked and bewildered leaning panting against the tree and went back through the French doors closing them behind them. Giggling started again as the officer regained his composure. Startled once more the officer saw the doors open again, to his relief the woman, still naked, just blew a kiss into his direction and mimed dreamily, "Thank you!"

When the officer reported in from his police post the Sergeant asked him if he had seen anything. The officer replied, "Nothing to report. All quiet. Sergeant. It was best not say anything else. He was still not sure if it was the Sergeant or the couple who had set him up. One thing was for certain he had kept control and not cocked up!

STORKY LEGS

We had a small police office at the rear of the multi storey car park in the town centre. We used the office to make up notes in pocket books, warm up on a cold day and telephone into the main police station.

At night the toilet in the police post was used in favour of the not so clean public toilets. So it was not unusual for two officers, an older officer and a bouncy, chatty, full of beans probationer went into the police post in the early hours.

The probationer was ripe for a set up and removing his trousers was meant to quieten him down so the peace and tranquillity of the night would be kept undisturbed.

At 3.00am the town was deathly quiet. The only disco that the town had was closed two hours before and the entrance doors that could be seen from the police post were locked tight.

As the two entered the police post and three heavy figures pounced on the unsuspecting probationer. Realising very quickly that it was not real assailants but members of his shift, attacking him the probationer foolishly relaxed from his violent struggling.

Had he known what was going to happen he would have continued to push his attackers off him but his softer defence allowed the dirty deed of trouser removal to be accomplished. His belt was undone and the trousers slipped from his thin stork-like legs, even the large gleaming black boots did not stop them from being totally withdrawn from his body.

The door to the police post burst open as the officers decamped, running in all directions from the pursuing probationer. Still wearing his helmet and in the full regalia of a Police Constable, defender of the Queens Peace, there he was trouser-less with the whitest, gleaming, thinnest legs ever to light up the darkness of the town centre, trying to focus in the gloom to identify the officer that had his trousers.

The trousers had been placed on a parking meter directly outside the disco door. Tantalisingly close to the officer but dangerously close to the more probability of him being seen by a person walking the High Street.

Care had to be taken not to be seen resulting in embarrassment, so he decided to creep along the brick wall of the tall building. His blue serge would melt into the grey brickwork but stealthily the white legs stretched out one after the other in a sideways crab walk following the contours of the wall and its supporting pillars. Any sound that momentarily broke the silence would cause him to halt his movement and stand motionless, like a preying mantis, before continuing his quest.

Seeing his opportunity he leapt from his wall camouflage and bounded the four steps to the parking meter just as a taxi came round the corner and stopped directly outside the disco door and the blue serge statue of a police probationer. Two young ladies got out of the taxi. The taxi door conveniently obscured the lower half of the still life frozen in the position of replacing trousers.

The fare was paid, the driver thanked, the door slammed and the ladies walked passed the prone officer. The trousers slid back onto the wiry legs as if greased, as the ladies turned with gaping mouths, astounded and not fully appreciating what they had just witnessed.

The disco doors opened allowing them into the private party that unbeknown to us was taking place inside. The door went to close but then suddenly opened as four heads popped out to see once again the police officer standing outside.

By this time the trousers were back on and the officer was quite confidently able to wish them a good night and continue his patrol. As he swaggered off he clasped his hands behind his back, in police stance, and exclaimed, "Shit!"

He then realised that in his haste he had not completely tucked the long tail of shirt inside his trousers. Twelve inches of the longest light blue shirttail, in the country, lit up the night as it hung from his backside below his tunic.

The faces at the disco door burst into laughter with one girls voice saying, "I told you. I am sure he had his trousers round his ankles!" "No. Not one of our coppers", a male voice confidently stated.

THE TORCHED RED HEAD

Pranks of this type were not always completed on such a funny note. Although none ever resulted in serious consequences, the adrenalin rush that some experienced took them past the point of acceptability, that was expected of a police officer.

All part of the learning curve and perhaps part of the intent of such exercises but painful for the officer who suffered the wrath of the probationer.

I probably should not have dressed up as an old woman and warned the young officer before, but when he hit me with his torch, as I identified myself to him, the force he used and the venom of the blow, released a tad more excitement than I could ever expect.

The event had started with me donning a red wig, pouring myself into a black skirt, borrowed from a WPC's locker, and covering that with an old raincoat. Black Wellington boots poking out from below the raincoat crowned the effect of turning me into a nutty old lady.

BOB CRAVEN

My partner in punch-ups, a very tall imposing officer, was talking to me at the top of the cliffs, a lovely expanse of winding paths and ornamental gardens, that led down on to the seafront.

The young probationer had been picked up by another officer in a panda car to assist their colleague and "check this strange old woman out"-. They screeched round the corner just as the old lady knocked the checking officers helmet off, kicked him in the balls (a feigned blow) and then ran off (legged it) down into the myriad of pathways and open spaces.

The keen and enthusiastic probationer had seen this heinous crime take place and was climbing out of the approaching panda car before it had stopped. Sparks flew off the studded soles of his boots as he tried to gain a grip on the road and give chase. Egged on by his colleagues he flew into overdrive in hot pursuit.

In the peak of winter and dressed in heavy police great coat and carrying everything imaginable to carry out his duties, it was no mean feat to run at full speed at the best of times, let alone up and down the winding paths of the cliffs gardens.

Shouting as he went, "Come back here you silly old cow". To be replied by the old dear, "Leave me alone. Leave me alone". (Not an easy task to speak in a high pitched woman's voice when you are being chased but these were the days when I was young fit and healthy).

He was now in his shirts-leaves having discarded his burdenous clothes and equipment as he continued the chase. As he approached the stooped exhausted figure of the old lady bent over a park bench, watched by all his shift colleagues from bushes and other vantage points, he shouted, "I am arresting you for assaulting a police officer. You are not obliged to say..........." At that point the old lady whipped off her wig and said, "John. It's Bob Craven. You've been had!"

Instinctively the torch hit the head of the wigless old lady as the probationer launched into a stream of expletives and his mates surrounded him with pats on the back and offers of congratulations. Fond memories of an aching head!

BRAVE AND BOLD

A well-deserved commendation was the end result of another set up.

Outside the then Ritz Cinema the probationer had been called upon to assist another officer, who was tipping up a suspicious character again at 3.00am.

As the probationer approached, the suspect hit the officer checking him and ran off into a small alleyway that lead onto a large car park behind the seafront amusement arcades.

The probationer was shocked to see that the assaulted officer was bleeding profusely from a head wound (a large lump of tomato ketchup in fact – splattered as the officer held his face after being hit).

Being slightly indecisive at first as to whether he should tend to his injured colleague or give chase, he hesitated, until encouraged by his mate, "Get after the bastard".

He took off like a bat out of hell, shouting something that sounded suspiciously like, "Banzai!" and then disappeared down the darkened alleyway. Out onto the car park, crawling under heavy goods lorries with sleeping drivers inside and shining his torch under chassis and into cans eventually disturbing the assailant, who disappeared down yet another of the numerous alleyways that interconnected the back streets of the area.

He reached a "T" junction at the back of some shops and had to make the split decision of what direction he had to go.

The suspect had turned left and gone out onto the next road but the probationer heard noises coming from the right hand alley. It did not disturb him that there were now two sets of running feet.

Neither he nor the burglars knew that the alley was a dead end. The probationer was a large fellow, tall stocky and not one to be messed with. He saw the two shadows trying to climb a fence where the alley finished and launched himself at the bodies with arms outstretched ready to grab them and disable them.

He did not want to suffer the same fate as his mate back outside the Ritz. His determination and tenacity froze the burglars into a very early stage of submission. They did not fancy taking on this heavy aggression and very quickly appreciated that they were, no match for such determination.

They did find it strange that he arrested them for grievous bodily harm, when all they had done was steal some radios from a shop and had not hurt anyone. But when they were only charged with the burglary and not GBH their fears were allayed.

The officer was put fully in the picture with the events that lead up to his heroics but never found out who the suspects were for fear that he would seek some retribution. We had seen him in full flight and did not want to chance our arm with him any further.

Set ups seemed to take a halt after a too realistic one backfired in the County Force area.

A probationer was stripped to his underpants by a man with a handgun and dumped in the wilds of the Essex countryside. The near naked officer woke up the occupants to some farm premises. His frantic story of woe caused them to dial 999 and alerted the whole of the County Police Force. An Emergency clamp down was set in place throughout the area. The Force Information Room Inspector telephoned his boss, who telephoned the Force Firearms Unit, who telephoned the Deputy Chief Constable, who telephoned the Chief Constable who did not like his peace disturbed at any time let alone at 3.00am in the morning.

None were best pleased when the truth finally came out and no officer had the bottle to suggest a set up again.

It was just as well as the nights began to get busier with the opening of late night discos and the use of the motor car gave the less well even more freedom and a greater sense of security for night time travel.

Only once after the naked probationer incident did we suspect that we were being set up.

Real police work continued as normal. At 2.45am all officers on the night shift were called to attend the Cemetery at Sutton Road. A van had been found abandoned and unattended in a side road and footprints in the freshly fallen snow could be seen clearly leading away from the van, across the road, into the Cemetery and over the graveyard in the direction of the industrial estate on the other side.

Six men were detailed to walk around the cemetery perimeter on the road and the remaining four, were to follow the footprints. The cemetery was used quite a bit for set ups and as you can guess we were expecting the worst. Ghosts, skeletons, angels, what was it going to be?

A flock of pigeons flew up from a conifer as we passed a tombstone depicting an angel in prayer. "Spooky and coincidental", I thought. But we were unperturbed, looked at each other, nodded confidently that all was still well and continued our pursuit.

"Watch out for the empty graves", one officer whispered as we reached a mound of earth beside the hole for the next days internment. "Christ! Fall down that and you would never get out", said another. "Wouldn't matter if you are dead", said a third. "Yea but if you weren't. You would not be able to get out anyway would you?" said the younger of the two.

"Shut up. We've got enough to worry about here with a living bloody burglar", said the first and more senior officer.

The footprints led us to a factory on the other side and through a hole in the wire fence. A window had been smashed and the lock released but there was no sign of anyone inside. The officers approaching from the road joined us as the snow begun to deepen and cover the footprints that were leading away from the factory.

"Two stay here and the rest of you come with me. We've got to catch them before the snow obliterates the footprints", ordered the Sergeant who had condescended to leave the warmth of the police station and join us.

As we left the factory the footprints grew wider apart indicating that the would-be burglars were now running. The fittest of us took up the challenge and gathered pace, striding out faster and further than the others.

I had been used to this area as my old school had carried out cross-country races over the open ground that we knew locally, as the "prairie". Through the middle of this scrubland ran a small stream, known as Prittle Brook. At this time of year it was renowned to break its banks in flood and be quite deep in places.

Unfortunately some of the following officers were unaware of this obstacle and whereas, the two who were with me jumped across at one of the narrowest points, those that followed either stumbled into the water with a splash or narrowly missed a good ducking in the icy flow.

Two officers were soaked and others squelched in sodden boots as we met officers from neighbouring Rochford and a Dog Handler. By this time the footprints had all but disappeared and we were left to follow the faithful hound that tore off into a nearby housing estate.

Closely followed by eighteen officers the dog went straight into a front garden and pissed up against the front door. "Dirty bastard!" said the Sergeant. The Dog Handler said, "No. It's his signal to say there in that house".

The lights were on and the Sergeant peered through the window. "There's three blokes in there shivering their bollocks off, talking to an old girl", reported the Sergeant.

The old girl must have heard us, as the front door opened almost immediately. She stood with a shawl clutched around her shoulders and covering the top half of her long nightdress. Large fluffy slippers poked out from under the hem, as she looked at the gathered crowd of Southend and Rochford's finest. With a quivering voice she said, "Oh no! Has Alf, my husband, died? He only went to hospital yesterday".

For a split second we hoped that Alf was not dead and felt pity for the old dear. Then two officers with a sense of humour linked arms and mimicked a dance to a song, "Your husband is dead. Your Husband is dead. E I adio your husband is dead". Not in good taste but by then it was realised that her frail approach was a ploy to give her sons inside time to escape out the back of the house.

Pity, the dog and his handler were out the back, cutting off the escape route and causing some bite damage to one son who wanted to fight. Pleased to say, the dog was not harmed. The handler reported that he had been given a tetanus injection just in case he had bitten into something that was diseased.

The set up operations did give us all that extra edge for the unexpected and none of the officers, including myself, felt the worse for our experience.

Only too often now the first experience an officer has is the real one needing their full and utmost professional concentration and allowing no room for mistakes.

Unlike an Army recruit who is treated to the reality of live fire exercises the police raw recruit does not have that luxury.

Although the best is done at training schools to simulate life threatening situations, it can never compare to an actual experience, where the rush of adrenalin can cloud reasonable judgement or emulate the feeling of loneliness and despair, of being on your own.

Untried and untested with no rehearsal every police recruit has to deal with his first major test using his own basic instincts, innovation or initiative when he is actually on the street and in no mans land. It takes pure guts to do this!

HOME SWEET OFFICE

The security the Police Service offered in pay, pension and housing was a good reason for joining and something that Dorothy and I thought very beneficial to our lives together. However when we married it turned out that we could not get a house. Earning too much to qualify for a council house, not enough to get a mortgage and as there were no police houses available we had to turn to other means to find us a home.

The mother of one of our good friends had worked in a department store, in a road just off the High Street, for many years and recommended us for the occupation of a large flat on its second floor. I remember the owner saying that it would be such an asset to have a police officer living above them.

This wasn't to be proved the case, unfortunately as during our time there he was burgled once while we were away on holiday and audacious thieves committed a smash and grab there on the very night we had a houseful of coppers and in the middle of a party. The breaking glass was heard by two of my shift mates who chased after them, arrested them and retrieved the sheepskin coats they had stolen so all ended well.

A few nights later I was at home and the sound of smashing glass alerted me to two young lads running, chased by the owner of the Chinese restaurant two doors away. I recognised the two and followed them all into the High Street. The Chinese man had lost them but I saw them hiding amongst people standing in a bus stop queue. I arrested them, although I was actually off duty. The Chinese man was so pleased and delighted he would not stop giving us free dinners and drinks whenever we visited his restaurant. It got so embarrassing that we stopped going there.

Another time I saw two youths breaking into cars on the multi storey car park opposite and went and arrested them. Again off duty and at night! Although I received commendations for this off duty work it started to get a bit much living at the hub of the town where so much happened.

Even when assigned to duty in the quieter areas of Thorpe Bay I found myself driving back to our flat in the small hours. It was common practice to go poaching onto other areas when "all was quiet" on your beat but on this occasion I had left my sandwiches at home. I hid my panda car in the car park opposite and walked across the road and into the small alleyway at the side of the shop that lead to the stairs to our flat. The alley had a light but I did not bother to turn it on as I climbed up the wooden stairway to our front door.

Making as less noise as I dared so as not to disturb Dorothy I unlocked the door and went straight to the kitchen to pick up the lunch box. I could not resist going into the bedroom to check that she was okay and in doing so kicked the door causing her to wake up. I settled her down with a kiss and reassuring her that I had just come to pick up my "sarnies" and then left as quietly as I had entered.

Going down the stairs and into the dark alleyway was a little bit more difficult as I was walking directly into the glare of the strong street lighting. Slightly dazzled, I came out onto the street and saw two youths at the window of the small tobacconist / newsagents shop just along from the alleyway. They appeared to be startled to see me and walked off quickly into the High Street.

Suspicious of their sudden movement in the opposite direction I ran after them and stopped them a short distance away. They gave me the excuse that they were just trying to shield themselves from the wind to light a cigarette.

I asked them to turn out their pockets. Amongst a variety of items one had three small wood screws and a screwdriver.

Why I asked did he have these. He said he was doing some work at his sisters' place, but when asked to describe the work, it did not fit in with the type of screwdriver he had. The car, I had called up for support, arrived and the two were detained while I went to check the front of the tobacconists shop.

A wooden board that had been placed across a smashed window had three screws missing from it, so it was no surprise to the two youths when I arrested them.

With the magic words of arrest being mentioned the two tried to run off and put up quite a fight to resist us. In doing so my sandwiches, that I had worked hard to retrieve were squashed and trampled into the footpath.

My favourite egg and tomato in crusty bread now decorated the soles of the coppers and burglars shoes and trouser legs. Colourful and smelly!

The youths were taken to the police station.

The Detective Sergeant who had been with me on my first observation in the hairdressers was waiting in the charge room when we arrived. I did not think that he had been too enthralled with me, and I thought that he might still have it in his mind that my thumping heart had spooked the burglar on that occasion.

It was 2.00am and he, and the other detective with him, had obviously been out for an "after hours" drink in one of the many pubs that stayed open for the local CID, contrary to the Licensing Laws.

He listened as I explained to the Station Sergeant the circumstances that led up to the youths being arrested.

The facts of the case and the reasons why you arrested someone always had to be set out in front of the arrested person to enable the Station Sergeant to decide whether there were sufficient grounds to detain them further.

As I spoke I noticed the DS swaying and his eyes crossing with the occasional hiccup. He had obviously consumed!

"What a load of crap Sarge!" the DS blurted out, stumbling forward and reaching for the desk opposite which the burglars were sitting quietly.

He steadied himself with both arms clinging to the desk. You could feel the concentration he put into regaining his composure.

Pulling himself up to his normal height and taking a deep breath he eloquently said, "My candid opinion is there is insufficient grounds for keeping these persons in custody Station Sergeant".

I was astounded, even for a wet behind the ears probationer, that anyone would listen to such an idiot, was beyond me, but the Station Sergeant agreed and said, "I think we need to investigate this further and you two will be released to attend the Police Station at a later date while enquiries are made".

Not perturbed I dutifully released the youths. Not wanting to leave the situation there, I offered them an unofficial lift home. I insisted on doing so although they dearly wanted to decline the offer.

Taking another shift officer with me we arrived at the address. The large Victorian house was a rabbit warren of large rooms, cupboards and a garden with an old WW2 Anderson shelter and sheds.

This was the address they had given when arrested so it was awkward for them to deny they lived there. It was a squat and occupied by many of life's unfortunates.

We suggested a cup of tea would be in order and went in with them not allowing them to refuse us entry.

As we went in the first murmurings of other residents could be heard, "Is that you Fred?" a girls voice whispered. "Fred?" I questioned silently one of the youths as neither of them had given that name. He shrugged his shoulders and mimed, "Not me".

The other youth in the meantime looked as if he were going to burst and failing to contain himself any longer shouted, "It's the filth. Fucking get out!" Banging and crashing followed with doors opening, running footsteps, shouting and blurred sleepy faces appearing from every direction.

We radioed for assistance not knowing what to expect and managed to detain several occupants in one room including our two youths.

Finding out that the place was not theirs and that it belonged to a respectable couple trying to sell it we felt duty bound to protect the owners interest and arrested the entire group.

The shift arrived in force and we then made a search of the house.

We found heroin, syringes, and cannabis resin, a 14-year-old girl missing from Birmingham, two youths wanted for stealing a car and stabbing someone in London, one who had escaped from a Youth Detention Centre and boxes of cigarettes, tobacco and booze, the proceeds of burglaries in the area.

We were quite pleased with ourselves and even more delighted to have to telephone the drunk Detective Sergeant and get him out of bed to deal with these characters, as he was "On Call".

All this because I had forgotten my lunch box

Our flat was handy as a "tea stop" for colleagues on the High Street beats and fro keeping up with the football World Cup at Mexico in 1970 when all the matches were shown live at 2.00am.

Dorothy was not best pleased when 12 coppers were strewn all over her lounge shouting support at every move that the England team made and screaming derision at all the refereeing decisions made against our beloved team.

Although she was no fan of football she cheerfully kept us supplied with toasted cheese sandwiches and large mugs of tea.

The noise from the High Street was always at its worst of a night.

During the day there was a constant buzz of people and traffic and even the buses hissing air brakes and squeaking doors did not interrupt sleep during the daytime. But at night the streets emptied and any sounds made echoed through like it was the Grand Canyon.

The noise of police radios travelled great distances and one particular officer was renowned for having his personal radio on so loud that it was thought he did it on purpose to frighten off any potential burglars or wrong doers.

I did get fed up with this when I was on early turn and had to get up for duty at 6.00am. Having had a hopeless night trying to get to sleep the last thing I wanted was one of my own colleagues keeping me awake. I had been late every morning of this seven day tour of duty and the Sergeant had warned me that a seventh would result in me being put on a discipline charge.

I left a note to the "loud radioed" officer, "Please keep the volume of your radio down low". He took no notice. Round the corner he came, radio blaring out but this time I was prepared.

As he sauntered past underneath our bedroom window and out of the protection of the shop canopy, he was soaked by the contents of the bucket of water I had kept by the bed, should he ignore my polite request. I was on time that morning and looking forward to seeing him go off duty as I reported in.

He had a befitting nickname and the soaking gave the opportunity for the one officer to ask him, "You are very wet "Goldfish". Have you been swimming while on duty?" I never heard a loud personal radio in the vicinity of our home after that day.

My enthusiasm for doing the job even from within the confines of our home was soon to backfire as can be read in the Bank Holiday chapter. I was forced to rethink that carrying out my duty so close to home could have drastic consequences.

I was never able to identify the characters that we heard at the rear stairs to our flat but it was enough to convince me that someone was trying to locate where I lived.

With so many occasions where I had arrested people or taken action against someone in or near the flat, both on and off duty, it was no surprise to have them make some investigations. "He came out of here somewhere", I heard a male voice whisper as I went to find out who was at the back of our flat late one evening.

A bad enough situation when I was at home but dangerously unacceptable for Dorothy, on her own when I was on duty. It was time to move.

A police house in a pleasant road in Westcliff had just become available and our occupation of it coincided with Dorothy expecting our first child.

Chapter Six
ILLUMINATIONS DUTY

Southend has been the playground of the East Ender from London since the late 19th century. From taking in the sea air and a promenade on the longest pleasure pier in the world to "kiss me quick hats", sweet seaside rock made locally and the local delicacies of cockles, jellied eels and delicious ice cream made to the secret family recipe of the resident Italian vendors.

The stunning cliffs, award winning gardens and pleasure parks full of thrilling rides such as water slides, helter skelters, carousels and the wall of death where a motor cyclist mastered the law of gravity by riding a shear circular wall at hectic speed to the wonder of those watching.

The attraction to the town was exemplified by the illuminations that lit up the seafront for about a mile from the gas works in the east to the open-air swimming pool in the west. Known as the golden mile, the lights showed set pieces of clowns juggling, fish leaping, bouncing balls and hundreds of others.

The Never-Never Land filled part of the floodlit cliffs with an assortment of model railways, fairy castles and nursery rhyme scenes.

The Pier was lit from end to end and sported dance halls, bars and amusements at its head and pleasure ships docked regularly to take holidaymakers for trips to see the shipping that regularly passed en-route to the London Docks and cruises to the Kent ports and beyond to Calais and Boulogne four hours away on the French coast.

With fifteen pubs in that short seafront and many more on the roads leading to it the area brought out the best and worst of the day-trippers who came here on the works outing or beano as it was called.

Thousands of coaches dragged already inebriated occupants after visiting every hosteliery between London and the Borough. Our public were very happy before they arrived.

Coaches, or charabancs, using their historical name after the horse drawn coaches of the turn of the 19th century beano, were given specific routes into the town that took them to designated coach and car parks. When these were full they were allowed to park on the seafront roads either side of the golden mile. On busy weekends it was not unusual to see them parked nose to tail along the seafront all the way to Shoebury some two miles to the east.

In the late 1960's, with the town and seafront heaving with day-trippers in various states of euphoria, our task was both enjoyable and exciting.

Violent behaviour had to be dealt with but also the hilarious and mostly harmless drunken antics and colourful characters made the task of policing the area so enjoyable.

On these busiest of occasions the numbers of police officers on the beat were boosted by the extra hours we all had to work. Fours hours were added to each tour of duty so if you were on early turn from 6.00 am to 2.00 pm it was extended to 6.00pm, late turn 2.00 pm to 10.00 pm extended to 2.00 am and nights 10.00 pm to 6.00 am started at 6.00 pm.

These twelve-hour shifts provided the manpower to have a police officer on every corner and road junction on the town centre and seafront, all on overtime. Although we were allowed to have time off in lieu at an enhanced rate or payment, I cannot remember ever being paid for doing these extra hours.

It is no wonder that people these days refer to going back to the old days when police were seen in plenty and demanding more officers on the beat to prevent crime. This was only successful because the cost was minimal compared to now that overtime is fully and fairly paid.

The Patrol Sergeant would warn every one on parade before duty of the beano's that were heading our way. The Metropolitan Police and Essex Constabulary Officers to the west of town would report to out information room any incidents that had occurred had at pubs and cafes on the roads leading the Borough.

Most coaches would set out to time there run to coincide with pub opening hours of premises en route.

9.00am was the norm from the City of London usually meeting at a transport café. Huge fried breakfasts, called train smashes because the mostly red congealed contents of the plate resembled such a scene, were dished out to prepare the stomachs for the onslaught of alcohol that was to follow.

Northern or Midlands beanos would set out earlier. We would receive messages from Forces, like Birmingham or Leicester, as early as 6.00 am that trouble was on its way.

Regular troublesome visitors usually held their beanos on the same weekend every year. The Sergeants would always give us fair warning of what to expect.

The ladies from a matchstick factory in the east end of London were renowned for their love of a good time, not always at the expense of others, but it lacked in certain areas of decorum.

The toilet facilities both on the roadways towards the town and in the town itself were never quite sufficient to meet their needs. The sight of a long line of thirty plus women squatting in a row, with a variety of types of knickers around their ankles, relieving themselves at the road side in full view of other travellers was greeted with hilarity, and somehow was more acceptable than having them do the same in the street of our town, in the close proximity of many hundreds of other trippers.

It took a very brave officer to take any action against such behaviour and usually resulted in a further scene of unpleasantness. Such was the case when our young Police Inspector witnessed a group of ladies urinating in the gutter in full view of decent holidaymakers.

He remonstrated with them saying that such behaviour on our golden mile was totally unacceptable. One offending lady said that it was probably called the golden mile because of the yellow piss that flowed. Another noticed that the Inspector had fair, almost golden hair, and asked if his pubic hair was the same colour. This caused a snigger between the two older officers who were with him, as the Inspector had recently returned from the Police University and was often referred to as "Golden Bollocks"!

A crowd gathered as the ladies, about ten of them, moved closer to the Inspector and started to touch his crutch area, with some making for his belt buckle. Realising the predicament the two officers went to intervene, but were then occupied by similar advances from the remaining women.

The Inspector was easy prey for the ladies. He was large enough to fend them off by using normal restraint methods, but in his public school upbringing, could not use such force against females, so he tried to use polite requests to persuade them not to do him any mischief.

Even the enforced use of, "Madam please?" did not hold water with the girls as they forced him to the ground. He grabbed hold of his belt so tightly, but the dig in the ribs they gave him released his grip and gave them sufficient time to whip his trousers down to his ankles.

His large boots saved the day and stopped the trousers from being completely removed from his legs. Trousers inside out and wrapped around his ankles he stood up to the applause of his assailants and the crowd that had gathered.

The girls clasped hands and did a dance around him as he tried in vain to break their circle and escape to less embarrassing climes. The two accompanying officers could only stand helplessly by, held at bay by the others and the large dense crowd that was jockeying for a better view.

Realising the hopelessness of the situation the Inspector stood silent for a moment, breathing deeply in frustration and waited patiently for the humour to die down.

The girls' drunken drone of a song dissipated into giggles and laughter as they made to disappear into the crowd. The Inspector realised his ordeal was about to be over and bent down to start the difficult job of pulling his trousers back up.

His red face and neck deepened in colour as he bent double to reach the distressed trousers but a gasp of shock and pain struck him as one girl reached through his open legs from behind and grabbed his genitals saying, "Fucking hung like a donkey you are you lovely boy" and then releasing him to slap his backside with the other hand.

Finishing off she shouted "Yee Ha!" in cowboy fashion from underneath her Stetson "Kiss-me-quick" Hat and skipped off into the crowd.

The crowd dispersed smiling as the Inspector replaced his trousers like a tired busker, silently retrieving his props after his act.

This not so impressive display of the Towns' finest, in his underpants was in complete contrast to the spectacle of the dominant line of law enforcers that stood opposite every pub on the seafront, at closing time in the afternoons and late evenings. This line of two officers at least to every pub, and five at each of the most likely trouble spots, ensured that any drunk intending to cause a disturbance was deterred from doing so by the threat of such a visual display of force.

The white helmets stood out in the middle central reservation of the dual carriageway Marine Parade, in the sunshine and the illuminations later in the day, head and shoulders above the crowds as a warning that any moves to create trouble would be stamped on immediately, and with strength of numbers to provide support at the time it was needed.

The powerful display of stern faced officers did not stop the odd individual from being stupid and violence was always a regular problem, but it hardly escalated further than a few swings of the fists. It very rarely involved weapons and the use of a smashed glass or bottle was something I had never seen or experienced.

Incidents were usually crushed by the sheer weight of numbers of officers, and in some instances the officers far out numbered the assailants, to the point that it was embarrassing.

However the system worked and when questioned once a senior officer said that given the choice what would you choose, the cost of over policing with numbers to swallow up trouble or the cost in money and health of more victims in hospital and the extreme expense of court appearances and its knock on affects.

"We are here to prevent primarily, not pick up the impossible amount of pieces later", he added. I think he had the situation about right.

The fights occurred for a wide variety of reasons with beanos from all quarters of the country, rivalry and revenge from previous years altercations, pinching someone else's girl, spilling a drink.

Nine times out of ten the situation could be defused by officers talking to the fighters, giving friendly advice and smoothing the volatile with the warnings that a cell awaited for them if the did not heed what was being said.

It was always handy for the officer to be able to point out the numbers of colleagues, who were waiting in the wings to carry out the ultimate job of arrest if he did not take any notice.

I am sure that the assailants respected this approach, and many a temporary hot head continued to enjoy his day trip peacefully, and without the reminder in future years of the day by way of a criminal record, for committing an act of violence.

Being able to communicate with people was a craft that was learnt by young officers from their elders during such incidents, and the ability for an officer to use his own common sense and have authority to verbally warn offenders, not only prevented crime but kept stupid misguided people out of the courts.

Persistent offenders were watched and concentrated efforts were made to lock them up. Having been given the luxury of a warning and then flown in the face of such kindness always resulted in a no compromise response from arresting officers.

Always assured of a swift court appearance the following day while the crime was fresh in the mind the courts were far more committed to protecting the public and punitive sentences were meted out.

If the offender was unfortunate to appear before certain Magistrates he could expect no quarter. The fact that one Justice of the Peace was nicknamed "Hangman", gives you some idea of the thoughts he had when sentencing defendants who stood before him.

The seafront traders were so appreciative of the support that their officers gave them. Most were known by their first names, particularly by the long serving officers, whose job it was to introduce the younger of us to the traders. There would be an open invitation to eat at their restaurants, hot dog stalls and shellfish bars.

Sometimes I would be so full up from the food on offer that I had to gamble with the possibility of insulting a trader by refusing his wares. Although not receiving the official consent of senior officers, this was accepted as a genuine practice to keep in touch with an important part of our public and sources of intelligence and information. Building bridges and keeping in touch with our locals was considered to be a very important part of the job and had to be done to provide good policing.

Sometimes the use of an officers' initiative would take the turn of using some physical efforts to assert the necessary authority on offenders.

Yobs and generally young people would try the patience of officers on the beat with antics that were a nuisance and at worst anti-social. A flick around the ear from an officer would suffice but occasionally a boot up the backside was used to get the message home.

One sunny afternoon a senior colleague and me were walking our beat on the seafront at a point where the Pier created a bridge over the footpath. Two youths were throwing stones up at the windows to the Pier Train station and were caught by us before any damage had been done.

One of the youths, a fat lad of about 16 years, kicked my colleague on the shins as we grabbed hold of their coat collars. My colleague winced with pain and turned the youth around holding him an arms distance from him and gave the lad a heavy slice of boot leather on his rear.

"Don't be stupid lad", said the officer, "If you want a further taste of my leather and end up in court then just carry on the way you are. I can accommodate you whatever". The lad half crying shouted, "I am going to make a complaint about you and police brutality".

"Be our guest. It is your right! My Sergeant is just over there. Go and tell him" the officer replied. Our Sergeant at that time was standing at the bottom of Pier Hill some 100 yards away and the youths approached him.

The Sergeant was the exponent of the swift response and was known to use such methods himself to deal with matters.

"The Ways and Means Act is common sense attitude towards behaviour that could construed as bordering on youthful exuberance and the minor criminal. It is a question of getting to grips with the actions of the "swiftness of the hand deceives the eye", he would say.

"Otherwise hit the little shit to teach him a lesson, not put him in hospital, but sting him so he knows he has been hit but doesn't know where it came from. Nip his behaviour in the bud so he won't do it again", was the philosophy of the Sergeant these youths were approaching.

The outcome was inevitable. The aggrieved youth, we saw describe how he had been kicked up the backside, and pointed to us as he remonstrated with the Sergeant. He stood passively elbow on hand, stroking his chin with the other hand listening intently to the youths' complaint.

He waited for the youth to finish and then asked him to show how he was kicked. The youth bent over in front of the Sergeant and pointed to his outstretched backside. The Sergeant scratched his chin and then quick as a flash booted the backside in what seemed a much harder strike than the previous one.

The youth shot up in the air holding his arse as if it was about to drop from his body ran off and into a café situated on the Pier Hill.

His mate stood stunned in disbelief briefly and then took the same route away from the now laughing Sergeant.

A few minutes later they appeared with a middle-aged man wearing a blue and white striped apron. "This will be interesting. That's his Dad," my colleague said.

The scenario was played out with the youth pointing at us, and the Sergeant, to his father and then to his backside with the nodding in confirmation to his story by his mate.

You could see the father saying is that true to the Sergeant and he replying that they were throwing stones at the pier windows and miming the action with his arms. The father turned to his son and asked the question is it true and the youth nodding his head.

The father enraged at his time being wasted put the palm of his hand against his forehead and then struck his son at least five times with his other hand across his head, far harder than any blows he had received before. He took hold of the boy by his collar, shook hands in thanks with the Sergeant and disappeared into the restaurant.

A short while later, we popped into the restaurant for a cup of tea and saw the youth with the sore arse and head, the son of the owner, and his mate standing at the sink washing up. They were only just visible amongst the biggest pile of dirty pots, pans, and plates, cutlery that you could ever imagine in the steamy washing up area.

The owner served us tea and shouted at the boys, "Think yourselves lucky that these officers just gave you a kick up the arse and didn't nick you. The two of you are washing up for a week now".

Rough on the kids really, especially, as the restaurant had over a hundred chairs usually occupied fully throughout the day.

Life was not always easy for the officers, although most day-trippers were out for a good time, the revelry would sometimes be played on the young probationers.

A group of panic stricken young ladies ran up to such an officer and in grief said that one of their number had fallen over the railings on the Pier and had gone head first into the mud.

Southend mud was well known for its healing powers and was used apparently in some beauty parlours for facial packs and this young lady had intended to try its qualities first hand, leant over the balustrade and toppled in some ten feet below.

The officer needed no second explanation, running at full steam he hurtled into the soggy mud.

His first strides took him some distance before the deepening mud slowed him. His legs sunk to the knees as he waded against the weight of the ooze.

A sizeable crowd had now gathered including the young ladies friends and a few police officers who seemed to be willing to stay in the background just keeping a watchful eye on the saga unfolding. The girls' two legs were all that could be seen wearing stockings and red shoes, with the frill of a pink skirt or other garment just protruding from the mud.

There was no movement of the legs and the worst was expected as the breathless officer reached the spread-eagled legs.

It was not unusual for pot holes of mud to be over three foot to six foot deep, as bait-diggers were notorious for digging for the rag worm bait, leaving the holes for the on coming tide to disguise.

When the rescuer reached the lady in distress he dived at the hole that was obviously keeping her down. His head hit the mud that was no more than a meagre foot deep.

Dazed and bewildered his face re-appeared like a black and white minstrel. Holding one leg fell over to his left and the other to his right, those in the crowd who did not know of the ruse, gasped in the horror that the lady had split in half.

The gallant officer realising that he had been had tugged at the ankles of a tailors dummy, lifted them clear of the ooze.

To rapturous laughter and applause, the audience whistled and cheered him as he held the legs above his head like trophies and made his way back onto the shore and away up the town centre and the police station showers.

As he climbed the steps from the seafront lower levels to the High Street he was a followed by a small entourage of ladies in flimsy blouses, tight mini skirts, stiletto shoes and "kiss-me-quick hats.

Apologising as they tripped after him for causing him to get so muddy, suggesting that they could help clean him up, grabbing sizeable handfuls of his rear end and begging him to met them when he went off duty at the Foresters Pub where they would "make amends for their crime!"

Not wishing to disappoint the ladies the officer did meet up and, being a gentleman, never disclosed if amends were suitably made.

ILLUMINATION BY FIRE

Three fires sent the old Golden Mile into some years of demise.

To my knowledge none were caused by arson or other suspicious circumstances. One at the Pier Head where the old pavilions and dance halls were destroyed, a mile and a third out to sea where no fire fighters could effectively reach.

The roller-skating rink and Pavilion at the land end was burnt to a cinder. This was eventually rebuilt as a bowling alley and again suffered a fate by fire and waits to be resurrected.

The third was on a day when my shift was on nights. Our illumination duties had come to an end and the crowds had disappeared from whence they came.

A burning piece of paper was seen to blow out of a waste bin on the Marine Parade and carried by the strong onshore window under the steel shutters of one of the amusement arcades.

One of our officers had seen this happen and tried desperately to stop it going under and into the premises, and then to force the shutters up to get at the now flaming paper. All his efforts were in vain as the draught from the strong seafront wind blew the flames back deeper into the premises.

Frantic calls were made to get assistance, as the glow grew larger from within. The shift soon appeared in numbers as the sound of the Fire Brigade bells could be heard in the distance.

The buildings above and behind the arcade were old converted cottages and now divided into a warren of small flats and bed-sits. We all had to empty the buildings as quickly as possible, as the flames crept towards the back lower ground floors.

The only way to get to these flats was by several steps from a service road at the back called Seaway. This road also had a large lorry park opposite the rear of the arcades.

Flames were now leaping up the front of the building and spreading along to adjoining arcades. Three were now catching alight and the heat was starting to build up. The whole shift was now kicking open heavy gates and running shouting hoping the occupants would hear them. The door that I went to had eight different doorbells. I was pressing them all and getting very concerned that I could not hear one bell ringing.

I started to kick at the door and was joined by my Sergeant who said, "We haven't got time for that" and smashed the door window with his torch. He released the catch and we both dived into the small corridor and up the narrow stairs.

Smoke was starting to fill the hallway as we thumped on doors and shouted at the top of our voices.

In all four men, two women and three children came out of the tiny rooms. All sleepy and bleary eyed in their nightclothes. In the noise not one of them panicked as they made their way out through the back yard and up onto the road above.

As we climbed the steps I could feel the heat from the flames on my back. Smoke was starting to rise from the wooden fencing that skirted the road, some twenty yards away.

The Fire Brigade had arrived and were pumping water onto the huge flames that now clawed at the sky. Wearing breathing apparatus teams were checking the buildings for any other occupants but fortunately swift action had emptied all the buildings and everyone was accounted for.

The blaze was taking hold increasingly with the full blast of the onshore wind and the old buildings were being turned into matchwood. Collapsing roofs and walls were reducing the height of the fires but this was increasing the heat at the back in the Seaway lorry park.

Many lorry drivers were sleeping in their cabs and most had been woken by the commotion. Those that were not had the hammering of fellow drivers getting them up and helping to drive their rigs to safety.

Lorries whose owners were in bed and breakfast nearby were left at first to face the music, however when one had its windscreen broken by the heat, it was time to bodily shift these last remaining vehicles away.

With the technical knowledge of several drivers who were able to release air brakes manually. We pushed and shoved four heavy goods lorries away from the fire and prevented causing further damage.

It took fifteen of us, drivers, police officers, firemen and other onlookers to push them. None of us seemed to give a thought of what the vehicles were carrying. We did remark about the possibility of fuel tanks exploding but it was not until a driver arrived to check his lorry that we realised the full implications of what risks we were taking.

He had been sleeping in a B & B nearby and was woken up by his landlady. He rushed over straightaway to check his load of paint and cleaning fluids.

If his load had ignited, he said, the whole car park and possibly many adjoining buildings would have been covered in inflammable liquids.

We had not got a clue! In our haste to do the work all of us professionals and members of the public had not had the common sense to check the signs that clearly stated the dangers of the loads. We were very lucky.

The fire took days to dampen down.

Some say that on that night the seafront lost, forever, its quaint, soft soul to the colder impersonal style of modern day-tripper entertainment.

KURSAAL SPECIALS

The Kursaal renowned to be the best, in its day, amusement park in the country with rattling scenic railways, big dippers and water shoots. Super structures made of wood vibrating and shaking as screaming day-trippers clung onto to life, boyfriend or anyone else they could grab hold of, as they hurtled through the ride.

Below its impressive domed tower, in the flowered gardens, trippers could have family rides of a gentler nature on wooden animals, small cars and buses, whereas the dodgems and racing cars were where the boyfriends could show off. The ghost train and haunted house with its wind blower that enabled even the coyest of girls to show off her stockings and suspenders Marilyn Monroe style to the delight of the spectators below.

Death defying acts of bravery by the motorcyclists who rode horizontally around the "Wall of Death" to the talent competitions that ranged from the ridiculous to the best quality in live amateur entertainment

Bars and bingo halls provided the obvious attractions and two dance halls provided shows and events all year round. One hall was reputed to have "the best-sprung pine floor in the country" and was a regular venue of the television programme, "Come Dancing". The haunt of dancing enthusiasts for lavish ballroom music, the popular big bands, singers and entertainers and its own Southend Scottish Pipe and Drums Band brought the house down every New Years Eve.

The Kursaal was the jewel in the crown of the town and needed the attentions of the Police to protect it and its guests.

Officers were hired by the proprietors to patrol inside the complex, in their white helmets and smart uniforms, and were a high profile that was a deterrent to would be troublesome elements.

These duties were called Kursaal Specials as the officers were paid for this service in addition to the normal pay. Using days off to supplement their pay, officers worked most weekends and Bank Holidays for reward in money and personal satisfaction.

Many of the traders in the Kursaal would provide refreshments just as they did in the seafront areas. You never needed a packed lunch and always had to have a bottle opener on your key ring. That way you never missed out on the strategically placed crates of beer that were left out for us as we patrolled the grounds. Care had to be taken not to over indulge, as the consequences of being too drunk to perform your duties were very serious even then.

The need to be in full control of your actions was of paramount importance both for the sake of the job and personal safety.

One officer found this out in a most scary way when he was called to number 5 Kursaal car park after an offence of rape had been reported to him.

I had just finished my tour of duty at 2.00 am and went to the canteen in the Police Station to get a supper of Mary the cooks' renowned fried potato sandwiches.

Bent over a table in the corner of the canteen was this officer, with a blanket around his shoulders and wearing a crumpled blue and white tracksuit. Head bowed low he was just staring into the large mug that was clasped between a weak pair of ghostly white hands.

This guy was normally a bouncy, jack-the-lad, gutsy, confident and lively bloke but he now seemed overcome with exhaustion as if the stuffing had been completely drawn out of him.

The canteen was empty him, and Mary who was busy frying away in the back of the kitchen. She came out to take my order and I asked her what was the matter with our mate in the blanket.

"He's been sitting there for ages. Won't speak. Won't go home. He's worrying me. I tried to talk to him but he doesn't want to know me. You try", she implored.

I took my mug of tea, placed it on the table and sat opposite him. I said, "What's up mate? You look all in. Where have you been?"

139

He took a long sip from his mug and without looking up said, "Fucking Kursaal Special".

"Why you under that blanket then? Too much booze?" I said.

"No, not now. I well and truly sobered up after what I've been through. I can assure you!" he replied and then expanded on the day he had just had.

"We were on the special as usual from about 10 this morning. No problems, the usual crap, old ladies wanting the photos with us, kids being told by Dads that we would lock them if they were bad and all that stuff. Took a few drinks over the day. Probably too much but in the afternoon I was okay. Sid (the other officer) and me split up and went about the place as normal when this girl came up to me, very upset, saying her mate had been raped in the back of a coach in the No. 5 car park.

I asked one of the traders to contact the office to get some back up as you know about the problems with No.5 don't you? (No.5 car park was where the most notorious coach parties were placed so keeping all the likely trouble in one spot). I knew that Sid had only gone for a piss and would get the message so I went over to the coach.

Three other women joined the upset girl and me as we went over to the coach. All were saying that the girl was in a right state and that the bastard better watch out cos if they got hold of him they would chop his balls off and things like that so I didn't suspect anything was wrong. But it was a set up!

They told me that the girl was at the back of the coach, and as I went up the aisle I saw a crowd of them round someone on the back seats.

I still didn't think anything was up as the driver was at the wheel smoking a fag and seemed normal. I didn't notice at first but the driver was a woman, I thought it was a bloke with a cap on and a white dustcoat like the coach drivers wear.

Anyway I got to the back and they just pounced on me. I heard one shout out, "Get going Mabel" and then the sound of the door closing and felt the coach drive off. These women were like fucking animals, all over me. I tried to roll up in a ball in the well of the seat.

My helmet went and then my legs were outstretched and trousers taken off. They were whooping and shouting, "What a lovely arse" and pulling at each other to get a better view. Some of them must have been drinking as I felt booze going down my back but then realised they were pouring drink down the cheeks of my arse and then I felt one of their lips slurping at my back.

There were so many of them enclosing me I thought, "Fuck it. Lay back and enjoy it, as long as they haven't got the pox. Ugly yes, but without the benefit of a paper bag I can close my eyes.

I thought it was only women who had to "lay back and think of England". I just let them get on with it. Look". He pulled the blanket down to his shoulders and showed several small round bruises.

"Fucking love bites they call them. I think they took chunks out of me, and some with no teeth.

It's bad enough at home, as it is, without this fucking lot. Is my missus going to believe me when I tell her what happened? That's what I am doing here. I can't decide how to tell her. If I hide these for a few days she is bound to notice them after a while. Then it will be worse". He stopped to ponder.

I tried of think of something to say or ask or show some sympathy but could not find the words that would help, but at the same time wanted to know more. This obviously showed on my face as he picked up his tale of woe again.

"It didn't stop there. I was on the floor and they obviously noticed that I had got a hard on. Never let's you down, does it? Horribliest fucking birds in Christendom and still old John Thomas wants some action, anyway what else could I do?"

He waited a short while for me to agree and then continued, "I lost count at the number that shagged me ("He's bragging now. But who could blame him?" I thought).

Do you know one didn't have a bra on, she was so fat and old her tits were touching my stomach as she rode me?"

BOB CRAVEN

The thought made me choke on my fried potato sandwich that I suddenly realised was being eaten at twice the normal speed, as I devoured what was being said and tried to picture the scene in more detail.

"I think they ran out of things to do. A couple of them tried to gobble me off. I thought dirty cows, me covered in the others love juices but there you are, no accounting for taste," he said thoughtfully and at this point appeared to show a sign that there were parts that he had enjoyed and could use some embellishment to boost his prowess a little.

He continued, "I noticed we were going over the flyover at Gallows Corner. I reasoned with them that I had been a good sport and wouldn't take it further and suggested they let me get off."

"Just one more duckie then", a bleached blond said.

Too late for me to realise that it wasn't a bleached blond but an ugly cow with a huge lump of candyfloss that was whacked onto my bollocks. Fortunately she had it in her hand and not on the stick as the sticky mass was curled over my privates and then face after face disappeared into it taking as big a mouthful as they could muster. A fucking nightmare! All of a sudden they let me get up and shouted to Mabel the driver. "Let the poor fucker off at Gants Hill mate".

"I couldn't get off quick enough. I forgot my trousers and just had the remnants of my shirt. Everything else was left on the coach.

I managed get to a TK to phone up for help just as two MET blokes came round the corner. They gave me this lot and got me a lift back to the borough boundary.

I've had a shower but it was not hot enough. The fucking candyfloss has gone to sugar and hardened. All my pubes are stuck together. I am in agony. I need to sit in a hot bath to soak it off.

That stupid bastard of an Inspector has said I ought to go to hospital to have it cut away. He is having a laugh.

Any chance you could get me home mate and help clear things with the missus?"

Tall order I thought but to his home we went, borrowing the police van and making sure no candyfloss and nothing else attached to it fell off.

I told his wife that he had been in a severe ordeal with some mad women and some understanding and sympathy was needed.

I am not so sure that he got what he wanted but they are still happily married even now and he never reminisces about the ride he had and I guess that he looks back on his Kursaal "Special" much differently.

POINT DUTY

"The roads of our fair land are the arteries of industry and commerce. If they get clogged up then the whole body of prosperity falls apart and dies", said the training Sergeant at the Police College, as he opened the lecture on the art of traffic management, which in those days meant, standing in the middle of the road, usually a junction, waving your hands and arms about trying to keep cars and pedestrians apart.

The amplifiers crackled into action as the whole class was swept backwards by the fanfare to the early fifties government cine film titled, "Keep it Moving". This was 1967 and the film was old then!

A lone policeman was depicted standing in the middle of a road with the odd black square shaped motorcar or box lorry passing by only interrupted by the occasional pedestrian needing to cross the road.

One lady pushing a large pram crossed the road twice from the same side within a minutes, such was the doubtful edited quality of the film.

One thing that stuck in my mind was the smart and precise manner in which the officer conducted the control of the situation. He was so meticulous in his signals to proceed, with the commanding wave of his arm. The erect holding up of his right arm wrapped in white elasticised armlet with white outstretched gloved hand, fingers reaching for the sky, dominating the air above him and clearly indicating to the oncoming motorist that he had to stop immediately. There was power and command at its best and most authoritive.

My mind was drawn back to this when the Patrol Sergeant gave out the duties for the Saturday illuminations. We were late turn and therefore prepared to work until 2.00 am on perhaps one of the busiest illumination days of the year.

The Sergeant warned us that many beanos's had been reported coming our way and several punch-ups had taken place at pubs on the Arterial road from London.

I am not sure why the A127 was known as the Arterial but it was reputed to be the first stretch of dual carriageway to be built in the country in the 1930's and it seemed to go well with the description given to our roads by the training Sergeant.

My allocated beat was Southchurch Road and Southchurch Avenue and point duty at the junction of these roads, which was commonly known as the Glen traffic lights.

This was a major junction with coaches following a blue route leading them from the outskirts of the town into the areas containing the main coach parks for the seafront areas. The coaches laden with revellers would come along Southchurch Road from the west and then turn right into the Avenue that took them down a hill to the seafront and the Golden Mile.

By the time I had reached my beat it was about 2.15 pm and the coaches had started to mass at the junction. The traffic lights could not deal with the weight of traffic and a jam was starting to build up causing mixed reactions from the trippers inside and the local motorists. Horns were being tooted and derisory comments passed between vehicles.

Duty called and my powers had to be exercised to avoid chaos and "keep them moving". I placed my white armlets over my tunic sleeves, took the fresh white cotton gloves from my pocket, carefully pulled them over my hands and pushed the fingers tightly into place.

I turned the traffic lights off with my special issue key and smartly marched to the centre of the junction holding my right arm up into the sky, clearly asserting to the drivers that I was in charge and taking full command.

What crossed their minds was of no consequence to me as I signalled the stationary vehicles to manoeuvre back or forward to rid the junction of the snarl up.

All was cleared and the smooth running of the traffic returned, but as the coaches were now appearing from the west nose to tail, I decided to remain in the middle waving my arms about.

The revellers inside the coach were always singing, shouting, swearing, arguing and generally above the level of noise due to excitement and the amount of alcohol consumed, so it was nothing out of the normal when this old green charabanc full of dancing ladies pulled up beside me.

The traffic negotiating the junction had been temporarily stopped to allow two elderly local ladies to cross the road in front. The coach, shuddering to the movement of the dancing females, was stationery inches my right shoulder.

I relaxed my commanding posture and waited for the traffic to disperse when the singing grew louder as I heard the squeaking sound coming from my right. The charabanc, being over 30 years old at least, had wind down windows and the ugliest woman I have ever set my eyes on was lowering the one immediately beside me.

She was huge. The pretty daintily floral patterned dress she was wearing could not compensate for her massive biceps and podgy bearded face. She clawed her way through the narrow gap between the metal bar that crossed the window and its lower opening, and thrust her enormous arms out towards me, as her equally immense breasts hung bra-less over the charabanc bodywork.

Too late for me to fully realise what was about to happen. She wrapped her arms around the top part of my chest and pulled me up against the coach side. This coincided with the traffic jam easing, and the coach started to move off.

145

"Come here you beautiful policeman. Give us a kiss," she gruffly spluttered. She planted her wet, soggy, beer swilled lips on my cheek. The horror of the kiss was equally as terrifying as the thought that the coach was now picking up speed and heading away from the junction and onto the seafront.

I was trying to keep my footing and run backwards with the increasing pace. The occasional foot making contact with the road as the lady cradled me against her. Shock retreated sufficiently for me to shout to her, "Let me go madam. Please!" Being polite so as not to antagonise her, I again asked her to let me go.

One of her mates said, "Doris you'll fucking kill the poor little bastard. Put him down there's plenty more down the front".

Doris fortunately took note of her mate and let me go quite gently allowing me to get my balance before releasing her grip saying at that point in such a cute girly voice, "Sorry dear. Perhaps next time eh?"

As the coach disappeared over the brow of the hill towards the seafront the ladies hung out of the still open window waving and blowing kisses with outstretched arms and gathered on the rear seats mouthing "I love you" with pouted Marilyn Monroe lips. Two others pulled their skirts up showing their bare bottoms, framed by their best lace under wear, probably worn specially, for the forthcoming days activities.

The whole incident only took seconds. I was able to quickly compose myself and run back the two hundred yards to the junction, which by now had ground to a massive halt with vehicles snarled up in all directions. Flustered but not deterred from what was expected of me, and my duty, I started to wave my arms about to efficiently untangle the mess.

Just when you don't need it an Acting Inspector turned up!

The chaos had affected the traffic approaching the junction and further down the coach route for a considerable distance of two miles, I later heard. I don't think it was entirely my fault but that was not what was on the Acting Inspectors mind when he marched up to my point.

Face like thunder with thoughts of a forthcoming promotion disappearing down the drain he shouted at me, "What the fuck do you think you are doing. This lot's (pointing to the snarling traffic) piled up to Cuckoo Corner because of you. You fucking idiot!"

I was caught between complaining about his language and saluting him. Neither was a good idea. Complaining, because it would not achieve anything and may even make it worse for me and in the words of the Training Sergeant, "You never salute an Acting Inspector". I suspected that he used to say this as he had some aversion to Acting Inspectors. I was not now surprised if his experience was the same as I was suffering now.

Not wishing to aggravate the situation I waved a floppy hand to my right in acknowledgement of his presence and got stuck into sorting the tangled of vehicles out.

Apart from a few very near misses from some impatient drivers, I managed to shuffle and shunt the vehicles back and forth, prising them from their predicament and sending them off on their way.

Under the scrutinising gaze and occasional tut from the grimacing face of the Acting Inspector, all was resolved and peace reigned over the junction.

With a sigh of both pride and relief I returned the junction into the capable automatic hands of the traffic lights.

The Acting Inspector marched off to a more prominent spot for displaying his supervisory skills in front of the senior officers who frequented the more populated areas of the High Street and the Golden Mile. The local dignitaries, like the Mayor and the Chief Constable were more likely to be in those places where he could pontificate and throw a few more fucks into other probation constables and prove his worth as a substantive, real Inspector.

Pleased to see him disappear I walked further into my beat and down towards the seafront. As I got closer to the razzmatazz, music and screams of the amusements and rides of the Kursaal, I saw that the junction to the main car park and the road outside was stifled with queuing coaches and cars.

Not impeded or put off by my last experience I leapt to the rescue.

147

Arms waving bedecked in white I soon sorted the problem out. "If only that bastard, Acting Inspector, had seen this man in action. That would soon shut the bastard up!" I thought.

I remained there in the middle of the road for some time directing and pointing, manoeuvring and ordering. I was in total command again, proud and very pleased with myself. Whilst I smirked slightly, I suddenly realised I had a little old lady standing immediately beside and below me.

She was so short and tiny I had not even noticed her. With hair net covering her wispy grey hair in tight curlers, she stood there in blue quilted housecoat and pink fluffy mule slippers. She held a neat tray containing a small china teapot, milk jug, sugar bowl, cup and saucer and tea plate on which were neatly arrayed a selection of biscuits including my favourite biscuits, "jammy dodgers".

"What are you doing?" I exclaimed in some shock, and a little concerned that she was in some danger from the traffic that I was continuing to control.

She said calmly using her free hand to nudge me gently, "Don't you worry about me dear. I do this all the time. You boys work so hard. It's the least I can do. I'll put this on the wall over there outside my B & B and you help yourself when you have got the time. Now don't let it get cold!"

She then shuffled off across the road oblivious of the dangers. The traffic stopped automatically for her without a command or wave of any hand.

As if to acknowledge her local fame and respect some tooted on their horns and a taxi driver leaning out of his cab shouted, "You spoil them Mrs B. Put some clothes on next time you sexy little thing!"

Mrs B waved her little hand in a feint, I like it but don't embarrass me gesture saying," Oh don't you rascal!" Then she went through the spotless and shiny red gloss front door of the house opposite the junction.

The thought of the jammy dodgers and cup of tea diminished the traffic crisis and I sloped off to the waiting tray of goodies.

As I went to pour the tea out the door opened and Mrs B's voice said, "Good. About time you had a rest. Now sit down at the table. (I then saw a wicker table and pair of chairs in the small paved front garden of the B & B) and I will bring you something to eat".

From the garden I could see the whole of the junction in all directions especially down towards the seafront from where any supervising officers might come.

It was the perfect vantage point for surveying my domain and a safe haven for devouring the mighty meal of eggs, bacon, sausage, tomatoes, mushrooms, fried bread, black pudding and Mrs B's renowned bubble and squeak.

Washed down with more cups of tea and an afters of home made jam and cream on freshly baked scones I was very reluctant to return to point duty work.

All that hand waving twisting and turning, engine fumes and droning noise was not likely to help my stomach. God I hoped that nothing else was going to happen. Neither mind nor body was going to be in tune after that lot.

Chapter Seven
BANK HOLIDAYS

Bank Holidays in the town were always busy. The day-trippers were mostly families here for a good day out. They came in there thousands by coach and rail from as far as Manchester and Liverpool on Special trains using the rail links that circled London. These trippers were always good for my sales when I had a part-time school job selling ice creams on the station platforms. Hot weather sold ice cream and cold weather tea, coffee, pies and donuts.

For a change the roads were congested which for those days was a rarity only to be seen at such peak times.

The town had survived the onslaught of groups of troublemakers over many years protected by the guile, ingenuity and forceful thinking of the Borough Constabulary.

The Officers were big, bold, given excellent backing and support by their senior officers, Exemplified, respected and admired by the residents of Southend who in return were given a dedicated service by a Force of individuals who had the freedom to take a balanced view of situations and make an instant decision to defuse an incident in the common interest of all concerned or who could be affected.

In the case of persons committing offences we were given more responsibility to deal with the offenders in a practical way. The old clip around the ear for those causing nuisance was still perpetrated although only by older, experienced and wiser Officers who understood and calculated their grounds carefully for doing so.

My first Bank Holiday duties were performed in the Easter of 1968. Mods and Rockers were still evident on the seafront areas but only those local and recognisable to Southend could be seen.

Mods riding their scooters with their feet protruding outwards from the footplates and wearing distinctive khaki American Army Parkas, edged in fur and the odd imitation foxtail attached. Mini skirted girls with heavily mascarered eye make up wearing leather caps on Mary Quant coiffure hair and thigh high boots hanging precariously onto their Beatle or Georgie Fame haired rider.

The Vespa GS and The Lambretta GT were the favourite scooters. None could race over 60 miles per hour unless illegally adjusted by the owners. Some of who had taken the bodywork off to expose the moving parts of the engine and expanded the exhaust pipes to give the sound of an approaching Second World War De Haviland Mosquito.

The out of date Rockers were fewer in number but were dressed in the leathers of the rebels of the 1950's rock and roll era that was drawing to a close to most. There were still a few hangers. The Rocker boys insisted on sweeping his hair back in Elvis rebel style, using Brylcream to produce that jet-black sheen and black leather bomber jackets and a variety of leather accessories. Girls in heavy make-up with backcombed hair creating the "beehive" much like Ma Simpson today.

Acres of tassels, chrome lone stars or wings and clan colours painted etched on the back of their jackets. Hells Angels were starting to take shape. Locally the Billericay Bastards were the main group but there were many others who sported the rebel colours of the American Confederate cause. How and why we will probably be told someday.

These would ride motorcycles of varying cylinder capacity from the huge engine Triumph Bonneville's to the Honda 50cc "hairdryers". Each rider would wear his colours with pride and ride his bike as if it were the strongest and mightiest stallion.

The mere presence of these opposing groups was a major concern of the senior officers who, every Bank Holiday, commanded members of the Traffic Department to cover all routes into the Borough and forewarn us in the town of the approaching hordes.

Motorcycle scouts were sent towards London on both the A13 and A127 trunk roads. They would then notify the patrol officers on the Borough Boundary check points, of the route taken by large groups of Mods on scooters and Rockers on Motorcycles.

Coaches and cars containing groups of these "undesirables" were also reported. All vehicles and occupants representing these groups and suspected of being a threat to the peace and stability of Southend Borough were turned unceremoniously around from whence they came or dispersed into smaller groups and sent westwards away from Southend. But it was not possible to turn all away. Some did manage to slip through the net to do battle on the seafront.

The town was not only visited by these type of trouble makers but we had to contend with many persons who binged on drink, if it was a hot day the level of possible incidents increased, numerous lost children tied up many resources and the town centre and seafront was usually grid locked on such days.

All of these factors committed manpower to dangerously low levels of effective policing and to allow hundreds of rival groups intent on causing injury to each other, criminal damage and serious mayhem would be a neglect of our lawful duty and unforgivable in most peoples eyes.

Many seaside resorts had been affected by such incidents including Clacton and Brighton and our Acting Chief Constable had been reminded that if damage and injury was caused as a result of a riot by these groups then he and the Police Authority would be held responsible for the costs.

To enable us to carry out this prevention work The Metropolitan Police would convey all intelligence received in their area to our force for dissemination.

Our senior officers and us, the lower ranks, considered that these large groups of opposing factions would cause a breach of the peace if allowed to proceed to the seafront where families and businesses could be subjected to violent and disorderly behaviour.

In the face of much criticism from Civil Liberties Groups we are sure that this action to avert such unacceptable behaviour and gave the vast majority of ordinary day-trippers the opportunity of a happy and peaceful holiday in the town.

Towns who did not implement such methods were soon identified as a soft touch and bore the brunt of any trouble.

With the assistance of The British Transport Police we were able to monitor all large groups of suspected troublemakers using the railway system into the town. The BT Police had long experience with these groups throughout their network and escorted trains where possible to ensure passenger safety.

We were notified of these persons and met them at the main Southend stations.

As the youths alighted from the trains they were separated from ordinary passengers and lined up to be checked and where appropriate searched. The usual offensive weapons used by gangs were found including knifes, home made coshes of various descriptions and some even had antiquated and home made knuckle dusters.

It was not surprising that large numbers of them did not possess a valid ticket to travel on the train. All those committing offences were arrested and taken into custody whereas the remainder were ushered onto the next train leaving for London.

These events were never more evident when the era of the mods and rockers melted away and the skinhead cult started to spring up from the East End of London and other similar areas of major inner cities. Rockers still existed but mods changed their parkas for smart suits and long lapelled shirts with brightly coloured kipper ties or totally hippy in the mode of the pretty people of California.

Skinheads were the less well offs' answer to the rebel image, but with a twist of military uniform, even Nazi bearing, clothing and attitude. Anti colour, racist insignia and tattoos, shaven heads, high leg Doctor Martin boots, tight jeans to just above the ankles, no belts but braces exposed over a Ben Sherman shirt was the dress code and in winter a dark blue "Crombie" overcoat with breast pocket from which would protrude a red handkerchief. Earrings and other jewellery were still considered "only for poofs".

Laindon Railway Station, Basildon New Town still did not have one, was apparently the place to be on a Friday evening when the units of the these bands of rebel brothers paraded in military ranks to alight the trains to London and "Do the Town".

They were so easy to identify and even wore the colours of their football club to enable us to establish where they came from. The majority who visited or tried to visit Southend were from the East and South of London supporting West Ham, Millwall, Charlton and other such football clubs. They even chanted their provocative unison football supporter songs as they went through the towns, usually ending in a spontaneous applause and self-gratifying roar of approval and dissent.

Local youths tried to follow suit with their experience of the North Stand at Roots Hall, Southend United Football Clubs' home ground but never seemed to reach the peak of atmosphere that the city boys managed to achieve. The local youths were easily controlled by the Police and occasionally arrested for simple breach of the peace offences whereas the city skinheads were a far greater threat to the community.

The Senior Officers stance on dealing with these skinheads continued in the same vein as that of the mods and rockers. On the Easter Bank Holiday of 1968 information was received from the BT Police of the imminent arrival of 400 plus skinheads at our local railway stations with many more gathering at other London Stations. They were met Southend Victoria Station by the Southend on Sea Borough Constabulary in all its massive glory. Not a thin blue line but a massive wall of blue serge uniform. A wall that seemed almost as thick as it was high due to the tall compact muscle of the officers. The white helmets topped the wall extending its height even further.

Admittedly there was the odd decrease in the height; where I stood in fact, but this did not stop the gasp that one skinhead gave as he got off the train to be greeted by us. One of his mates objected to being told to make the return journey to Stratford where he had come from. (Stratford apparently was the easiest place to "bunk" (not pay for a ticket) the mainline as you came straight up onto the platform from the underground trains whose entry stiles were easy to jump en masse).

"They can't do that. They just, fucking, can't do that", his mate exclaimed spitting with frustration. He went to push through the line of blue rock with his friend attempting to drag him back. Two huge arms took hold of his wrists and pulled him through and the immortal words were heard, "You are being arrested for conduct likely to cause a breach of the peace. You are not obliged to say…".

The caution continued, as per "The Judges Rules", with the youths' protests suddenly dulled to silence as he was taken by the standard police hold of the officers' left hand firmly gripping the youths left wrist and the officers right hand gripping the youths arm just below the left bicep muscle. If the youth struggled this grip enabled the officer to press into the youths arm at that point to a nerve between the bicep muscle and the elbow joint causing him some further pain and discomfort. Properly connected this pressure had the affect of stilling any further struggling. This procedure of executing an arrest was only successful if the arrested person was slightly smaller in stature than the arresting police officer.

Other arrest procedures were taught to us at training school in the forms of self-defence techniques. These included a wristlock where the officer took the hand of the offender and bent back at the wrist joint with the hand at a right angle to the forearm. This could be done with one hand with practice leaving the officers other hand to reach for handcuffs. I used this quite often, as a high level of physical strength was not required. This levelled the field of play for a short arse like me because the difference in size of the offender and me was usually to his advantage.

Large disturbances and fights were quite common in the Borough and self-defence techniques, "as per the book", were too time consuming and ineffective to quell the situation. Although we were many on the ground and our individual body size on average was much larger than our opponents. The alcohol they had consumed or the pumping adrenalin they were experiencing usually caused that very deep red mist that always clouds and compromises common sense.

To calm such incidents and keep the Queens Peace that we were paid to do and what was our sworn duty concise and instant action was required. Arrests were carried out only if absolutely necessary and in the case of serious offences however the majority of the time the offenders were treated to "summary justice" that resulted in the odd black eye or sore cheeks. On many occasions these melees would end with the perpetrators shaking hands with the officers, apologising to them for their behaviour and thanking them for not arresting them and dealing with the situation in a civilised way.

It could almost be said that their was an unwritten "Queensbury Rules" in these incidents and that only when someone stepped over the line where matters taken further. This would include the drawing of a knife by an offender and the over zealous use of a truncheon by an officer. Very rarely did this take place.

The Southend Constabulary were renowned for their intolerance to behaviour that was not conducive to the peace and enjoyment of others and when they were spat at by or threatened the offenders on the platform were immediately and unceremoniously arrested and hauled away.

Searches were made for offensive weapons and again arrests made without discretion and consideration for protests or excuses. That was for the Courts to decide but the immediate affect of such firm and positive policing destroyed the belligerence and threat of this army of undesirables. I have no doubt that there were innocent skinheads in the groups that were treated in this way but we had a duty to protect the majority of other law-abiding citizens who were in our town. The balance had to be in those peoples favour rather than that of a minority group of possible troublemakers.

Any further protests of being treated unfairly were quashed out of the mob of skinheads who remained on the platform. The mate of the arrested youth turned to his girlfriend, equally shaven headed and dressed, "Come on Doll. This lot will kick shit out of us. It ain't worth it".

Train after train, a small number of coaches and cars containing skinheads were turned away. This procedure continued throughout the year and the bank holidays of 1968. We obviously received the criticism of the then Council of Civil Liberties but this was dwarfed by the stupendous accolade we received from the newspapers, the law abiding public and the traders of Southend who enjoyed a profitable and largely peaceful weekends, suffering only the odd troublesome individual.

This was to change somewhat with the amalgamation of the adjoining Essex County Constabulary with our Southend on Sea Borough Constabulary. On the 1st April 1969 (no significance can be given to the date being April Fools Day I am told) The Borough of six foot tall plus officers were joined to the Essex five foot eight officers, jokingly referred to as "The Diddy Men".

The changes in tactics of the combined force were never more significant than in the dealing with public disorder. The Borough had 50 years of experience in sorting the situation out without any major problems but the realignment of thinking was not in the mode of a localised solution but that of a wider geographical concern.

Unfortunately a small number of the skinheads we had turned away from the town on a previous bank holiday had alighted trains in local villages en route back to London. Their decision to cause trouble and most likely vent their frustration and the fact that the areas were sparsely covered by the County Police resulted in some windows being smashed.

This did not go down very well with Chief Constable of the County Force who just happened to be the Chief Constable of the now Essex and Southend on Sea Joint Constabulary. Specific instructions were issued that no such action would be used to stop any persons from entering the town.

This attitude was completely in line with the liberalised type of thinking that was being introduced. The hippy era of "Peace not war" was becoming in vogue, dialogue not force, and persuasion not coercion, was being passed down from the government thinkers and planners.

Unfortunately nobody had told the skinheads or the organised anarchists and protestors who violently demonstrated against our democratic society and the police service was treated as the punch bag. The riots at Grovesnor Square had just occurred and we were all in the process of being trained in crowd control techniques yet we had to handle street criminals and disturbances with kid gloves.

The first bank holiday after the amalgamation was the Easter weekend. Good Friday was a normal quiet affair as usual; the Saturday was slightly busier with mostly families and coach outings enjoying the dry sunny weather.

Easter Sunday saw the arrival of a large number of skinhead gangs some 80 to 100 strong. They were allowed to come in as instructed and were accompanied by pairs of Police Officers who monitored their behaviour and movements. These officers did not have the bearing of previous days. No longer were they wearing the imposing white helmets and most were drafted in from other parts of the County. The majority did not have the local knowledge required for sending reports of locations and directions and their numbers fell far below that which the Borough Force would have allocated to a bank holiday.

Disturbances soon took place in pubs. Minor thefts occurred and reports of making off without payment from cafes and restaurants started to roll in thick and fast. The tactic was to use large numbers to confuse traders and avoid being identified. One inside premises it was very difficult to stop the inevitable scenes that followed.

Where action could be taken officers made arrests, but this took already thin resources off the street to deal with the time consuming taking of statements, interviewing offenders and other procedures that had to be carried out.

Some local officers continued to use summary justice tactics. However this did not achieve the approval of our new senior officers. One such incident took place when a Sergeant saw a group of skinheads throwing normal dressed girls and boys bodily off a jetty on the seafront into the deep slimy mud that was present on the shore when the tide was out.

The Sergeant along with three other local officers went onto the jetty and blocked the skinheads exit. The youngsters who were thrown into the mud protested that their clothes were now ruined and the Sergeant asked them how much their items of clothing cost. The skinheads tried to push their way past the officers claiming to be innocent of any wrong doing but the Sergeant cut short their protests and said that he and his colleagues had clearly seen the offences take place.

The question then arose of what to do about this conundrum should they all be arrested, ten of them in all, and waist time and manpower etc or can something else be worked out. One skinhead said, "Don't nick us mate. I've got money. I'll pay for the damage". The Sergeant assured the skinhead he was deluded if he thought that he was his mate but stated that the payment of compensation was a honourable gesture. He then asked all the skinheads to produce their wallets and the girls to empty their handbags.

The boys and girls who had been thrown off the jetty did not wish to take the matter any further mostly because they had been frightened enough.

There was a slight disagreement over the cost of an aggrieved girls leather coat but an agreed sum was decided. Unfortunately this left the skinhead gang with no money for the remainder of their stay but at least they still had their return tickets to take them home on a train to Fenchurch Street.

A substantial crowd had gathered to watch these proceedings and a few individuals had shouted their disgust at the leniency of the treatment of the skinheads. The Sergeant had noted their disapproval and asked to the skinheads what they would have expected in the way of punishment if they had gone to Court for this matter. All unanimously replied that they would have been fined at least and one even admitted that he would have expected a term at a Detention Centre because he had form (previous convictions).

The Sergeant told them the only way they were going to get off the jetty was from the sea end. They looked round and it dawned on them that he meant that they should take the route of their victims via the mud. A few remarks of disgust and momentary refusals followed by stern, meaningfully unsympathetic and intense lowering of the Sergeants eyebrows made the skinheads realise that the options were not for discussion. "On the count of three jump", shouted the Sergeant. He commanded, slightly hesitating as if to ensure full submission, "Oooone"! Large portions of the crowd joined in unison, "Twooo. Threee. Jump"!

Strangely some of the male skinheads decided to make a spectacular show of it and took macho dives and belly flops into the oozy mud but did not realise that below its one foot or so depth was a hard layer of shingle. Their spread-eagled bodies hit the seabed with a stomach jerking squelching thud, followed by a deep gurgling sound as the mud entered their mouths.

One girl with dyed black crew-cut hair and a tattoo of "WHU", believed to mean West Ham United, expertly followed the males. Two others turned from hard cases taking full part in the throwing of the other kids into screaming schoolgirls who were frightened of crabs and what other sea monsters there might be living in the depths of the slime. Another intense look from the Sergeant and the reassurance from one of the males already in the mud that it was bravado "luvverly" convinced the girls that to jump was at least in their best interest. Down they went trying to support each other as they descended. As they hit the greeny brown slime they bounced off each other and they sunk to their knees. The momentum of the jump threw them forward until their chin and upturned heads entered into it.

The crowd roared with laughter as two kind ladies gave the girls towels to wipe the mud from their faces. One said, "Here are love. Not funny now is it"?

The group were then ordered by the Officers to walk out to sea and around a fishing boat moored about 50 yards out and then walk westwards under the Pier and then along to a point where they would be met and escorted to the railway station. This they did and the group dragged their mud sodden boots and clothes in a painfully slow trudge to Southend Central Station.

Sadly their ordeal did not end there with a passage home, as the railway staff would not let them on board a train in such a state. The mud had to be removed. In despair they looked to the escorting Officers for help. They pointed them in the direction of the nearby petrol station that had a car cleaning hose. The attendant reluctantly allowed them to use the hose to spray themselves down along as they cleared away all the mud from his forecourt.

When they returned to the railway station they were allowed to return to their destination but in the guards van accompanied by two British Transport Police Officers.

The incident was recorded in the Occurrence Book for the day, "Criminal Damage – Marine Parade – aggrieved parties declined to prosecute – names and addresses of aggrieved and alleged offenders taken – no further action".

This was perhaps one of the last officially recognised instances of summary justice as senior officers, although thinking that this instant resolution was morally acceptable to the vast majority, they had to also be very aware that some, a very small minority did not consider that this was the correct way forward.

During that Easter Sunday there were more disorder offences, assaults and thefts committed than the previous three years of bank holidays and the public of Southend noticed and complained. The usual oil was poured onto the stormy waters by the politically tangled senior officers and a new apathy started to creep into the once proud Borough Force.

Easter Monday saw the brain wave that was to cause a further storm for the senior officers to settle with the libertarians. By the time the early turn shift had paraded for duty that day the word had got to the beat police officers that numerous complaints had been received from the traders, shopkeepers publicans, fairground owners and many of our friendly residents and supporters of the town that they had been let down by the Police. They now feared that their safety was in question, they were not to be protected, crime would escalate and perhaps more important to some they would loose valuable and essential trade.

The junior officers knew and sympathised with the senior officers' dilemma but were at pains to see how they could satisfy both parties.

One deep thinking officer suddenly had a brain wave, "Why don't we take their belts, bootlaces and their much loved braces off them. That way they won't be able to run, kick (the heavy boots they wore were used in many assaults) or punch because they will be shoe loose and too busy holding their trousers up".

We'll take them and then they will only go and buy others in the shops", said another officer. "Not if we ask the shops to take all the belts, shoelaces and braces off display they won't", was the reply.

With that after parade all the shops were visited and owners and managers gladly agreed to our request. The job was made much the easier as there were only a small number of shops open on bank holidays who sold such items.

The scene was set before any senior officers came on duty. The talk concerning the plan over the radio was kept to the minimum although those officers who were not aware in the first instance were quickly told by word of mouth.

Large boxes were arranged to be available in the front office of Southend Police Station to receive the items taken and then made available for when the skinhead owners arrived to pick them up before they returned home.

The first trains arrived with the skinhead hordes and they were met by a small but determined group of officers. Safe passage through the ticket barriers was secured for the many families who had travelled, some skinheads who did not have tickets were quickly apprehended by the BT Police and the remainder of our skinheads waited to be turned back.

To their surprise and our frustration they were allowed to come through the barrier. They were asked for their ticket and then to remove belts, braces and bootlaces. To our surprise they hardly questioned the request and meekly gave the items up. Some seemed to think this was fair trade to be let into the town. They were told to pick up the property up from the police station before they left.

Most did but some complained that there "expensive and irreplaceable belts / braces or bootlaces" were not in the boxes. They were advised that no matter where you go in the world there is a dishonest element in every part of society even skinheads. They were told that if they wished to send a copy of a purchase receipt for the items missing the Chief Constable would consider any claim for replacement. To my knowledge none were received.

The following day the newspapers heralded the action taken by us but as usual the liberals questioned our actions. The majority of the public who were asked to comment were full of praise and the traders and residents who suffered so much previously thought the good old times had returned. There were minor skirmishes of disorder but generally crime was down. Only one skinhead was arrested when he took a kick at another youth but forgot he did not have bootlaces on his loosened footgear. He only realised this when his boot sailed across the bar and went straight through the pub window. In mitigation his defence solicitor stated, "If the Police had not removed his shoelaces his boot would not have gone through the window". This was rather foolish as the Magistrate pointed out that according to witnesses if his boot had been securely fastened it would have made contact with the head of the person he was attacking and his client would have been charged with a more serious offence.

No Senior Officer would take the credit for having the bravery to set this procedure up but the Chief Constable affirmed that, "The Essex and Southend on Sea Constabulary would continue to provide the community with steadfast and resolute policing".

THE STICK OF ROCK

However things were due to change for the job and me in particular.

On the 26 May 1970, a Bank Holiday Monday I had been on early turn. The duties had been particularly frustrating as we were ordered not to participate in any methods that could be construed as contravening someone's civil liberties. New methods were being used to disperse large groups of troublemakers into smaller groups, in which they would be considered less harmful.

As a result instead of one large group skinheads that could be contained we had several smaller groups who were running us ragged by stealing and damaging property in several parts of the town.

I was off duty in the afternoon and returning home to our flat above Ravens Clothing Store in Clifftown Road with my wife when I saw a very large group of skinheads wearing cult pork pie type trilby hats enter en-masse the small Newsagents next door.

This little shop was no bigger than the average front room and by going in as they did the youths "were up to no good". The shopkeeper was a very elderly Scotsman opening his shop all hours to grab the limited trade that passed on the way to the main line Southend Central railway station nearby. Always jovial and chatty and being his neighbour I had many a conversation with him "putting the world to rights".

I heard a shout come up from inside the shop and the youths came rushing out laden with sweets, cigarettes, and drinks. You name it they had taken it! Swept the place almost clean! The elderly newsagent, who had not long come out of hospital for heart surgery, rushed out after them. He was knocked to the ground by the sheer weight of numbers of youths as they ran out clutching their goodies. Some stopped to kick him and then punched the air in celebration. Others threw handfuls of cigarette packets and other goods to those of their mates who could not get into the shop to help themselves.

All the time press photographers were snapping away to get the horde in action, passers by stopped in amazement and gawp at the show and even laughed at the youths' antics of leaping in the air sporting their ill-gotten gains. Nobody helped the old shopkeeper writhing on the ground.

I shouted out, " Stop, Police", or something similar and all the youths stampeded off and onto the nearby Central Railway Station. I picked the shopkeeper up. He said, "Fucking shits. I'm okay. Just get the bastards Bob!"

I ran off after them and as I did I saw two uniform police officers heading the same way. I quickly told them what had happened and continued onto the station where I saw these youths getting on a train to London. I dragged one youth off. I recognised him as one of the ringleaders. He was about my height, 17 years, medium build and still clutching a stick of rock I had seen him holding up above his head outside the shop.

I shouted to a ticket inspector to stop the train leaving and thinking the policemen were behind me I took the youth back to the station concourse. There was no sign of any officers there or on the road outside the station. I was starting to get a bit concerned with no support or likely assistance.

By this time the youth was sensing my despair and a group of his mates who had followed me out of the station were starting to get over the shock of my arresting him and becoming braver trying to get him free. I was kicked about the ankles. Fortunately they were wearing soft-toed Dr Marten boots and not steel capped like some were wearing that day. Even though I was used to receiving kicks during football matches the pain was starting to get worse as every blow made contact. I was determined to hang onto the youth and gripped him in an arm lock restricting his movements and attempts to escape.

Half dragging him I walked back to a point outside Ravens Menswear Shop next to the Scotsman's shop - still no sign of any police officers or no other support - the youth and his mates saw their opportunity and suddenly attacked me from all sides.

I was head butted from one side and punched in quick succession from the other. I went dizzy and dropped to my knees. As I did my grip on the youth stood firm and he came down with me.

I felt the full force of a ferocious kick to the back of my head. My head felt like it was going to explode and then this warm trickling feeling went down my neck as the blood came from the wound the blow had caused.

The blows continued to rain down and across me from all sides. I was starting to lose consciousness and could here the gang shouting encouragement to each other, "Fucking harder than that you tosser", after one blow and, "He's never going to let go of him. Kill the bastard!"

Others kicked me to the head. By this time I had fallen completely to the ground and was on top of the youth who seemed to be unconscious either by being kicked by his own mates or hitting his head on the kerbside.

Press photographers seemed to be everywhere busying themselves taking their scoop pictures and the usual large crowd of ghoulish onlookers gathered to watch the spectacle.

I curled into a ball on top of the arrested youth and could do nothing else but hope that assistance arrived quickly. I screamed in pain and shouted, "Dorothy!" Whether this was a cry to get help, panic or because I thought that this was the end of me, I do not know to this day.

I remember a local youth being there, that I had arrested on previous occasions at one time. He pulled some of the youths off but ran away when they turned on him. I found out later that he was the only person who phoned 999 for the Police to assist me.

I can still hear and fell the sickening thud as the blows hit, sunk into me and the boots stamped on my head. The pain was there but it was as if I was anaesthetised and all feeling had been removed.

The shouting and thumping suddenly stopped and reality returned with a loud wakening as if the volume had been instantly turned up to full blast.

Normal voices said, "Okay mate they've gone", and others talked to each other referring to me as if I was a stage show.

In the distance I heard the police sirens. I stood up; blood streaming from cuts and bruises to my head, making a real mess down the back of my new "Ben Sherman" shirt. My back and midriff racked with pain and I could hardly stand on my legs, as one of my ankles was now twice the size and throbbing as if it was going to fall off. A huge bump was forming on my forehead and my brain felt like mashed potato.

As I stood there astride the unconscious youth a photographers camera flashed and an old man said to me, "Leave the poor sod alone you bastard". I told the man I was a police officer and he said, " I know you lot are always picking on the kids of today".

Officers arrived and efforts were made to apprehend the ones responsible. An impromptu identification parade was held on the station platform. Skinheads of all shapes and sizes were lined up in an attempt to identify my attackers. Everything was buzzing around me and there was no chance of me recognising anyone.

The press were out in force taking photos of my every move and describing me as a "Hero".

I went to hospital and was stitched and patched up. I was advised to stay overnight for observation but I just wanted to get home and go to bed. I came home to Dorothy who like me felt a mix of shock and excitement. The night passed so slowly as I wrestled with the pictures of the assault and the need to sleep.

I must have fallen off to sleep as the next thing I remember is the doorbell being rung and my best mate and shift colleague, who was on early turn, came running into the flat in great excitement. He shouted, "You have made the front page of the nationals. Look!"

SEE PICTURES - DAILY SKETCH FRONT PAGE

There I was, on the front page, standing over the youth, in the "Daily Sketch" under the headline "Hot and Bovvered" - " Skinhead mob held at bay by one PC" - "PC Robert Craven arrests skinhead after stealing a stick of rock" - some accolade!

The front page described how the skinheads had returned to Southend to take revenge after the police had foiled them on the previous Easter Monday when we took their bootlaces and braces off them. It described how large numbers of skinheads had created havoc in other towns stealing, causing damage and being violent and disorderly.

In the days that followed, Dorothy was interviewed by a reporter from another newspaper on the effect this traumatic incident had on her.

I felt a strange feeling of both elation, disappointment and of course pain and discomfort as the weeks passed. My wounds healed, as you would expect. I was put on a pedestal by some as a hero but kept my feet on the ground because I knew I was not.

I had been in the right place at the right time as a police officer but was dropped in the shit by the two officers who I had told of the incident. Some weeks later I confronted them in the Police canteen. Both apologised and said that they did not grasp the situation and were more concerned about getting off duty on time. I was very angry but there was no point dwelling on the issue.

Senior Officers were quick to congratulate me when they visited to check on my progress although the DCI of the day disapproved of the press coverage and suggested that I was a "glory seeker".

With the help of the many press photographs taken at the time several youths in the West Ham area were arrested and charged with assaulting me and stealing from the newsagents. They received various sentences locked up in detention centres.

After three weeks off sick I returned to duty and as everybody else did, just got on with the job.

I never thought of me needing support, caring or other considerations. It did not cross my mind that I, or my family could be affected by such an incident or there could be any dire consequences for us in the future. Why should there have been? I was okay after a while wasn't I?

Time did heal the physical injuries and the occasional nightmare and waking up sweating profusely did not worry me. I received the grand sum of £120 from the Criminal Injuries Compensation Board so in financial terms we were being considered for any harm caused. The new dining room suite we bought with the money seemed to be ample compensation for us.

On reflection there was only one occasion that concerned me.

Some months later I was in an annual appraisal interview and inexplicably burst out crying for no reason whatsoever. It was a career interview with my Chief Inspector.

I had nothing to fear from the officer. My appraisal was first class with fine words being used by my supervisors and a rosy future forecast for me in the job.

I don't know if the Chief Inspector detected something was wrong or what but he said, "How are you in yourself? Coping okay?"

Dorothy and I had moved to a police house in Westcliff by then and she had given birth to our first daughter, Clare, a few months earlier. So the question was quite normal and to be expected.

BOB CRAVEN

The Chief Inspector was a very kindly bloke and the type you felt you could confide in. I was very relaxed in his company and started to tell him that everything was okay, I was happy with a lovely wife, family and home when I started to cry. I was shaking and uncontrollably blubbering, having to wipe my nose and eyes from streaming tears. My guts churned over as I felt a massive build up inside me that would burst out any minute. I had to rush to the toilet only making it by the skin of my teeth.

It was most embarrassing for both of us and one that I could not explain until now.

I had no warning apart from the previous night when I had woken up in a pool of sweat after some intense dreaming. I put it down to the normal stresses of pre-appraisal nerves coupled with a busy time with the new baby.

The run to the toilet caused a great deal of joking and leg pulling but as the months passed I sensed a major change in my life but with a new family and house this was no surprise.

Chapter Eight
THE FIZZERS

The fizzer was what officers commonly called a discipline notice. These were served on an officer against whom a member of the public had complained, or when a senior officer suspected that the officer had breached the discipline code or Police Regulations.

Just like all officers, who served at the front line, throughout my career very rarely did a week go by, without me having one of these notices hanging over my head. Some were quite serious allegations but most were petty.

Some senior officers, whose main aim in life was to rid the Service of officers who they considered to be undesirables, also issued fizzers. Using their position to pursue their own agenda and personal vendettas. These individuals spent more time pursuing their own officers than concentrating on catching real villains. Some of us considered that they did so because they were not capable of taking on the real criminals.

This kind of oppression on usually trivial allegations detracted and depleted attitudes towards rooting out bent officers who should have been investigated on specific suspicions of corruption and caused officers to close ranks more often to protect their colleagues.

Fizzers were issued after Defence lawyers encouraged clients to make complaints against the arresting officers to enhance and delay the case. Any smoke screen was helpful to disguise the true intention of bringing criminals to justice. The lawyer, who tells a jury that the client is waiting the outcome of a complaint, and/or accuses an officer that he is a liar, when he is standing in the witness box, can produce enough doubt to get his client off.

Typical of that tactic was one solicitor who defended a man who I had arrested for attempting to importune males for sex.

I received a complaint from a sixteen-year-old boy that this man had taken him in after he had run away from his home in Leicester. He told me that the man had raped him but he was terrified of what would happen to him if he gave evidence. He was medically examined and the Police Doctor stated that he had been sexually assaulted and his internal injuries were compatible with being raped but it could not be specified or corroborated when the assault took place.

The boy was not willing to go to court therefore we were left with having to keep an eye on the male rapist. Resources even in those days only allowed us to do so much so concentrated surveillance was not possible. But coincidentally a few weeks later I was passing some public toilets that were some miles away from the rapist's home when I saw him going inside.

I decided to wait for him to come out, just to see how long he stayed in there. It was December and late evening so dark, damp and dismal. I radioed for back up whom after half an hour found his car was parked nearby. Several males went in and came out as normal. One who did not want to be involved said that this bloke was in there standing at a urinal for ages but was still there when he left.

Another said the same but again did not want to be involved. Do we disturb him or let him stay in there to possibly do harm?

Our mind was made up for us when a young boy of fourteen went in after he had been in there for over two hours. There was no way that we could allow, even the slimmest of possibility, of anything to happen to such a youngster.

As we went into the toilet the boy came running out, so quick that we were unable to extract what had happened from him. Whatever had happened was enough to make him keep running for two hundred yards flat out and way beyond the point that any of us could have given chase. We never saw him again and subsequent appeals in the press were unsuccessful.

When we went into the toilets the rapist was standing at a urinal above which, written on the wall in clear black pencil were the words, "I am for sale", with an arrow pointing down into the direction of the spot where he stood. "Have you got a medical problem?" was my first question to him as he hurriedly fumbled with the flies on his trousers.

"It is none of your business", he retorted as I replied, "Well why have you been in here for over two hours?"

"Going to the toilet. What do you think?" he argued. "Well you have either got something wrong with you or you could go into the Guinness Book of Records for the longest piss ever", I said.

I pointed to the wording on the wall, "What's the idea of this?" to which he replied, "Oh! I hadn't seen that".

We were clutching at straws but he had to be arrested and with the Crown Prosecution Service agreeing to take the matter before the court were satisfied that we may be able to save some kids from this monster.

He made a complaint against me and the other officers for harassment and beating him up in the toilets before he was taken to the police station. One of the officers who were with me was incensed and particularly aggrieved as he was a lay preacher at a Baptist Church and just could not understand that he, of all people, could be falsely accused of such a thing.

Although completely untrue the rapists' solicitor used this at court as part of the defence case. The rapist was found not guilty as we expected. Without the complaint being brought up the evidence was flimsy and not enough to gain a conviction.

It was enough though for him to realise that we were behind him and watching his every move. That was how we wanted him to feel but in truth we were not able to keep him under surveillance but he was sufficiently warned off and moved away from Southend. Unfortunately we could not guarantee that he would not do this again wherever he moved to.

All too often we were accused of perjury by a solicitor whose only defence was to attack the Police. The papers were blazoned with the headlines "Cop Liars" and even though the criminal was found guilty and we were exonerated, there was no redress and certainly no compensation for the harm done to our families who read about our alleged misdemeanours.

It went with the job and we had to take it on the chin.

The stories that follow give a small example of the fizzers dished out so readily to keep our police service so clean and tidy.

MINOR MISDEMEANOURS

My first few brushes with the Police Discipline Regulations were more, down to lack of experience, than a deliberate effort to evade my duty and responsibilities.

The Regulations were there but I did not realise the full implication of what they stood for. It took me a few fizzers to realise that in this job, you didn't receive just a bollocking if you did anything wrong, it could cost you money in fines or even an appearance at Court or worse.

My first fizzer was when I made the mistake of feeling sorry for a taxi driver who was accused of failing to ensure the safety of his passengers. He had just left Southend Central Station with a fare, a man and his four-year old boy.

The Station Approach road was a hill leading down to the High Street. The taxi was a Ford Consul, a large saloon car with the old bench type seats back and front. The wearing of seat belts was not legally required then.

As the taxi turned the corner at the junction of the High Street, the nearside rear door flew open and the boy fell out.

When I got to the scene the crying boy was being held by his father and an ambulance was in attendance. The ambulance crew said that he was uninjured but suggested to the father that he went to hospital for a check up.

I asked him what had happened and he said that his son was playing up in the back and scampered across the seat, opening the door before he could stop him.

The distraught taxi driver confirmed this. I checked the door for any faults and then asked the father if he wished to take the matter further. He declined and went with his son to the accident centre. The boy was checked over and declared to be fit and healthy.

I reported the incident on an "injury accident card" that went to our senior supervisors. A few days later I was served with a fizzer for neglect of duty, as I had not reported the taxi driver for the offence of "failing to ensure the safety of his passengers".

My Chief Inspector explained that this was an "absolute" offence and had to be done. He let me off with an official caution and ordered me to go and report the taxi driver.

Unbeknown to me, until I went to his house, the taxi driver had not worked since that accident and was now suffering from a heart condition. When I saw his son I could quite empathise with him when he said he could not hurt anyone. His son was a three-year old thalidomide child and required twenty-four hour care.

I reported the taxi driver and suggested an official caution when I put the prosecution papers into the Chief Inspector. He refused and the taxi driver went to Court where was fined £10. No justice was served by this court case. The fine was of no significance but what it did to the taxi driver was incalculable. The taxi driver was destroyed by the incident and never drove again.

Two other fizzers followed in quick succession.

Before personal radios we had to keep points with our supervising officers. To miss a point was a serious dereliction of duty in some senior officers eyes and "failing to keep a point", was a particular hate of a newly promoted Inspector who was out to prove his ability to command and control his men without fear of any kind.

BOB CRAVEN

I made my point under the railway bridge in the High Street. To my annoyance the officer, who was on the beat that covered the lower end of the Street, was also standing there.

I said to him, "You should be the other end at Pier Hill". He said, "No. You should be up at Victoria Circus". We argued the toss for some time. Neither of us had brought our beat books, that would show who was right.

It was no surprise when the Inspector met us and said, after we had both smartly saluted him, "You should not be here. You should up the other end!"

We both looked at each other in the same mode of, "Told you so!" The Inspector said, "What have you got to say for yourself then Craven?"

I could not bear to look at the glee on the other officers' face and just replied, "My apologies Sir". "Report to my office when you go off duty", the Inspector ordered.

I acknowledged his command with a nod and shaky salute. Another official caution!

Marriage took over my concentration, particularly where getting out of bed was concerned. An obvious situation to get to grips with for any job but early turn seemed to be that much more difficult to come to terms with. Getting up in the middle of the night to go to work seemed so unnatural and leaving Dorothy at the same time was even harder.

Three alarm clocks did not do the trick that would force me out of bed and onto duty. Early turn lasted for seven days on the trot from a Friday to Thursday. Weekends were excused by most Sergeants, even mine who was at the Police Station at 5.00am, one hour before he was due to go on duty.

His idea was that he would leave his home, in time, so that if he had to walk for some reason, he would still be able to get into work well before his designated start time. He was therefore less compromising to those who did not live by his standards.

The first three days, being late, were excused by him with a curt warning, but by the fourth and fifth, his patience was reaching boiling point. The sixth resulted in a last warning, "If you are late tomorrow it's a fizzer!"

The seventh morning the discipline form was already typed and signed before I reported on duty, half an hour late. The Sergeant just handed me the form saying, "Report to the Superintendent at 10.00am".

The Superintendent was stern but amused at my excuses of failing to get my new wife off of my nightshirt. He let me off with another caution. One that I heeded as I was never late again. Probably because I stopped wearing a nightshirt!

THE VENDETTA

Even with an efficiently run Complaints and Discipline Department, who investigated cases and the advent of the Police Complaints Authority, successes against dishonest police officers and those failing in their duty are minimal and limited.

A completely independent body with appropriate powers to investigate allegations would be more effective and rid the service of the cancer of the bent or racist officer and bring those deserving such treatment to justice.

The public would have more confidence in an independent body that has no political, racial or police service bias.

The Police would be released from the encumbrance of internal investigations that are almost always destroyers of morale and bring the service into disrepute even when the complaints are found to be unsubstantiated. Just as person's subject of all investigations, by the Police, should be kept anonymous so should any carried out by an independent body.

Such a procedure would stop any unnecessary publicity that has the permanent affect of ruining not only the lives of those investigated but also, their family and friends. It is totally wrong that any person should have to bear the full force of media publicity before they are convicted in a Court of any offence. There should be a total news blackout until the trial is finished and a conviction or acquittal reached.

The thousands of honest hardworking coppers, that are let down by the odd few who do cross the line, deserve the protection of such an independent body who can concentrate on complaints and allegations that merit investigation.

Their careers would not be affected by unsubstantiated complaints some of which have lasted for years because the investigating officer only deals with it on a part time basis, fitting in with his normal job of a serving police officer.

It would also stop investigations by senior officers who went on personal crusades against individual officers.

A senior officer subjected me to such an attack over a number of years. I grew up in the neighbourhood where he lived with his family and used to play football with his sons, sometimes in his garden or in the local park. I cannot say that I ever gave him any reason to dislike me but on several occasions he showed me that I was not his favourite person.

The first time happened when I was first in the CID at Southend. He was a Superintendent at HQ and in a very powerful position; able to dictate to the lower supervising ranks matters requiring an internal investigation.

One Boxing Day morning I was off duty and at home and about to enjoy a festive day with the family. I had been at work the previous day, Christmas Day, so it was a surprise to receive a telephone call to return to work.

Thinking that there had been a murder or other serious crime, that was normal for such a "call out", I dutifully attended the CID office where I was met by a Detective Inspector and Superintendent. I noticed that my desk in the office was completely empty whereas it was covered in paper and investigation files when I had left the day before.

Knowing that this was the usual procedure for an internal investigation team I realised that something was up. I raked my mind to think of what had happened to warrant such action as I was led to an office further into the building.

I knew I had nothing to fear from the Superintendent as he was a kindly bloke and deeply religious. I had recently been to the funeral of one of our officers who had tragically died at the age of 24 from cancer and the Superintendent showed a lot of emotion. It greatly impressed us all that he was a sincere and honest man.

The DI, I was not so sure of, as he had not long been promoted and needed to impress. He was a bit fiery and prone to losing his temper. It did not help that I was the captain of the Southend Police Football Team and had suffered his wrath a few weeks earlier because I had dropped him from the team. He did not like that one bit and I could not be sure that he had cooled down sufficiently to apply an independent view of things.

On top of that I, amongst others, had laughed at him when some very large bouncers threw him out of a local disco after he had the audacity to barrack and interrupt the comedy act of celebrity, Bob Monkhouse. Mr Monkhouse was his usual rhetorical self but the derisory comments made by the DI, who had perhaps consumed a little more alcohol than he should have for a man in his position, were too much. A raised eyebrow, a nod and a flick of the head by the comedian, in the direction of the DI, whilst looking at the bouncers was obviously a pre-arranged signal for an ejection to be put into operation.

The DI, being much shorter than the bouncers, was held a foot off the floor with legs pedalling in mid-air and protested, "You can't do this to me. I am a DI!" The bouncers knew him and his position well but had a duty to perform and the DI left the premises unceremoniously to the laughter of all the audience and the witty comments by Mr Monkhouse, "I know policemen are looking younger but are they taking on junior school kids?"

At this stage, as the three of us we walked through the corridors, I wasn't sure if the DI had seen me laughing at him and wondered if this could be his opportunity to get his own back.

We entered the designated interview room and I saw papers displayed in piles across the desk in the centre of the carpeted floor and over the cabinets on the side.

We all settled down in chairs around the desk and the allegation was put to me that I had forged a signature on a witness statement. A very serious allegation and if true would have meant a court case and imprisonment if found guilty. My heart sunk and my guts filled with bubbles.

The statement was by a man I had got convicted for burglary and was now serving three years imprisonment. As I was not his favourite person could he be telling lies about me to get revenge?

The allegation was preposterous and involved a statement that the burglar made regarding being punched and being put in hospital by one of his accomplices. There was a fight over the stolen proceeds of one of their burglaries and the stupid idiot made a complaint against his mate thinking that his mate would keep quiet about the reason for the punch up. After I had arrested and charged them they became bosom buddies again and the first burglar withdrew the assault complaint.

A statement had to be obtained from the aggrieved that withdrew a complaint to keep our statistics on reported crime in order. If this were not done then the crime would be undetected. The burglar made the necessary statement of retraction and signed it accordingly.

All the papers were then sent to HQ for recording statistics.

The person who supervised the statistical procedure was the Senior Officer who did not like me.

I was cautioned that I did not have to say anything unless etc.... and the allegation was put to me that I had forged the signature on the retraction statement. I was shown copies of the statements and saw that the signatures were slightly different. The burglar had signed his long foreign name with a squiggle going above it on the first one and a squiggle going below it on the second.

Apart from that the signature of the name looked the same. Even to a layman it was obvious that a forger would not have made such a mistake but here I was being accused of doing just that. I did point out that, if I had been that way inclined, I would have made a better job of it.

The Superintendent said that the statements had not been sent for scientific analysis and the burglar had not been seen and the interview was designed to get my side of the story. I was extremely angry that there was no substance to the allegation and that no investigation had been made to obtain any evidence or corroboration of the circumstances. Even though there was a risk that the burglar would be "anti" me he could have still confirmed that it was his signature on both statements.

But no, a decision had been made to drag me in on a Boxing Day Bank Holiday, away from my family whilst off duty. I thought that there must be more in this situation than was obvious.

The interview ended and I walked back towards the CID office, fully aware that the next course would be for the burglar to be seen and hopeful that he would confirm the truth. The DI attached him to my side by gripping the cuff of my coat and to my astonishment said, "Off the record Bob. Did you sign that statement?"

Even though this maddened me, I kept my composure and sternly replied, "The basic skill of a detective is to check out the facts and evidence before you interview an accused. You have ruined my Boxing Day. I am due compensation for a cancelled day and double time overtime payment for the four hours I have been here. I am also making a formal complaint, via the Police Federation, to the Chief Constable about this as I believe it was instigated from HQ without any foundation or evidence at all."

I got some satisfaction for this statement but it did not stop the worry of how the investigation might turn out. I hated the thought of being in other person's hands even though I knew that I was completely innocent.

Some months passed before I was told that the complaint was unsubstantiated. No reason was given, you were never told who had made the original complaint or given any redress. I knew that the Police Federation had taken the matter to the Chief Constable but they were none the wiser and could not tell me how, why or by whom the allegation was made.

Three years later I was back in uniform carrying out the area officers job in Westcliff. You will read about this work in a later chapter. I had voluntarily transferred out of CID but realised that soon after I had made a mistake and at the instigation of my previous CID bosses had re-applied to return.

On fourteen separate occasions I had been asked to return to CID by the Detective Chief Inspectors of the Southend, Rayleigh and Basildon Divisions and on each time I had got this mysterious knock-back from HQ. No reason was given to either the DCI's, or me as to why I was not granted the transfer. Several of them said they suspected the Superintendent at HQ but no one could be specific.

I was having a good time as an area officer and been commended by the Chief Constable, twice for my work so there was no real ground for refusal.

During this time I was called into Southend Police Station "to have a chat" with the Superintendent from HQ about a case file. This job was one that would go through him to the Director of Public Prosecutions. It was quite complicated involving allegations of theft by a wife against her husband. I had submitted this some weeks before.

I was on night duty so I arranged to go into the police station later in the afternoon after Dorothy, our two daughters and me had been shopping in the town centre. We did not have a car then and pushed the girls in their prams from Westcliff to Sainsbury's in the High Street. There were no large local supermarkets outside the town centre then so laden with the weeks shopping we would then trundle back home, sometimes getting a taxi if funds allowed.

This Thursday was just a normal day and I was just going in for a "chat" so Dorothy, the girls and shopping waited in the police station front office whilst I went to see the Superintendent in an interview room in the CID office.

During the two hours that followed I listened to the Superintendent tell me what an incompetent person I was and how sloppy the case file was. He gave no real reason for these assumptions but at one time questioned how long it had taken to interview the husband. I explained that it was difficult to get support when the husband, who was known to be extremely violent, was found but he rattled, "We've got the uniform branch, area cars, the CID, the Regional Crime Squad, traffic bastards who are always sitting around on their arses doing fuck all, police women, dogs section, licensing department, front office staff and even a fucking mounted section. How come its difficult getting support? I will be checking the duty sheets for the days when you should have got support to see what everyone was doing"

I thought that that would take a lot of man-hours and that it was unlikely that he would do that personally. He would give it to some underling and waste more precious police time. There was no arguing with this demented attitude and I decided to let him ramble on without annoying him.

Two hours into the "chat" he gave me a break to "think deeply". About what I did not know! This gave me the opportunity to arrange a lift home for Dorothy, the girls and the shopping. I took great delight in watching as all of our shopping was loaded into the boot of the marked police car, immediately below the very office where I was being interrogated, followed by Dorothy and the two excited girls. It was a little bit of justice, as civilians were not allowed in police cars and to give a lift to one was a discipline offence in itself, let alone two kids and numerous bags of shopping.

To add icing on the cake this was being done under the nose of the most hated senior officer in the Force, by a mate of mine who had been fined £5 by this Superintendent for having a cup of tea whilst on duty. Not much a fiver? But in those days it was nearly a weeks housekeeping so it was a very expensive cup of tea.

The interrogation continued with the Superintendent ranting on, from one minor point to another, for nearly another two hours. He had a habit of facing the window or the wall as he made his statements. Cigarette dangling from his mouth, he rarely asked a question but made announcements of how he was going to get rid of all the bent bastards in the force.

Several times I was tempted to say, "Can we get back to the main thrust of the meeting", but did not dare for fear of him finding something that would stick. It was not unusual for a major discipline enquiry to falter through lack of any evidence. The Internal Investigation Officer would then scratch around for some other lesser charge. Many a serious allegation has been quashed but the officer disciplined for failing to complete his duty pocket book or missing out the refreshment times in the daily duty book. Both of these books were supposed to be kept up to date but it was always inevitable that a busy officer, as we all were, would forget to complete something in them. An investigating officer who had failed to prove a substantive charge against an officer would make a beeline for these books "to expose the officers inefficiency" and prove his own personal worth as an investigator.

The Superintendent was no exception to this and would check my books. I knew this and could not guarantee that he would not find something on me so I kept quiet.

I switched off mentally, held my head in my hands and placing my elbows on the table, focusing my eyes on anything but him, and let him carry on with his tirade of abuse and demeaning accusations without making any comment or movement that might make him think that he was getting to me.

There came a pause with a silence that enveloped the room as he started to pick up the papers from the desk in front of me. I woke up from my concentrated stare at the tabletop and realised that the interview was over.

As I dragged myself up from the chair that seemed to have moulded to my backside, he stood at the door with one hand on the door handle and the other arm with the pile of papers tucked underneath. He said that I would be reported for neglect of duty and gave me the official caution of, "You are not obliged to say anything", etc. etc and then before I could answer continued, "I have known you for a long while Craven. As far as I am concerned you should never have been allowed to get into the Service let alone get into the CID".

With this, and before I could answer or even give any thought to this statement, he flew the door open. The interview room where this "chat" had taken place was within the CID office. It was sound proofed sufficiently to stop the likelihood of anyone hearing what was being said inside but with the door open anyone in the CID office could clearly hear any conversation coming from the room.

This was an obvious ploy by the Superintendent to get me to explode and say something that he could use and this was confirmed when I went through the door and saw the Superintendents "Bagman", a Detective Sergeant from HQ gagging for promotion, sitting immediately outside. He was sitting at a desk normally occupied by a Southend detective, whose nameplate was still displayed on his in and out tray. The Bagman had been planted there with his pocket book open and pen poised, obviously, to write down verbatim exactly what I said in reply to the Superintendents caution and outrageous comment, which I am sure he would not have heard from behind the closed door. He was there to record my reaction.

Although I was seething and shaking with anger I kept quiet and just left the office. I went straight to the toilets, kicking the door open and knocking backwards the figure of someone was about to come out.

I apologised and sunk onto the toilet seat. My guts were churning and heaving as I emptied the contents of my bowels and bladder in what seemed to be one single huge downward thrust. What was left came up so suddenly I barely had time to get up, turn round and throw up into the splattered stinking pan. My heart was pounding and sweat streamed from every part of my body.

I grew angrier and angrier as dizziness took over me. My thoughts swung around inside my head, "What had I done to this bloke to make him hate me so much?" I knew I had trampled on his roses when I was a kid. But I was only about seven or eight years of age. I knew I had not been dishonest or done anything wrong but now here he was digging so deep into my work. Hadn't I worked hard enough? What was I supposed to do to make blokes like him happy?

My head just spun and spun until I heard this soft woman's voice coming from the other side of the door, "Mr Craven. Are you all right? Do you want the doctor? You sound ever so ill."

"A woman in the men's toilet?" I thought but then as I turned to take some toilet paper to wipe myself I saw the grey sanitary towel disposal container. In my rage and haste I had gone into the ladies and it was the Southend Chief Superintendents' secretary that I had nearly bowled over as I bounded into the toilet. The ladies and gents toilets were side by side and the mistake was easy to make. I just hoped that she would appreciate the situation and I had not landed myself in the shit, literally, any further.

The Secretary was a very slightly built lady in her late fifties with silver hair. Employed by the police ever since she was a teenager, she was well respected for her kindness and I am sure looked upon some of us young officers as the children she was never able to have.

I don't know how long she had been outside but when I came out of my stench ridden hovel she was standing with a pretty lace trimmed handkerchief held up to her mouth. With a very worried and concerned look on her face she was holding the door to the corridor shut. As she spoke the door opened momentarily as ladies tried to enter. As it did so I could see a few tensed female faces through the opening. The secretary opened the door; slightly enough to push her head through, and said in her usual eloquent and steady tone, "Ladies. We have an officer in here who is very ill. Please give some space and use the toilet downstairs for the time being."

She was the right person at the right time for me to have. She was lovely, underneath her small demure stature was a comforting authority that quietly commanded and received respect even from the toughest of people.

The doorway cleared and she took me to her office further down the corridor and next to the Chief Superintendents. "Don't worry the Chief is at a meeting. Take your time. Would you like a cup of tea? It may help", she suggested as she led me into the Chiefs' room and placed me in one of the comfortable armchairs he used for informal meetings.

I spread myself out and stretched to release the tension that wracked my whole body. I had to be careful not to over do it, as I had not been back to work for long after the incident, "The Loaf of Bread", that I describe later. I had been off duty for over ten weeks after arresting two blokes who then set about me punching and hitting my back and causing damage to my vertebrate and discs between my shoulder blades and neck. I had only returned to normal duties at the beginning of that week and the physiotherapist had told me to avoid excessive movement.

I stretched and lay back with legs splayed out as the secretary served me with a cup of tea and a plate of biscuits on a small tray.

The heavy pounding in my head and heart subsided as I scoffed the biscuits and gulped the tea.

The Secretary came in now and again to check on me until finally after I had finished and got up to go she said, "I think you ought to go and see your Chief Inspector and tell him what has happened today. I think it is disgusting what that man has done. Mr (she named my C/Insp) is in his office at Westcliff and is expecting you to call". As she waited for my reply she held the telephone and pointed it in my direction. She held her head down with approving authority, confirming what she thought was the right thing and what she wanted me to do.

I took the telephone and rang my Chief Inspector. He insisted that I met him immediately and to clear my head I walked the mile or so from Southend Police Station to Westcliff through the quiet of the leafy tree lined back streets. When I got to his office I had calmed down sufficiently to tell him as fully as possible what had happened. He showed no emotion or gave any indication of how he felt about the actions taken by the Superintendent but listened intently to my story.

When I had finished I felt a sudden surge of emotion and cried uncontrollably. I once again cannot explain why this was. Was it the result of the released pent up and suppressed feelings of anger or frustration or was it part of the lead up to the post trauma stress disorder that manifested itself more seriously later. It was an incident I will never be able to put my finger on.

I few months later I was exonerated from any discipline charges.

I was somewhat compensated when I received a commendation for "Outstanding work in relation to detection of crime over a long period" and the local paper printed an article on the commendation stating that a "Miniature police whirlwind had hit Westcliff" when it described the work I had carried out.

I did think that the vendetta had stopped until I was yet again asked to go back into the CID and got a mysterious knock-back from HQ. I was so incensed that I made a formal request to see the Chief Constable asking for some explanation.

When I went to see him all I wanted to know is why I had been refused so many times, having been asked to go back to CID by the senior officers and having such a glowing backing and support from my immediate supervisors. He said he would look into the matter.

A week later my Chief Inspector at Westcliff asked me to come to the police station where I was to see the Senior Officer from HQ, who had interviewed me. He assured me that he would supervise the meeting.

I did not know what to expect but when I arrived at the police station I was met by the Admin Sergeant who said, "The Chief Inspector wants you to wait outside his office until you are called in".

I went up the stairs and waited outside his office as instructed. I could clearly hear what was being said between the two senior officers.

I heard the Chief Inspector say, "PC Craven is highly recommended for a return to CID and has been asked by the DCI's at Rayleigh and Southend to return and on two occasions actually started when this mysterious knock back came down from HQ. Why is it that?"

The Superintendent replied, "He is not being flexible enough. He only wants to go to Rayleigh or Southend".

I thought, "The bastard knows that I have not got a car and that to go anywhere further would cause me hassle. But in any event I had not been offered anywhere else".

The Chief Inspector called him by name and said, "It is the consensus of opinion of all the senior officers of both "H" and "J" (Southend and Rayleigh) Divisions that you have a personal vendetta against PC Craven for some reason. He is a highly regarded officer and in no way deserves such treatment".

I was gob smacked and did not hear the reply, if there was one. It was a rarity for any officer to show such strong support for a lower rank in the face of a higher-ranking officer, let alone a Superintendent. My Chief Inspector showed tremendous character, the like of which I would never forget, particularly as he himself could have been putting his own career on the line.

I went in at the designated time and was told that the next vacancy for the CID was at Basildon. I knew this to be a lie as Southend wanted one and that the Superintendent was still putting the boot in but, determined not be put off by him, I accepted the transfer.

I did not hear much from the Superintendent after that accept one time when an Inspector friend said that he had overheard him slagging me off to other officers saying that I was, "thick and incapable". The Inspector said to me, "The one way to prove him wrong is to pass your promotion exams. That would stuff him!"

This did spur me into action and determination to pass these exams. Dorothy, just as eager to prove him wrong, helped me to get my head stuck in the books and discipline myself to study. Sometimes not even allowing me to go to bed until I had convinced her that I had completed my study course programme for that week. It became an obsession to show that bastard what I was worth and I succeeded in passing both the exams for Sergeant and Inspector within one year.

RACIAL TENSION

Racial hatred is something that I detest and still cannot understand why people should think that way. From my very early days as a schoolboy I have always thought every human being is privileged to be part of this world and no one has ownership of a land or any rights over another human being. Neither colour of skin, country of origin or religious preferences should determine what rights we have as individuals on this earth. We should all be treated as equals and prejudice is totally unacceptable.

I could never understand why at school assembly the boys who were Jews, Catholics, Jehovah's Witnesses and other sects were segregated from the main body of the scholars. They were trooped in at the end of the service to hear the announcements made by the Headmaster like a latter day line up of suspects. I always thought it was degrading for them to be paraded like that but when asked they would shrug shoulders and say they were used to it.

BOB CRAVEN

It came as quite a shock to me when as a young officer I was accused as being racist. I was stunned when this Asian man told me that there was one rule for the blacks and one for the white.

I had gone to his house after he had complained about a large van that was parked outside his front room window. The small terraced house where he lived only had a small front garden and then a narrow pavement onto the road, so when vehicles parked outside they were close and blocked out the light.

A large white Luton box van was parked in front of his house, in this busy road that had vehicles of all descriptions parked nose to tail on both kerbsides. The Asian man demanded that I get the vehicle removed immediately.

I told him that I had no authority to remove the vehicle unless it was causing a dangerous obstruction. I was about to go further when he started shouting and remonstrating that there was "one rule for the blacks and one for the whites". I quietened him down and explained that it was the law and nothing to do with race and asked if he knew whom the driver or owner was. He still did not seem to accept what I had explained but he thought the owner lived two doors away although he was not sure, as they had only moved in a short while ago.

He was surprised when I asked him if he had tried to find out who the driver was, to ask him if he could kindly move the vehicle so it did not block out his daylight. He said that was my job to do that. I pointed out to him that it was not but just to show good faith I would make some enquiries to do just that.

Five front door bells later I found the owner who, when I explained my dilemma, graciously agreed to try and find an alternative parking space away from the Asian mans house. I took the owner to introduce him to the Asian man. I will never forget the look on the Asian mans face as I introduced the van owner, who was a huge black guy from Jamaica.

I did not have to say anything to make the Asian man realise what I was thinking.

Both he and me were a bit more educated on racial issues.

During my service I did meet two officers who were seriously flawed with racialist attitudes but these were far outnumbered by the vast majority of us who detested their ideals, attitudes and covert insults.

You could make the excuse that it was considered by most to be freedom of speech but we should have realised the hurt that they caused to our black colleagues. I do believe that most of the banter and humour, they were subjected to, was no more harmful than that of the stage and TV comedians of the day. It was common for religion, race, sex and gender to be the subject of jokes and ridicule but a line had to be drawn.

Although I did not witness levels of unacceptable, at one time I suspected that one black detective officer was suffering the wrath of a white, racist Detective Sergeant. The officer would not confide in me and brushed away any suggestion of racial motivated supervisory excesses. I was powerless to do anything without the officers' consent. It annoyed me intensely that nothing could be done however the situation was resolved with the unexpected early retirement of the Detective Sergeant.

The Sergeant died suddenly a short while later. Perhaps someone else was working on the same issue!

Sometimes even if you lean over backwards as far as you possibly can to make sure you do the right thing, someone will find fault.

I had formal complaint of racial abuse made against me by a white social worker from a London Borough. I was the Office Manager supervising the Incident Office on the investigation of the murder of a Nigerian woman. Her body had been dismembered and her head, torso, one arm and a leg had been found on the council rubbish tip.

The rubbish deposited came from a number of places within the vast area of London and efforts by the Murder Investigation team to identify her had drawn a blank. The usual channels of missing persons' registers, press and media releases did not help to identify her.

We enlisted the help of an expert to reconstruct her face from the skull that had been found. As anyone can imagine this gruesome investigation was highly emotive and fully charged concentrating on the sensitivity for the feelings of the relatives and friends of the victim we were yet to meet. Any actions we took were planned with as much compassion and understanding as we could give.

It was with this intention that we consulted every Embassy and High Commission in the country on how we could best describe the lady depicted on a photograph of the reconstructed head. The main purposes were to identify the country or even region where she could have been born, as her facial lines were quite distinct.

Each, and everyone, of the predominantly black Ambassadors that we consulted referred to her as being of Negroid appearance and most likely to have come from Nigeria. To make sure of our wording we consulted the Race Relations Officers and our own black officers who confirmed that the description of Negroid was acceptable to use. Just as Nordic could be associated with peoples from Scandinavia and that area of the world so Negroid was a description of people from West Africa.

Satisfied that we were according with accepted practices, as Office Manager of the Murder Incident Room, I arranged for posters with the description and photograph of the reconstructed head of the victim to be circulated throughout London with the hope that we would identify her.

One of the first telephone calls we received regarding the poster was from the complaining Social Worker. She objected to the use of the word, Negroid, saying it was degrading, disgraceful and inflammatory. I allowed her to rant and rave for sometime over the phone, having some difficulty in interrupting her from the full blast of getting her disgust off her chest. At one time she took her breath and must have thought that I had hung up as she spoke to someone else and said, "The pig has hung... hello, hello".

I then saw my chance to answer. It was difficult not to be a little cynical but I tried my best stating the huge lengths that we had gone to ensure that we dealt with this matter in a sensitive and understanding way. While she was on the telephone I arranged for a complete list of all the Embassies and High Commissions we had consulted to be drawn up.

I suggested that if she felt so strongly about the issue then it would be helpful that she complained to these people so that the same mistake was not made again. I faxed the list to her at her office in London and did not hear anymore on the subject.

The victim was identified when her relatives from Nigeria reported her missing to a police station in London, a few months later. An officer recognised her description from one of our posters and contacted our Murder Incident Room.

Her husband, an airline pilot, was later charged with her murder. He committed the atrocity in a hotel room in Kensington and disposed of her body in refuse bags that eventually ended up on the rubbish tip.

There are obvious instances of racialism but there is still very difficult area that requires a balanced approach. In this instance one persons' perception of racialism is another ones accepted attitude. There is no hope of appeasing this situation!

FORTUNATE ACTION

Wary of the need for absolute control and the last PC who was put on a fizzer when the prisoner he was guarding at the hospital escaped, stole a car and crashed it and himself into pieces. There was no way that I would suffer the same fate and be charged with neglect of duty when I had to do the same some weeks later.

My poor shift mate had been "escorting" a prisoner who had broken his leg and was lying in hospital recovering from a serious and complicated operation. He was desperate to use the toilet and left the man unattended for what he said was a split second in bed in a locked ward, two floors up. There was no way that you could allow for the ingenuity of the prisoner who with one leg plastered to his hip, climbed out of the window, down a drainpipe and then hot wired a nurses car parked nearby.

Not being local he did not realise that when he drove out of the hospital he should have turned right towards his east London home and not left in the direction of the open countryside and extremely dangerous bendy roads.

The likelihood was that, whilst obviously travelling far too fast, his plastered foot caught between the brake and accelerator pedals causing him to go straight on and not negotiate the sharp left hand bend. He hit the wall of Stambridge churchyard with such veracity that he was killed outright.

My poor mate was distraught and put on the fizzer.

I decided that my prisoner was not going to escape so in the slim possibility that I should need to use the toilet or be called away for something equally important. I handcuffed his ankle to the bed, as he lay asleep.

The toilet did not call but the young nurse offered the comfort of their rest room and a nice cup of tea and hot toast. I could not refuse, as it would have been discourteous. No sooner than I had taken my first mouthful when I heard a loud crash from the prisoners room. He said he had wanted to go to the toilet but the nurse said he must ring the bell for a bedpan, as his stitches from his appendix operation would not stand the movement. While we helped him back into bed I subtly removed the handcuffs and the possibility of a fizzer.

I am not sure if the nurse realised what had happened but she did say that the latest latex blankets had holes in them that occasionally caused the patients to catch their arms or legs in. I was fortunate!

THE FIZZER THAT STUCK

There had to be one that stuck. Twenty-six years at the sharp end and countless disciplinary notices later the law of averages dictate that one must hit me where it hurt.

It was not bad but annoying and only resulted in an official reprimand. It was a blemish that I could carry without fear of being considered dishonest or degraded.

We were one month into the new Police and Criminal Evidence Act, commonly known as PACE. This was a new Act of Parliament that gave, us not only new powers but also more strict procedures that had to be followed.

I was a Detective Sergeant and carrying out a virtually permanent role as an Acting Detective Inspector at Benfleet. Our area was suffering from criminals, who were breaking into houses in side roads adjacent to the main trunk roads leading into London.

Large amounts of jewellery were stolen but we were lucky to have had a witness who gave us a description of some suspects and details of a car seen near to a break in.

The details fitted a well-known burglar, who specialised in such raids, living in an adjoining county so we obtained a search warrant to gain entry to his house with the hope that we would find some tangible evidence.

With officers from the local area I led my team of six officers to the villains house. This was a beautiful thatched cottage in a small village and just the type shown on the cover of chocolate boxes.

The usual 6.00am knock on the door produced no reply and we were left with having to make a forced entry. This was never the most ideal situation as the damage caused, no matter how careful you tried to be, was always far worse when the owners came home and submitted their claim for repairs.

The large oak medieval front door was discounted without even touching it however the side kitchen windows were of the modern softwood type and the least likely in expense to repair.

A swift lift of the crowbar not only removed the small sash window but the whole of the surrounding woodwork and part of the wall. After the dust, brick and rubble settled we were able to get in and search the cottage. No jewellery was found but we found several receipts from petrol stations and papers referring to our area on the dates of the break-ins. We knew we were on the right track.

We also found details of a luxury motorboat that the villain had moored at a marina nearby. After securing the cottage and arranging for it to be repaired by the local council we drove down to the marina.

We located the boat and two officers and myself stepped aboard. As we did so the boat started to move away from the mooring jetty. A Woman Detective Constable had placed one foot onto the boat just as it moved away, leaving her other foot on the jetty.

Their had been comments about her tight short dresses and the inappropriateness of such wear on searches but she wished to impress and up till now it had not caused her any concern. But here she was with her high heel shoed feet drifting apart, legs splaying outwards, skirt riding up her thighs and deep panic setting in as she screamed for help.

Sympathy for her plight was not immediately forthcoming as the rest of the team, being male, momentarily looked on with the expression of "told you so" or "what do you expect - dressing like a Barbie doll". Her dilemma did not last long as the one gallant detective we had with us, was the first to get to her and pulled her onto the boat before her legs split too far and she fell into the greeny brown soupy river.

Panic and laughter over our duty continued but not finding anything incriminating on the boat our search was a failure.

One consolation was that the burglaries suddenly stopped so perhaps a victory of sorts was won.

The thirty discipline notices I received from the Complaints and Discipline Department were trivial and contained accusations of damage I caused were so grandiose it was a wonder that the cottage still stood and was habitable.

But like the claims that insurers get you always expected the damages to be bumped up to gain that little bit more money. It was a fact of life but it did not deter us from trying to keep inconvenience and disruption to the minimum when carrying out searches even though we always knew that it would be exaggerated afterwards.

My only problem with the boat incident was that I should have got a separate search warrant as per the new legislation. I didn't so I was reprimanded.

SLEDGEHAMMERS CRACKING WALNUTS

Throughout the years it has always been an unenviable task for any officer to investigate another for corruption. I was seconded on a number of occasions to do just that but only once was I put in the position of having to discipline one of my own officers.

Not a heinous crime, malingering, but one that I considered to be lacking in appreciation of your own colleagues and letting the side down. I was the Detective Sergeant at small but busy station and had a team of four Detective Constables. We were short staffed due to officers being taken away on murder enquiries and the officer concerned was off duty, sick, suffering from severe back problems.

It had been a particularly busy week with myself and the other remaining officer working long and arduous hours of overtime investigating a string of burglaries. Being football fans we decided to take some time out at one of the local football clubhouses beside a pitch where our Police side were due to play.

We had not been there a few minutes when the teams came out of the dressing room and to my disgust the malingering officer was leading our Police side out.

I felt I had to do something but did not want to place him on a discipline charge.

I found the task of creating a discipline notice distasteful and spoke to the Detective Chief Inspector who removed him from our station to the divisional headquarters where he could be more closely supervised. Not the most satisfactory solution but in the circumstances I was glad to see the back of him.

It is not always possible to deal with discipline informally as I have found out when investigating such matters with senior officers. You are nobody's friend. The aggrieved parties do not trust you even though you have to assure them that you will be impartial and carry out your duty without fear or favour, they are rarely convinced that one police officer can investigate another to the satisfaction of all.

The officers who are the subject of the investigation treat you with contempt and suspicion and are never willing or comfortable enough to be co-operative. No matter how balanced you try to be, you are the accuser and unfortunately the perpetrator of someone else's fury at being arrested or assaulted. All too often the complaints made against police officers were malicious and had no reasonable foundation but they all had to be investigated in the slim chance that we had a bad apple.

And all too often good police officers were treated as criminals by internal investigators intent on proving their own worth rather than carrying out an independent assessment of evidence and then a robust but focused investigation.

Some officers would use internal investigations to feather their own nest. Using over zealous and vigorous methods to prove their own worth knowing that they could treat the police officers being investigated with a less than fair attitude, without fear of being criticised or served with a law suit.

It was always "in the public interest" for complaints to be investigated thoroughly but many investigations lost sight of the need to appreciate that officers had their individual rights. In some cases internal fizzers destroyed valuable and skilful officers' careers.

Senior officers, who were able to steer an investigation to suit their own personal opinions that clouded the possibility of fairness and unbiased independent assessment of evidence, could orchestrate investigations.

Old scores could be settled under the banner of routing out corruption. I was subjected to such treatment and numerous other officers suffered the same fate. On rare occasions a "bent officer" was identified and appeared in Court under a hail of media publicity. Rightfully so when found guilty they received sentences that reflected the crime committed whilst in public office.

Some officers did receive sentences without going to Court or having the chance to appeal against accusations at Disciplinary Hearings held in front of the Chief Constable.

In the case of serious allegations against an officer suspension from duty is considered the normal course. Being on full pay and having the luxury of home life can never compensate for the worry and strain that such a situation brings. I never had to suffer this treatment but so many of my colleagues have had their lives turned upside down unnecessarily by this action.

Two friends where suspended from duty when an anonymous letter was received alleging that they were corrupt and dishonest.

I was serving as an Acting Detective Inspector in The Regional Crime Squad at the time. The friends where the squad Detective Chief Inspector and the Detective Inspector, the DCI was on rest day and the latter was on annual leave hence the reason for me carrying out the acting rank. Both were hardworking career officers, popular with their officers and a credit to the service and the RCS

I was on a surveillance operation with the team of 15 officers we had on the Squad. We had been out from early that morning and had a lull in the "follow" we were doing when, over the radio, I was ordered by the Detective Superintendent from RCS HQ to return to our squad office.

A local force Chief Superintendent and officers from an outside force met me there. I was told of the allegation and that I had to be present as they searched the whole squad office, the desks of the individual officers and every other nook and cranny in the office complex. The internal investigators took every conceivable item that could be moved from the office away. Including notice boards and "nobo" boards that contained confidential graphs and link charts of our operations.

Any obvious personal items owned by the squad team were left but the office echoed with the emptiness after they had gone. Soon after the DCI and the DI were suspended from duty and I was left to pick up the pieces.

The whole team of squad officers were devastated and morale dropped to an almighty low. We were all individually interviewed and asked for any details we may have that would corroborate the anonymous allegation. It was obvious to us all that the investigators were scratching around for scraps trying to identify the author of the letter to give the matter credence.

High calibre Regional Crime Squad officers are hardened to any and probably all types of investigation tactics and this over the top attitude could have been counter productive. If the officers in the squad had been less professional, and not cooperated as they did, the enquiry could have been obstructed and lengthened quite easily.

All of us in this squad where determined and honest enough to provide evidence against any bent officer even if it was their own bosses but none of us knew of anything that could be damning or hint of dishonesty.

The enquiry dragged on for months, no stone was unturned by the investigation team to deduce evidence. We were barred from any contact with the DCI and DI but officers, who were allowed to see them, told us that they were suffering.

When your wife and family ask what is going on and why you are suspended, what do you say to them?

The DCI was never charged with any matters relating to Discipline Regulations or the Criminal Law and later suffered a total mental breakdown. He was a tough, hardened detective, respected by his officers. The treatment he received was abysmal and unfounded and I strongly suspect senior officers, he had rubbed up the wrong way in the past, subjected him to this.

The DI was charged with a minor offence but the case was kicked out of Court on the direction of a Crown Court Judge who stated, when doing so, that the whole allegation was based on a tissue of tenuous evidence, was a waste of public money and should not have been brought to the Court.

The DI resigned from the Police Service in complete disgust and is now a successful businessman.

Chapter Nine
THE AREA OFFICER

Two years as an Area Officer in Westcliff taught me how essential it was for The Police Service to mix and communicate with the public it had a duty to support. The Area Officer lived where practical on his area and worked from his own house that served as an office and mini police station, very much like the village bobby but centred in a town environment.

Projecting oneself into the community, mixing physically with the locals, good and bad was the main aim of gaining their confidence, finding out what they wanted and finding out by first hand knowledge what was going on and what required our attention and action was the main priority.

The down side was that having the front line of policing on your own doorstep clashes became close to home and personal.

It was perhaps the first time that I recognised that policing was for the community and should be dictated by what the community wants.

My falling into the job of the Area Officer was more by accident than desire. I had spent the four previous years in the CID at Southend and found the long hours comfortable to work with but unacceptable for both the family and me as it was very rarely rewarded financially. Dorothy had accepted the time I spent away from her and the girls but questioned the fairness of not receiving pay in proportion to the work carried out. I decided to transfer back to uniform to give me more time with them.

The Area Officers job was offered and I took it willingly.

COMMUNITY PLAYER

I suppose the fact that I now had a family, two lovely daughters, a house and neighbours at the police house we lived in, the natural course was to be involved in issues that had not been staring me in the face as a young flat dwelling, disco bopping long haired detective.

The first heady years I had served in the CID had to be put behind me and the important role of being a pillar of society at ground level appealed to me greatly. I wanted to make my mark and was determined to make the area, where I worked and lived, a safer place for all my residents and our family.

The police bicycle I had been issued with was black, big and an extremely heavy machine to push around the streets but it kept me fit. As we had sold our car to make ends meet so the bike was my only form of transport to and from the police station and anywhere else I had to get on my beat.

Our pay at that time was extremely poor and so low that I qualified for the then supplementary benefit from the Department of Health and Social Security. It was a very strange situation standing in the queue, in the DSS office, to apply for the benefit. Me and two other police officers stood in line with the very criminals we were locking up from time to time.

Our salary was difficult to live on and had to be supplemented in some way. Many officers were forced to do spare time jobs even though this contravened the Police Discipline Regulations and you could be in serious trouble if you were caught. Painting and decorating was popular, driving jobs were close behind and gardening work was in great demand. I had a job driving punch cards around between offices for some large companies. The cards were used for record keeping and data storage before the days of computers. The work just about paid the running costs for the car itself. Both had to go in the end and I took up gardening and growing our own vegetables.

I made a wooden barrow that I could pull behind my bike on my trips to my three allotments where I grew the vegetables that provided us with much needed meals in those money strapped days. The girls took great delight in riding in the barrow in which I had made two small wooden seats for them to sit on. They would wear little straw hats and sit there chatting like two little old ladies, waving to passers by as we trundled along with my garden tools and bags of vegetables and flowers stuffed beside them.

Living and working from home gave me the opportunity to be not only close to the family but also to those connected to them. The girls went to a playgroup at a church hall nearby. It was whilst dropping them off one morning that the Playgroup leader asked me if I could arrange to come and see them one day in my uniform. Her idea was that the kids, even at their very young age, should recognise a policeman and be able relate to the work an officer does.

This was perhaps the first time that I started to identify the need for forming a connection between very young children and the law. The Playgroup leader and I discussed the need to level the connection to the age of the child but both agreed that the earlier it could be done the better the understanding as we knew that once the child had reached the teens the task would get harder.

The children at the playgroup were between 3 and 5 years old, very impressionable and a delicate and soft presentation with fun and games should be the appropriate approach.

After discussing this with my Chief Inspector, the playgroup leader and I arranged for our first visit.

I arrived at the playgroup to the delight of the children in a panda car, a white mini with one of our policewomen and a Police Dog Handler and the fluffiest, friendliest Alsatian and puppy under training.

In the hour we were there the twenty-five children took it in turns to stroke, cuddle and play with the dogs, they tried on our helmets and hats, blew our whistles, banged the floor and one window with our truncheons, fortunately without breakages. They ran around "deedaaing" the sounds of the police sirens and then clambered in, over and around the police cars outside.

The grand finale was to stand all wrapped in their winter clothes and wait on the church hall car park for "Windsor" the dapple-grey police horse to arrive. The appointed time was 11.45am that Windsor was to be standing in the car park. Parents and guardians arrived at that time to pick their children up so it was an ideal opportunity for everyone to see him.

There we stood all in a long line in anticipation. Parents gathering as we stood there but there was no sign of Windsor. Nerves got the better of me as heads and necks arched to look up the road towards the police station and teachers and parents shrugged shoulders to explain to their charges that, "he was not here yet".

Taking my official tone I talked into my personal radio, "Control from PC169". "Go ahead PC169. Control Over", came the reply. "Can you contact our Mounted Section to get his eta (estimated time of arrival) at the Earls Hall Playgroup please", I requested.

"Horsey One, Horsey one are you receiving, over", the controller called.

A garbled reply to the background of a clippety clop came back, "Receiving Horsey One over".

The controller, "Your eta at the playgroup please, over".

"I am in Victoria Avenue so about five minutes, over", Horsey One replied.

Parents waiting hearing this started looking at watches and thinking of picking their other children up from school as the controller said, "You are on talk through PC169 to Horsey One". I said, "Obliged if you could get a move on as those waiting here have other pressing engagements, over". "Will do PC169", he replied and continued to command his steed to, "Come on", with the clippety clop increasing in momentum.

With increased anticipation all the waiting crowd of kids and grownups craned necks to look up the road and saw to tremendous gasps of amazement Windsor and his rider Horsey One at full gallop, hurtling towards us. Horsey One's cape flowed behind him horizontally, his cap hung onto his mouth by the chin strap and his hands gripped the reins urging Windsor to keep going by rattling them against his front flanks.

Sparks flew from Windsor's shoes as they gripped the tarmac road, his nostrils flared and eyes rolled with the excitement of what may have appeared to him as a chase of life and death.

The kids were leaping up in the air, cheering and screaming with the spectacle of this beautiful animal in full flight and seemingly enjoying every minute of occasion. It seemed so natural for Windsor to be doing this, the grace and poise being no different from the stately fashion we would normally see him in.

It was a glorious sight, as he eventually pulled up in front of the crowd of ecstatic kids and grown ups. A few sparks flew up from his skidding hooves as Horsey One pulled him in to calm him down. Training and soft commands from his rider were enough to quieten him down for allowing the now Windsor fans to pat and stroke his panting skin.

Thank you letters came into the police station thick and fast after that day. Children even wrote and sent pictures to Ben the police dog, Bert the puppy and Windsor the horse along with one parcel containing a carrot and a bone.

The word got round and many other playgroups requested and received our presentations. These were never high on the list of duty priorities but with a combination of some off duty time and give and take by supervising officers we were able to attend every school that requested our presence. Windsor was always on time but nobody could expect the gallop of the first episode to be repeated.

The then children, now parents themselves, stop me now and tell me the affect that the visits we did had on them and wished it could be repeated for their kids.

This was a point in my career where I probably woke up to what was needed for a police officer to do his duty to the full, preventing crime, protecting the public and keeping the peace. It did not seem that we were ever able or likely to achieve this with the Fire Brigade policing that we were forced to carry out.

We were catching the criminals but as soon as one was locked up another would take his place. We never seemed to get to the very young potential villains to stop them before they got to the point of no return and committed their crimes.

It was not an overnight experience where I suddenly decided to dive into the community to find out what they wanted but a gradual enlightenment started to be gained by talking and meeting people as I went about my daily duties on my bike and walking around instead of driving faceless in a panda car. Making time to stop and chat to shopkeepers, people as they worked in their gardens, speaking to parents to give advice and guidance help with their kids, calling in at schools and exchanging views with teachers in their staff rooms.

It was amazing the reaction you got and the praise from them saying that they did not have to wait for ages on the telephone to talk to an officer at the police station. Here was one that they could moan to, pass on ideas and report on who was doing what in the area.

I was able to transfer this mixing with the community to performance on duty and through a large number of arrests and convictions and some hard work was rewarded with a commendation for "outstanding work in relation to the detection of crime" by the Chief Constable and a small article appeared in the local newspaper that a "mini crime busting whirlwind" in the guise of a police officer had hit the area.

I did not have to work longer hours. I just changed my approach making it more open and available. At times, like most successes, the level of work would snowball but then the Chief Inspector would allow other officers to help and take some of the strain.

All very nice stuff but the piss taking, by the other equally hard working dedicated officers at the nick, became a bit boring after a while.

THE LOAF OF BREAD

My duties at Westcliff were enhanced by the freedom given me by the Chief Inspector and Inspector to work discretionary hours in accord with the problems of the Area. To this extent I rode around in plain clothes on my bike, at times looking something like a French onion seller whilst wearing my then fashionable green and white striped button collared T-shirt.

This paid dividends with me targeting a number of persons responsible for crimes and many arrests followed.

As time went on and my enthusiasm continued I would work for hours and hours on various projects being carried on by a massive amount of energy. This over ran into running a football club, helping charitable associations and carrying out talks and presentations at local schools and playgroups.

However everything would come to halt when I went into inexplicable lengthy periods of total exhaustion completely opposite to the powerful strength I had most of the time.

None of these feelings seemed to seriously affect me although I was once described as a workaholic.

One night at about 3.00am another Area Constable and I were given a lift home by the Inspector. The Inspector thought it a good idea to drive in the opposite direction to our homes and ride along Victoria Avenue passed a bakers premises. The baker was always complaining of having freshly baked loaves of bread nicked from his cooling trays by yobs returning home from the late night disco nearby. The Inspector was being hassled by him to do something about it.

As we turned into the Avenue we saw three youths, one very muscular one known to us, eating freshly baked loaves. We confronted them and the Inspector told them they were being arrested. With this the muscular one, who had a string a very violent pre-convictions, did his usual and wanted to fight the world.

The Inspector and the other Area Constable tried to restrain him and a very violent struggle ensued. The other two smaller youths took advantage of the situation and made to run off. I grabbed them each around the waist in a rugby scrum type hold and pushed them against a parked car. I bent double with my head between them at waist level.

My head was protected but they punched and kicked me about the back and chest. My arms went numb as the blows hit me but I held onto the pair of them for what seemed to be an age until other officers joined us. The violent struggle between the muscular youth and the Inspector and other officers continued until he was subdued by the weight of numbers of burly officers.

I was taken to hospital after with a total loss of the use of one arm and severe pain in my back and abdomen. It was discovered that I had frayed nerves in the arm and my upper vertebral discs were torn. I had dislocated two ribs and was off duty for two months. Though during that time I did manage to get a few presentations in at some playgroups. The kids gave me the lift I needed to regain my confidence in society and what my job was really about.

The yobs received sentences of fines and ordered to pay me some compensation. For years after I received the odd postal order of £1 or £1.50p as and when one of the yobs paid into the Court. One even apologised to me a few years later at the football club I helped run. He said that it was the lowest point of his life and something he would regret for eternity. Nice words and more than I got from the Inspector who wanted to impress the baker.

Even now nearly thirty years later I have to carry out regular exercises specifically to keep my muscles built up around my neck and upper back to compensate for the damage to my spinal column in that area.

Any aftercare that I received was from friends and family. I did not expect to receive counselling or other forms of care from the Service during the following months that I was off duty and eventually time healed. I did not really notice any change in my life but some sweating and the occasional sudden jolted awakening from sleep did not cause me any concern.

I put this down to the natural pain of movement or lying in the same place but I now suspect that this may have been a slight rumbling of the more serious condition that was to come.

CRIES FOR HELP

Being in amongst the public and in a position can also have its down sides. In my earlier years as a beat bobby I had arrested lesbians who had been shoplifting. One was a girl from northern England who had come down to Southend to escape her violent father.

She was small, diminutive and covered in tattoos including the L.O.V.E and H.A.T.E letters scarring the tops of the fingers of both hands. Her neck and arms were festooned with the manly tattoos usually associated with macho figures wanting to make some statement and succeeding, in her eyes, of saying to the world, "Look I am a man, I've got the trappings to show it!"

She would dress in the clothes of a male, usually open neck shirt - collar high, suit jacket, trousers or jeans and male Chelsea boots. Hair slicked back in "teddy boy" cut with Boston back, her small stature would epitomise a boy in his early teens.

In her own group of friends, she was at home, normal and "top Johnny", a leader even revered. Outside she was a very lonely figure and very vulnerable, often left in a pool of blood after drinking heavily and getting into a fight with some thug who questioned her manhood. Even though she and her mates worked as manual labourers and even Dockers at the port of Tilbury nearby, the tough exterior she showed in defiance very rarely matched the size of her mocking opponents.

Never backing out of a fight she would often end up unconscious before she could be halted from taking on impossible odds. It was after such an altercation that I found her slumped in an alleyway. I had been sent to investigate what the telephone caller had reported was a "bundle of moving rags". The alley was just round the corner from a pub that was one of the girl's regular drinking places when she wanted to prove her worth in the "mans world". So it was no surprise to me to find her in a vomit stained heap with blood oozing from a deep gash to her forehead and the rest of her body crumpled and bruised over ripped and torn clothes.

She slurred at first, "Piss off!" then suddenly, realising she knew whom it was, apologised saying, " Oh it's you. I am sorry. I've fucking done it again, haven't I?"

She then spewed blood and booze and fell into unconscious. I put her into the recovery position, always the best for drunks so they don't suffocate on their own vomit, and went to the nearest house to use the phone. The area was a radio black spot and communication was very poor if at all existent.

I knew the woman who lived at the house and as I waited for her to answer I hoped that she had her clothes on this time. The last time I had visited was on a house-to-house enquiry during the investigation of a murder some years before. She had answered the door completely naked except for the skimpiest towel wrapped round her. She apologised for her state of non-dress but upon hearing the nature of my enquiry insisted that I come in and continue to complete the questionnaire that was attached to the clipboard I was carrying.

Her ample figure waddled with towel wrapped round her into a room to her left. She shouted for me to come through which I did assuming it to be her lounge or other room but not her bathroom. The towel lay on the floor beside the bath and there she was lying in a foot of bubbles completely covered except her head with shower cap and one foot holding onto the tap at the other end.

She said, "Now what were you saying?" I regained my efficient composure and explained the questionnaire. She answered the questions and asked me if I would like a pickled onion. She explained that her idea of relaxation was to bath in her favourite bath oils eating pickled onions. The two combined cleaned out the outer surfaces and the inner pores and internal organs.

I was not prepared to disagree in case the agony of the situation was lengthened and the combination of the smells of both oils and digested onions was not one to be tolerated for any length of time. It was almost the like the smell of death, another stench that cannot be shaken off and takes ages to leave the nostrils and senses.

I had left the place with haste and hoped that she was not still in that bath as I stood there waiting. The door opened sharply to reveal an elderly man in bathrobe. Horrible thoughts did cross my mind but I put these to the back of me and apologising for the call at such a late hour asked to use the telephone for an emergency call.

He waved his hand to come in and I went straight to the phone in the hallway to summon an ambulance and report to my station.

I returned to the still prostrate young lady, checked her breathing and waited for assistance. Minutes later she was whisked off to the Accident Centre to be patched up until the next time.

I saw her several times in the street and the pub and found out that she was now alone having split up completely from her group of lesbians. She deteriorated very quickly into alcoholism and heroin injecting and no matter who tried to help her she refused advice, guidance and support from police, social workers and probation officers. She had a massive independence that was impeded from seeing sense by an even bigger chip on her shoulder. Her enemy was the world around her but it also trying to help her.

People turned their backs on her. Her only contact with people was the arrests for drunkenness and stealing, as she became a recluse this contact disappeared. She would ring the police station to speak to me and we would talk about all and sundry but her brain was not listening. You could tell that she just wanted company.

When she drank, she became violent and suicidal; on three occasions she jumped off a railway bridge but landed on the soft embankment causing her no real harm except on one occasion when she broke her leg.

In a funny way she found some solace in hopping around with leg in plaster and walking on crutches. People took notice of her, sympathized, held a conversation, became a temporary friend and she felt wanted.

I had seen her that day and she was in high spirits. She may have given herself a boost of H but she seemed pretty happy, perhaps in hindsight too happy and she was hopping off to the pub to meet "me mates". Laughing and taking the piss out of me the "friendly copper" as she told her mate as they walked arm in arm off down the road.

Late that night Dorothy took a telephone call from the station to say that the girl was in hospital again and could I go and see her. She had asked for me to go. This was unusual as she always rang for me after she had got out. It was a short walk for me to get to the hospital and I got there in only a few minutes.

She lay in an anteroom that I knew was for the patients for whom there was little hope of recovery. Her mate I had seen earlier was in tears seated by her side and holding her hand. She was covered in dirt and dust but had no signs of being punch or cut as was the normal sight. Instead she had a large burn to her neck that was open and exposed red and sore flesh. Monitor pads were stuck to her chest and forehead and a saline drip hovered over her.

An oxygen mask covered her mouth and nose. She was so still. She was not the grotesque figure of wannabee man anymore. She had returned to being a small young lady.

Her mate told me that she had been "pratting around", they had had a few drinks, and "Not too many" and she had climbed on the top of the railway bridge parapet to show how she had fallen down when she broke her leg. "She was just pratting about like any bloke does. Just trying to prove something as usual", she continued.

The face moved slightly from under the mask and turned towards me. "I am sorry Bob. I really am. You must think I am a bloody idiot". I noticed her voice had changed. It wasn't the gruff male rasp tone I was hearing that she always came out with. I did think at one time she was taking hormone tablets to enhance her male features but here she was now speaking like a young woman, soft and endearing.

She tried to talk some more but could only whisper incoherently. Her mate explained that she lost her footing and fell over the bridge onto the railway line some fifty feet below hitting the electricity lines as she went. It was one of these that had nearly severed head neck and caused the burn.

She died shortly after without being able to express her feelings once more. I met her distraught parents at the funeral who looked like any other Mum and Dad. Giving my condolences and wondering if her Dad had been as bad as she made out I looked for some reaction to confirm the situation either way. After the normal exchange of feelings her Mum could only say that she "Was a complicated girl that we never understood".

I still think that such complications could be identified and sorted out at a very early age and save so many people from such heartache. Perhaps that is aiming to have a too perfect world.

EARLY WARNINGS

A number of people would tell me about the clip round the ear that they got from a copper did them the power of good and the one they got from their Dad when they went home and told him about it was just a reinforcement of the need to behave and respect that is now missing from everyday life.

I still remember the clip round the ear I received from a copper who was doing point duty at a school crossing. I was fooling around with my friend as we walked home from school to have tea at his house. We were pushing each other and taking it in turn to dig our fingers into our ribs. It had started to get a bit rough and out of hand and we were not concentrating as we crossed the road. The officer was standing there with one arm raised skywards and the other outstretched at a right angle holding the traffic up. We were adjacent to him and a push from my mate made me stumble and virtually fall to the ground. As I regained my balance the copper swung his hand across my ear and in a windmill movement hit my mates ear simultaneously. We stopped in our tracks and looked in shocked and slightly pained dismay up at the huge policeman who said in a kind but authoritive voice, "The roads are dangerous places, and certainly not playgrounds. Always concentrate when you cross the road and you will not get hurt".

We walked quickly across the road holding our ears and then ran like mad to my friends' house never to talk about it until later years but remembering the wise words every time I cross a road, even now!

As an Area Officer you were very much like the old time copper that these people depicted, but time had moved on and any one clipped round the ear was more likely to know their rights and make a formal complaint against you, so subtle changes had to be made to strategy on such issues.

An old school mate of mine called me over to his house one day. He was a single parent having lost his wife a few years previous. He had a son aged 9 years and a daughter of 13 years, who just about tolerated her father as a number of teenagers of that age do.

My mate was suffering from cancer and in need of regular chemotherapy. He quite openly smoked cannabis to give him some respite. Although never in my presence the sweet smell was always lingering over his rooms when I visited.

"I can't doing anything with the little shit", he despaired as I walked into his always-open front door. "He's in the fucking shed. I locked him in. Here's the key. Go and give him a good hiding Bob will you? If you don't I am going to fucking kill him", he continued before I could say anything.

I ascertained that it was his son who was in the shed and that he thought it was part of my job to give him a slap. When I explained that I could not do that he said, "But you said that you would help me get him on the straight and narrow and would help me at any time. I am too fucking weak to hit the bastard as a normal parent would and he knows it, so he takes the piss and I am asking you go and hit him on my behalf. It's your duty to prevent crime and I am saying you are preventing him from committing crime in the future. He is going to be a statistic in the future. Most criminals come from single parent families, so they say. I am not going to be here then they reckon, so it's down to you mate to sort him out before its too late".

I was stunned at his thinking. Here was a guy who had been the source of much of the trouble on our estate when we were kids telling me in no uncertain terms to sort his kid out of the mess he himself was in not so many years ago.

While he was drawing breath I explained to him that I could not do that it was tantamount to having a police state and that I would be breaking the law if I did it and that it was a job for social services. He said, "Fucking social services are not worth a wank. He does something wrong we have to have a meeting, then case study then period of mediation, then fuck knows what and then we have all forgotten what we have got together for. What he needs is a fucking good slapping immediately after he has done something wrong. Not fucking years later. It's too late. I can't do it. He's too quick for me. Even at 9 years. I'm asking you for help Bob. You know I have not got a lot of time and I just don't want him turning into "a wrongen". He then melted in crying and holding onto me.

I went down to the garden shed, the door of which was hanging on by a couple of hinge screws and had obviously been kicked open.

The son was sitting on the shed floor at the opposite end with his arms crossed and face frowning defiantly. As I closed the door he got up and brushed passed me. I tried to say something to get him to see some sense but he just snarled, "Piss off copper". He then climbed over the six-foot garden fence and disappeared.

My mate passed away two months later and his son has been in and out of prison ever since despite the efforts made by successive unpaid volunteers, overworked social workers and elderly grandparents.

Here was a cry for help that those who were supposed to assist were incapable of stopping the tragedy that continues to this day.

Some people you cannot help because they are too thick to realise that you are caring and not just being a copper and locking offenders up.

An elderly gent reported to me that his dust caps from his car tyres had been taken. He did not wish to officially report such a trivial matter but he identified the two young boys who were doing the same to a number of cars in the street.

The two five year olds were walking down the road looking very furtive and lowering their eyes when I looked at them. I said to them, "What have you been up to then?" They both swung their legs at the ground as this uniform questioned them, "Your pockets are a bit bulgy. What have you got in them?"

"Nothing", the fair-haired one said as he cuffed his snotty runny nose. "Let's have a look. Shall we?" I said bending onto one knee to be at their same height.

The other lad pulled both his pockets out and a large number of dust caps fell to the ground. The other reluctantly did the same and revealed even more. I said, "Now you both know that you should not take anything that is not yours. Don't you?" The other lad said, "His brother said he would give us a 10p for each one and said people wouldn't mind us taking such little things". The fair boy did not say anything.

I knew both boys from the neighbourhood and after getting them to place the caps back onto as many tyres that they could remember I walked them back to their parents.

One lad came from a decent family and when I handed him back and explained what had happened they were grateful, apologetic and assured me that they would deal with him appropriately. The lad is now a Doctor, credit to his parents and can always be seen taking part in events raising money for various charities.

I do not know what his parents did to correct him but whatever it was they saved him from a very dismal future.

However I knew the fair-haired boys family and that I would have a problem with them. His Dad was a casual lorry driver, drinker and convicted of being the driver in armed robberies, Mum was a shoplifter and local prostitute and elder brother was a car thief and into "ringing" stolen cars, altering their appearance and placing false number plates on them. The only saving grace may be his elder sister who worked in a local shop and seemed to be carving a normal life for her self in such mayhem.

Hopeful that the sister would open the door I called at the house with the boy still at my side. Bad start, Mum opened the door and blurted, "What the fucking hell are you doing with my son?" I said, "Can we go inside. I do not want to talk about it out here in earshot of all your neighbours?"

I explained to her what had happened to which she retorted, "He is not of criminal age, he's only five, and so you can't prove a thing." I said to her that this was not the issue here and that my main concern was that she taught her boy the meaning of right and wrong. To do so at this early age would stop him from getting into trouble in the future.

She said, "As far as I am concerned he has not done anything. You have no right to arrest him". By this time I knew it was useless to continue. Her attitude was intransigent and so set to be anti-police and not tuned to appreciate that I might be trying to prevent her son from becoming a criminal.

She went to the police station and made a formal complaint of false imprisonment, putting more effort into that than bringing up her offspring.

The complaint against me was unsubstantiated.

The boy some years later is regularly arrested and charged with drugs related petty crime and has been convicted of begging on the streets of London.

The daughter gave up on the family and immigrated to Canada and is married to a dentist.

The elder son has two children from a partner ship with a woman who has convictions for stealing from shops and fraud. Their son of 9 years of age has already acquired notoriety as a car thief and regularly rides a scramble motorcycle around the council estate where they live.

The cycle of a bad life continues!

THE SCHOOL VISIT

The lack of support can manifest itself in the most unlikely places. You would expect a school head master to give some encouragement or at least cooperate with the Police but a return to my old school showed me what difficulties there were in that direction.

I had been caned once by this headmaster for "talking in an exam" after I picked up the pen belonging to a classmate that had fallen on the floor. I gave it back to him and he acknowledged me and thanked me. We were first years and 11 years old and knew none the wiser.

The form master dragged us both by the ears to the headmaster who then whacked us with his cane three times each across the backsides.

Drugs, I thought would be far higher on this Headmasters level of discipline and dealt with on an extremely higher plain.

With the knowledge and painful experience of this mans attitude towards rules and regulations and no doubt the Law I made an informal visit to the Old School.

I told the Headmaster that a boy had reported to us in the presence of his father that drugs were available from a Sixth-Former at the school who kept his goods in his locker situated in the corridor opposite the physics lecture room. I continued that we intended to deal with this informally and that the six-former had not been previously convicted so a formal caution could be administered.

Quite a straightforward procedure, no fuss and no likelihood of embarrassment to anyone, I was even in plain clothes as was normal when visiting schools for that very reason.

The Headmaster asked what was the alternative and could he deal with the matter himself. I told him that this was a crime of supplying controlled drugs on a scale that could not be ignored by the Police. In addition the father of the informant boy had reported this to the school and that the supplying was continuing unabated.

I continued that I needed the Headmasters consent to search the locker concerned and his cooperation to eventually detain and interview the Sixth-Former if drugs were found. If I did not receive the Headmasters consent then I would obtain a search warrant from the Court. I stressed that I felt that this should not be necessary.

To my astonishment the Headmaster refused to give his consent and stated categorically that, "There are no drugs in my school whatsoever", and told me to go and get the warrant.

Having no alternative, I dutifully got the warrant but was not surprised to find that the locker in question was swept clean of everything. It was completely empty as was all the lockers in the whole corridor, some thirty in total.

Later that day I went to see the informant boy and his father. The boy told me that the whole of the Sixth-Form were instructed to take all their belongings out of their lockers that morning, as they had to be moved to another part of the school.

They never were because after I had searched the lockers the boys were allowed to replace their gear back. The father was rightfully appalled and removed his son from the school.

My Chief Superintendent sent a letter of complaint to the Education Authority but the matter was not taken any further.

The Sixth-Former went onto university but dropped out after he was accused of drug pushing. He went to work in the financial markets in Docklands in London and was caught and convicted of supplying cocaine. Such a waste of a good life but more concerning is that it is incalculable whose lives he had ruined on the way with his illicit damaging trade.

GOOD, BAD AND THE UGLY

The funny side of life inevitably came out as I did my duties as an Area officer.

The size of the big old police pedal cycle I was forced to ride was soon appreciated the first day I took to the road. Resplendent in new uniform, hair cut short, white gloved hands protruding form freshly pressed jacket I rode out of the police station yard on my first patrol of my new beat.

Sitting bolt upright on the hard leather saddle I negotiated each turning with impeccable skill and forthright commanding hand signals impressing the public even though I was on a pedal cycle, "That I ruled the road"!

I rode onto the main London Road and towards the busy shopping area of Hamlet Court Road. Looking behind me to check for vehicles approaching from my rear, seeing that all was clear I gave a right angled signal with my fully outstretched arm my intention to turn right at the forthcoming traffic lights.

Moving to the centre of the two-lane road seated on my faithful steed I towered above all the cars waiting at the red light. I could sense the public confidence in this stalwart blue serge protector of the peace as I pulled to a halt.

Keeping my back straight to keep as much composure as I could my right foot reached for the safety of the tarmac road and the balance of the stop position.

My ego drifted, at first slowly and then in blind panic, downward as I suddenly realised that my foot was nowhere near to the road. The bike was far too big for me and my short legs had no hope of making contact with the road without causing severe pain to my groin area.

In my haste and excitement to impress I had forgotten my first experience with police cycles. Too late, composure gone my right shoulder hit the tarmac, helmet rolled forever across the busy road, traffic dodged me and the helmet alike and I was left with the bike tangled between my legs.

Momentarily I thought of going for the sympathy vote and make out that I was seriously injured but from a bus queue opposite strode a young boy and two old ladies who insisted on helping to me to my feet, dusting me down and raising a cheer from a passing lorry driver.

Thanking them and saluting them I decided to wheel the cycle round the corner and out of sight to regain my composure before returning to the station and swapping the bike for a smaller version.

The bike was the brunt of much comment by my mates at the station and on one occasion was stolen by persons still unknown, whilst I was on an enquiry. Searching unsuccessfully all likely places in case it was a prank by yobs in the area I eventually had to reluctantly report the theft to the Sergeant.

When I did so he quite nonchalantly said, "I've just seen it out in the yard!" I went outside and could not find it anywhere. The sergeant joined me and just said, "Look at that lovely full moon!"

Thinking he was going mad didn't stop me from looking up to see my bike strung on wires between the two separate buildings of the police station. I had forgotten it was Halloween and then realised not only kids did trick or treat in Westcliff.

No sooner than I had got my bike down when we were ordered off to Canewdon Church, a village just north of Southend.

The pagans were at it again and annoying the villagers with their cavorting in the church graveyard.

Canewdon village was renowned for witchcraft in the years gone by and still had the witches ducking pond and open jail next to the church for locking up the wicked people. Not used in these days it was still an attraction for the weirdo's, young inquisitives and drunks who wanted to experience the Halloween atmosphere.

There was always a possibility that dancing rings of nude maidens would be seen so most officers were keen to get there to protect them, of course. None were ever seen and on that night only a few local teenage girls and boys with alcoholic courage were found. The various states of dishevelled clothing were more to do with the juvenile heavy petting rather than the magical although to some at that particular young age the experience was obviously mystical.

Having no bearing on this it is true to say that Dorothy and I got engaged at Canewdon Church or the road along side it. It was a peaceful place with a lovely viewpoint northwards across the River Crouch and southwards towards Southend and one of the prominent places in this part of Essex. I did not know about the witches but it was a magical moment for us.

This part of Essex is renowned for its ghost stories and one still exists for the so-called Boxing Day apparition of a Prior who appears in the ruins of the Priory Park in Southend.

Apparently the Priory was dissolved on a Boxing Day and the Friar put to the sword by Henry the Eighth's men at arms and the Friar appears regularly on the anniversary of his death.

The Park was part of my area and it was my responsibility to ensure that nobody crept into the park on Boxing Day night. Some damage had been caused in the past but most of the problem was just nuisance value and protecting the museum in the grounds.

One night an apparition did appear and terrified girls and boys come streaming across the park fields and vaulted the pointed iron railings surrounding the park as if their lives depended on it.

We went to the ruins and found a discarded luminous sheet and facemask but no body. Many persons, even myself, were accused of being the apparition but the culprit was never found.

I was telling this story to my elderly neighbour some days later and she said that the tale was true and, in fact, she had experienced other spooky goings-on in the years she had lived in the area.

Across the road from her used to be Coleman's Hall, a large stately house believed owned by the Coleman's mustard family. I knew the house reasonably well as I was born in small terraced house beside the Hall grounds.

The Hall a long been pulled down to make way for a small housing estate and care home. There used to be a pond and menagerie of various farm animals including geese.

In medieval times a tunnel linked the Hall to the Priory and the geese would take refuge in there during the cold winter months. When the Priory was raised to the ground the tunnel was filled in at both ends trapping the geese.

She said the cries of the geese could still be heard on some cold winter nights in streets above the tunnel.

True or false I did not hang about when a cycled home through those streets just in case!

Time as an Area Officer was not only a great learning curve but also a good time for the family. Even on duty we found time to laugh together especially the winter that it snowed when Dorothy and the girls threw snowballs at me as I stood waiting to see the children across the road.

The School Crossing Patrol (Lollipop) Lady was off sick so I had to stand-in. The look of horror on the faces of the parents and children as they saw this uniformed policeman being attacked by this mad woman and screaming kids was a picture. And their faces when the policeman started to throw snowballs back at them were even more so. Soon everyone was joining in. The excitement stopped and everyone went about their way with a few Mums complimenting, "How nice it was to see a human policeman".

I wasn't so sure that my bosses would have thought of it that way, but what the hell!

At the Queens Jubilee Celebrations during the following summer I am sure the same kids who threw the snowballs took great delight in throwing wet sponges at me, in full uniform, as a sat in the village style stocks. I suspect some of the local kids also put heavier objects in the sponges to seek a little retribution as I felt quite punch drunk after the event. But it was all for charity and the beer I consumed soon after helped to relieve the pain!

Duty had to be performed and a small number of families and individuals did not appreciate my position in the community. Mostly because I had arrested them or used my powers to stem their enthusiasm for making life hell for those living near them.

You could not please everyone and enemies were made. An arrest for a burglar at his home turned nasty when his brothers decided to try to stop. The burglar escaped and one brother threw a heavy tiled coffee table at me flooring me instantly in a hail of splintered wood and shattered tiles. My PC colleague had a narrow escape when the other brother lunged at him with a six-inch sheath knife. I saw the knife blade disappear into the PC's stomach and both fell back into a heap.

I kicked the debris off myself and leapt to help my mate but before I could do so he was up on his feet and hitting the knife-wielding brother with his truncheon. "Take a knife to me you bastard", said the PC as he hit him across the wrist and then punched him in the mouth with his free hand.

I could not understand how the PC was still standing and neither could he but all was revealed when we saw the large split in his leather belt. The knife had gone straight through his uniform jacket and been stopped from going any further by the thick leather belt. The PC was quite thankful saying, "Good job a did not wear my bracers instead, wasn't it!"

Both brothers were arrested and the burglar caught some days later and when they went to Court one of them said to me, "Think your God's fucking gift. Start thinking about moving. It may be better for your health!"

Another family were equally notorious but this time it was the mother and one son who were the main problem. She would protect him no matter what and even gave him an alibi when he driven another car off the road and killed the other driver, a young mother of twenty five, and leaving her five year old child in the crashed vehicle.

It was one of the most tragic jobs I had to do when I had to tell the dead girls parents what had happened and something that will stay with me forever. The boy responsible was caught and on the evidence of his passengers who had also decamped, six independent witnesses who identified him and forensic tests on the vehicle he was convicted. The mother still insisted that he was at home.

When he was sentenced to three and a half years for manslaughter the mother leaned over the balcony of the Crown Court public gallery and said, "You better be careful that your daughters look both ways on the road, Craven. You never know what will happen!"

Colleagues wanted to arrest her for Threats to kill but it would have been futile. I by this time had transferred back into CID so a move was probably the best solution.

Chapter Ten
THE APPRENTICE DETECTIVE

Starting work in the CID of the then Southend on Sea Constabulary was, even in 1970, like stepping into a time warp to the 1950's. Seasoned detectives in trilby hats and double breasted suits with silk handkerchiefs in breast pockets during week days and only allowed to change to tweed sports jackets and cloth caps or other head gear on weekends seems now a long way from later days when suits are rarely seen and casual clothes, T Shirts and jeans are the norm.

"The art of being a Detective had to be learnt and you won't be one for many years", explained my first day advisor in the Department. With greased grey swept back hair parted in the middle and crumpled ash stained light grey pin striped suit the middle-aged detective, a throw back from a Humphrey Bogart film, stooped over me as I sat nervously on the day a joined this illustrious Gods gift to the Police Service.

"You're bloody lucky son", he spluttered as he chewed upon a dog end that hung from the corner of his mouth, "Most blokes don't get a sniff of CID until they have got 10 years in".

I knew this was not right as many younger officers were in the Department but the "old boys" of many years service liked to think they were more elite than was their true standing. I had a lot to learn so I let him continue.

He drew closer to me, half whispering and screwing his lips up so that the contortion allowed him to talk out of the side of his mouth. (Another older officer told me later that this method was used to enable you to direct your speech to the person you were talking to and no one else. Thus keeping your secrets safe.)

My advisor continued, "Some advice son. Get out to the pubs and Clubs, put yourself about and get as many informants as you can." He pulled himself up and inhaled, pushing his chest out, changed his expression from a scowl to kindness personified and invited," If you need any help or advice then you know you can always come to me. I will see you alright".

I thanked the senior detective for his indulgence and put my head back into the piles of filing that I had been given by the Detective Sergeant to "help show me the running of the office". Remembering the warnings I had received from friends on my uniform shift about the officers who would ride on the backs of those who got information, they could be bent or get to the bosses with it before me.

Even in my limited experience I had seen officers steal intelligence and information and use it for their own advancement so I'd better learn how to speak secretly out of the side of my mouth. What a joke!

The grey suit had decided that the filing was not for me and said, "Get your nose out of that lot and get your coat on. I'll show the real town!" Born and bred in Southend and now 23 years old I thought I had seen most of but he was to prove me wrong in many senses.

I had done all the pubs that younger people do but he took me to the private clubs that were allowed to sell alcohol outside of lunch times and evenings. Smoke filled dungeons with a clientele of life's unfortunates whose average age was well above what I considered to be the real fraternity that were responsible for committing crime in the town. But these were places where you could get a drink at anytime during the day and would come in useful.

He loved showing me places that I had never been to and revelled in that fact that he was able to teach this young "no it all up-start" that he was lucky to be in his world. I doubted that I would ever be completely accepted by him as a fully paid up member of "his department" but I do not think he fully appreciated that I didn't want to join the "crumblies" anyway. It was outdated and I did not care. The action for me was elsewhere in the vibrant up and coming discos and modern clubs that were popping up in the town.

Pubs were being revamped with décor that was supposed to attract customers with more discerning tastes. Pseudo wooden beams, white artexing and piped pop music turned dingy hovels into popular drinking holes. Consumption of alcohol took off to new heights; drugs became more available as the venues increased in popularity and our job became more arduous.

When I joined the Police it was surprising who gave me the pat on the back and wished me well. The Uncle who had done time in prison who said it at last brought respectability to the family, the mate who was always in and out of trouble who said it was brilliant and others who, as far as I was concerned, had no hang ups with the Police but turned their backs on me, never to make contact again.

Keeping in touch with my mates helped me to keep my feet on the ground and maintain a sense of proportion of what was happening in the world outside of the job.

The regular pub I frequented most, with these mates, was also the meeting place of a few hard nuts or those who liked to think they were the toughest crew in the town.

Mostly misfits they comically called themselves "The Firm" and being slightly older than my mates, they were more associated with the "Teddy Boy" age. They nearly all sported "Elvis" type hairstyles; they drank heavily and invariably were the cause of any bloodshed that occurred in the place.

Two of this gang stuck out in the crowd, one was a pathetic looking bloke with podgy face, squat beer bellied body and short legs disproportionate to the rest of his frame.

He and I went to the same junior school and I can clearly recall him coming to school with no shoes and dishevelled dirty clothes. It was easy to take pity on him but even now grown up, he would still look as if he had just crawled out of some rubbish tip. He seemed to have work of some sort but his attitude was that the world owed him and he did not care how he got repayment.

The other was an extremely violent character with a short fuse temper when sober and uncontrollable when intoxicated. He had the misfortune, although brought about by his own youthful stupidity, to have lost his lower arm when he touched the electric power lines on the London to Shoebury railway track. His arm had an attachment to which he could screw various contraptions to give him the ability to carry out a useful life.

These were metal tipped and pointed, sharp or heavy, depending on the use to which they were needed and were also used by him to inflict horrific injuries to those he attacked.

I can still see the blood splatter across the bar and the optics behind as he hit the face of a man who crossed him and the head of the victim explode as he hit him again with the steel rimmed club on the end of his arm. The blind veracity he used was frightening, stunning and shocked the on-looking witnesses to silence.

He ran out making his escape while we attended to the injured man but was as meek and mild when we arrested him at his flat at 3.00am the following morning.

The proverbial silent "three wise monkey" attitude followed with every one of the fifty or so eye witnesses in the pub either not noticing or being "in the bogs". It worked out that the pub toilet consisting of one urinal and one cubicle had 35 males in it at the same time. We did suggest to some that the only way that it could have happened was if they were joined together in a homosexual embrace. Most preferred that label than the dangers associated with giving evidence at court against the assailant.

He pleaded guilty and spent a few years in prison but the victim has never been able to carry on a normal life since then. Even then I started to realise that there was not a lot of justice for victims.

As a junior detective I was usually tasked with the younger element type crime. Stolen bikes, motor vehicles taken without consent and gas meter boxes broken into whereas the more senior detectives got the cream jobs.

If you arrested a youth for one cycle it was always expected and often turned out that the youth had taken many, many more. The Detective Chief Inspector would be delighted if you had got a youth to admit to nicking several bikes or cars. The hype in the Divisional Detection Rate would lift your esteem and the promotion prospects for the DCI.

I was in his particular good books when a scrawny kid admitted to me that he had stolen 193 bikes over the last year. It did not matter that he could not tell me where he had put them as, although none had been recovered, our crime detection figures went through the roof that month and the DCI was my best mate.

The boy pleaded guilty to stealing all the bikes and had 193 similar offences as TIC's (taken into consideration). The sentence he received of 3 months at a detention centre only helped him to hone his skills as a thief still further and become a house burglar and later an armed robber. "Bloody waste of time", I thought but "We weren't to worry about what happens after they are nicked", my Detective Sergeant said. "Aren't we supposed to prevent crime?" I argued but it fell on deaf ears.

My ambition was to be a detective on a murder squad and really harped back to the excitement of arresting a suspected murderer when I was in uniform. I had been parked on the seafront when a shout went up over the radio that two of our detectives where chasing a car that was being driven by a man suspected of murdering his wife in Blackpool.

I could hear the approaching wail of police sirens as a Ford Consul hurtled past me on the busy seafront dual carriageway, Marine Parade. The Ford was going so fast it just barged other cars in front out of the way. The grey CID Ford Cortina chasing it seemed to lack pace for some reason and was being balked by the debris of the hit cars.

I was driving a brand new very fast Mini Panda Car. These were very nippy, manoeuvrable cars and suited to making way through heavy traffic. Saturday afternoons in the summer were always busy on the seafront and the chase debris caused even more problems for the pursuing CID car.

Lights blazing, hand on horn I drove across the central reservation and onto the opposite carriageway. The road ahead was clear so I drove the wrong way and overtook the CID and Consul to my left. A roundabout at the Kursaal amusement park soon came up and the Consul was forced, by the heavy traffic, to drive straight on. He then did an immediate first left. By this time I was along side of him in a narrow two-way road that 100 yards ahead turned a right angle.

The Consul hit my new paintwork and I wondered what the Sergeant would say as we slewed around the corner. It then tried to clip my rear wing as I drew slightly in front of him. We whipped by a couple of parked cars and I saw the approaching T-junction. I had my nose just in front and had to do something or I was going to go straight head on into the terraced houses at the junction.

I slamming on my brakes and pulled the wheel over to the left. The Consul, instead of just pushing me out of the way, braked hard and sent itself into a spin. It lurched to the left and then to the right and hit the corrugated fencing surrounding the amusement park. The metal panels flew upwards and outwards some landing on top of the car and others somersaulting across the cindered waste ground of this part of the park.

I skidded to a halt as the CID car drove through the gap made in the fence. I reversed up to see the driver of the Consul slowly get out and rest his arms on the roof in submission. I arrested the driver for murder!

The elder of the two CID officers thanked me and said that they had not covered the back door of the hotel when they went to arrest the bloke. He said, "You saved me some embarrassment there mate. Ever get into CID and I'll look after you."

He kept his word and many times supported me through the paper work millstones and practicalities of the Department. A kindly bloke he seemed to be more aware of the causes of crime and often used to say to me, "If only we could get to the kids before they went bad. Instead of mopping them up from the gutter where they have landed."

Something I strongly believe in now but did not fully appreciate then.

But my time was taken up too much by the high life of a detective, the priority of locking villains up and keeping the "streets safe" than to look at the deeper issues.

I sought the lighter side of life to relieve the tension like putting the Special Branch Officers telephone inside his security safe in the office, waiting for him to return then calling him and watching him looking for his phone and having that quizzical look on his face as he tried to work out how we had got the combination numbers to his lock.

Dressing in the latest fashions and parading in the clubs and discos in my bell-bottom flares, kipper ties, huge collared paisley or multi coloured shirts and stack heeled shoes. I even had a three-piece suit complete with waistcoat in the audacious colour of aubergine. Pandering to the dress code of the detectives on TV, smoking 60 cigarettes a day was the "cool" of the time and alcohol was never a problem especially as the landlords expected to provide you free booze and did not charge you for entering their clubs.

This to me was the epitome of what was expected of the detective.

The CID Courses we attended at cities around the country were as much to teach you how to cope with the demands of high consumption of alcohol and keeping your senses and private life on an even keel as learning the rudiments and intricacies of the criminal law. Those who succeeded in controlling all these subjects could look forward to a fruitful and rewarding career. Many fell by the wayside suffering broken marriages or drink related problems. A minority were not affected but many of us teetered on the edge. Responsible camaraderie and huge amounts of support, understanding and some suffering from wives and family kept the wheels going.

Going out at 9.00am each day and not getting home until the small hours, being called out at all times of the day and night, coming home stinking of booze and smoke and sometimes strange perfume was not something that many marriages survived so it took a very strong relationship to keep the lid on. Many detectives were not so lucky as me and the CID was renowned for nasty divorces.

Dorothy was aware of this and even though threatening me once with, "Either it is the CID or me," stuck by me throughout my service.

How she did I will never be able to understand. Lonely nights at home on her own not knowing when I would come home, having heaven knows how many days off spoilt because of leave being cancelled, having no social life outside the job and mopping up after I had been assaulted did not make for a perfect life.

When co-opted onto murder squads she would be able to understand more for the need to work so many hours as the news headlines would contain a blow by blow account of the investigation and identify the horrors whereas the every day tribulations of detective work was less in your face and therefore less able to be understood.

I would not be able to say a lot to her about the exact work I was doing but the funny side I could relate.

Like the Murder enquiry that was being held up by a "Queen Bee" homosexual. He was the manager of a pub where a number of witnesses were being reluctant to come forward because he would not allow them to speak to us. Sounds ridiculous but he was such a strong character and violent to his subordinates they were fearful of the consequences if they talked to us.

It took ten of us to convince him that his ways ought to be amended. The biggest detective, a six feet five rugby player and the Force boxing champion took the Queen Bee to his office and said that we were carrying out our lawful duty and gathering evidence and any obstruction by him would be treated with utmost diligence. He was under no doubt what they meant and we were able to establish the evidence that was eventually used to convict the murderer.

The Queen Bee went into a childish sulk that lasted for many weeks until he left the town for a "quieter life in Ibiza". He was not best pleased when the boxing champion bumped into him whilst on holiday on the island some years later and wrote to the Chief Constable complaining of harassment. I am sure it was an innocent coincidence and the champion categorically denied stalking him.

SPOOKY

Every murder enquiry receives the offer of help from spiritualists and sadly persons who want to confess.

A serious approach has to taken to these as every avenue had to be tried to apprehend suspects. Personal opinions had to be put aside and the element of doubt forgotten no matter where the information comes from.

"My spirit can identify the one who did it!" the voice said on the telephone.

It was getting to the end of the enquiry and all possible leads were drying up and another detective and me knocked on the door of the Psychic Medium who had sent the message.

A man in his early twenties answered the door of the small terraced house. White, short and stocky with light brown thick hair stuffed under leather cap, floral patterned shirt tails hanging outside his dirt ground concertinaed trousers and flopping along with larger than required woolly slippers and without a word, he beckoned us in.

In silence we followed leaving the small entrance hall and going through a door to a large room that seemed to extend the full width of the house and into a further room at the rear.

A large bookcase and staircase filled one side the room. In the centre of the room and the only obvious furniture stood twelve evenly placed dining chairs in a semi-circle. They looked intriguingly lonely and my detective mate was also looking at them curiously.

The medium did not speak and looked at us waiting for some reaction. Only after I told him who we were did he alter his gaze through us and say, "My friend was out on the night the lady was murdered and saw this man leaving her house with a bloodstained crowbar in his hand."

At any stage in an enquiry we had to be careful not reveal any item or fact that only the murderer would know and we were aware that the medium would have been able to ascertain a lot from the heavy press coverage. The crowbar had been released so this took us no further.

"Who is your friend then?" said my colleague. "That one there", replied the medium, pointing to one of the chairs in the centre of the room. We looked at each other. "There's no one there!" I said, hoping my mate would agree and that I was not going stupid.

"I know that. You can't see him but I can", the medium replied.

Not wanting to antagonise him and not knowing what this guy might be capable of, I said, "So you can see him but we can't. Is that it?" "Yes. I'm qualified and you're not", he said reassuringly.

Not wishing to show any scepticism I said, "Well how does this medium business work then? Do you talk to your friends? I assume that all the chairs are occupied?"

He took us by surprise and sat on one of the chairs, waiting for a ghostly yell of pain or shout of, "Get off my lap!" we looked at each other and sighed in relief when no sounds came. The medium paused and indicating with both arms said, "Most are here but some are out. They all usually go out at night but it's a bit early just now".

I cringed as I said it and wondered if I should at all but it was out before I could stop it, "Perhaps you could introduce us to your friends".

I waited for some caustic remark but the medium gestured to each chair and said, "The officers would like to be introduced. They are from the murder squad so just tell them your names". What followed was an amazing exhibition of voices coming from the mediums lips, differing in tone, pitch and gender, each speaking a name Henrietta, Alfred, Simpson, Agatha and so on. I was stunned and obviously gapping as he then said, "And this George who saw the murderer".

Such was the impact of the situation that I found myself almost stepping forward to shake the hand of this invisible being. Regaining my composure and showing some startled cynicism I tried to be as conciliatory as possible and said, "I am not sure how this thing of yours works but would it be possible that George could know the name and address of the murderer?"

To my astonishment before the medium could reply, George said, "Bill Smith 20 Fairview Road Colchester". "How do you know that George?" I retorted. There was no reply.

I then radioed through these details to our Control Room to get the details checked out.

The most uncomfortable situation followed. It was spooky that my second name is George and I lived in Fairview Drive. Could this medium be for real but slightly off track? We entered into niceties of conversation, avoiding George and his friends, even eye contact with the chairs and their invisible figures.

The radio crackling into life startled us and the message received with accompanying laughter that there was no such road in Colchester and that there were over 150 thousand Bill Smiths in the country.

The message was loud and clear and did not to break the silent atmosphere until the medium, arms folded and sighing quite nonchalantly said, "He's a bastard like that. Do you know this is not the first time that he had lied to me! I think he is attention seeking. Now if you can excuse me I want to have a quiet word with him".

Trying to stifle our laughter we left him to his spirits and wondered at the audacity of his performance. He was real and excellent entertainment but useful witness? I think not!

SPECIAL OVERTIME PAY

We received special paid overtime rates on murder enquiries that encouraged the detectives to work longer hours to get the evidence needed and the conviction required. It was no surprise that murders were invariably solved and a high number were detected.

During the early seventies Police Pay was being reviewed and officers were being canvassed for their views on how dedication could be recognised and rewarded.

Police Pay was abysmal and overtime payment virtually non-existent. In the CID we only qualified for overtime payment if on average all officers worked 96 hours overtime per quarter. If that was achieved then we received the grand sum of £36.

If the average was below this then you got nothing. It worked out that you as an individual could be working your butt off and doing many, many hours and some others doing none. You would either get the same money or nothing at all! It was an unfair system and unreliable. A referendum in Essex dictated an increase in this allowance instead of paid overtime i.e. being paid for the hours you worked individually.

It was unfair on my family and me to continue. Our salary was barely enough to live on and the compensation I received for working such long hours and being away from them was not enough so I decided to return to Uniform Duties as an Area Officer.

BASILDON AND BEYOND

After the successes of my stint back in uniform the new town of Basildon was to show me another side of policing. Basildon with its sprawling award winning estates of houses, flats, dwellings and open spaces was filled with many decent people who just wanted to live their lives as normal and peacefully as all the other people do.

In amongst these honest people, mostly over-spill residents from the East end of London were not those who could not care less for their neighbours nor have any respect for the law.

The East ender has a rough diamond reputation, villainy could be acceptable and even out and out criminals looked upon as Robin Hood characters even if they robbed the poor and made themselves rich. To be a "grass", police informer, was a greater sin than to be a robber of old ladies.

Coming from a London family with many relatives still living there, I had sympathy for the residents who were tarred with the same brush as the villains and criminals who exalted in the reputation that

Basildon was hard-core and had no room for the honest and even less for the weak.

There was an inbred distrust of the law and it was even harder to find witnesses to incidents who were prepared to attend court and give evidence. The fear of retribution should they do so was much higher in Basildon than I found in any other town that I worked.

For three terrific years I was partnered with a black detective who was born in the town, quietly spoken he and I had the delight of working together until I was promoted and moved on.

I started off with him driving me round the area in an attempt to acclimatise me to the myriad of alleys, terraces and multi levels of sixties buildings that made up the town. He showed me the factory estates that made up the industrial backbone of the supposedly self sufficient town

I pointed out the places that I knew and, driving down one road, found to both our surprise that we had gone out with the same girl and working out that she went out with him after me. Both of us had very nice thoughts of her and a joint natural respect stopped us from discussing her further.

Other officers in the Department equally made the work at Basildon both funny and enjoyable. One in particular who was prone to drinking a lot was affectionately named "Uncle Weeble" by my girls who met him one day when I took them to the office.

He kept them busy, giving them a pencils and paper to draw pictures while I had a meeting with the DCI. Because he was rather fat with a small head they drew a large circle with a pea-sized head rather like the television characters, "The Weebles", of the time who were similar in shape. In drink his shape used to come to his aid, as it was very much like the toy you get in the bottom of a budgerigars cage. When it is pushed over it's heavy base always manages to stand it back in the upright position. It did not matter how much the Weeble drank he never fell over and stayed on the ground he always stood upright again.

The Weeble DC took the girls to his heart and kept this drawing for years and produced it from his drawer every time I visited Basildon.

Although at the time he had a weakness to drink Weeble was one of the best detectives the Force had. His interview skills were second to none and his meticulous energy to detail when submitting his case papers were the cause of many a villain to be successfully convicted in many complicated and serious cases.

He had the detective "nose" and instinct. He spent hours just talking to a man that had been arrested for a fairly minor matter because he "felt there was something more about him".

It was when he was interviewing a man, to get his antecedent history required by the Court before sentencing, that Weeble sensed something was wrong. The man could not speak about his family or other acquaintances and emotionally refused to speak any more.

After talking for hours the man confessed that he had raped a woman, a family member, and was living under an assumed name. Checks revealed that he in fact was wanted for this offence.

The man insisted that he spoke to the trusted Weeble further and then admitted to murdering a woman earlier. This murder was in another Force area and the man would never have been implicated.

Weeble would have his words of wisdom for us all! Varying in degrees of success.

Two gypsy boys had been arrested for shoplifting, one a teenager and the other no older than six years of age who was obviously under the age of criminal responsibility although he had all the attributes of a hardened criminal.

They had been with an adult who had made good his escape. The two youngsters stayed silent throughout their arrest and the subsequent interviews with Weeble and myself.

The teenager was detained to go before the Court and we took the six year old out to visit all the gypsy sites in the area in an attempt to identify him and hand him back to his parents. We toured several sites in the area until we drove onto a vast open stretch of land near Tilbury.

There were in access of fifty caravans and from the reaction of the first on-looking gypsies we calculated that the boy came from this site. A crowd gathered around our car and the boy started to hammer on the door shouting he could not get out. He screamed and cried alarmingly as the crowd grew even more hostile. We kept our doors locked and shouted that we had to see the boys parents.

The hostility continued and then suddenly went quiet as the gathering parted allowing us to see across the field where in the distance I saw the head of a man loping along from a lower level where the field dipped. The head got closer as the body revealed itself further and further getting taller and bigger as it came.

As the huge mountain of a man sloped towards us his black eyes on a red angry face grew more menacing. His muscular arms filled the dirty tweed coat that looked slightly too small for him and the pickaxe handle his was carrying swung threatening at his side.

"Keep calm, Bob. I'll radio for back-up", said the Weeble. He tried but failed, "We must be in a dip. I can't get through", he exclaimed throwing the microphone back onto the radio unit.

By this time the Hulk had got to the car and was swinging the pickaxe at the car. "Christ. Those windows are strong", I said as yet again he swung the weapon and it bounced off.

"Keep cool. Can we drive out of here?" the Weeble calmly asked.

"Not without taking a few gypsies with us", I said as the car started to rock violently from side to side. The Hulk had now taken a grip on the car roof gutter and was bodily pushing it backwards and forwards. Assisted by the baying crowd we were bouncing about with two wheels at a time coming completely off the ground to the extent that our heads struck as we met in the middle.

The boy was being equally thrown about and by now very distressed. This had not gone unnoticed by the Hulk and his crowd. The rocking abated and the Weeble said, "Well there is nothing else left to do. You are going to have to go out there and talk to them".

By this time I had realised that no form of communication was possible with these people. They spoke a language that had no bearing on English and were in no mood for conciliation.

Whilst I was contemplating my next move the Weeble said, "Use your hanky!" I thought, "Why the hell should I have to use a hanky for?"

He saw my perplexed look and said, "The international sign for surrender. You've got a white hanky haven't you?"

I had to get out of the car to open the passenger door to let the boy out. Releasing the central locking system and waving my white hanky at the time I gingerly opened the car door and entered the arena of angry gypsies. In one movement I leapt out and opened the door and let the boy out.

The Hulk was on the other side of the car and in two strides he was on my side as I closed the door, got back inside and locked the doors again. The Hulk glared at me and then lifted the boy up the six-foot or so on to the top of his shoulders. The cheering crowd then followed the hulk and the waving boy aloft back down from where he had come.

After they had walked a safe distance I felt I could do my duty and winding down the window shouted, "Make sure he does not shoplift again!" A quick first gear and a belt across the field took us onto the road and out of harms way.

The Weeble said, "What chance does that kid have now!" I had to agree, although we had notified Social Services, we did not know the boys name, his parents or even his caravan address. He was bred into theifdom and unlikely to know anything different in life. He was only six!

Even though we knew their identity there were many other lost causes. A young lad was being interviewed by a junior detective who was not getting anywhere with him.

The detective with short tight curly ginger hair, horned rimmed spectacles and bushy moustache resembled more like a schoolteacher than one of "Basildon's finest". He remonstrated with another detective saying, "I can't understand it. Last time he was nicked he coughed loads of jobs. Now he won't say anything".

Weeble's words of wisdom followed, "Cuff him round the ear! Always works, never fails. His Mum will always agree. She's with him isn't she?"

The young detective left the room only to come back a short time later holding the side of his face with one hand and his broken spectacles in the other. "What happened? How many jobs did he coughed?" he was asked.

"Fucking shit hit me back!" said the detective. He took his hand away and a nasty black eye was starting to develop. "Do you know?" the Weeble said, "It must be 5 years since I interviewed him. I suppose he is getting too big for a slap now".

THE SHOPLIFTER

I had not long been at Basildon when on a Saturday afternoon I received a phone call from Wickford CID, about 5 miles away, that there had been a shoplifting at one of their supermarkets and that the offenders had made off with a very large quantity of groceries in a car the registered owner of which lived in the Basildon area.

My black detective partner went to check the details and any possible associates of the registered owner in our intelligence files and I took a young probationer constable on his CID attachment to check out the address on what seemed a usual routine job.

There was no sign of the vehicle near the address. The area was relatively new with terraced housing interlinked with open grassed areas and alleyways giving access to numerous parking areas. We made a sweep of the surrounding roads and found the car parked three streets away.

The engine was still hot and inside we saw several goods labels from the supermarket in Wickford. As we looked at the vehicle, a door opened at a house nearby and a young woman approached us asking if she could help us.

She must have suddenly realised who we were and started to back towards her door. We got to her doorstep at the same time as she closed the door leaving both her and us standing outside on the step.

I looked into the front room window and saw a large pile of groceries and other goods on the floor of the front room and a number of persons climbing the fence out of the rear garden.

I told the probationer to stay with the woman and made my way round to the back of the house. I called for assistance on my personal radio. As I went towards the rear alleyway a swarthy looking man in his twenties came out onto the front footpath. I recognised him as one of the persons climbing the fence.

I approached him and he ran off down another alleyway. I pursued him and saw him disappear round a bend in the alleyway and as he did he threw something into some long grass to his right.

I ran up to the bend and stooped down to pick the object, a calculator, up. Just then I felt this tremendous blow to the side of my head. The lights went out for a few seconds and when I came round I felt several more blows to my head and upper body. I was being kicked it seemed from all sides. I felt the crunch of bone cracking as he kicked my nose and forehead.

I tried to get up and was hit again and again. All I could do was curl into a ball and protect my head. Blood streamed from my mouth and side of my head and ran into my eyes blurring my vision. I could here voices saying, "Don't follow me you bastard". I passed out momentarily as everything went very hazy. I came round in time to see a figure running further down the alleyway.

My head was spinning as I tried to stand up. Blood was running down my face into my eyes and mouth and dripping onto my shirt and jacket. I retrieved my radio and asked for urgent assistance. The usual inability of the radio operator to receive through interference followed but this was as much to do with the top of the radio filling up with my blood. I could not remember exactly where I was which did not help them locating me.

I ran in the direction the swarthy man had gone. A respectable looking middle aged man was entering the alley. I asked him to telephone for the police and he told me to "Fuck off". A few streets later I met the two-man crew of a police area car.

We searched the streets wider and eventually I again saw the swarthy man walking quite nonchalantly along as if nothing had happened. I got out of the vehicle with the other two officers and arrested him. He just laughed.

I just wanted to give him one good punch but as I tried my whole body seemed to go to jelly and I must have lost consciousness as the next thing I remember is coming round in hospital.

The doctors and nurses did their usual wonderful bit. I was stitched up, 35 stitches in all over my eye and lips and inside my mouth, nose filled with cotton wool, X-rayed and advised to stay in for observation.

Although my head felt as if it was three foot wide and throbbed like hell all I wanted to do was get home.

Before doing so I was visited by the DCI and an entourage of other detectives. The jokes and laughter were all meant in good spirit and solely intentional on cheering me up.

I could not focus on what was happening round me. It was almost as if I was a ghost in the room just observing the proceedings form afar. It had no effect on me. I was in a different world distantly apart from this group of well meaning friends.

The Weeble and another senior detective drove me to my house in Westcliff. The family, my two little girls and a very concerned Dorothy greeted me. My eldest daughter all of four years old, standing with hands on hips, told me off saying, "Daddy you are in a mess. Look at your jacket and shirt. I don't know!" It was such a lovely greeting. Funnily comforting but so warm and innocent.

It is hard to say how they felt when they saw my face with the stitches and bruising but as the days off sick followed I found the cuddles and caring by all of them was the best therapy I could ever want.

The customary bottle of scotch appeared a few days later, delivered by the Weeble, who naturally devoured half of it before he left. A welcome visit later by another DC and his wife, also a WPC at Basildon and the laugh we had when they presented me with a book on self-defence for women will stay with me as a warm reminder of the occasion.

SEE PICTURES - FACIAL INJURIES

I saw many friends from inside and outside the job during the time I was off but somehow I was never able to find the opportunity to tell them my feelings. My black partner visited and could not stop apologising for not being with me. I kept telling him that it would have happened anyway as one of us would have had to have gone round the back of the house. I did realise that if it had of been him it was quite likely that the swarthy man would have ended up in hospital as my partner was at the peak of his career as an accomplished karate expert. Such is life!

After this I did start to have short periods of the fear of being alone, unprotected, unsupported. Occasionally I would wake up crying and curled up like a ball. My mind would be running crazy with, it seemed, millions of thoughts of all different things running across my brain sometimes till it hurt my head. I put this down to a bit of concussion and after returning back to work these feelings receded slightly.

I was physically fit and healthy still playing football regularly for both Basildon Police and Southend Phoenix, the old Southend Police Saturday side. I did start to feel pain and tightness across my chest however but I put this down to a football injury, when after a tackle the opponent fell on top of me. Even so I did go to the doctors and have the situation checked out. He told me that I was perfectly healthy with no heart problems etc.

This did not stop rumours of me suffering heart problems reaching one of my best mates who telephoned me asking if there was something I should be telling him.

My activities on the outside of the job increased with me helping to run the Southend Phoenix Football Club. I had times of boundless energy and felt I could do many different things for long periods, especially those things that I liked. I was described as a workaholic but the people doing so were not about when I had my down times when I felt so drained and exhausted of everything and my only redress was to go to bed.

Dorothy was getting concerned with this and several times warned me about taking too much on and the consequences but I seemed to have the uncontrollable urge to fill my life with so much almost as if there would be no tomorrow. Sometimes I would feel that it was a "runaway train" that I could not stop but then it would, with a "down time".

I took the job on of being the Secretary of the Basildon Police Sports and Social Club. I had no option really as the whole committee had resigned when two of us held a referendum to get the club to buy a television. They lost and resigned so I was left with building the Club up again.

I got a headache but we had a TV to watch Saturday night football in our Club Bar. I also got involved in raising money for a local hospital burns unit and arranged dinner dances and boat trips on the River Thames in London.

Great fun and a lot of money raised! But it was taking its toll as, now I look back a few bad days started to happen. Muzzy heads and periods of total exhaustion mixed with massive highs of power and strength.

Better was to come, though, as the pressure from Dorothy to study for promotion paid dividends. I had proved to that bastard in HQ that I wasn't thick and passed my exams to Sergeant and Inspector.

At the first time of trying I was promoted to Detective Sergeant.

"SLEEPY" CHELMSFORD

After serving in Basildon, the so called "crime capital" of Essex, with it's notorious Eastenders I was looking forward to the rather more staid and relaxed posting to sleepy Chelmsford.

Working at Southend and then Basildon stupidly gave me naïve arrogance, that nowhere else could be such hard graft.

However the same difficulties of the job continued. There was no concrete jungle but the market county town suffered just like any other division, the beautiful countryside surrounding it just made it a more pleasurable atmosphere and experience.

It had its problem areas, run down housing estates with its honest decent residents, treated to the rough, indifferent and uncaring attitudes of a minority. A local council that made all the right overtures to get elected but rarely delivered the manifesto that put them there.

These were echoes of discontent that probably rattled through every borough in the country.

The Police were forever looking to improve the quality of life of the people we served and reinventing the wheel at the behest of some "new" management initiative that spelled the rise rank of some officer in the promotion race. In the eyes of those more experienced officers, "This has been tried before but it stopped because we had another governor with different views".

It, therefore, came as no surprise to me that being the new Detective Sergeant I was put in charge of yet another attempt at trying to stem the tide of criminal behaviour and appease the people in the rural parts of the division who were suffering from "severe criminal behaviour".

I was now the Detective Sergeant in charge of the Chelmsford Rural Section and given two Detective Constables and one Woman Detective Constable to cover an area almost the size of Greater London. Thatched cottages, palatial mansions, wild flower filled country lanes muddy farm yards, tweeds, green Wellington boots and sherry parties with the country set was my expectations.

The DCI said, "Big problems out there Bob! Get stuck into it. Get these complaining nobs off my back. Antiques are going left, right and centre". It was probably no coincidence that this DCI had a hobby and small sideline occupation as a dealer in Antique Clocks

I spent the next few weeks driving round with the local village Bobbies who gave me an insight into the country coppers job that I had never realised or fully appreciated. Their knowledge of their patch and the people on it was invaluable. Gutsy and dominant in their approach, they ruled the roost or fell flat on their faces.

With back up nearly always a good twenty to thirty minutes away it took a brave calculating officer, on his own, to stop and check a vehicle containing a suspicious heavy mob late at night. "Gift of the gab" attitude and being able to read a situation came with only experience and a long hard look at the options and dangers.

It was something a city or townie copper had no understanding, as his back up was virtually always "just round the corner".

On my tours they pointed out the residences of the "big" villains, most emanating from the "smoke" and the houses having the type of décor that no self-respecting "countryfile" or person of similar taste would entertain. Ornate Grecian figures and fountains, gaudy coloured painted walls and plastic Father Christmases gave certain villages the tag of "Costa Del Essex".

Some of these villains had been accepted into the community and even belonged to the local fox hunting set. One hunt meeting I had to attend, "To stop a breach of peace between the hairy saboteurs and the gentry", in the words of my Chief Superintendent, was no more than a gathering of yobs in red coats with a smattering of local horse-riding enthusiasts.

I counted five known London villains in the pack. During the next three years two were found shot dead in a gangland feud and much later another two were convicted of fraud and money laundering.

All parts of society have their bad eggs but unfortunately the close proximity of London and the attractive countryside made the area I had to cover too uncomfortable for the other residents.

Building a trust and ties with the "friendlies" was what the village Bobbies' achievements relied on and they were the first person I would turn to when I wanted anything.

We soon had some successes with making arrests but I must admit that it was not due to any new approach or fantastic new style of detective work. It was down to the fact that we were concentrating our efforts on the subject of crime committed in the rural area.

While we were doing this other areas of the division were neglected and troubles increased. The same old story as elsewhere prevailed. There were not enough of us to cover every possibility, thin on the ground resources could only be targeted effectively in specific areas at the loss to others.

When a brace of pheasants and later boxes of apples, new laid eggs, local honey and myriads of vegetables started to land in my office I knew that our rural public had started to appreciate us. Aware of the possibility that the pheasants may have been delivered by someone who did not like me and twinned with the fact that I did not know how to "hang them to mature" to prepare them I threw them in the dustbin. Discretion being the better part of valour!

Disappointments, with the Law and our inability to do the best for our public, still came.

Trying to explain to a man, after he had seen his neighbours' son burgle his house, that we did not have enough evidence was a very difficult job. He had been woken up one bright sunny summers morning at 4.00am by some noises downstairs.

He looked out of his upstairs window and clearly saw the bright ginger haired boy of 19 years coming out of the kitchen door below him. He had known this boy for many years and had no doubt that it was him, and even noticed that the he was walking very stiffly and looked in some pain with every step he made.

The man checked downstairs and found his wife's handbag open in the kitchen and her purse was missing from inside.

The boy was arrested and the officers found that his peculiar walk was caused by severe sunburn on the back of his upper legs but the officers could not find any trace of the missing purse.

He was charged and put before the Court but the Judge ruled that without any corroboration, even though we thought the sunburn issue and that the aggrieved knew him might suffice, the identification of the boy was not safe and the case was dismissed.

The man and his family were distraught and felt defiled by their neighbour. The man could not believe that the court was saying that he had lied. He saw the boy and there was no doubt in his mind. He decided that to seek his own retribution would be the only way of getting justice. All we could do was advise him that this would have more serious consequences for his family and implored him not to take the law into his own hands.

As life went on this was being more and more thrown in our faces, that justice was too much in the favour of the accused and sufficient account was not being taken for the aggrieved parties and victims.

THE WATCH STRAP

I had been on the Chelmsford Rural Section for just over a month when on the 20 December 1979 two DC's asked me if they could follow a woman to London.

She was going to meet her boyfriend at Enfield railway station. He was wanted for committing several burglaries on our patch, a shotgun had been stolen from one at the Hawk Pub in Battlesbridge.

Her boyfriend was a man in his 40's and a bloke I knew from my days at Southend CID. He wasn't a violent man as far as I knew so the job was to be fairly simple.

The detectives added that he was driving a stolen car, a light blue Ford Escort and had been staying at numerous hotels throughout the country leaving them without paying. No heinous crimes to be concerned about!

The Detective Inspector gave the okay and I telephoned the CID at Enfield and gave them the details of our little operation.

The three of us then followed the lady on the train from Battlesbridge to Liverpool Street Station in London. We kept some distance from her as the boyfriend could have met her anywhere on route. She then caught a connecting train to Enfield.

We did not have radios that worked in such conditions and mobile phones had not been perfected then. Unbeknown to us as we settled down to our journey a bank at Enfield was being robbed by a man with a shotgun and he made his getaway in a light blue Ford Escort.

Enfield Railway Station is situated in the busy main street shopping centre of the town. At its front there is a "D" shaped access road allowing vehicles to drive in and out with parking bays to make pick ups In the centre of the "D" is a grassed area with flowerbeds.

The woman came out of the station and stood immediately outside the front doors by the parking bays. She was in her late 30's, brown long hair wearing a plum coloured winter coat. She was nervously fiddling with the handle of her leather handbag and looking furtively for signs of her boyfriend.

Standing in places around the "D" were a number of men, conspicuous in dark trousers, white shirts, black ties and bulging winter jackets. Even the uninitiated would have recognised these as policemen in "civvie" jackets. The bulges signified to me that they were a firearms team hastily put together to cover some operation. We were in the middle of something that we did not know about?

The two DC's placed themselves at a distance either side of the woman and I approached the most important looking bulging jacket. He was somewhat startled as this corduroy capped character in brown sheepskin coat spoke to him and broke his tense concentration on the movements of cars and people going on around him. He relaxed a little when I told him who I was and introduced himself as a Chief Inspector from the Metropolitan Police Support Unit.

He explained that there had been an armed robbery earlier committed by a male with a shotgun and our suspect fitted the description. I took his advice and went to the other side of the main road where another more casually dressed man greeted me. It was the Met DS who I had originally spoken to on the telephone earlier that day.

The main road was very busy with heavy traffic going both ways and Christmas shoppers thronging the shops and footpaths on each side. I was standing with my back against iron railings separating the footpath from the main road I saw the stolen Ford Escort drive into the "D" access road. I recognised the driver.

He drove round passed the woman and stopped. The bulging jackets then surrounded the vehicle. Guns were being pointed at the driver who seemed fixed with a stunned look on his face. The jackets were shouting when suddenly the vehicle revved loudly and hurtled across the road causing several vehicles to swerve. The front bumper of the Escort nearly pinned me against the railing. Thankfully it stopped before it hit me and paused momentarily. I laid the palm of my hand on the windscreen showing the driver my warrant card. I shouted out his name and said, "Its Bob Craven from Southend, don't be stupid".

Little did I realise that it was me that was being stupid! The car suddenly reversed and the windscreen wiper blade ran up my arm underneath my metal watchstrap. There it lodged, stuck between the wiper arm and blade. I was wrenched forward and then it stopped for a very short spell. I tried desperately to release the strap but he then drove off into the stream of traffic dragging me with him.

The only thing I could do was to climb onto the bonnet of the car, still struggling to release the strap. We picked up speed, the engine was screaming underneath me, I was being thrown across the bonnet from side to side, and my brown sheepskin coat was ripped on the mirrors and at one time got caught on a lorry as we passed it. At the same time I felt terrible pain as my left leg was hit by lorry.

My brown corduroy cap, my pride and joy, and subject of much hilarity in the office, was blown off my head never to be seen again. We smashed passed cars, lorries, vans, going in both directions as we bounced from side to side along the middle of the road between the congested two-way traffic lanes.

I hung onto both the windscreen wipers desperately trying to stay on the bonnet and keep myself from sliding off into the path of the passing traffic as we picked up even faster speed. I tried to shout but for some reason could not get the words out. I was losing my breath and my chest was starting to ache. My left leg had gone completely numb and lifeless.

A traffic island with two striped poles and keep-left bollards loomed upon us. We drove straight across the top of it. I thought I was going to be cut in half but the car just demolished it with metal and glass flying everywhere. I felt the shudder of the underside of the Escort as it passed over the concrete kerbing.

As we picked up speed again I could feel my chest sucking or being pushed inwards, I could not shout, I had no air inside me, I started to black out, I thought I was going to die. The thought of never seeing my wife and two lovely daughters flashed across my spinning mind. The other windscreen wiper came off in my hand but the one stuck under my watchstrap stayed put.

It was almost like a surreal dream as we pulled over into a service road. A queue of people, elderly ladies, young mothers with pushchairs, smoking old men wrapped up against the cold, standing quite unaffected by the sight of me on the bonnet, outside a cinema or bingo hall and the look of disbelief as we drew up.

I could hear the sound of distant police two-tone sirens. Help was on the way!

It was obvious that the driver was letting me get off. Any hopes of releasing myself from the wiper were dashed when he revved up and we were off again.

Back onto the main road, then a sharp right hand turn. We hurtled down this long road at one hell of a speed. Gripping the only windscreen wiper I had recovered my composure, my chest had settled down and I could breath a little better. I seemed to be even relaxed in the anticipation that I was going to die. Seeing a "T" junction coming up convinced myself that at this crazy speed, when he braked, I would keep going straight on with the wiper still attached to my watchstrap.

I braced myself for the pain of losing my arm and landing in the gardens opposite. We turned the corner and unbelievably I stayed on the bonnet. This was followed by an almost immediate turn left and we ploughed into the back of a stationary Transit van. A stomach wrenching thud and the twisting and grinding sounds of metal on metal brought us to an abrupt halt. The deafening whining of the engine died to a gentle hiss.

There was this eyrie ghostly silence with the faint sound of the two tones in the distance and the gentle warmth of smoke and steam coming from the engine. For a moment I thought I had died and was on my way to peace and tranquillity. I was in heaven.

A flicker of a flame and feeling a little more heat coming from underneath the bonnet made me realise that it was not my time. I had to get off the car.

The wiper was still stuck between my arm and watchstrap but it was now released from its mounting and there was the possibility that the car was on fire and could explode. I leapt off the bonnet, angry and intent on committing a murder.

My feet met the ground and I crumpled in a heap into the gutter. It was only then that I realised that my left leg was broken and my left foot was at a right angle to my leg. I crawled away from the steaming wrecked Escort and deposited the contents of my stomach on the pavement just as the reinforcements arrived.

The driver, who had not been wearing a seat belt, had hit the windscreen and was slumped unconscious over the steering wheel. The officers who were now with me, some just wanted to angrily get their hands on the driver, to enable an arrest to take place, smashed every window.

The Met DCI relieved that I was still on this earth, pulled me to him and gave me the biggest hug I have ever had from someone of the same sex. He said, "That was the most amazing act of fucking bravery that I have ever seen. Well done mate". I was still angry that I had not been able to get at the driver but also perplexed as to why he had driven like a maniac and nearly kill me.

I exclaimed to the DCI, "I didn't fucking do that intentionally." I held up my arm with the windscreen wiper still stuck to it. "This was why I got caught out," I retorted.

My two DC's then joined us, one of them was wiping his face around the mouth and the other said, "One of these idiots started shooting at the car. He even shot at it when it was across the road and you were on the bonnet. He went loopy! All we could do was throw ourselves onto the floor."

It did not really register with me what he said but I was glad to leave the mayhem of the scene to others but was a bit dubious about travelling in the same ambulance as the lunatic driver who actually appeared to be worse off for injuries than me.

It certainly concerned me as to why he had driven like that and put me in so much danger. In the ambulance I was more concerned with my leg and the pains I was getting in my chest to worry about the whys and wherefores of the incident.

Even when my mates came to the hospital and said that a high level enquiry was being held into why the guy had shot at the car and me it did not register. They were very angry especially as they had shouted to the officer who was firing, but in the end they could only throw themselves onto the ground to avoid being hit by the bullets.

A visit in hospital by the then Metropolitan Police Commissioner was nice but had no real calming effect as I laid there with fractured leg, cracked ribs and numerous bruises and grazes all over.

I was patched up and my mates took me home. I had purposely asked that no one tell Dorothy about the incident because I did not want her to be worried or upset. Her actually seeing that I was okay, although injured was far better than having someone knock your door, informing her of something and causing unnecessary worry.

Exactly the opposite happened as one of my so-called mates, who had no involvement or in-depth knowledge of the incident, decided to go round and tell Dorothy that "there had been a shooting" and that I was injured. Whether it was ghoulish curiosity or a well-meaning attempt to help, I have no idea, but the tense worried look on her face told the story. I will never forgive that guy for sticking his nose in when it was not wanted. It was more traumatic dealing with Dorothy's grief and worry than the bloody windscreen wiper.

Close friends and family helped over the following months and the physical scars healed very well after physiotherapy and a strict exercise regime. But inside I was feeling betrayed, let down, questioning my own sanity and judgement, blaming myself.

Even then I needed someone to talk through what I had experienced. When you are at work you have your mates and people who you have so much in common with to talk to, have the piss taken out of you and even argue with you. You have the opportunity to rinse out your thoughts and feelings, although you do not realise you are doing it at the time. At home it is completely different, telling your nearest and dearest the inner most thoughts would place an unfair burden upon them and likely to put further strain and anxiety upon relationships

Neither Dorothy nor anyone else at home could have done anymore for me.

I find it now hard to describe how I felt about the situation. I was intent on getting back to work but trusted my bosses to find out what had happened. I could guess that the MET wanted to keep it quiet to save face. I did not want to rock any boats and it did not cross my mind to make a formal complaint against the officer who had shot at the Escort and caused the driver to act the way he did.

I needed some answers but never made any fuss, I just wanted to get better, so I have to take some blame for not getting them. No senior officers contacted me or visited me and I was never informed the result of the high level enquiry or even if there was one.

I suppose I should have shouted from the rooftops but I was not that sort of bloke.

At the trial the MET DCI, who had cuddled me, asked if I would agree to accept a plea of guilty from the defendant of "ABH", assault occasioning actual bodily harm, rather the more serious charge of "GBH", causing grievous bodily harm. I realised that the defendant would probably not have driven the way he did if the idiot had not been shooting. In fairness I agreed and he got two years imprisonment.

During my sickness leave I did get visited by the Essex Police Force Welfare Officer of the day. Unfortunately we did not speak as he turned up unannounced one day when I was on my own in the upstairs toilet. I answered the door as quick as I could (very difficult with your whole leg in plaster) and sliding down the stairs on my backside only to see him driving off up the road.

I suppose the lack of aftercare I received reached its climax when I requested the replacement of my sheepskin coat and prized cap. This was turned down by the Assistant Chief Constable who said that such an expensive item of clothing should not worn whilst on duty. I was very disappointed at this treatment and found it hard to find anything that the service did for me at the time.

I remember my father saying, "I thought the Police Service looked after and cared for their own. If they can't do that what chance do us outside stand?" I had no answer for him.

Looking back I do not think that I ever totally got myself together after this incident. Life seemed to take a new turning. My attitude to life, the job and colleagues was different. I started to see the closest of friends as enemies, competition for points with the promotion race taking particular prominence. I had little trust in anyone at work apart from close friends. I felt a tremendous need to prove that I was capable of so much. I was dazed and living in some sort of dream that would not go away.

I learnt to deal with these feelings and pressed on with my job and even had time to play football and manage the Chelmsford Divisional Football team.

I continued playing on Saturdays for my Southend Club and also arranged exchange football trips to Holland with a team of life long friends called VVZ Zaandam.

These pastimes helped me keep my feet on the ground and my brain on an even keel. But the deep feelings and senses stayed with me often manifesting itself in violence and loss of control.

My attitude changed to the job, with having times when I could take on the world and even think I was bullet proof. On an annual staff appraisal, when the boss gives you an assessment of your work during the previous year, my DI wrote down that, "Bob Craven goes where angels fear to tread."

At first I took this as compliment, I had guts and could brave a lot after all. But when he told me how he had come to this conclusion it made me think far differently.

"What about the Chelmsford Club fracas?" he asked. Some unsavoury members had spread the word that the private club was a "no-go" area for coppers and they would do what they wanted, when they wanted and how they wanted.

The Licensee was caught between the two by being held to ransom by these members and wishing to keep in with us, the Police.

I took four detectives with me to the club to show the membership that exclusion of the Police was not an option that they could afford. A large body of burly members surrounded us as we drank at the side of the bar making derogatory remarks, spilling drinks over our jacket sleeves and pressing against us. I took the lead with the officers and said, "Hold your ground men. Do not be intimidated. Just hold your ground!" Faces got closer as the squeeze on us continued. We could hardly move the beer glasses to our mouths as I continued to keep the "thin blue line" encouraged and together as one dominant unit.

The pressure suddenly rescinded and I found myself to be in a wider space. Turning to say, "There, told you acting together would result in us winning!" I realised that I was in fact on my own and the officers had deserted me. Glaring eyes, looking hungry for some violence, peered at me. I made an executive decision to make a tactical withdrawal. Identifying the exit and the obstacles between it and me I hurtled forward with fists and feet flying. Bravery or panic the speed had the desired affect and two punches one member and a swift kick in the bollocks to another saw me to the door and out onto the street. My officers, two doubled up with pain met me outside. "Sorry Sarge but we thought you got out with us. It got a bit nasty so we had no alternative but to burst out. We thought you had heard us," explained one of them who were still standing upright.

"We've got the troops coming to sort the bastards out," said the other one standing. I said, "Cancel them. There's a better way to do that!"

The busiest night for the Club was a Saturday and it was by coincidence that my friends in the Force rugby team were playing a friendly match against another a Midlands Force rugby team the following day.

As I was an honorary member of the Club I invited both teams to have a drink with me after the match. With an average weight of 17 stone and height of 6' 2" and at least 30 in number the unsavoury members did not stand a chance against such opposition. There was no violence, just a bit of gentle persuasion and some "leaning" as one player from the Midlands Force put it when he came out of the toilets with one of the main exponents.

As you probably guessed we did not have any more problems from the Club after that, particularly as two members of the rugby team would regularly visit them just as a reminder.

Normal duties involved terrible tasks, having to use a pitchfork to dig out the head and brains of a poor woman from the railway track points who had committed suicide. Putting the various parts of her dismembered body into a coffin piece by piece.

Remonstrating with a freelance reporter who had gone to the sister of a boy, who had stabbed their elderly parents to death, before we had the chance to see her and break the news gently. The reporter complete with cameraman had found the name out from the deceased parents' neighbour and then asked, "Can you give us your reaction to the fact your brother has killed your parents?"

The reporter was unapologetic falling back on the words, "The public has a right to know." The sister was distraught and inconsolable, within an hour of her parents being found murdered and her brothers body located submerged in a nearby lake she had to deal with this leech on society in the guise of the free press. A complaint to the Press Council was upheld but the toothless authority was incapable of repairing any hurt or distress caused and the reporters scoop story deepened the wounds already suffered by the sister and the rest of the family. An apology was never received or offered.

The Press and Media have a lot to answer for in their quest to sell newspapers and make money on the backs of other persons' misery!

A good sense of humour is essential in a job where pain and suffering is always just around the corner and regularly blown in your face. The following is just one story of many that will be told perhaps in another book.

THE REVOLVING BOOB

Detectives were renowned for their jokes and fast lane talking, characters with the "gift of the gab" and able to think on they're feet whilst drunk, tired or under extreme pressure was a pre-requisite for a successful and productive officer. The immense energy that was needed to carry off the role was difficult to suppress during those relatively quiet spells that fell upon us in the office whilst catching up with the mountain of paper work that always accompanied law enforcement.

The peace and tranquillity of the office full of detectives, heads down into their administration, was interrupted by Fred, a rather large detective known for his subtle and methodical almost scientific approach to his work.

Although in his mid 40's Fred was a childish figure and treated as such even by the more manly officers half his age. He had a cherub face that always looked odd with a roll-your own cigarette sticking out of his mouth.

Opposite Fred sat Jasmine, a buxom blond mid-twenties detective, single and always beautifully turned out in smart suits and blouses that showed off her curvaceous body without showing an unacceptable glamour that would not appropriate to the job and position of an officer of the law. Always showing decorum and authority Jasmine was not one to be taken as weak or gullible.

Fred took a sip from his mug of tea, flicked the ash off his stubby cigarette, took a concentrated drag from its seemingly sticky end and said, "Strange what you come across in this job isn't it?"

Jasmine looked up, somewhat indignant at having her concentration interrupted and nodded slightly in agreement.

Having got her attention and the raised heads of the remainder of the office Fred continued, "I was at this woman's house today, she was a psychic or something, but she could make things move by just looking at them. It was amazing". He paused and glanced to see the reaction from the others and said, "She showed me how she could move parts of the body without touching them". A ripple of disbelief echoed round the audience. Fred tried to convince the doubters, "Not legs or parts that move anyway, but boobs". "You've got to be fucking joking!" someone shouted.

"No straight up", Fred exclaimed, "she got her mates boobs to turn round clockwise and anti-clockwise just by concentration and waving her hand in front of them. It was amazing".

More disbelief rained while Jasmine sat in silence until Fred turned to her and said, "Jasmine, you're a pretty feet on the ground type of girl could you help me demonstrate. The woman showed me how to do it. It was quite simple really. I'll show you all".

Jasmine immediately replied, "You have got to be joking. That is impossible". Fred persuading said, "Honest it is possible. I saw her do it. It can be done". Jasmine still hesitated in disbelief to Fred who was now standing at her side, "Go away I am not entering into your juvenile world".

Showing some hurt at that remark Fred said, "Look, Jasmine. Would I embarrass you in front of all these people?" She looked round the room at the men and women, all seasoned honest hard working trustworthy detectives, her friends and seemed to console herself that she was safe and in good hands. She shrugged her shoulders and said, "All right then but you touch me you bastard (half smiling in a friendly tone) I will kill you!"

Fred instructed, "Just stand here in front of me". Taking her shoulders he placed her immediately in front of him, put her arms down by her side and did likewise with his. "Look into my eyes and continue to do so". He stood an arms length away from her and both stared motionless into each other's eyes.

Some of the audience vacated they're desks and drew closer to take in the intricate details of the spectacle of the boobs moving. Fred's concentration moved up a peg as his eyes closed. Jasmine faltered not from her gaze at Fred.

A stony silence enveloped the office broken only by Fred saying, "I am now going to move your left boob clockwise". Still with eyes closed his right hand formed a cup shape and came up level to her left breast.

Jasmine twitched slightly and then her patience broke, "You are going to touch me. Not too close with that hand of yours. I told you, I'll kill you if you touch me!"

Fred eyes open slightly reassured her, "Jasmine, we're mates, colleagues, I am not going to touch you". "All right then. But I warn you", Jasmine nodded.

"Look, just to show good faith, if I inadvertently touch you then you can have this", Fred slammed his open hand onto the desk and revealed a 10p coin. Jasmine stared at it and like us all thought, small change but the right approach.

She nodded to carry on.

He closed his eyes again and raised his hand. Reaching a point where the silence fell and the concentration on all faces returned Fred started to move his cupped hand clockwise. Jasmine still looked very suspiciously at the hand and then her boob, waiting for some reaction as the crowd around them deeper and closer.

Now whether it was a deliberate act or a push from behind that caused Fred's hand to cup over her boob we will never know but cup it did and with disastrous consequences. No sooner had the dirty deed been done than Fred was laying on the office floor holding his bleeding nose that had just been struck with the full force of the powerful, no nonsense blond, who was well known for her physical attributes and fighting skills.

Writhing on the floor with both hands holding his nose, his balls were open for assault and violently received the most almighty kick from the sharpest of shoes supported by the full force of a very angry woman who always calculated the level of force she wanted to apply. The shoe disappeared an extraordinary depth into the groin lifting Fred's prostrate body as it struck.

The audience were cavorting into all different forms of laughter, hanging onto desks in tears and looks of disbelief at what they had just witnessed in a CID office in a police station.

Jasmine satisfied with the punishment she had meted out sat down at her desk and pointed at the still flaked out body of Fred, "You ever do anything like that again and I will cut you bollocks off!"

Fred had regained a small piece of composure and croaked, "Jasmine, honest I did not mean to touch you. I am sorry". "Not half as much as you would be if you did it again", retorted Jasmine who defused the situation by grabbing her bag and walking out to the ladies room followed by a small escort of serious looking fellow female officers.

The office door no sooner had closed than it opened again as Blossom entered. She sensed that something was amiss and looked inquisitively around the now quietening room.

Blossom had been at this police station since she had joined 28 years ago. She was a very large lady in her fifties, a spinster, very straight-laced, churchgoer and very good friend of the Chief Superintendent of the Division. Everyone treated Blossom with respect just as you would your own mother. Kind, never seeing much wrong in anyone except villains she was not one to insult or undermine.

"Fred dear. What on earth has happened?" she exclaimed as she placed her extraordinary large handbag on the desk next to Fred's doubled-up body. "Oh nothing Blossom. Nothing", he replied. Unconvinced Blossom helped Fred to his feet and sat him on the desk.

Loco, a less responsible detective came over and said, "Go on Fred, and show Blossom that experiment. She would enjoy it!"

Glaring at Loco in disbelief Fred said, "No she won't be interested," hoping that she wouldn't.

Oh come on Fred. How does it work?" said Blossom in an almost girlish voice.

Fred then reluctantly explained what it was all about. With this Blossom positioned herself in front of him to take full part in the adventure.

The crowd formed again around the couple as Fred closed his eyes and cupped his hand in front of Blossoms large left breast.

Silence reined and Blossom lifted her head to look upwards in submission. Time went by while the concentration continued. Once again Fred moved his hand clockwise. Blossoms' left eye glanced downwards and suddenly she lowered her shoulders and said, "You won't touch me, Fred, will you?"

Fred replied as before, "No of course not but just to show good faith here is ten pence. If I inadvertently touch you it 's yours."

Reassured Blossom stuck her chest out, put her head back and upwards, closed her eyes and said, "Okay I'm ready."

Once again Fred closed his eyes and cupped his hand. Silence returned and the crowd drew closer.

Was it a push or was it deliberate? The boob was touched, Blossom screamed, the office was like a bomb had burst, bodies flying for cover, doors opening as every soul tried to escape the melee at the same time. Fred stood in stunned disbelief. Blossom released her grip on the ceiling and came crashing down and one move grabbed her handbag and hauled herself out through the office door and out of sight.

It took sometime before normality returned to the office and everyone returned to go about they're duties in the quiet and industrious manner that had been previous but gradually we all got back into the business of paper work.

A nervous silence descended as we waited for the return of Blossom. Where had she gone in such haste and upset? The Chief is her good friend. Were they writing out statements for a discipline hearing?

After all he had not taken too lightly to the cling film that Loco had put across his private toilet. It was not the nicest thing in the world to be sitting there for your morning constitutional dump to find that your excreta is not leaving you to the depths it should normally do.

He was not happy but never did find out who had done the dirty deed. We had heard that fingerprinting the cling film was considered but doubted that any scenes of crime officer was brave enough to take on such a demanding task.

The demise of Blossom could be the revenge he was so longing for?

Hours seemed to pass until Blossom re-entered the office, serious faced and looking very flustered. "I've got something for you Fred, you dirty dog!" she announced. Here comes trouble we all thought as she went into her handbag.

"I've been queuing at the bank for ages," she said, " but finally got some." She slammed a £5 bag of 10p coins on the desk and continued, "Can we carry on with the scientific experiment in private without all these looking on?"

Fred's head hit the desk top as we could all imagine him thinking, "How the hell do I get out of this one?"

These humorous interludes and refreshing change of place of work did not stop the strange feelings I had experienced before. They never really left me but returned together with waking at night with the feeling of a ton of bricks on my chest, my windpipe totally blocked, fighting for breath and every ounce of air being taken out of my body. Terrified that I was at deaths' door, soaked with sweat and paranoid that a return to sleep would result in passing away for good.

I managed to cope with the situation, thinking it will pass and putting it down to over work, giving up smoking, hangovers but never ever thinking that it was anything more sinister. The busier I was the less I suffered until I was hit again by these feelings again. The quieter I was the more likely they would return.

The Criminal Injuries Compensation Board gave me the grand sum of £1200 for the watchstrap incident and we decided to put it towards buying airline tickets for a trip to Australia, life seemed to get a bit better. I had also been accepted to join the elite Regional Crime Squad, to me the ultimate unit for the professional detective.

Chapter Eleven
THE ULTIMATE DETECTIVE

I had achieved one of my goals of being an undercover detective on the "Queens Regional" as the DI at the time would exclaim when we mounted another operation to bring high-ranking law-breakers to justice. Long hours of mobile and static surveillance operations, armed with fast cars, electronic gismos, cameras and invariably firearms in the hope that we could strike at the heart of the organised crime gangs. Without exception the twenty squad officers would "get behind" the cars driven by our targets in the hope that eventually we would gather enough evidence to put them before the Courts.

A DCI and DI supervised the Branch Office with a Detective Superintendent and Detective Chief Superintendent who were based at the Regional Crime Squad HQ in Hertfordshire. The HQ staffs were accountable to a committee of representatives from the Police Authorities in the national police region.

Our branch office was in the No.5 Region that covered the counties of Essex, Suffolk, Norfolk, Cambridgeshire, Hertfordshire, Bedfordshire and Thames Valley (the joint police areas of Berkshire, Buckinghamshire and Oxfordshire). The RCS received their funding from the Police Authorities.

We had the capability and authority to follow and investigate any serious criminal activity in every corner of the United Kingdom but it was a natural process that, as we skirted the borders of the "smoke", our concentration was invariably drawn into London.

This did not bode very well with the top bosses in Essex and many a time we were criticised for being an extension of the Metropolitan Police and thus failing the public of our county who were paying us.

I was just so pleased to be on the "Squad" and did not give any thought to it being other than efficient and effective in its role in fighting crime wherever it was. In the first instance, getting used to the equipment and operational jargon used on surveillance was my main concern followed by gaining an acceptance within the twenty or so seasoned officers.

It did not take me long to find that we were subject to the whims and fancies of our immediate bosses, a DCI and DI, with the direction of the work depending on the results of static surveillance on a major distributor of amphetamines and other drugs, the illicit copying of video tapes, the lucid intelligence of a dodgy police informant and the occasional information provided by the more professionally capable officers.

I did not have any informants at the time and being the new boy was not in a position to openly find fault. I did however question in my own mind whether the level of work we were looking at was of the high grade you would expect of the top most investigative body and most costly in the country. Shouldn't' we be aiming higher and looking at the real Mr Big's? Making a real impression, effecting significant damage and not just picking at the pieces on the lower levels.

It was early days for me and I had a lot to learn.

TO AUS ON A SHOESTRING

When the handout from the Criminal Injuries Compensation Board landed on our doorstep we had decided to spend it on a trip to Australia. After all, the chances of us saving the grand sum of £1200 pounds were nil so we decided to blow it in one go on a holiday of a lifetime seeing Dorothy's sister on the other side of the world.

During the last few months of working at Chelmsford all the overtime I had worked, the days I had worked for other officers and two weeks unpaid leave allowed me to get 8 weeks off for the holiday. The Chief Constable had given his consent for the leave of absence after my DCI had approved it, saying that, "I had received the money as a result of bravery in the line of duty and that it was only fitting that the job reciprocate and allow the application."

My secondment to the RCS came up in between and the fact that I was going to be away for such a long period and that the branch were going to be a man short, did not go down well with the DCI and DI. The latter wanted me to cancel the holiday for three years until after my secondment but I would have lost the money I had paid for the paid tickets.

The holiday was brilliant as we expected but a lot more expensive than anticipated. It was just as well that we had cashed in an endowment policy to help pay for the unforeseen extras. Although we had struggled the whole experience was worth the effort.

We went swimming in shark-invested waters, snorkelling and just soaked up the sunrays in between barbecues and visits to the Blue Mountains and beyond. Only one thing disturbed me whilst away.

We were camping on a site beside the Cola River, west of Sydney, Dorothy's sister and brother-in-law had sailed up to us in their large power-boat that they moored just off the bank on which we had pitched our tent. We had a barbecue and whilst Clare and Karen, who were 10 and 9 years old respectively, settled down to sleep inside the tent, we had a beer and coffee with the others.

The river at that point is very fast running and about 50 yards wide, shallow with a small sandy beach on the campsite side but extremely deep on the other side. The water treacherously sweeps around this part and through mangrove roots that grow out of the outside edge of a very tight bend. Swimming in all parts of the river would dangerous and utterly stupid.

It was dark across the campsite with only the laughter and chatter of campers around their small fires when we heard the sound of splashing from the river and a muffled gurgling sound. Dorothy's brother-in-law said, "There's someone in the river!" and ran towards his dinghy moored a few feet away. Sister joined him and they rowed out to their powerboat. The engine roared into life and the beams of their spotlights filled the river surface all round them.

The light then caught sight of a man clinging desperately to some mangrove roots on the opposite. They coaxed the powerboat over to him and both dragged him with great difficulty onto the boat. It would have helped if the man had been clothed in something and could help himself. But almost paralytic drunk and without a stitch of clothing, the job was made that much more difficult.

Gripping wrists and then an ankle they eventually poured the collapsed figure into the well of the boat. By this time several mates of his had joined us on the riverbank, nearly all in the same condition but fortunately clothed they were offering inebriated advice and abusive suggestions on what could be done with him. He was delivered to their safe custody and we settled down to our coffee.

Sister and brother-in-law told us that it was not unusual for a group of blokes or women to shoot off to a campsite out in the wilds to have a binge or "beano" as we would call it. The raucous sounds of them enjoying themselves dissipated not long afterwards and we turned in for the night.

What seemed like only minutes later we were suddenly woken by the loudest blast of heavy metal music that I have ever heard! Being a fan, under normal circumstances, this would not have mattered to me but the girls shot up out of their beds terrified and on looking out of the tent door saw that so many couples with young families were having the same problems.

The source of the noise was a huge 4 x 4 truck beside which I could see a large tent with figures rolling about. I got dressed and walked over. As I approached in the darkness four shapes formed into two women and two comatose males lolloping on sun beds. One woman had her eyes open in a glazed dream and held a spilling glass of wine in one hand and cigarette, half burnt to two inches of hanging ash, in the other.

Intending to be as polite as possible but having to shout above the din of the blasting music coming from the 4 x 4 next to her, I said, "Can you turn the music down?" A broad gruff slurred Australian male voice replied, "Say please, you pommie bastard!" I turned to the grimy, dishevelled "T" shirt and fly-open shorts where the request had come from and said, "You've woken up half the campsite now do us a favour and turn the noise down. Please!" "No. Now fuck off!" retorted the voice.

I opened the 4 x 4 door and turned the radio off. The creaking rubber of flip-flop sandals then disturbed the peace and quiet as the voice flew towards me from his pit. "You stuffed-up bastard. Think you own the place", he screamed as he threw a punch at me.

Being sober, I had the distinct advantage and ducked to one side, kicking out I felt my bare foot sinking into his open fly and groin. The thought of my skin touching his revolted me but a smack with the back of my hand across the side of his face helped him to go further downwards. He thumped to the hard ground and moaned as the woman and the other couple joined us.

My immediate reaction was to prepare for an onslaught but the woman venomously booted the prone figure on the floor saying, "You stupid, ignorant fucking bastard you deserved that, now have some more!" She then laid into him, kicking, punching and finally sitting on top of his prostate body slapping him and causing his head to rock from side to side. It was almost as if she had been waiting for this opportunity for years and now it was here she was taking full advantage of it.

I had achieved what I had wanted and went back to the tent and bed. Daylight came quickly and the noise of voices and sirens filled the river valley.

Dorothy looked out of the tent and announced, "You've gone and done it now haven't you? The place is full of police! I told you that it was stupid to hit that bloke. Now you are going to spend the rest of the holiday in prison!"

I went into a cold sweat as I saw the officers outside but then realised they were searching the river and the banks on both sides. One officer then said to the two heads poking out of our tent, "Some idiot went swimming in here last night and hasn't come back." We told him about the naked bloke and he said that the same guy had gone back in the water.

As he spoke one of his colleagues shouted from the bank opposite, "He's here. Bring the boat over." We took the girls over to the camp café while the Police got on with their work.

A little later I saw the heavy metal guy walking towards the water with a lilo under his arm. A child with him was begging to have the lilo and the guy was hitting him saying, "Piss off. I'm having it!" The kid in tears ran back to his Mum who again had the half ash cigarette. When the guy passed me I saw a lovely black eye that he had to go with his obvious hangover. I was sure that it was his wife that had given that. To my relief he did not take any notice of me and walked passed me to relax on the river.

The remainder of the holiday went well but it did ponder at one time if there was something about me that attracted trouble. Like the time a few months later when me, Dorothy and the girls were walking through Nottingham City Centre during a visit to relatives. One of the Nottingham Football teams was playing at home and the opposing supporters had decided to kick shit out of each other in front of us and the other Saturday lunchtime shoppers.

A uniform WPC and her taller but younger male colleague were struggling to restrain a drunken shaven head youth whilst his girlfriend was shouting obscenities and trying to prise the youth away. Other friends were joining in trying to release the arrested youth from the grip of the two officers. The male officers' police helmet went up in the air as the struggle became more violent. I could not see any help arriving so stepped in to help the officers.

Pulling the main instigators off the officers and advising the girlfriend that more support was just round the corner I held onto the youth with the male officer while the WPC radioed for more assistance.

A few minutes later the youth was arrested and placed in the back of a police van along with me. The officer who took hold of me would not listen to the explanation that I was just helping and I did not have the opportunity to show my warrant card and police badge. I could see the girls and Dorothy, by this time, looking quite bemused by my predicament but offering neither solace nor verification. The original male officer turned up at last and took me out of the van.

He thanked me and apologised for the mix up and the van sped off with the youth. Dorothy uttered words like, "Serves you right for interfering" and "perhaps you'll learn your lesson one day." I said I did not think I attracted trouble and I was just doing my job. She did not reply and we continued with our shopping.

TO ARMS!

I was a qualified "shot", trained in the use of firearms, when I was seconded onto the Squad but I was so pleased when put on a firearms course to give me an insight into the use of guns by the RCS. My experience until then was rather jaded.

Ten years previously I had passed a firearms test and been given the authority to carry firearms on duty. I got my "name on the wall" to be one of the elite "shots" soon after I had joined.

The "snowdrops" were short of young officers trained in firearms and relied on the expertise of the many older officers who had served in World War 2 and done National Service in the armed forces.

The former were now less fit and National Service had long been abolished. It was 1969 and the troubles in Northern Ireland had started in earnest and this had spilled over to the mainland. Police Forces had been instructed to train up officers by the Home Office in readiness for an escalation of the problems.

A boyhood hero of mine was the firearms instructor. His sister was our next-door neighbour when I was a boy and my mates and I used to look in awe when he drove up in his Police Jaguar and parked it outside her house whilst he went in for a cup of tea.

One of the reasons for me joining the police was now standing before me about to instruct me how to be a copper as good as him. He was by now somewhat, worse the wear for years of sitting in a police car and had a large paunch belly but he still had that authoritive bearing I so much admired.

In khaki combat trousers, open neck shirt and calf length brown American Army boots he had a holster strapped to his left thigh with an automatic handgun poking out of the top. I was late for the two days of training as I had been to Court and apologised for not being to attend earlier.

Although he was standing in a small trench below me he was still an imposing figure as he held a rifle in his hands across his outstretched arms. Cordite smelling gunfire echoed around us as other trainees fired rifles from prone positions in the trench either side of him.

He threw the rifle at me saying, "Catch this. You missed small arms this morning but you can soon catch up." I caught the rifle across my forearms and hoped that this was the correct way of doing so and trusted that it would not go off.

"See those targets down there?" he shouted above the din. I could not see anything threw the sea mist and gun smoke that was slowly covering the firing range, except a grass mound some two hundred yards away. The only reason I saw it was that the others were firing in that direction.

"Get eighteen shots out of twenty in that target and you are through to the next session", the admired instructor screamed. He must have seen me screwing my eyes up to get a better idea of where he meant, as he added, "Those white round discs on the bank." I could just about see some white plate size dishes on wooden boards.

"You should have no problem hitting them with that. It's a 303. You can hit a pimple on black mans' bum at that distance. The best rifle the British Army ever had!" he proudly announced.

I took a long look at the piece of army surplus that weighed heavy across my arms. The only gun I had ever handled before then was at the Kursaal amusement park rifle range and that was a toy air rifle compared to this killing machine.

The instructor reassured me, "You won't have any trouble constable!" and helped me down into the trench. Twenty shots at "Christ knows what" later and the green flag from the marker officer at the grass mound shouting, "Nineteen", and I passed the first session. "Pistols, tomorrow", commanded the instructor. I was sure that he had taken a shine to me and allowed me to pass the test, as I was his sisters' ex-neighbour, until we all got back to the nick. All the trainees had the same exclamations of disbelief that qualifying was so easy with the 303 being "that easy" to use. I was not such a hotshot!

It did not stop me from being proud of myself when I got home and over the dinner table exuded confidence, as to how well I had done. My Dad was not so convinced. He did not say much, frowned at my excitement but only politely and wryly laughed at my success. I did not know until some years later exactly what he was thinking.

The following morning we were back on the training range. Just on the eastern edge of the town, the range was on land known as Shoebury Barracks. Ministry of Defence land since the 1870's I was elated to be following in my Grandfathers footsteps who was stationed there when he was in the Royal Artillery in the early 1900's.

"Same procedure as before, son", the instructor said as he held, in front of him, a revolver pistol that resembled something out of a wild-west film. He slapped the automatic in his holster and said, "Get one of these when you grow up!" He smiled and showed me how to load my six-gun. Putting bullets in the chamber he then swung it shut and handed it, handle first, to me.

"Get in the pit there and fire six into the target", he pointed at the mound we had been firing at the previous day. Facing us stood the crouching cardboard shapes of an oncoming enemy. Only twelve feet away and not likely to hit back, it was easy to get six out of six. Okay one went into his foot but another did hit him straight between the eyes!

"Well done. Now rapid fire!" he went on further and demonstrated a quick draw, western style, from his holster and shot so many bullets into the target with his automatic that I lost count. The centre of the cardboard figure was obliterated.

With no holsters to wear, revolvers were held at the hip and swung upwards as the trainees drew their weapons in a host of different stances and shot at the enemy in a machine gun staccato lasting just seconds. It was like a hundred crackerjack fireworks set off at the same time. Without ear protection or goggles, the sharp cracking lingered on indefinitely in my ears while the gun smoke hung in the air above and debris and splinters floated down from the targets.

"Safety first", said my hero and, "Lower your weapons." With gasps of both relieved tension and anticipation we pointed our guns to the ground, checked our chambers and individually shouted, "Clear."

Another instructor checked what was left of the targets and with the exception of one target that had twelve shots put into it, he reported that all but two Pratts had passed the test.

"Right." Shouted the hero, "With the exception of the two pratts who hit the same target. Everyone back to the firing range at base for cleaning and safety procedure. You two bastards get in the bloody hole and try again."

The afternoon continued in the indoor firing range at the police station and that evening I was told that I was a fully-fledged "shot" and my name was "on the wall." This meant that my name was now on the list of authorised firearms officers displayed on the office wall in the CID. I was licensed to kill, well not quite, but it did mean that I could go out and shoot people when or if the time came. That night I lay in bed in a less than euphoric mind contemplating if I really wanted to be with other guys with the same inexperience as me.

The chance came no so long later when I was called out early one morning. The uniform officer who rang on the doorbell said, "Report in straight away. All shots are wanted at the nick. They reckon the IRA is digging a tunnel under the garrison wall." As I got dressed I thought, "Typical Irish don't they know that there is no guard on the sea wall and you can just walk into the garrison after ducking under the wire fence as all the school kids in the area regularly did!"

Dressed in full uniform I arrived at the nick to the comments, "Why have you got your uniform on?" from my mates who were all dressed in civvie clothes. Strange but most were dressed, uniformly, in woolly fisherman's roll neck jumpers. All the same colour of creamy white and all smelling like a damp herd of sheep. "Buggered if I am going to get my own gear messed up!" I replied but knowing that I did not have a woolly jumper anyway.

We were all issued with a revolver and sealed envelope containing six bullets. "Don't take the bullets out of the envelope until ordered to do so", said the leader, a very serious bushy eye-browed Sergeant dressed in a dark blue boiler suit. "What if they start shooting at us?" came the obvious question from a woolly jumper.

"Then you ask for permission to load up", he replied. "Fuck that. If he think that is going to happen, then he must think we are stupid!" someone else muttered.

We all then climbed into the old J4 Austin Van with our guns in one pocket and the bullets in the other. Some complaints that the duty driver had not washed the van out after he had taken the last lot of lost dogs to the pound. We sat either side on the bench seats rather like a group of parachutists waiting for the off in their air transport on some clandestine operation.

One shot commented that it would only smell of the overpowering "Jeyes" toilet cleaning fluid if it had been washed as the bushy eye-browed Sergeant peered into the pitch black of the van. Quite calmly but strongly he said, "What the fuck are you doing in there, Smith?"

We all turned and looked at PC Smith who was curled up in the corner behind the drivers' seat and until now had not been noticed by any of us. Smith considered himself to be a cut above the rest, having served in the British Transport Police and then a short while in the Armed Forces.

Although he had showed only mediocre prowess at training school, he was always extolling his own virtues in the opinion that there was nothing else that the job nor the world in fact could teach him that he didn't already know.

Slightly older than me but with the same length of service of just over one year, he was not a popular person with his peers.

The Sergeant anticipated the reply before Smith could open his mouth, "You are not an authorised shot! You were bloody hopeless and failed the tests miserably. So give the fucker back to me!" Smith protested and remonstrated that he was just as good if not better than us but was persuaded that the Sergeant meant business when threatened with a fizzer if he did not leave the vehicle straight away.

Smith clambered and stumbled through and over our legs as we tried to make way. As he was doing so he clumsily delved into his pockets to retrieve the gun as instructed. To the horror of those assembled in the tight space he drew the gun out and his passage was made all the more awkward as we dodged the pointing barrel.

In a huff he jumped from the van and strode off still holding the revolver. "Gun?" the Sergeant shouted. It was more like natural reaction that everyone saw what was likely to happen. No! He didn't fire it but the next worst thing.

The gun sailed through the air from Smiths' hand with no chance of it being caught by the Sergeant. Unused to such situations, I was mouth opened and awe-struck but the rest of the mob in the van tried to find what cover they could in the tight, sardine can we were sitting in.

The Sergeant missed the catch, the revolver hit the concrete of the police station yard car park and one shot rang out above the shouts of men in panic. "The stupid bastard had one up the spout!" shouted someone from cover.

Smith disappeared into the Police Station followed by the Sergeant intent on murder. We waited a few moments until the Sergeant returned saying, "He's locked up until I get back. Let's go and get some terrorists."

The IRA was not digging a tunnel. The Irish couple living in the terraced house backing onto the garrison had decided to knock down an internal wall during the night much to the annoyance of their neighbours.

When I got back to the Police Station I struck my name off the typed list of authorised officers on the wall and noticed that the handwritten name of Smith had also been erased and the Sergeant's signature was beside the alteration.

I did not like the idea of being a "shot" until I could feel confident that my own side would not hurt me. This did not change and my opinions were even more reinforced by the behaviour of an armed Regional Squad Officer who attended a kidnap scene a few years later.

I was returning from Court at Southend to Westcliff Police Station when a call went out over the radio that a deranged man, armed with a shotgun, had attacked a woman in a house on our patch and had ran off into the streets still brandishing the gun.

I picked up two other officers and unarmed, as all other converging patrolmen were, made our way to the area where the gunman had last been seen. En-route we were ordered by the Police HQ Control Room to contain the man but keep a safe distance from him while an armed unit was raised.

Within seconds of arriving in the area we saw the man running, still carrying his shotgun, down the road in front of us. The police radio airwaves were in constant use by the controller instructing patrols to set up roadblocks at strategic points around the town. We then saw a Police Traffic Motorcyclist ahead talking to a uniform patrolman who was sitting in his parked patrol car about 200 yards away. The gunman was running straight towards them with shotgun poised menacingly.

The officer with me frantically tried to interrupt the outward radio messages to warn the patrolmen but the gunman was on top of them in seconds. The motorcyclist shook, startled as the nozzle of the shotgun slid under the rim of his helmet and edged against his neck.

In silent compliance the motorcyclist hesitantly raised his arms away from his controls as the gunman kept the gun to his neck with one hand and opened the patrol car rear passenger door with the other.

Leaving the motorcyclist suspended with arms aloft the gunman sat on the back seat and transferred the direction of the shotgun to the neck of patrolman driver in the front. The passenger door closed and the patrol car sped away with the driver held hostage.

My mate finally managed to get through on the radio and the ensuing instructions were to follow at distance so as not to alarm or antagonise the gunman. The patrol car made its way onto the main dual carriageway road heading towards London.

We were joined by other police cars all keeping a respectable and safe distance behind. We blocked the road off to stop any other vehicles passing and causing any possible complications, quietly intent on ensuring that our mate in the patrol car in front came out of this unscathed.

The car turned off to the left and entered a small industrial estate and stopped a short distance in amongst a conglomeration of factories, waste ground and work yards. The control room instructed crews to take up positions around the perimeter, still containing the situation so as not to endanger anyone, particularly the patrolman who was still being held at gunpoint.

My car crew and me took up positions in a stonemasons yard and had a good viewpoint where we could see the patrol car still with its two occupants. People in the yard were starting to get inquisitive and a closer check made us aware that many of the workers were within gunshot distance and in danger themselves.

Some of them had seen that the gunman had now got out of the car and was sitting on a wall with his shotgun held at the head of the officer beside him.

Realising what was now happening in front of them some less sensible workers were making comments, "Shoot the bastard" and calling to their workmates to come and have a look. One crane operator was sitting some 30 feet up gleefully shouting that some TV filming was taking place and inviting others to come up and see. As quietly as we possibly could we coerced indignant workers away from the unrealised dangers for themselves and the kidnapped officer.

As our efforts took hold, work stopped in the yard, and the owner objected strongly to our demands for quiet and responsible behaviour. He ordered us out of his premises even though we tried to explain what was happening. We ignored his requests and his threats that he would complain to our "Superiors" and tried to encourage restraint on the excitement that was now spreading across the yard. Our only thought was for the traffic officer and what he was going through.

Two other workers had joined the crane operator who was still shouting from his vantage point. All were refusing to come down and receiving encouragement to stay put by his co-workers. I started to climb the crane rigging but was aware that to do so would put me, and my uniform, in full view of the gunman. I did not want to worsen the situation but felt I had to do something about the men on the crane for their own safety. The running commentary by the crane man suddenly changed when he said, "Some fucking idiot is walking up to the copper."

By this time I had got to a point where I could see clearly, the gunman, the patrolman and a tall bloke in a suit approaching them. It was a Regional Crime Squad Officer who I knew had been on witness protection duty. I stretched a little bit upwards and saw one of our senior officers', a DCI standing nearby.

The RCS Officer was talking to the gunman, and after a while the patrolman got up and walked away. The RCS Officer then sat on the wall a short distance away as the gunman still held the shotgun. This time pointed at the RCS Officer.

I ducked down to keep myself out of sight and continued to try and get the men down. Suddenly the crane man and his two mates were clambering down in panic. "That idiot has given the shotgun bloke a gun", he shouted as he pushed passed me, treading on my fingers as he went and followed by his two mates in equal fearful mood.

I peered over from my cover and saw the RCS Officer still talking to the gunman who now had the shotgun on his lap, but pointing at the Officer. I then saw a handgun lying on the wall between the two of them. I could not understand why this was but hoped there was a rational explanation.

It was pandemonium in the yard below with the owner and the workers in total disbelief at the inaptitude and stupidity of the police in giving the gunman another gun and endangering them further. We were more concerned that their feelings were nothing compared to the officer talking to the gunman and the need for us to keep things quiet whilst the incident was resolved.

The gunman eventually gave himself up and all was sorted out fortunately without any injuries. The RCS Officer was commended for his bravery but all of us on that day thought that what he did erred on the side of stupidity, was completely unnecessary and put so many others in danger. We could not understand why he did not wait for the firearms unit and trained negotiating officer to attend. Everything was safely "contained". The only time that panic came on board was when he "gave" the gunman his revolver and the opportunity to use it in addition to his own shotgun.

The yard owner was dissuaded from complaining about the RCS Officer and us and apologised for his attitude. One of his workers explained that the owner had lost his teenage son not long before. He had gone on a fishing trip and not returned. All efforts to find any trace of him had been unsuccessful so he was particularly sensitive.

The same RCS Officer was subject of an enquiry after he shot at an innocent passing car in London some years later. Nothing was done about it but his colleagues presented him with a bullet-ridden car door at his farewell night just to remind him of the incident. It was all a laugh and more twinned with the theatre than the reality that I considered important where firearms were concerned.

With this and my nasty experience at Enfield after the misuse of a firearm by a police officer, I still had to be convinced that the RCS was going to have a more responsible approach to firearms.

Officers on the Regional Crime Squad carried firearms with a regularity demanded by the surroundings and the areas in which they operated. Banks, post offices, betting shops and every place where there was the likelihood of ready cash were a target for the criminal. London where we spent most of our duty time suffered upwards of three armed robberies per day and guns were the recognised tool of the defence of criminal turf.

Headlines in the press regularly showed the latest robbery. Even nine years before, in 1972, the Daily Sketch headline article next to me being "Hot and Bovvered" reported an armed robbery in the West End. It was a commonplace occurrence and therefore something I had to contend with if I was to be an effective member of the RCS.

The Firearms Training Course I went on was a very pleasant surprise completely different and professionally organised unlike the previous training course led by my hero. Teaching wide reaching and secure methods of ensuring that all the firearms team were safe and secure from the unlikely event of "friendly fire". The emphasis was on close operational and personal issues and the wider areas of safety that could involve the security of innocent bystanders and passers-by.

A psychological assessment of all trainees was taken seriously and many did not come up to the grade required. Control and mental aptitude was of the most paramount importance. Essex Police was the forerunner for the effective but secure use of firearms by police officers in the country at that time and I was delighted and confident to carry a firearm with my colleagues.

This was not the case though when on joint operations with other branches from forces outside of Essex. The training and skills were not compatible and at times dangerous attitudes jeopardised many and undermined safety.

GUN CRAZY

Whilst working with officers from the Metropolitan Police "Flying Squad", a nickname for a unit that specialised in the investigation of armed robbery offences, we played cards and other games to pass the boring time spent on static observations, or stakeouts.

Some guys used to take their games seriously, although the money stakes were quite low, the prestige of winning and beating someone from the "Constabularies", as we were known, would be a far greater prize. Arguments would get out of proportion and egos dented at the drop of a hat.

When the threatening Flying Squad detective drew his gun and pointed it at the Essex officer saying, "If you take a card off the pack that way again I will shoot your fucking balls off!" We knew something was amiss.

Not that we had cheat in our midst or someone that could not take the competition but a dangerous mind blown potential killer in the disguise of upholder of the law. After we emerged from our sheltered places of cover, common sense prevailed, much to our relief, and the DI, "stood us down for debrief". This meant that the operation was terminated and had to return to our branch office where we would talk through the days work. We did not have any joint armed operations with MET officers again during my secondment.

Whatever the training methods the number of armed robberies took a significant drop after it was made obvious to those who were committing these offences that we meant business and some of them were shot, fatally on occasions. There was no "shoot to kill" policy but more and more police units were being armed as a matter of routine as gun crime increased.

No nonsense "hitting them on the pavement" became a catchphrase as more gangs were taken out. These villains had considered themselves invincible until the risks outgrew the profits. The takings from robberies of banks started to drop with the advent of the credit card so the soft target was the betting shop and street corner off licences. Profits were smaller but the risk was also small. Until they started to get shot by the police!

We had received information that a team were going to hit a Scandinavian Bank in the City of London and carried out weeks of observations and surveillance to put together the evidence to get them for conspiracy. A much better option was to charge this offence to cut down on possible injuries or fatalities but you had to have the luck.

One of the gangs' girlfriends worked at the bank, they had put together their "happy bag" containing the guns, masks, gloves etc and stashed it in a lock-up garage near their addresses in east London and information was being monitored for the signs to identify when they were going to do the job.

A tunnel was mentioned and thoughts went towards the possibility of a hit on one of the banks' security vehicles in one of the many tunnels that existed in the London area. Blackwall and Rotherhithe were too close to their homes so it could the Dartford Crossing under the Thames between Essex and Kent. Since it was built it was a robbery waiting to happen, nearly two miles long between two county police areas and a known radio "blackspot". The ideal, extremely busy road network waiting to be clogged up to add to the confusion and assist a comfortable getaway if planned right.

They could not have planned it better, as the day they decided to do the robbery was when half our staff was off sick with the flu and the remainder were at Crown Court giving evidence.

We could not field a surveillance team and reluctantly had to pass the operation on to the Metropolitan Police. They rarely appeared enthusiastic to carry out operations passed to them from outside the MET, possibly as the info came from the "Constabularies, Yokels or Swede bashers", coppers considered to be of a lower class than them and therefore not so worthy of their efforts.

It is sad to reflect in this way but unfortunately this was the attitude of too many MET officers at that time. Also we did suspect that they were still bruised by an internal investigation, called Operation Countryman, led by Essex Police senior officers into alleged corruption in the MET CID and Serious Crime Units. This had left a bad taste in many a mouth and reflected in attitudes at lower rank level, even though we had nothing to do with the enquiry.

The operation was taken on and the surveillance team "got behind" the villains. I met the DI in charge of the team the following day in the bar at New Scotland Yard and he told me his tale of woe.

Holding his heavily bandaged arm he related the story, "We took them to the M1, there were two cars, the red Ford with four in and an old Avenger, with the plates of a Volvo following on behind, with two others and the happy bag." I didn't interrupt and let him continue after he took a sip from his glass of scotch.

"They then took off, like shit off a shovel north on the M1. I tried to get through to your lot at Chelmsford to find out the current SP but it was fucking hopeless." (These were the pre-mobile phone days and radio was the only form of contact). He continued, "You can imagine. We did not know what to think. Your info did not say anything about leaving London. I had to send one car off at the services to buy maps but the bastards just kept going. We were touching 120 mph at one time. Through fucking thick fog. I nearly called it off. It got quite hairy. The fog was awful, a pea souper. Wish we had the gear from Aldermaston to slow them down."

"What is that then?" I asked. He replied, "They're working on some computer that we can put into the targets car to slow them down. Only trouble is that it can also make them go faster and you could crash them. Come in handy if you did not like them. Wouldn't it?" I agreed wholeheartedly.

He took another breath and continued, "We were tooled up so you know the score. We had to get permission to carry arms through each Force Area but on the M1 we went through three areas in the space of 30 minutes. By the time we got permission we had gone through and hit another. It was fucking manic!" I could imagine the problems, Chief Constables asking the most in depth questions before giving consent while the incessant radio talk of a mobile surveillance was taking place.

He went on, "Anyway between Birmingham and Manchester we turned off and ended up in this little town nearly into Wales. Thank fuck they spoke English."

I looked for him to explain and he added, "You know what the Welsh are like. Speak English normally and change to Welsh when a foreigner is present. You know?"

He didn't wait for a reply and started off again, "They stashed the Ford and struck out, all of them crammed in the Avenger. That motor couldn't half shift! It must have been sup'ed-up. No sooner had we got to the town centre than they were out and hit the security van."

"We had a bit of time to get the locals and they got there quite quick but not before we put the challenges in. We had to, we weren't happy with the way it was going. It would have been nice to leave it until they got back to the Ford but one of Security men started to put up a fight. The one who had the sawn-off pointed it at the guard. One of my blokes heard him say, "That's it. You've asked for it!""

I thought, "Very convenient! Exactly what you want to hear when you want to start shooting. Protection of life and prevention of injury and all that!"

One of ours took a pop shot at the sawn-off target and then all hell let loose. It was like Tombstone, fucking lead flying everywhere. That's how I got this", pointing to his arm, "Bit of shrapnel they reckon."

"Who was shooting from their side then", I asked. "Two with handguns and the one with the sawn-off, although he was hit on the first shot. He's dead and the other two one slightly hurt and the other critical – not expected to make it. Shame! Stupid bastards shouldn't have started it" he relished and smiled.

All sorts of things were going through my mind, "Did they put in a challenge? Did the robbers have the chance to lay down their weapons? Before I could ask he said, "They've already started the enquiry. Yorkshire Force is doing it. Bastards started asking questions before we could properly debrief." I thought, "He meant before they could get their story together!"

He must have read my mind as his next words were, "Better get your books in order as they will be coming to you to verify the info you gave us." He gave me the doubting look of, "You're in the shit mate if you can't give the right answers!" I told him not to worry, that it was rock solid but knew that I had to check the operational files to make sure all the "T's" were crossed and the "I's" were dotted". There was always an element of doubt of a possible loose end that could trip you up on such enquiries.

The intelligence files of Essex HQ were my immediate next call.

The ensuing months and several interviews later by the internal investigation team saw us all vindicated and verdicts at Inquests verified our authority and that we had carried out our lawful duty.

Gradually the attitude of the robbers changed as more were shot however it was more apparent that we, the perpetrators of the law had to get our their act together and formulate a joint strategy in the use of firearms. No longer could we do our own thing within our own borders when the travelling gun carrying criminal had no such boundaries.

A TURNING POINT

I could not put my finger on the exact reason I felt the way I did but I always had the feeling that I could never reach the stage of complete acceptability from the other officers in the RCS Branch. I found that the less adept officers were being castigated by the stronger ones. Officers I had known for years as good reasonable people would pick on others who had not come up to scratch whilst out on surveillance. These outcasts were often given menial tasks and isolated or even ostracised "to get rid of them" as one of the bosses would say.

One officer was terrorised by an exploding firework that had been placed inside the engine compartment of his own car. A gallery of officers stood at the upstairs window overlooking the Branch Office car park as the victim went to his car. "Wait for it!" said the DS, who had planted the "bomb". The firework exploded and the officer leapt from his car in such a state of shock that he fell over on shaking legs.

He pulled himself together in total defiance of the baying crowd. He fanned the smoke as he lifted the bonnet to check for damage. Finding none he slammed the bonnet down, gave a finger "V" sign to the still laughing figures at the window above and drove off home.

Playing practical jokes was part of the natural morale boosting and high-spirited banter throughout my time in the Service but this episode was beyond the point of acceptability. I am sure that my comments, regarding this incident to the bosses, was the start of a rot that was to set in a few months later. I considered that much harm could be done to the individual who was an excellent officer and could split the opinions of the officers, some of whom had stated their disgust but had not been eager to say so to the bosses.

I took my feelings to the bosses about this incident. They did not take this too well and accused me of stirring up trouble unnecessarily. I had also expressed concern with the DS who I believed was not conforming to standard procedures with a registered informant under his control. There were strict guidelines set down by the Home Office in any dealings with paid police informants who had to be registered and controlled by senior supervising officers,

Alarm bells started to ring when I interviewed one of the persons who had been arrested on the basis of the DS's informants' intelligence. It was obvious that the arrested man had been set-up by the informant but unfortunately it was his word against the informants' without any evidence to support his accusation. At Court his version was not believed and he was sentenced to imprisonment.

In the situation where results were the key issue and not how we got them it was very difficult to convince the bosses that something was wrong without putting myself on a pedestal. I was about to be knocked off!

I was not popular with the DI on the squad and had been told that he did not want me on it. Another detective told me that at the time I was seconded the DI wanted one of his closest friends, another DS, to take the vacancy but had been over-ruled by our HQ. Until then I could not understand why he was so caustic towards me and unappreciative of any work that I carried out.

Another situation was to seal my fate.

The DI had been late to a meeting with some senior officers during a major investigation into a bank robbery. I, like others from our Squad, was asked why he was not present. None of us knew.

When he arrived he received a bollocking for being late and then decided to take it out on me. I would not accept his tirade of abuse directed at me in front of the other officers and we adjourned to an office where a violent, verbal and physical, argument ensued. At one time the Chief Inspector, whose office we were in came to break us up, but he was given short shrift and told to, "Fuck off!" by both of us in unison.

I had seen enough of the RCS and decided reluctantly to return to CID. It did cross my mind that in the league the RCS worked it was just as well to be leaving relatively unscathed. It could have been worse, "being fitted up" with a crime or accidentally injured or even shot may have been the result. Such was the way I felt! It was certainly a safer prospect to leave.

A strange coincidence occurred shortly after I had left the RCS when I went to my bank. An old school mate of mine was an Account Manager at the branch and we would usually have a laugh and chat when I visited. On this occasion he had quite a serious and concerned look on his face as he asked me into his office. As far as I could remember my overdraft was not too excessive and although the Australia trip was costly my finances were pretty sound.

He sat me down, cleared his throat nervously and said, "I don't know how to put this. But I had a telephone call from someone, who said he was the head of the RCS, while you were away in Australia."

I was quite intrigued as it was quite often that banks and other financial institutions were contacted to gain intelligence on criminals but was astounded when he continued saying, " He said he was carrying out an enquiry regarding police corruption and wanted to know if you had received any large sums of money."

I was shocked and angry and blurted, "What did you say?" He said, "I told him to go through the legal channels and asked him his name, rank and where he was based. He didn't reply but said you had gone to Australia, which I obviously already knew, and honest policeman didn't have that sort of money. He did sound a bit tipsy!"

I threw lots of questions at my manager friend to try and identify the caller but really could not satisfy myself however I did have suspicions who it might be.

The next day I went to the Complaints and Discipline Department at Essex Police Headquarters. This would be the investigation team who would carry out such an enquiry. I took with me copies of my bank statements to show my finances. I told them that I knew I did not have to prove my innocence but felt I had to. They insisted that there was no need to and vehemently and categorically stated that no such enquiry was taking place.

I was grateful, but the fact that someone had made this assertion, upset me terribly. I tried several times using different methods to try and identify the voice, even visiting a pub, visited by the RCS officers, with my bank manager mate but to no avail.

I had gone through so much, worked hours and hours to get the time off and tried to get some repayment for the horror of the "Watch Strap Incident" but been kicked in the teeth from all directions.

But now I had to let the matter rest, forget it and get on with normal CID work.

Chapter Twelve
THE SHERRIFF OF CANVEY

Canvey Island renowned for its Holiday Caravan Parks, oil refineries and gas terminals all on a spit of land reclaimed from the middle of the River Thames over the previous fifty years. Devastated by the horrendous floods of 1953, the island was now a thriving community living on plots of land that once were the holiday homes of Londoners between the two world wars.

With land at that time costing, sometimes, as little a £5 per acre, Canvey was somewhere that people could spend quality time away from the smog and dirt of the city. As time progressed wooden shacks turned into brick built bungalows and houses and shops and industry followed close behind. It was a place you either hated or loved to bits.

I fell between the two, I loved to work there but could not live there, preferring the sanctuary of the high ground of Southend, at the same time ensuring that I kept abreast of the regular flood warnings that were posted on the police station notice board.

With an Inspector in charge and a complement of about twenty men and a CID of four detective constables and me we were all well known in the village and treated to respect from the majority of our law abiding citizens.

In one pub the publican, who insisted on calling the Inspector, "Marshall", gave me a rapturous welcome to his customers as, "the new Sheriff of this one horse town". I was assured it was their way of accepting me into the community!

The Island did have its fair share of villains but as usual these were by far outnumbered by the honest people who relied upon us. Once again it was the very small minority who run the majority of others ragged with their criminal behaviour.

THE UNSAVOURY

The unsavoury was not confined to the public especially when confronted with police officers that would sail close to the wind and use individuals' frailty and weakness to line their own pockets and improve their personal prestige.

On Christmas Eve I received a teleprinter message stating that a prisoner had escaped and requesting that we made a visit to his wife and family who were living on Canvey.

It was strange that this prisoner had decided to run away as, in three months time he would have completed his sentence. Our curiosity was answered when we saw his wife and three year old son. The woman coughed and wheezed from a bronchial infection and the boy had chicken pox spots all over his body.

A clean house, but in disarray, greeted us with brightness in a corner of a cheap plastic Christmas tree decked in tinsel and bright coloured paper chains drooped in the corner, as if about to collapse. A half smoked cigarette burnt in an ashtray on the arm of a tatty armchair beside a small coal fire.

"Smoking is not good for you in your condition. Is it?" my detective mate said to her. "I don't smoke", she replied with a splutter and then tut her lips as she realised her mistake.

"Have you heard from Tony?" I asked, as I looked at the Polaroid photograph of her, Tony and their son, displayed on the mantelpiece. Dressed in the identical outfit she had on now and the photo depicting the very same droopy Christmas tree gave its' obvious conclusions.

She sat arms crossed, pulling them up against her chest and shrugged her shoulders. She gazed into the depths of the floor, not wanting to look at either of us officers for fear of giving something else away.

"Look at me please?" I asked and she reluctantly pulled her face up frowning with annoyance. I continued, "It's Christmas. I do not want to be running around after Tony over the holiday. Tell him to be at the nick before 6.00pm on Boxing Day and we can be friends. Okay?"

Her face lit up, she leapt up from her chair and threw her arms around me, planting a smacker of a kiss on my cheek she said, "Thank you, We need him here just now." I nodded in agreement, "I appreciate that. Just make sure he gives himself up in two days time."

Whether he was there in the house or nearby did not matter. My partner said nothing but his silence was sufficient for me to know that he agreed with my Christmas spirit.

At 5.45pm Boxing Day Tony turned up at the police station. Holdall of clothes and Christmas presents in his hand and tuned into returning to complete his sentence.

As normal I interviewed him while we waited for his escort to take him back. We had to find out where he had been, what he had been up to, how he had survived without food and shelter and what offences he had committed whilst he was a fugitive.

"Friends all over looked after me. That's all!" was his reply, knowing that if he said his wife had looked after him she would be in serious trouble. I shook my head in disbelief and he took this as, perhaps, a reason for saying more because of my festive lenience. He leaned forward across the desk between us, even though we were in a room on our own, he looked from side to side to make sure nobody else could hear us and said, "You better watch out for (he named a bloke). He wanted me to do a blagging down near Brighton. He had a shooter and a car already for me to do it."

I asked, "What sort of blagging?" He replied, "Some rich gits house. Loads of smutter apparently. I told him to fuck off. I've only got three months to do. With the extra week or so I will get for going over the wall. He'd got to be fucking joking. You know me. I am not a blagger and guns put the shit up me."

After a few more questions and in-depth discussion the prison van arrived and transported him away.

The following morning a Detective Sergeant from the RCS telephoned me asking, "What's happened about the bloke, Tony, who is over the wall on your patch?"

I had a suspicion that this was going to go further and smiling said, "He had his Christmas at home and gave himself up yesterday. He's gone back to the nick."

"Fuck!" was the response, "We heard that he was going to do a burglary down in the West Country. We've been on stand-by with the firearms unit all over Christmas. Fuck!"

"Well he obviously hadn't got any intention of doing it. His missus and son were ill and he gave himself up yesterday," I said and allowed myself a smirk of satisfaction.

I continued as the caller at the other end went silent, "Are you sure your information was correct and it was not a set up?" There was no response just thoughtful silence!

"Or was it that you fancied a Christmas earning lots of dosh on treble overtime!" I said with an obvious bitterness that he knew reflected my disappointment of having to come off the RCS.

I wanted to say more and accuse him of the set up and earning overtime by false pretences but decided to report the incident to my bosses. I knew that such an operation would cost thousands of pounds and would have to be authorised by a Chief Constable. The DS was now in deep shit!

I had my doubts that it was legal and had to be investigated by our Complaints and Discipline Department. I never did know the result of the enquiry and was not really that concerned to find out, assuming that the powers that be would take appropriate steps to ensure that this would not happen again.

THE ROPE

The next episode of my experiences is perhaps the worst. After it I certainly changed my attitude to life both in and out of the job.

Early after my transfer to Canvey my ridiculous desperation to prove myself manifested itself to the extreme nearly claiming the ultimate penalty.

I had received information that a group of drug dealers were operating out of a flat in the East End of London. Arrangements had been made for me to meet them with a view to purchase cocaine in the future.

Having done similar tasks before I was quite happy to carry this out and after talking through the operation with my DCI and DI was quite confident that I could meet the dealers, verify the information and arrange for the deal to go down when they would have a Metropolitan Police reception committee.

When I arrived at West Ham Police Station I was informed that the MET Police Drugs Unit had been pulled away to another job.

The local CID officers would cover me while I went into the block of flats to keep my meeting. I did not look upon it as foolhardy. I had the right cover and the backup if I needed it. With the confidence I had gained in my previous experiences before, it did not cross my mind that I was in any danger; I was just doing my job.

As usual and essential we had looked at all the options and calculated the possible dangers. Someone had to make the first move if we stood any chance of taking these dealers out, they were expecting me, there was no harm in meeting them as arranged, it had to be!

I felt at home as some of my relatives had lived in these blocks of flats in Stepney. They had moved out but I still remember good times here and confidence exuded from within me.

Even the memory of my cousin stabbing the best man at a family wedding didn't worry me. I was six years old and could still clearly see the blood splattered over the brides beautiful white dress. The lace getting matted together as it dripped down from her brothers' wound as she held him to her chest.

293

Mum gathered us kids up as the reception hall erupted into punching, kicking and screaming mayhem. We piled into the back of an open back pick-up truck and hurtled away from the brawl, down the Bethnal Green Road and into the City and the safety of Liverpool Street Station and the train home.

As I drove with the two MET DC's, who were to cover me at the meet, my tongue felt for the sand and cement we kids had left in our mouths as we got off the back of the pick-up.

We passed the flats where my aunt once lived and I told the story to my backup team. An honest but down to earth East end girl, she would have been appalled that drugs, especially cocaine, was being dished out to the kids in her old neighbourhood. I took a bit of more pride in what I was about to do.

High self-confidence and my knowledge of the area had a very settling and calming effect as I made my way up the stairs to the fifth floor flat where I was to meet the dealers. The building was one of those built between the wars, dilapidated on the outside but surprisingly clean and recently decorated in the foyer and stairwell. Some graffiti had been scored on the grey stippled effect walls but the freshly green painted iron balustrade seemed to be untouched. Someone had recently washed the floor with disinfectant, probably to wash the local drunks recent urine away and this mingled with the acrid smell of new paint, causing my already slightly nervous throat to dry up a little.

It was an early autumn evening, getting dark and the stairway, although only lit by the occasional low wattage light bulb was surprisingly bright and friendly. I could hear voices and laughter coming from above me. As I went up the stairs Five black men all in their mid twenties stood across my path stopping me from going any further.

One, wearing a Rastafarian woollen hat over long matted dreadlocks, shouted inches from my face, "What the fuck do you want, white trash?" I went to say, "I am going to a friends flat", until interrupted by another, who had a very distinctive drum tattoo below his left ear. He shouted at me, holding his face with his nose touching mine, "You're a fucking "Cozzer!" Being as polite as I could and making out that they were mistaken, I said, I was visiting friends and made to go passed them.

As I did so I was grabbed from behind and felt something being put around my neck. I tried to free it until my arms were held to my body from behind. All these men were screaming at me that I was the filth and such like but the rope I now had round my neck ensured that I could not talk even if I had wanted to.

One of them said. "Let's hang the pig" and with this they half threw me over the balustrade. "If he lives. He's the old bill. If he dies then who fucking cares!" another screamed.

I was kicking and trying desperately to grab hold onto the balustrade or anything else including the clothing of the gang members but I could not get sufficient grip. I tore at the shirt of one of them but this only made them more determined to throw me over.

They prised my fingers from the metal side rods and my hands went numb, my head filled with a cotton wall and the voices went muffled as I started to black out. My stomach heaved and the most enormous fart came out that caused hoots of laughter from the gang.

My ability to struggle and fight back waned virtually to a halt when a door of a flat on the landing opened and a woman's voice screamed out at the gang to stop making a noise.

I felt the rope go limp and grabbed hold of the balustrade. The gang separated and I saw a middle aged black woman standing in the doorway with a black very large male standing to her side.

He bawled at the younger blacks saying he was expecting a white visitor and the gang skulked off. The black couple helped me back over the balustrade, apologising for the business and saying that, "You could not be too careful these days with so many troublemakers about!"

They took me into their flat, calmed me down and they gave me a cup of tea and being genuinely sorry about the incident apologised that, "Not all people round here are like that!"

I could not believe that this lovely couple, my lifesavers were the target of our drugs operation. But as we talked more about the purpose of my visit it became more apparent that they were not as innocent as they first appeared. The subsequent following weeks were to also prove that the couple were a positive link to a major cocaine supply ring.

The subsequent raids that took place revealed a lifestyle far beyond their meagre surroundings of the flat in Stepney. Illicit thousands of pounds in the bank and property abroad were masked by their "Mumsie" style.

After my "hanging" I returned to Essex and told my DCI of the escapade. I had no real physical marks or cuts although my neck was very sore. We put it down to experience and had a few laughs about it later.

I had felt a bit groggy but the adrenalin was still running and the potential success was enough to stave off any thoughts of going off sick. Two months later the euphoria that followed when the Met raids took place, arrests were made and a large quantity of cocaine seized, provided enough consolation for my discomfort.

Any remaining after effects temporarily flowed away with the copious quantities of alcohol that we consumed to celebrate the success.

THE FEELINGS

My return to Divisional CID duties at Canvey was followed by a sense to throw myself at anything likely to create enjoyment for family and myself. I seemed to have such powerful energy and an insatiable appetite to want get involved, do things, be accepted and be a part of anything that cropped up and on other times I would be completely drained of all strength and ability even to put one foot in front of the other.

The complete contrast of energy and weakness did not worry me and it did not occur to me that it could be something that I should be concerned about. I just ploughed away at the job, improving my already good reputation on CID and working toward a new goal of getting promotion to Inspector.

Many disappointments would follow with having my hopes for promotion dashed, even though I was always recommended. Each time I would pick myself up and jettison into yet another project or initiative, still with that powerful, self-possessed and motivated push to prove the bosses they were wrong. It became an obsession within my own mind, but the harder I tried the higher I would fall.

Again in hindsight I recollect starting to get nightmares, inexplicable twists and turns of the mind like riding a continuous helter-skelter. I would wake up in a pool of sweat, with heart pounding and body shaking. I became to accept these as a normal part of life not knowing why I had them or when to expect them. After these periods I would get extremely tired and irritable with the lack of sleep and these caused obvious problems between Dorothy and me.

I did go to the doctors on occasions and he offered Valium as a remedy. I hate taking pills anyway and the thought of taking Valium, "the mad woman's pill", was completely unacceptable.

My back and upper neck stiffened and ached sometimes going into spasm and then I would get shooting pains and a tightening cramp across my chest. I went to see my doctor, he would check me over, tell me nothing untoward was wrong and prescribe painkillers and massage cream. The chest pains were quickly discounted after X-rays, blood pressure and heart checks. This was a tremendous relief but did not stop me from feeling the pain.

These low periods did not seem to coincide with any specific times and I put them down to overwork or the normal stresses and strains of the job that everyone must suffer in their own way.

One of my best mates in the Job contacted me saying that he had heard I had heart trouble. I had not told anyone for fear of being thought being weak especially as the doctors had said there was no problem. He took some convincing before he believed me that I did not have a "dickey ticker."

I desperately tried not to show any signs of my problems and considered that I had well hidden them until one day when an older Detective spoke to me in the canteen area in Canvey Police station.

297

BOB CRAVEN

I had had a bad night of the sweats and was deep in my own thoughts when he asked me if I was okay. I told him that I felt very floaty and my head felt like it was filled with cotton wool. He was an ex-miner with a broad northeast accent and always had a kindly, understanding and caring word for all people who were in need. Whether it is a young probationer constable who had got himself in a pickle with his paperwork or a villain who needed to be pointed into the right direction to change his dishonest ways.

He stooped over me and I felt his vice strong grip, firm and assuring tighten as he placed his hand on my shoulder. He softly said, "I reckon you have suffered a "miners gliff".

I did not feel like speaking and found it somewhat annoying that he had interrupted my relaxed mind but realising he was perhaps the first bloke that had noticed my state, I questioned, "What is a "miners gliff". Trying not to appear to be rude and offend him but still feeling some irritation.

"I didn't expect you to know Sarge but I really think you have suffered this. In the mining villages up north there are often miners who walk around with strange expressions on their faces, looking into space, sometimes outwardly angry but inwardly tormented. Kids in the street would take the piss out of them unknowing that they had suffered some catastrophe down the pit like a rock fall or gassing. Usually the women would put the kids straight by saying, "Leave him alone. He's had a gliff".

"You've had a few problems so I here. I think you've got that glazed look! So I would not be surprised if you have had a gliff."

I was quite surprised that he had taken such notice of me to come to this conclusion and out of respect for his consideration did not like to say, "I did not know what the hell he was talking about". I still thought that I had just been over doing it, that's all, and needed a bit of space.

He was kind, but I just carried on without giving his "gliff" theory a second thought.

AGGRESSION

Returning home one day my daughter, Clare said that there was a book on aggression at her school. The book had my picture on the front page and inside depicting various forms of aggression by animals and questioned the reasons for the pictures.

The picture was the same one of me that had appeared on the front of the Daily Sketch some years previous. Deeply upset about this, as the situation was completely out of context, I arranged for The Police Federation to take this up, with the publishers on my behalf.

Although the situation was more humorous than threatening, one of Clare's friends did remark that she did not realise that I was a violent bloke. At the time I was giving lectures at her school on drug awareness and other issues during Sociology studies. I am sure that Clare had told the girls that I was embarrassed and upset with the book so no mention was ever made of it by them.

The School Head Teacher was very kind and gave me the book and said that she will make sure that the Education Authority would be informed to have it withdrawn.

What was most upsetting for me was the reference on the inside pages to violence and asking the reader for their views, the alternatives and the Christian point of view on such things and inviting a Christian Minister to talk to them about it. The comments were completely out of context and had no bearing on the incident. I was infuriated. I did get an apology and received £500 for the upset but this did not help me get over the indignation of the situation.

SEE PICTURES – ENQUIRIES BOOK FRONT PAGE

SEE PICTURES – ENQUIRIES BOOK PAGE 43

THE PERMANENT ACTOR

Trained in the skills of H.O.L.M.E.S, the Home Office Major Enquiry System, state of the art computers designed to make the task of detecting murders and solving complex crimes that much easier, I was more than often whisked away to manage Incident Offices in the rank of Acting Detective Inspector.

Ho! How I longed to gain the substantive rank of Detective Inspector, becoming more frustrated as I failed only to see some "wanker" get the job that I was obviously so much better qualified.

My own DI would be off on courses to teach him how to be a better senior officer leaving me to run his sub-division. I had the pleasure and inspiration of excellent experienced detectives all of whom took great pride in their vocation. Some of the older officers could detect a major crime and put a faultless complicated file together without any supervision whatsoever. All the DI had to do was put his name at the end of it and take the praise from all and sundry. The job was easy but getting it for myself was the hard part.

Murder and sex crimes were not commonplace but the public of our division suffered too many.

Parts of a body and torso found on a refuse tip, a social worker who befriended a released murderer and ended up as one of his victims, girls walking home from school dragged into bushes and brutally assaulted and an escaped mental patient looking for food but ending up assaulting a lady occupant as she got out of her bath were some of the many operations we solved.

The sight of such scenes of carnage had little effect on me or the other officers who worked on these investigations. Even the post mortems were considered as part of the job and never a problem for me.

There was only one murder scene that did affect me and that was the senseless killing of a young newly married couple in their home. They had disturbed a jewellery burglar, the young man had caught him, and the burglar drew a knife and stabbed him and then did the same to the girl.

I did not actually go to the scene of the crime but watched a video of it, as did all the other members of the Investigation Team. Several of us were physically sick for the first time and remarked that it was also the first time we had seen a video of the crime scene. I visited every scene in person after that and did not suffer any such sickness reaction again.

The demands of the bosses were never ending with league tables for detection rates being more important for personal promotion and prestige than the wishes of the public.

We devised a variety of plans for stemming the tide but none made any significant difference to the crime figures. Very rarely would we detect any more than 20% of the offences committed, which basically meant that 80% of the villains got away. Blasting into touch the saying that "crime doesn't pay!"

A novelty crime would turn up from time to time, one that was different and created a rare piece of interest. The armed robbery gang whose getaway car was a three wheel Reliant Robin. More like a three wheel motorcycle with a car body, low speed but who would have thought they could succeed.

They got away with the money from the petrol station but in their haste to dispose of the Robin and any forensic evidence, the centre front wheel dug deeply into the muddy field, that lead to their hideout, none of the robbers had brought any matches to set light to the petrol tank and to top it all, the field belonged to a copper, whose horse chased the robbers, minus the cash, away.

The team who perfected the demolition of shop premise walls by using a hydraulic jack to force the brick inwards in almost total silence but forgot when one wall collapsed on them after they had taken out the reinforced steel joist.

One was hospitalised by the ton or so of bricks and mortar that fell on him. It was unfortunate, as they had done the same at shops in many adjoining areas, but they had not suffered flood damage, like many buildings in Canvey. Soft mortar and bad luck brought about their demise.

In a way I was also the subject of some bad luck when putting together a video for the Court showing the hydraulic jack doing it's work. I arranged to use the jack on some old buildings in the derelict part of Shoebury Barracks.

I met the Colonel in charge as arranged with all the necessary equipment and we strolled down to the building we were to use. A smart man, resplendent in full uniform we marched towards the sound of crashing, banging and shouting. He said to me, "Some of your chaps down here, Officer. Practicing crowd control or something like that. Comes in handy all these old buildings. Plenty of ammo for the yobs they reckon!"

As we turned the next corner and entered a road between two brick buildings we were confronted by the full compliment of our Force Support Unit. Fifty men in full riot gear thumping shields in unison and seeing off a small gathering of hired rioters who threw the odd brick missile in nigh-on placid defiance.

To their right stood an ensemble of "scrambled egg", Chief Constables and Superintendents and from what I could see the bulk of our political representatives currently serving on the governing body of the Police Authority.

Everyone was smiling with approval as the Chiefs and politicians turned to walk toward us following by the motley Force Support Unit. Our Chief Constable made a bee line for me and greeted my like a long lost friend, taking my hand and shaking it enthusiastically he said, "I haven't seen you for a long while, Sir. How are you? Everyone at home okay? We must get together for that drink sometime. Nice to see you." He then turned to the Colonel, acknowledged and saluted him and went on his way.

The expression on my face must have been a picture, smiling senior officers holding back laughter and full-blooded comments from the lads I knew on the FSU, "Didn't know you were a Mason, Bob!" one remarked. "Bloody dark horse you are mate", said another as the Colonel, who by now had removed the shocked expression off his face and stopped gaping, said, "He rather made a pratt of himself. Didn't he?"

Jolted out of silence I replied something in agreement but my mind was firmly fixed on the prospect of me appearing before that same Chief Constable on my promotion board interview in two weeks time.

Needles to say, another disappointment was on the cards.

This coincided with a new Detective Inspector being posted as my immediate boss. I was doing my usual Acting Rank when I met him in what was to be his new office.

Shaking my hand and introducing himself his first real words to me was, "Bob Craven. I've heard a lot about you. I'm told you put my predecessor on the right road for promotion. I hope you will do the same for me!"

I didn't say a word but just let go of his hand and left the station. It was time for a change I decided, Acting Inspector for nearly five years, knocking my head against a brick wall without any reward. Told for two of the previous years that I was the top Sergeant on the Division yet seeing nothing to back up the bosses' promises of promotion.

The new Detective Chief Inspector on the Regional Crime Squad had asked me to return "and show the bastards what I was really made of". I needed to get back, I had so much to give to the RCS and was not allowed to do so on my first tour.

A Senior Officer friend tried to persuade me that it was the wrong move being the number one DS, but my answer, "That if I am the number one it should not matter where I was serving. I could be promoted from any department." He didn't say it but I knew that my chances were slim if I transferred, if only because I was bucking the system.

I was right, it took another five years before they would promote me. Such was the ways of the Police Service.

While I waited patiently to be transferred the new DI carried out the usual management ploy of "throwing everyone up in the air and waiting to see where they land to identify their loyalty and commitment". A stupid attitude to have in the light that, the officers we had were so long in the tooth, with masses of experience, any motivating techniques would be met with a tide of resentment and suspicion.

Re-inventing the wheel some called it. Putting in place an initiative that had been tried and tested years before, perhaps under a different heading, and failed to make any significant difference. Only to be put to bed by the next innovative supervisor and another project put in place to annoy and confuse the troops.

Unlike the permanently based lower ranking officers, senior ranks were more like nomads on a travel through the promotion trail, stopping momentarily to come up with some "look at me Chief Constable" innovation, not staying around to see it fail but passing on to higher ranking pastures.

In all no real changes or improvements proved any more successful than those carried out on a decade-to-decade basis by all officers.

Detectives from the stolen vehicle branch formulated one innovation that did have the smell of success. A Ford Escort, the favourite of the young male car thief, was fitted with devices that would signal that it was being stolen. A radio alarm would be sent to officers nearby, the doors would automatically lock, a siren would blast and all its lights would flash as the culprits were locked inside.

To put the fear of Christ in them an addition was made that would bring about its demise as an effective model of crime prevention and detection. The Chief Officers did no think the smoke bomb led us towards that objective.

Pandemonium ensued when the two 17 year olds were locked inside, the deafening siren, eyeball blinking flashing lights and the locked doors were enough to bring on panic. Let's face it; even the likelihood of imminent arrest can do the same and even cause some to shit themselves!

But the smoke pouring into the car from under the bonnet was a step too far. The psychiatric report on the boy, who had dissolved into a whimpering wreck by the time the arrest team arrived, stated that the smoke was held by them to be a punishment and not a means of arrest. It therefore should not be used.

The sad thing is that the decoy car was withdrawn from active duty never to be seen again. It must have been a shock for the lad, who had been spitting, punching, kicking and screaming at the windows of the car in desperation to get out. But as one of the hardened detectives put, "That's one little shit who won't be doing any more harm!"

SWANSONG CAR CHASE

Two days before I was due to leave Canvey I had one of the worst car crashes that I ever experienced.

With a probationer PC driving on the main London to Southend road, known as the A13, a report came over the radio that our Police Surgeon's car had been stolen from outside his surgery in Southend.

His pride and joy, a classic bright red sports car, had disappeared with its keys in the ignition along with his surgical bag containing drugs, prescriptions and all the other doctor type stuff they carry.

Within minutes of the message going out, the red car passed us going towards London. We turned round and tucked in behind it, three or four cars back.

The PC had been only in the job for a few weeks so I had to help him first, to calm down then stick to proper radio procedure through the excitement of his first chase.

I said to him, "Now the first consideration is that we do not we alert him to our presence. So get on the radio. Tell Information Room that we have located the car and that we are on the main A13 in Hadleigh heading towards London. Suggest to them that they set up a road block on the A13 just before the junction with the A130 at Sadler's Farm."

With impeccable confidence the young PC carried out my instructions. I only detected a small amount of nerves in his young voice as he gave our position and speed. Momentarily losing the car in the early evening did not deter him from his concentration and the calm commentary continued in factual and precise mode as we regained sight of our quarry.

The calm was interrupted as we waited at the traffic lights at a junction known as Tarpots, named after a pub situated on that corner. A Traffic Police Officer in full uniform walked across the road from his parked patrol car towards the red car that had also stopped at the lights. All was going to plan, we knew that the roadblock should be in place and the rush hour traffic would calmly take the car up to the waiting officers without any fuss or unnecessary bother.

I said to the PC, "That man is a Pratt and is about to ruin all the good work you have done!"

The Traffic Man nonchalantly placed his hand on the drivers' door handle of the red car. The locked car door provided both discomfort and humiliation for the officer and as the car drew away from the line of waiting vehicles and hurtled off across the junction on the wrong side of the road, the officer could be seen saying, "Fuck! Fucking fuck!"

It occurred to me that this officer might have been the roadblock.

We shot passed, not having time to shout or even glare at the now stranded Traffic Officer.

The red car had now joined the vehicles on the other side of the junction, still heading toward London but at a speed that would demolish any vehicles straddling the road.

He slowed in the inside lane baulked by the weight of traffic. I managed to get in the outside lane stopping him from overtaking and slowing him down further. Our car was a simple Vauxhall Chevette plain unmarked car but my PC, sitting in the passenger seat, was in full uniform.

A momentary glance in our direction showed the red car driver who we were and the threat we posed. He turned his wheel violently to the right and smashed into our nearside.

To take evasive action would have meant driving into the path of the heavy oncoming traffic to our right. An option I could not take as the road is a four-lane carriageway with two lanes going in either direction both with heavy continuous rush hour traffic.

We had to keep our ground and stay in the outside lane. He hit us again but it did not manage to budge us. Turning the wheel slightly in his direction I was able to keep the Chevette steady in a straight line as he tried to push us out of his way.

At a point where the road narrows the two lanes of each carriageway are very close and normal driving conditions dictate a slower approach. This rough neck attitude was not conducive to the width of the road and a last gasp push by the red car to get passed resulted in both of us going into a spin and locking together.

I glanced the side of a car coming the other way and several cars behind that one shunted into one another. Fortunately the cars behind us, had an early warning of the possibilities of a crash, held back and were able to avoid colliding with us.

The PC leapt out of our car like a jackrabbit, my side was blocked and I scrambled out of his side. I went to the crashed car taken out by us to help the lady driver and her passengers while the PC took hold of the groggy, now docile, driver of the stolen red car.

The red car, Chevette and the lady's car had such extensive damage it was a wonder that we only had relatively minor cuts and bruises.

When we got back to the police station the Traffic Man greeted us with streams of apologies and gestures of sincere sorrow at being, "so stupid". The rest of the officers had a field day with comments and remarks but I didn't care really.

Three days later I was back on the Regional Crime Squad.

Chapter Thirteen
BOUNCING BACK

Life in the RCS had not changed drastically in the four years I had spent back in the CID. Although we had some great successes overall the criminal was still out in front. We worked hard to catch the ones we did but chasing too many shadows the majority of the time and never likely to make that level of significant impact on the crime our public were suffering.

Faster cars, better technology and updated methods of tactics and surveillance made little difference to the numbers of criminals. "Fire Brigade" policing was fast becoming the norm for Divisional local force efforts, attending crimes after they had been committed rather than preventing them. The numerous initiatives and innovative brainchild projects to reduce crime made no recognisable difference.

The RCS was formed to get in front of them but more than often only succeeding in slowing them down.

The crime gangs were organised like a limited company having a Managing Director, Company Secretary, Accountant, Bank, Works Managers, Foreman and shop floor workers. Able to mask their activities under a blanket of deception they had moved with the times, whereas we had not.

With the added bonus of fear, blackmail and violence they were able to dictate their own terms with impunity, safe in the conviction that the legal system would protect them if they were unfortunate to be amongst the low percentage of their kind that were caught. They would calculate the profit levels of their crimes, comparing it to the term of imprisonment they would receive, even allowing for the, almost, certainty of being able to manage their operations from inside the cells! I heard, for the first time, the stock phrase, "If you can't do the time. Don't do the crime!" A business approach and calculated philosophy!

They were not concerned where they earned their profits. If it made money and it was viable then they would hit it. They would learn their craft and we had yet to read and understand that.

Organised criminals would look upon any method whether it was honest or not as a viable commodity. Prostitution, cigarette or alcohol smuggling, protection rackets, lorry hijacking, major fraud and drugs trafficking and anything else that did not put them in danger of being shot had become their field of play. The villain diversified but the Police, Customs, Serious Fraud investigators and all the other agencies had not followed suit. Still being cloned to specialise and failing to talk, or even cooperate with each other and with the likelihood of capture heavily stacked in their favour, the villains were still winning.

I was pleased to find that carrying guns was now the task of dedicated Firearms Units from Headquarters who would work tactics independent and in front of our lines, so there was little danger that I would shot by my own side.

In the past the offices and other police units were tasked with investigating specific types of crime, in the provinces we had dedicated drugs squads, lorry squads and fraud squads. In the MET they were divided into even more specialist units and with the other agencies like Customs and Excise, Government Benefit Fraud Squads, Inland Revenue, Immigration and Ministry of Defence Police, British Transport Police it was a hotchpotch, disjointed law enforcement group.

Nobody had told the villains that they were to stick to the "Queensbury Rules" of crime and only commit one type of offence at a time so the situation of lacking coordination and direction had not changed for decades.

RIVALRY AND DISTRUST

Lengthy operations were marred by bitter rivalry and distrust between different law enforcement agencies, even between branches of the same agency would not talk to one another or even exchange information to help. On the rare occasion it did happen just token liaison would occur to show an outward ability to co-ordinate. Inwardly the level of trust and commitment to work together was just above nil.

A visit to look up an old school mate of mine who was a high ranking officer in Customs and Excise early on my return to the RCS proved that any liaison with that agency was going to be heavy going. A tourist type tour of Custom House in Lower Thames Street in the City of London, a token hand shake for closer cooperation in the future and a pint at a local pub, was all that followed in the way of jointly focusing our teams to bring criminals to Court.

The successes we did chalk up were hard fought efforts with all too often our concentration having to be more in the direction of other agencies not compromising our operations.

On one raid for cocaine we saw a vehicle, belonging to Customs and Excise with two men inside, outside of the premises. As we went up the garden path to break the door down, two other men were coming out of the targets house with armfuls of cigarettes and bottles of booze.

They had just confiscated these items from him, after he had been across the Channel and returned with over the limit contraband. We went in and found that his amphetamine and LSD laboratory in the attic had not been touched, neither had his bank accounts. He said afterwards in interview that he was about to burn and destroy everything, after they hit him for the booze and fags but we got there before he could. The Customs men nearly spoilt our operation, they had not checked with the local police, who knew of our interest.

It is true to say that every agency would have a similar story to tell, but the under riding fact is that the criminals were earning as a result of our intransigence and failure to realise that our intense, over calculating security was hindering, rather than complimenting the fight against crime.

Villains would use this to their advantage, "playing one end against the middle", was a common way for them to wriggle out of trouble and cause rifts between the different agencies. One even wrote a book about his life and referred openly, even stating in evidence at his trial for drug trafficking, that he was an informant for the secret services.

This drugs baron, spent a lifetime, after a failed attempt at gaining a university degree, evading capture and prosecution because he managed to convince investigating officers that he was more valuable to them outside, giving them information than rotting inside prison. After doing so he would keep his head above water and provide officers with only the level of facts that would keep them off his back.

He could then engage himself, unhindered, in the worldwide drug trafficking that netted him millions and caused thousands of innocents to become addicts to his dose of the happy drugs.

PULLING THE RUG

During a meeting, at Scotland Yard, of representatives of law enforcement agencies from 32 different countries his name came up consistently, as the centre of the numerous operations we were individually investigating. He was the pivotal force behind the trafficking of huge consignments of drugs, measured in tons rather than pounds, throughout the Americas, Asia, Europe and Australasia. He was therefore our major target.

After much discussion and debate about the way forward, an officer from a leading drug enforcement agency, who had been investigating this man for a number of years said, "You have no need to worry about this man." He raised his hands and gently waving them from side to side whilst fluttering his fingers, he continued, "He is like a cloud. He drifts in and he drifts out. He drifts in and he drifts out. He is of no harm to you!"

I found it unbelievable that such a distinguished law enforcer would speak in such a way in the face of everything that had been said by the other participants. He either had not been paying attention to the thrust of the whole meeting or was totally disinterested in our joint purpose and honest intentions.

My unit on the RCS had spent over a year investigating an offshoot of this trafficking ring. Using the computerised HOLMES system of disseminating, sifting and prioritising intelligence and evidence we had worked closely with the forces from Australia, Europe and Asia we had identified the essential significance of this baron and the need for very close cooperation to secure his arrest and conviction and as many of his associate major international criminals.

To facilitate the best result and successfully take these persons out of their illicit activities, we needed to put faith and trust in each other. My DCI, Detective Superintendent and I knew that what the finger flutterer was saying complete rubbish, but not wishing to alienate him, or the MET team he was working with, we came to an "amicable" agreement. When they were ready to arrest this baron, they would inform us so that we could do the same with our targets throughout the rest of the world.

It would have been a mammoth task but we all agreed that to arrest them all would close down the largest international criminal organisation we had ever known. Our operation had reached the imminent stage and we drew out search and arrest warrants in 13 different countries, to coincide with arrest of the "cloud baron".

Keeping tabs on the numerous criminal targets throughout this time was costly and time consuming. Many officers worked hours and hours of their own time, following the subjects around the country. The targets that had several false identities were more difficult to keep track of.

Obtained in the "Day of the Jackal" style – assumed names were taken from headstones in church graveyards, duplicate birth certificates sent with passport application forms and false signatures acknowledging their identity. After that process it was no problem to open bank accounts, become directors of companies and have as many credit cards as you would ever want. They were all well ensconced in their false identities.

In the initial stages of investigation we had taken photographs of suspects at meetings throughout the UK and in several European cities. When the officers from the other countries saw these, we were astonished to find that so many were found to have false identities. Five had been certified dead in their own countries and others had just disappeared never to be seen again. Here they were alive and kicking with their new faces, delivering their profit making misery to our people.

In addition to the normal problems of fatigue, morale and focus in deterring boredom, questions were being asked of our bosses as to the validity of our direction twinned with the huge cost and drain on our funding that such an operation dictates.

"Was this operation going to directly affect the people of Essex?" "Is it fair that the Hertfordshire taxpayer pay for the detection of crime in other countries?" were the type of criticism that we had to contend with.

We knew that to take this gang down would significantly reduce the drugs being imported into this country. However, it would take a huge amount of persuasion to convince blinkered senior officers of insular County Police Forces and the local police authority, accountable to local electors, that a drugs bust in Canada involving criminals from Australia and Pakistan would achieve that result.

It was inevitable that this would happen and perhaps we were very naïve to think that such support and cooperation would be received. The rot started when some of my international police colleagues and me were sitting watching the early evening news at our branch office. Plastered over the screen was the "exclusive" that the "cloud" had been arrested by the flutterers' men and showed pictures of the hideaway and a stash of several tons of his drugs.

Shock, anger and dismay did not stop us from entering into a whirlwind of activity to retrieve some compensation from this catastrophe.

We had not been informed or given the chance to organise our teams to search and arrest. No early warning or any prior information had been passed to us of what was being screened before us to the world. It was so frustrating to feel that no one from the other agencies who were supposed to be cooperating with us had had the courtesy to keep us informed.

It rubbed salt into the wound that even the television station had been given the nod prior to us. It appeared that they trusted the TV Company over and above us!

We could see nearly two years intensive and concentrated work going down the drain but were still determined to see the job through. Warrants were executed and arrests made in several countries however only mediocre success was achieved and certainly nothing like the effective result we had hoped for.

Seven tons of cannabis was found in a ships container at a North American port but with no claimants or persons likely to turn up, having been scared off by the arrest of the "cloud" it was unlikely we would have any success there. All we could do was incinerate it without intoxicating the area!

All the millions in assets that we had traced disappeared within hours of the televised arrest and one bank even reported that their clients had taken their cash away in large holdall "cricket" bags.

Even the visit by a Government Minister from the Home Office and his congratulations for a "splendid job" did not stop the inevitable demise of the operation.

With the return to duty of a Detective Superintendent who was more spirited by local issues, the operation was wound up and the team sent back to their original branch offices.

The "Cloud" and his cronies were sentenced to an abysmal term of seven years, serving only three and were back in business within weeks of their release. Those that were never swooped up just carried on as if nothing had happened.

Drugs continued to be the main source of income for the organised criminal, more profit and less chance of being shot. Ex-lorry thieves and armed robbers turned to drugs running, using the expertise that they had acquired in their previous trade, learning and gathering experience as they went, advancing profits and confounding us.

The need for better communication and sharing of information was frowned upon unless the bosses could guarantee that, "the rug would not be pulled from under us". A term used when another agency took possession of information provided by you and then used it to forward their own operation, disregarding and most likely compromising and eventually destroying yours.

Intransigence, personal ego trips and deeming the other agencies to be as much the enemy as the criminals themselves, became the norm as we all ran after the same criminals.

When success was mediocre and our haul of drugs was not of the quantity that our senior officers and public would expect from such an expensive unit, the case file would be "glossed up" to mirror "a significant dent in the criminal fraternity!" "Add three noughts onto the totals!" one boss would order, "It goes down well with the Press and does our future budget requests the power of good!"

The problem was that when a real sizeable operation was successfully concluded, the result would be watered down by the previous inflated job. And once the press and governors knew the situation, we could never be believed or trusted.

DRACONIAN FEATHERDUSTER

New legislation in the Drugs Profit and Confiscation Act went some way to give us the ability to hit the villains where it mattered, in the pocket. Blazoned as one of the most draconian pieces of legislation ever put on the statute book, it empowered us to be able to look into bank accounts, and for the financial institutions to inform of us of suspected drugs profits, without the knowledge or consent of their clients.

The complicated methods that the gangs used to disguise their moneymaking ventures needed the close cooperation of all businesses and agencies and their individual respective expertise. This was a major advancement and gave us a small edge toward our goals of locking these evil persons up.

I say evil, as throughout this part of my police career I was questioned about the validity of assertions that drugs created harm. It would be correct to say that many people who take drugs or even alcohol do not become addicts, but too many do become dependent and therefore slip into the abyss of social deprivation, steal to supplement their demands, fail in family life and suffer extremes of health.

I have witnessed all these in such innocent beings. Uncontrolled drug taking is evil and the supply and profiteering dominated and promoted by criminals is unforgivable.

CABBAGE COCAINE AND ECSTASY SOUP

We did take great satisfaction when an operation did come to fruition especially when the gang where highly organised and we had beat them.

Our tactics included what was termed then as "country covert". Suitable observation points in towns and cities had always been hard to find although numerous buildings, tower blocks, offices and houses were always there.

Finding that vantage point with the required line of vision and ability to provide the right amount of detail for a photograph or evidence of top quality was difficult in the urban areas. The sparse countryside where many of our villains lived in huge mansions provided even less opportunities.

Many brave officers had infiltrated gardens and outhouses to get that important bit of evidence. One detective had been stabbed fourteen times by a suspected drugs baron whilst doing observation in the garden of an illicitly gained palace.

The baron was charged with murder and pleaded self-defence, although not suffering any injuries to himself, he was unbelievably found not guilty at Court. The jury must have been in cloud cuckoo land or "got at", threatened or paid off, to have not convicted him. I wonder what their conscience was like a few years later when the baron was convicted of another murder. Their indecision caused the death of another person. Not something I would like to live with!

As a result of the officers' murder, Chief Officers put strict guidelines in force to ensure the safety of those going on country covert operations. Even so weeks were spent holed up in ditches and woods, dug-in, hoping for the arrival of the evidence.

It took 14 days of working in shifts, patiently lying in a wet soggy hole, amongst trees, opposite a small airfield just off the busy A303 road in Hampshire, before we heard the soft drone of an aircraft. We hoped our targets were about to drop a sizeable package of drugs.

Previous to that I had been to Amsterdam and working with Dutch officers had located the warehouse where "E's" were being manufactured. Ecstasy was not considered to be a hard drug by the Dutch Authorities and these relaxed, possession of drugs laws of Holland had allowed the country to become a drugs haven for users and suppliers.

The Dutch officers detested having to allow these traders to use their homeland as a stepping-stone to the rest of the less tolerant parts of Europe. But their sufferance did not stop them from working with us, when they were allowed, to stem smuggling to our country and hopefully identify illicit drugs manufacture in their area.

We knew the plane and the pilot. We knew the moneymen and the ground workers, runners and distributors. All we needed was a large batch of drugs being delivered and picked up by our villains.

My mate in the hole with me was from Lincolnshire and I thought well used to the rigours of country life and the creatures associated with it. The previous night he had frightened the life out of me when he leapt out of the hole in frenzied terror, throwing his arms all over his clothing, dragging at the neck of his polo-neck sweater and rubbing his hands over his Barbour coat. "Get the fucker off me!" he screamed.

In the gloom I couldn't see a thing. "What are you on about?" I quietly tried to shout. "I fucking snake! It's gone down my neck. I can't fucking stand them. Get the bastard out!" he replied, in panic, as he shook, removing his layers of clothing.

I stepped forward to help as he took off his jumper and saw a long slender form wriggle from underneath and fall to the muddy floor. I confidently picked the animal up and said, "It's a bloody slow worm.

It won't do you any harm at all. Calm down. You'll wake the whole fucking world up!"

We settled down again in our hole and I thought back to the previous year when we had found two grass snakes in our back garden. I did pick one up to save a frog that it had in its mouth, but dropped it, as I could not tell the difference between that and the adder, which is the only poisonous snake that lives in the British Isles.

Looking in our natural history book to confirm the markings of the reptiles then had given me the confidence, that my mates' slippery visitor was a harmless slow worm, a lizard without legs the book said. I didn't tell him this and let him think that I was braver and perhaps more intelligent than he originally thought.

The sound of the planes overhead was not unusual, as a small airfield for light aircraft lay only two miles further down the road but, as the Dutch had tipped off, that "our" plane was on its way, we were hopeful.

This site had been used before; it was near to London and the major road systems that gave the opportunity of easy access and a quick getaway if necessary. We had pre-empted the situation and had surveillance units and firearms teams plotted up around the area to cover any probability. We could never account for everything so our nerves were still on edge, as the drone got closer.

We heard a splutter of engine almost immediately above us, followed by a rocket type whoosh and then a tremendous thud to the north. We reported this to our colleagues but also commanded that they were to "stand-by" as the plane was turning round back towards us again.

Another splutter of the engine and a whoosh followed by a muffled explosion, this time coming from a field next to us. A white cloud mixed with green leaves flew up from the cabbages in the field next to us. My Lincolnshire mate said, "Fuck me. Hope he hasn't got a third one. It could land right on top of us. We could be killed or end up permanently as high as a kite!"

The plane disappeared in the direction of the airfield and the units there reported that it had landed. Shortly after a Range Rover with three guys inside parked in the lay-by next to us on the A303. All three had the stature of disco bouncers two with balding heads and one with swarthy greasy long black hair.

The shiny fluorescent bright multi-coloured shell suit he wore stood out like a beacon in the beam of passing headlights They hopped over the wooden paling fence, pushed their way through the bracken and small trees that lined the cabbage field and walked towards the white cloud.

"Fucking hell the box has split. He will go fucking ballistic! How we going to take this lot away", said the shell suit.

"Nothing we can do about that. Pick up what you can in the rucksack and lets go and get the other one", said a bouncer.

They scurried around clawing packages from the ground and put them in the bag, then walked through the cabbages to where the other thud had come from. As they trudged through the dark I noticed one of the men looking down at a small box he was carrying, held by a strap around his neck.

It was a direction finder. We had wondered how they could have been so precise and quick in picking the packages up. Each one must have contained a small transmitter.

Some of our blokes had placed themselves nearer to the other package and saw the men standing in the ploughed field and then kneeling, reaching into, what appeared to be a very deep hole. The top half of his body disappeared into the abyss. He came back up as one of the others kicked the ground in temper. All three walked back to their car.

The sun was just starting to rise and the first rays of dawn silhouetted their figures as they trudged through the mud, then taking kicks at the cabbages, before climbing the fence once again onto the lay-by.

The shell suit muttered as they got into the Range Rover, "We'll need a fucking digger to get that out! I hope he's not going to be too pissed when we tell him!"

Hours of daylight passed as we waited for them to return. A surveillance team followed the Range Rover and its' disgruntled crew to a café nearby and watched and listened as the shell suit remonstrated, cursed and played out his dilemma to the receiver of his numerous telephone calls.

The other two in the meantime had ordered, "full-works breakfasts" and settled down at a table. When their mate returned from his problems on the telephone he said, "We've got to wait here. He's going to sort out some stuff to dig the bastard out!"

"You've got to be joking! I've got to open the gym in a fucking hour", a bouncer protested.

The shell suit was just about at the end of his tether and pointed at him saying, "You fucking well go and tell him then. If you've got the bottle! Because I ain't."

Stuck in our ditch we could not move without the possibility of being, "sussed", seen by someone and spoiling the operation. Stick at it we must. Toileting was not too bad as the country ditch offered several areas where you could "cut and cover". That is, dig a hole, do your business and then cover it.

In the towns it was a bit more difficult and all sorts of receptacles were used. An experienced officer could cope with placing the contents of his back passage even into the small hole in the top of a Coke tin. That took some engineering!

When you've got to go, you've got to go! The bushes where I hid, some months previous, on a busy industrial estate, did not offer any such containers. My need to go was so dire and pressing that I had no alternative but to squat where I was. Any disturbance would have ruined the operation, an armed robbery that was reaching a crucial stage.

Ten feet away two ladies, standing at a bus stop, complained of the smell of drains. I dearly wanted to make my apologies but for obvious reasons, could not. A few minutes later the call went up to hit the robbers, as they approached the security wagon. I threw myself out of the bushes frightening the life out of the two ladies.

I said assertively, "Armed Police. Please move away from the area." They swiftly walked away as the operation went into full swing. The robbers were blocked in and arrested. I often wondered if the ladies put two and two together later and realised the smell was something to do with me and some increased tension!

Back in the ditch we were able to get some sleep and wait to be alerted by our "eyeball" that our diggers were returning. Never sleeping soundly, or at the same time, in case something else happened, one of us would watch the area occasionally using the high-powered binoculars to "bird watch".

Couples were often seen, the boss with his secretary invariably, finding a quiet corner in the company car or even a romp in the field. Romantic? Yes, but when we checked them out, usually to identify if they are suspects, it can be quite embarrassing and delicate approaches had to be made to defend the innocent and harmless.

The safer alternatives of high tech equipment, such as CCTV were in its infancy. We experimented with TV surveillance at one operation to research the saving of resources and reduce danger to ourselves. A camera was set up facing the front door of a suspect in a housing area and relayed the picture to a screen we had in our observation van, parked some 500 yards away.

It was too dangerous for anyone to keep static observation on the estate and the TV project had to be tested on a live operation. Disaster struck soon after we had set ourselves up, for some canny, even laughable reason, every television set on the estate now had a picture of the suspects' house on its screen. The local postal communications office was inundated with complaints. We made our escape before any embarrassing questions could be asked. The project was aborted. More expertise and technical help was required!

Telling this story In the hole we talked through what we could do to save ourselves from such discomfort, "Surely the SAS have got a better way of doing things?" my Lincolnshire mate implored as he smacked himself to remove yet another mosquito from his neck.

Evening was now approaching and our surveying of the field became even more difficult. Our night vision glasses were limited and only enhanced our view of the field by a small amount.

Radio messages had dissipated as the surveillance team were led away by our targets. We had kept our transmissions to a minimum to conserve our batteries and only double clicked to the operation commander every half an hour. As it grew dark we listened for the teams return and were ecstatic when the message came over "Target one mile from lay-by!"

Stretching and tensing ourselves up from the cramp of inactivity we positioned ourselves to get our eyeball. Replacing a few branches from the bushes around us just in case they had separated by the breeze that softly passed over us, we readied our reception.

Now dressed in gear more appropriate for labouring and digging the trio returned. Large laced-up boots of the type that weight lifters wear, jeans and donkey jackets replaced the carnival colours of the shell suit. Spades, a pickaxe and a garden fork in their hands they made their way to the cabbage patch load. One carried a sack as my mate whispered, "Do you think they are going to take the cabbages away?" as he giggled, "Cabbage and Ecstasy soup. That's a new one!"

They dug around the cabbage patch, put some parcels in the sack and then went over to the hole in the next field. Our other team watched as they dug for the next four hours thirty-two minutes, moaning, groaning, telling each other off for lighting up cigarettes and piling the earth up at the rate of an accomplished grave digger.

On the road, the surveillance team reported a red Ferrari passing slowly and taking a great interest in the lay-by and the fields beyond. All was going to plan even our main target was on "the plot."

Sweating and grunting with stiff pain the three stooges finally dragged themselves and their heavy bags across the fields to the crater in the next field. More digging followed, slower and deeper this time, filling more bags and then they laboured, sloping and dragging themselves, back to the Range Rover. Throwing their kit into the back, driving to the next intersection, u turning and then followed by the Ferrari they sped off with our surveillance team in tow.

Two hours later I was having a welcome shower at the nearest police station where the cells were being filled with the stooges, the Ferrari man and an entourage of hangers-on swooped by the support teams.

The Scientific Officers had field tested the white powder and reported traces of ecstasy and cocaine.

The cabbage farmer had been told about the contamination. He filled the hole in but the cabbages were harvested a few days later. He promised, faithfully, to destroy the ones that had been covered by the white powder.

The next year I went passed the cabbage field, now ploughed over it did have a large patch of white powder on it but I put this down to a covering of lime that is commonly used in farming.

I never did satisfy my curiosity as to the qualities of the crops that did have the benefit of an ecstasy fertilizing. Were they better? What does a spaced out cabbage look like? Are white powdered freshly ploughed fields covered in ecstasy, cocaine or lime these days? Would the EU sanction such a crop growth method? I queried.

NO THANKS - NO REWARD

After serving on special operations I returned to my previous office at Brentwood to find that the DCI had now changed. The DI, I had major problems with on my first tour, was now promoted and replaced the DCI who had asked me to return.

As I walked into the office an older DS met me and pulled me into a small room we used as a kitchen. Pretending to make coffee he said, "Don't get stewed up. He's changed. Whether he has been warned or not, I don't know? But I am sure you will be pleasantly surprised".

He was right. The DCI had certainly changed, polite and complimentary of the work I had carried out on the special unit he welcomed me back and, "Looked forward to working with me again".

The following months were perhaps the happiest days I had on the Squad. Considered to be the most senior of the Detective Sergeants, I was often asked to do Acting Inspector when either of the two bosses was away. The DCI even recommended my promotion and this also received the support of the senior officers at RCS Headquarters. My prospects were looking up.

The branch officers worked well and hard on a variety of operations from drugs trafficking and manufacture, armed robbery, major fraud and even the large-scale theft of aluminium beer kegs. The latter was not the type of offence that I would normally consider to be of the level we should look at, but as the booze trade were loosing £18 million worth of kegs per year it was considered by the bosses to be appropriate work for us, but not a priority over the other more important ops we had on.

During this time I was sent on a course to learn rudiments of the new legislation and procedures for investigation and confiscation of criminal profits, money laundering and the analytical dissemination and evaluation of intelligence.

This opened up a new concept of investigation, giving us the opportunity of hitting the criminals "in the pocket". Cutting them off financially would disable them where it mattered and hurt the most.

The powers the new Acts gave us innovative methods of investigation would also help to dispel the need for hours and hours of wasted time and effort sitting waiting for something to happen and the hurtling around at break-neck speeds following the shadows of suspects in their fast cars, with little gained.

Like the time when we followed a target in his Porsche, in thick pea soup fog at death defying speeds of 120 mph and over and another when we drove from Nottingham to London beating the train that carried our suspect. It was life threatening and a danger, not only to ourselves, but the people that we were supposed to be protecting.

These new tactics were more cost effective and less wearing on the officers but they needed dedicated expertise of officers more bound to a desk and computer than a motorcar.

Just as important was the safety of our own officers. Crashes were frequent no matter how well we trained to avoid them. Trained and highly tuned in "Pursuit Driving" and "Advanced Driving" that taught how you were to avoid any, yes "any" event that would likely cause injury, did not stop horrible accidents occurring.

In two adrenalin charged operations I crashed vehicles.

The highly tuned driver was not immune to accidents. Our motorcyclist, a cool and calculated professional first class traffic officer, was wiped off the road. A young member of the public, decided to do a "u" turn, without warning, in front of him, as he hurtled to catch up with a target that the surveillance team had lost. Barely surviving the crash our colleague suffered inoperable brain damage and is now crippled for life.

I recognised the value of being released from such risks by alternative but effective methods of investigation. But the macho detective would take a long time being convinced.

Using computers and the technology now available and improving all the time we could make an effective impact on the criminal fraternity. Convincing the old school detectives who were not technically minded and the equally uneducated Chief Constables, who were being asked to supply resources, was going to be a main stumbling block.

It was to take forever for the Chiefs to be persuaded, as one major problem was that any proceeds from assets confiscated would go to the Government coffers and not the local Police Authority who were supplying the manpower. Not the type of initiative that would create the degree of enthusiasm that was required to augment success!

Even so the RCS pushed forward and trained officers in these advanced methods of detective work. I trained officers to use a form of analytical charting and evaluation called ANNACAPPA and its successor on computer. ANNACAPPA was a manual method of creating flow charts and association link charts from the intelligence and information we obtained. It simplified our coordination and control of operations enabling us to use our resources more effectively.

These showed what target was meeting who, where their assets were, times and places of meetings and telephone number links and patterns. It gave us the capability of being able to forecast events before they happened and produce easily readable evidence in complex Court trials and proceedings. Much needed when the juries we had at Court were made up of ordinary people unused to such complicated formats.

I could see the benefits but realised that it would take a complete change in detective culture and suppliers of resources to make any difference in attitude and sophistication.

Our DCI and DI fortunately were very forward and modern thinking, encouraging the work of the "DPC" officers, as we became known and soon massive charts started to appear on the walls of the office depicting the activities and associations of our targets in clear and unambiguous form. Some less able officers were left behind but most extolled the methods capabilities and potential. In fact their was a sudden rush of volunteers to become a "DPC", I suspect that quite a few could see that this was the new "earner" and attracted the most potential for officially sanctioned overtime.

DPC was a ground breaking innovation but had a long way to go, to catch up with the organised criminal, who was streets ahead in his knowledge and experience in the world of making huge sums of money by any means.

The sums of money that were stolen by gangs dwarfed our previous efforts to maximise results and perhaps, were not taken seriously because of our previous bad habits of "adding a few noughts" to improve our standing. It backfired when information was received that over £100 million was to be stolen from an unknown finance house.

All the officers, including the higher-ranking supervisors, fell around laughing at the incredulous prospect of such happening. It did not matter how much the reporting officer and myself tried to convince them that the information was reliable, they just did not have the capability of comprehending that this was going to happen.

We were refused consent to take up a more in-depth operation to identify the forthcoming financial trail that would have to be implemented, by the gang for them, to succeed in laundering the money. All we could do was inform our Central Intelligence Team at C11 in New Scotland Yard and wait for the fraud to happen.

When it took place, some months later, it took several years of painstaking work before we could trace the money, masked by a network of laundering enterprises, as it was transferred from bank to bank throughout the world.

The main participants in the theft were arrested and charged but the bulk of the millions were never recovered and went on to finance large-scale drugs trafficking involving the Russian Mafia, Columbian Cartels and European Crime Syndicates.

The money floated from country to country. No local or national law enforcement agency had any desire to take the mantle of tracking the cash. And with no existing international law enforcement agency the villains were able to work unhindered in purchasing and distributing their drugs. On either side of the Atlantic small pieces of information were received but the trail went cold and our part of the operation was closed down. I continued to monitor the progress of the operation as it played out in other countries.

THE SHIT HITS THE FAN AND EVERYONE GETS COVERED

Bitter disappointments were there all the time but not as high as that when our two bosses were suspended for alleged irregularities in expense claims and I was ordered by the DCS to take complete charge of the Branch Office.

The shock of seeing the whole office stripped of every item except the furniture was an appalling experience. Even the wall charts had been taken along with all records, documents, personal belongings, the whole office contents had been swept away. Every single officer felt as though they were accused as they checked their stripped bare desks for personal items.

The common tactic of so many senior officers of hitting everyone hard had reduced a vibrant lively office to a grey morgue.

The Detective Chief Superintendent told me to continue in charge and build the morale up. Morale was at rock bottom, usually vocal, officers were reduced to silent disbelief and the lady Branch Office secretary, normally so calm and collected and hardened by 25 years of tough speaking, reduced to tears.

Cynical attitudes and collective condemnation of the actions of the internal investigators brought the team together and directing our efforts away from the demise of our supervisors and focusing on the operations gave us a fresh impetuous and outlook.

The weeks drew away and we managed to get a few successes under our belt before a replacement for the DCI arrived. We all made sure that our suspended bosses were giving the appropriate accolades for these operations. It was their leadership that had brought about these results.

My position as Acting DI was tenable but, promised by the DCS that I would be promoted and be given the post permanently I continued, even though I knew that two of the Detective Sergeants on the Branch felt that they should be given the opportunity of doing the Acting job.

As was normal when you have to supervise I made enemies of individuals. There was an issue on, who had been the anonymous informant that had accused the two supervisors of bumping up their expenses. I suspected that some put this down to me as I had had the fight with the DCI, when I was on the squad the first time. It was of no consequence that this same DCI was now recommending me for promotion and this blip had put a question mark on his current support.

One DC had taken exception to me when I suggested that he might be gay. He had a macho image, scruffily dressed at virtually all times and a renegade against life with a chip on his shoulder probably brought about by the fact that his wife had left him to live with a man twice his age. He would constantly castigate and cagoule and woman detective as "the bint" or "the dike" and was proving to be an unnecessary bad influence on the rest of the office. I hated any form of discrimination or homophobia, feeling that it could never ever be justified and that gender had no bearing on any officers' capabilities.

I pulled him to task on this and he made no apology for his comments as the woman had lived with another girl for a long time. He took umbrage when I suggested that he might be in denial, and have an underlying motive, as he was himself gay as he lived with another man and did not want to "come out".

I told him my views, that gender was not an issue with me. He protested that he was not but could not see my point by saying that two blokes living together was a different situation. He did not like it when I said, "So two blokes living together are "good old boys" but two girls doing the same are lesbians". I left him with the warning that any future behaviour would result in him being disciplined.

Some days after, I made the mistake of leaving my Psion pocket computer on my desk overnight. It contained comprehensive lists of contacts and data on DPC, none however that could not retrieved without a lot of hard graft. Someone had removed the battery wiping the whole data off. The "gay" DC had been paralytic drunk that night and had slept in the office. He was number one suspect but I did not to take the matter further. The last thing I wanted to do was start a war of juvenile behaviour in an already volatile office.

I had now been back on the RCS for five years and probably experienced the ultimate in detective work. Adrenalin had run at an alarmingly high rate continuously, with me hardly having a break to take account of where I was going and what I wanted further in the job.

I wanted to be an Inspector but only on the RCS not anywhere else.

THE RED MIST AND BLANKS

I had been carried along on a crest of a wave in those years and the feelings I had suffered before had been very much in the background. Casting an eye back as this account does, a red mist starts to appear.

On the special operation, near to its' end and the loss of so much ground when the rug was pulled from under us, I went to the DCI in charge and offered to become a "bent officer" and infiltrate the drugs cartel. My demise would be publicised in the media. I could be sent in as a "Trojan Horse" with the carrot of my expertise and knowledge of their organisation dangled in front of them. They would accept my usefulness and would get the evidence to convict them.

The most stupid, thoughtless, dangerous, ill conceived, unpractical, unworkable etc. etc piece of shit that I have ever been party to. Yet here I was making out it had a serious prospect of success. I really believed that I could do it. Thank goodness the DCI was not that desperate and turned my idea down. I put this episode in the perspective of over zealous behaviour and the passion I had for the job, not being mentally unbalanced at all!

I had some blank periods, usually when I was on my own and found my mind running wild with a myriad of thoughts all bundling and tumbling on top of one another. Sitting at my desk, at my computer, suddenly realising that it had turned dark and an hour or so had passed without me writing a thing. I was working sixteen hours a day, driving 80 miles to and from home and doing my charity work at weekends so fatigue was the answer.

After returning to my Branch these feelings dissipated for a while then came back in earnest. Several times I woke slumped at my desk not knowing how I had spent the previous hours.

Frighteningly I had a black out when driving on surveillance. The follow of the suspect had been manic with him darting from one place to the next at break neck speeds, down narrow lanes and busy main roads. In the process I had cut up and dangerously weaved in and out of several cars, nearly causing accidents and infuriating other drivers. Our target had come to a halt at an associates' house and our surveillance team rested up waiting for his next move.

Relieved for the rest we parked up in a local park in amongst numerous other cars. I had been driving and my partner, a DS, I settled down by adjusting the seats to lay back and wait for the next move. With the engine running keeping the heater going to keep us warm I drifted into a sleep. My heart started racing as my temperature soared. My mind tumbled into a torrent of thoughts and I fought to get my breath until an almighty crash. I shot up from my prone position put the car in first gear and shot off out of the car park in sheer panic.

I turned into the narrow residential road as my partner screamed at me, "What the fuck are you doing?" I looked at his ashen face as he continued, "Are you okay?" I did not know what to say. I felt stunned and drained but gathering some of my senses drove round the block and back into the park.

Some of my team were standing near to a car with damaged rear lights and bumper. The look of disbelief and perplexity on their faces could not explain to me what had happened although seeing the damage to the back of my car threw light onto the fact that I had hit this other car.

I could not remember doing it. My seat was still in the lying position. The surveillance had come to a halt and the target still at his mates' house. No one had given the "off" and I had no idea why I drove backwards, apparently with scorching tyres, like that. Something told me to do it but what I don't know who and I could not explain it?

I left the surveillance and drove gingerly back to the branch office. I was completely drained and totally exhausted. In the quiet of the office I drifted off to sleep until the noise of the returning team woke me up

My tenth attempt and the promises of the DCS did not get through to the Chief Constable who turned me down yet again for promotion to Inspector. It appeared to me that no matter how hard I worked or how loyal I was it did not amount to zilch in the eyes of those in power.

At about that time I received my medal for 22 years of good and meritorious service. If it had not been for the fact that my proud Mum, Dad and Dorothy had been with me at the presentation. I would have told them to stuff it up their arse.

"Return to Divisional CID. It's the only way to get your pips!" said the replacement DCI so reluctantly I returned to Basildon. Having almost continuously carried out the Acting Rank of Detective Inspector for eight of the previous ten years I was once again back to being a Divisional Detective Sergeant.

Chapter Fourteen
RETURN TO BAZ

Not much had changed from a public perception in the policing at Basildon. Detection rates were still abysmally low and did not reflect the advances that had been made by the police service to bring more criminals to justice.

The latest "management speak" and initiatives taught at the Police College and faithfully transferred to the practical policing on the street by candidates for higher status in the service, did not make one iota of difference to the public.

They still suffered burglary, robbery, rape and theft. Performance indicators designed to warn of us of pending trends in crime and anti-social behaviour made no significant change in criminal behaviour. The changing of names, like the DCI was now a Crime Manager, did not reflect on the statistics, although, they, as usual, were manipulated and could still be read to accord with the senior officers beliefs, that we were winning the fight against crime.

I am sad to say that upon my return from the RCS, and desperately wanting to gain promotion, I joined the ranks of the selfish career police officer and looked to feathering my own nest. Encouraged by colleagues, who had done exactly that, I was told that I would be promoted the following year if I carried out projects for the Chief Superintendent and kept my nose clean.

Old mates from my early days in the CID at Southend now occupied senior positions at Basildon, each one said that I had been given a raw deal and not been rewarded with promotion that was, "long over due". It was totally against the grain for me to do so, but also because it would have been unfair for me to let them down after such support, I put my head in gear to do what was necessary to get promoted.

Accompanying the Chief Superintendent on a large investigation into alleged serious assaults by other police officers and carrying out a survey of the future population of the division, I was focused to succeed.

NO CHANGE HERE

I found conferring with local council officials, in an attempt to forecast the growth of the area, an enlightening experience and showed me exactly how our approach to development is so badly flawed.

In our areas an estimated additional twenty five thousand houses were due to be built but in none of them was the balanced infrastructure of schools, doctors surgeries, shops, places of work, recreation facilities, open spaces or roads.

The plans were a recipe for disaster and a policing nightmare. There appeared to be no coordinated attack to the problems that had been identified as early as the beginning of the century. This was the 1980's, housing was being built for a selected few who could afford it but the people at the lower end of society would receive little to improve their lives. No lessons had been learned in eighty odd years!

The local authorities projected plans did not look at the social structure of the area and the affects of social depravation previously experienced. Planning did not take account of the views of Police Officers, Social Workers, Teachers, Doctors and other Community Workers who would have such first hand knowledge. No one I spoke to could answer why this was not happening.

Acting Detective Inspector continued to be required and produced the same problems. Having crap soiled toilet paper put into my desk drawer. Someone sticking the pages of my police note book together caused a problem when I was about to give evidence at Crown Court. I was sensitive to these but considered it was all part of the process of leaving being "one of the men" to becoming a "Guv".

I managed the incident office investigating a series of rapes in the area. Young girls and women were put through horrendous ordeals by a man on footpaths near the railway line passing through the town. We to identify the man spent hours and hours, and we felt we were so close, as we had positive samples for scientific analysis but without the advances in DNA we stood little chance.

With the drying up of likely suspects the team was cut down to just me and one other officer. We continued on the slog to eliminate over 150 suspects and search through the mountain of investigation documents in the hope that we could find something that we had missed. I worked 12 hours a day on that and kept pace with the responsibilities I had on normal CID Divisional work. After all there was nobody else to do it! I even managed to keep pace with my charity work.

FUZZY BRAINED AND EXHAUSTED

I took up jogging for the first time to clear my brain of the fuzz that seemed to fill it from time to time. I also started to get the shakes, so much so that at one time I had great difficulty holding a pen and not being able to write. Another time I shook so much that I dropped a full cup of tea over a pile of papers. Fortunately I could run copies off the printer to replace them.

The thought of Alzheimer's crossed my mind but I was too busy to consider doing anything about it.

Exhaustion used to be a problem; my head was a ton weight and felt like it was full with cotton wool. If I closed my eyes I would go into a spin. A good slap round my own face brought me round and then I could carry on.

Halting the supply of drugs in a public house and the laughter of the woman detectives who like the men had to take their turn watching hour upon hour of videotape to see the transfer take place in the gents' toilets. Only authorised if the cameras showed the top half of the men as they stood at the urinals, the tapes still caused a titter or two amongst the watching ladies. One remarked, "How can you do that? Have a conversation with a guy standing beside you while you've got your todger in your hand?" I couldn't do that from the next-door cubicle. Could you?" questioned another WDC.

Their concentration was not thwarted from the search for evidence and a nice result when drug pushers were taken out of circulation.

CHARITY AND COMMUNITY

It was difficult to know exactly where to put this part in the book, as being in touch with the community in a natural way was part of the everyday life of every Police Officer, no matter what department he was in.

Taking your kids to school, contact with other parents, talking in the pub and so on was rarely looked on as purposely projecting yourself with any specific intentions.

For me it was a gradual realisation that to mix and communicate with people as a Policeman would improve our understanding of what our democratic society wanted from us. It also gave you the opportunity of telling what you were actually doing for them.

I had been brought up in the Southend area so had plenty of friends, relatives and acquaintances to tell me what was wrong with the world and how, in my position, I could put certain things right. Transferring outside the hometown to Basildon and Chelmsford was a more difficult situation. You had to start from scratch and rely on the locally bred officers to kick-start your knowledge and the particular aspects of the local population.

"Familiarity breeds contempt", they say but the benefits far outweigh the pitfalls when the depth of local knowledge is so important. Gaining their confidence you can find out so much. Who is suffering? Who is doing what and when? The local Bobby should be a fountain of information and a positive link with his public and is the most important and essential part of the Police Service. Take him away and you lose your ears and eyes on the outside world and possibly everything!

In my teens I had helped elderly people as part of the Duke of Edinburgh's Award Scheme but in all honesty had probably looked at that as a means to an end and part of the process of getting the award.

Playing football for clubs outside of the police, prior and during my service helped me to keep in touch with the community but this was more by accident than desire.

In the days when Police pay was abysmal the CID used to hold stag nights or "Gentlemen's Smoking Evenings" for charity. Officers went round to traders, publicans and other businessmen to "mump" for items that could be raffled. To "mump" could be described as "to invite a member of the public to donate a prize of some description". Usually the request was preceded by, "all proceeds going to the Police Widows and Orphans Fund."

At one time, it was accepted, by the donors, that the Police Widows and Orphans Fund was a worthy cause, but as conditions in the service improved other worthier causes became apparent and traders, rightfully, were less willing to help. One of the main factors being that they were earning far less than us!

Some I suspect continued to donate to curry favour with the Police in the hope that they would be seen in a different light if they ever got on the wrong side of the law. There was always the danger that this could be considered, a bribe by the back door!

The practice of mumping also continued by some officers to line their own pockets, using their position to get items cheaper, a percentage off or even not paying for it at all. One officer had the audacity to keep a large cupboard in the CID office stashed with a veritable Aladdin's cave of goods that he sold as a sideline.

This culture was to seriously affect our standing with local business when we took a later professional approach to partner with them on joint crime prevention and detection initiatives. Sadly the business community were even more suspicious, as to our real motives, when we approached them for help on legitimate charitable projects and had to be convinced of our honest and noble intentions.

In the future, realising the probability of creating a counter productive situation, I shied away from asking for "freebie" handouts from business and tried to look for areas of joint advantage.

Mumping even for the benefit of charity is not the way forward. We, as Police Officers, were supposed to be putting something back into the community not taking something out. What was the purpose even of taking something out, like a prize, only to put it back somewhere else in the community. The credit we gained was by deceit as the supplier of the means to get the credit was part of that same community.

My efforts to raise money for charity involved the creating of trust and then working with the business, charity and sporting communities in a common purpose, thus each putting in the same effort and achieving the same amount of credit. The Police would not benefit financially but kudos and standing would be much improved. The trust we gained would be invaluable.

Like the many officers who were always raising money for charity, in their own time, I was in it for the enjoyment and sometimes the challenge. My first real effort, apart from the occasional school fun run or walk with my daughters, was to help build a dedicated Burns Unit at Billericay, a town in central Essex. This would provide a much-needed care and treatment centre for sufferers in our region.

In 1976 I was Secretary of the Basildon Police Sports and Social Club and best placed to get annual dinner / dances together for its members. Officers, civilian staff and their families were brought together socially and as a bonus, it turned out to be the ideal way of getting cash in. Dorothy got involved and we then arranged for boat dances to do the same. We coached 250 to 300 people from the area to Tower Pier on the River Thames in London and sailed up the river providing a buffet and disco dancing.

It was a roaring success and we were able to give the Burns Unit several hundred pounds each year for four years. When I moved from Basildon to Chelmsford it was harder to keep the popularity going and the last one we actually lost money, paying the deficit ourselves.

I blamed myself for not promoting it but some years later our own nephew was to receive extensive treatment at the Burns Unit for serious injuries he suffered in a terrible road accident, so our efforts had not been in vain and any losses we incurred were insignificant in comparison.

I became the manager of the Chelmsford Police Football Team and kept in touch with football in the Southend area by playing and being Treasurer of the old Southend Police side, now called Southend Phoenix. This team now had many players from outside the job and had to be self-sufficient and not reliant on the finances of the Police Social Club.

I set up a 100 Club fund raising venture that took regular payments from the members and provided cash prizes each month. A percentage allowed by legislation was paid into the Club and went towards purchasing kit and enabled us to keep the members' costs down. After a short while I took over as Secretary of the Club and whilst at a League meeting was asked if I would take on voluntary the running of their clubhouse bar and function suite.

These premises were made up of a number of timber buildings comprising not only the suite and bar but toilets, changing rooms and a large meeting room. The whole complex had been built by the efforts and financial support of the footballers of the town. The project had charitable status and a disabled group came to the suite once a week and played a variety of indoor and outdoor sporting activities.

Our daughters, Clare and Karen and some of their friends asked the committee of the project if they could supply refreshments and snacks to the footballers at weekends. This was agreed and got so popular that Dorothy helped them to manage the kitchen. They were asked to do weddings and other social functions like anniversaries and birthdays. They were happy, getting pocket money, stinking of burger fat and eyeing up the footballers legs.

I, in the meantime, managed the bar, increasing profits for the project, legalising staff pay and conditions and started to look at ways of promoting the use of the suite for other purposes.

Members made suggestions how we could improve the project. One player had a daughter who attended the disabled group evenings. We would come and help when we could at their gathering and were amazed how the people dealt with their disabilities.

Fit and healthy footballers, who were constantly moaning of being hard done by, were pushed into the background by these happy faces that overcame their adverse problems, as if they were not there.

We would laugh along with the disabled group when the deaf boy played around with his blind mate, jokingly telling him to throw the dart into the crowd, in the opposite direction to the board. He would turn his blind mate around and say, "Okay David. Up a bit. Right a bit. Ready", he paused as the rest of us dived for cover. There would then be a roar of laughter as the two jokers shouted, "Gotcha!"

Apparently they did the same trick during the summer when they went outside on the playing field to do archery with real bows and arrows!

The girl in the wheel chair who could wipe the floor with me and everyone else, fit and disabled, at table tennis. To this day, I am still awestruck with the ease that she moved across the field of play in her wheel chair with one hand and the bat in the other.

I admired the dedication of the elderly lady who was the secretary and the wheelchair bound slightly deaf man who was the treasurer of the group.

I felt that there might be a way that we could put football and disabled sport together in a joint venture, extending the complex and the objectives of the project. The member with the disabled daughter and I researched the possibilities for the future.

We got together a group of businessmen and builders to look at the building of a complex housing a bar, committee rooms, changing rooms, function / activity suite and gymnasium that would be designed so that the facilities could be used by both able-bodied sportsman and disabled people. Preliminary arrangements were made to set up a working party and a feasibility study.

Football was taking a pasting in the press as its supporters rampaged in gang warfare so any ideas like these would be a refreshing change and show that all those in the sport were not the same.

This was such an exciting prospect, even though I was busy working 16 hours a day travelling to the RCS offices at Harlow every day during the week. I was on a massive high and revelled in the situation. Every Saturday and Sunday, playing football both days and having a few pints of Abbott Ale to wash down my favourite, crusty roll with mature cheddar cheese, Spanish onion and Bovril filling. It was a kind of utopia, exhausting, fulfilling, satisfying but needing huge amounts of boundless energy that I seemed to have coming continuously.

Clare, Karen and some of their schoolmates distributed leaflets around the vicinity to start a club for pensioners, inviting over 50's to attend one afternoon to discuss the possibilities. 80 people attended, none of course wanted to run the Club, as I could not do so my Mum, Dad, father in law and mother in law formed the first committee. I put together the constitution of the pensioners Friendship Club. It continues today with my Mum only recently retired after 18 years as the Treasurer.

A few of my police colleagues and friends saw the opportunity to use the complex and sports field for charity events and formed a committee to hold a Fair.

I was at the height of extreme enthusiasm and had, it seemed, massive amounts of energy for both police and voluntary work. The two combined perfectly and the faster the pace, the harder, the challenge, the more I enjoyed myself.

I looked upon my duty as being as much about throwing myself into these "hobbies" as well as detecting crime. Both were exhilarating, addictive and had a passion that took me beyond the sensible, because, there were frightening times, throughout, when I would drop into an unexplained, total exhaustion.

I often got heart palpitations, chest-tightening pains, diarrhoea and vomiting after nightmarish sleepless, sweat drenched nights. I shrugged this off thinking that overwork caused these. When I did go to the Doctor, he reported everything including heart, blood pressure and stomach, okay.

These were never a mystery to me, just ailments that had to be endured if you lived the way I did, in the fast lane of the active detective and charity worker.

The Fair committee consisted of twelve volunteers, two footballers, six Policemen and two of their wives and two members of the disabled group, all mixed together to work to raise money for the good causes. The Project would have the takings from the bar, charities would be invited to have a stall pitch with any money raised going to themselves, an admission fee would be charged for everyone attending that would pay for arena events and other expenses with a funfair of dodgems, Wurlitzer's and other rides that would be charged a fee to attend.

Over a two-day period the football ground was turned into a massive entertainment park. It was a resounding success, hundreds came to watch the "Honda Imp Motorcycle Display Team", high wire acts, and jugglers, Punch and Judy Shows and we made a profit.

We did not think that for a first untested year we would make a serious profit but after expenses, like repairing the burnt patch caused by the flaming hoop used by the motorcyclist, we were able to vote for £200 to go to the disabled group.

Our success appeared to eclipse the football fraternity who were perhaps not so wide or forward thinking and a rift started to appear.

In addition to this incident Dorothy came to me very upset one day when she said that the Committee Member of the main clubhouse project was shouting at the disabled group treasurer. I went to the Bar. Before I got there I could hear the Member shouting," You will give that money back or I will throw your group out and you will not be allowed to come here for your meetings!" I was horrified that he could treat such a vulnerable person in this way but as I entered he stopped talking and went out of a door opposite and onto the playing field.

The disabled group treasurer was distraught and in tears. When I asked him what the argument was about he said that the Committee Member was demanding the cheque back that the Fair Committee had given his group, as one charity could not give donations to another.

I took this up with the Committee member, saying that it was a group of volunteers not the Project that had raised that money, we then argued about the pitch repair and he added that the "disabled so-in-so, s" did not deserve to be there and "were too demanding." He went on to say, "The Project was for football only and no other organisation should allowed to get the benefit." I was both shocked and disappointed with his attitude, feeling that it was cruel, selfish and blinkered, but he would not be moved.

That night, I resigned from the clubhouse project not really coming to terms with the fact that a charity could be so selfish and self centred towards the disabled group that formed a large part of it's own bid for charitable status. I did not want to be part of such a deception.

It was sad but the experience of the Fair stood me in good stead when I was asked to help out with the fund raising event that took place at Essex Police Headquarters each year.

The Essex Police Fun Day, as it became to be called, was started by Officers to raise money for the Great Ormond Street Children's Hospital in London. It's popularity had spread and now it supported charities all over Essex.

These were invited to set up stalls on the playing field at our Police Headquarters in Chelmsford. Off duty officers, families and friends volunteered to sell goods for designated charities and an events arena entertained the crowds to fun and games, speciality acts and displays by various police departments.

The event raised many of thousands of pounds for charity and gave the Police the opportunity to show the public what we were all about and raise awareness to the many various law enforcement issues of the time. In terms of public relations it was a huge success and showed us in a light that was rarely shown in public.

Much heartache went into the project, particularly when scathing criticism came from various ranks of officers who had no interest in such public projection.

Some even suggested that it was a ruse for officers to gain promotion.

However all the traumas of arguments and differences of opinion were pushed into insignificance when we attended the presentation of the cheques that was held at Police HQ just before Christmas each year.

The organisers, supporters and representatives of the hundreds of charities that we raised funds for were so grateful and appreciative. They showed such humility when they were given cheques at a reception we held at the end of the year

Dorothy and I were always reduced to tears of admiration for the bravery and strength that they possessed to overcome their individual difficulties.

Many a time we returned home in silence unable to take the evenings experience in and humbled by the affection shown by these people in the face of such adversity.

It was during one such Fun Day that I was standing with a volunteer detective constable and the Chief Constable watching the day's arena events when the detective said, "What would be good here, you know, is a football tournament".

The Chief contemplated the idea and then turned to me and said, "Sounds an excellent idea. Look into that Mr Craven will you?" Not wishing to upset him I acknowledged his request with a nod of the head and turned to the detective and mouthed silently, "Thanks you bastard".

In the weeks that followed I held meetings with teachers and secretaries youth football clubs and, not wishing to leave the ladies out under threat of severe punishment from my daughters, the chairwoman of the Essex Netball Association. I sent letters to every junior school in the County for their views on the project and received a tremendous response.

Competitive sport was not part of the curriculum in some schools as it was considered to be unfair to those who could not take part and sent the wrong message to children, apparently. "Total rubbish", said the remainder and only, "bred wimps and softies not able to make their way in life that had so much natural competition."

Not wanting to embroil myself in the politics of the education system I was just interested in getting together an event that attracted kids, parents and as many people as I could in one place to promote crime prevention, drugs awareness and everything else that Essex Police wanted to get across to children, throwing in some sport and raise money for charity, if I could.

A friend of mine was the Chairman of HiTec Sportswear and through sponsorship set up by his marketing director we provided trophies and sportswear for prizes.

SEE PICTURES - CHILDREN, POLICE, BUSINESS AND SPORT IN UNISON

A police officer, usually the schools liaison officer, from each division was appointed to co-ordinate a venue in each police area of the County and the winners, would take part in the finals to be held at the major Essex Police Fun Day at Police HQ.

At each divisional venue charities were invited to attend and raise money for their causes, the junior school kids would participate in the football or netball, HiTec would have a stall advertising their goods and provide celebrity attractions and the Police would promote awareness of road safety, crime and drugs misuse aimed at the junior school age children.

It was perhaps the first time that the Police, Business, Charities and Education had got together to jointly promote connected interests in such a way.

The initiative was met with differing attitudes, some senior police commanders were head over heels in favour and gave it top priority others had no enthusiasm and in one case open hostility to it. Some only agreeing to it because to go against the Chiefs' idea would not be conducive to promotion prospects. The actual success of it was always down to the determination, industry and enthusiasm of the individual community police officers that put their backs into it and made it work.

We started to add the numbers up of children who took part overall in the County and gave up at 8000.

Clare, Karen and their boy friends helped out to organise the events. The local Football Association supplied referees, the national body of the Football Association never replied to my letters, and the Netball Association managed the netball tournament. Police Officers attended to mix with the children and show them their real side. It was a very satisfying sight.

The grand finals at Police HQ were graced by the Tottenham Hotspur FA Cup Final winners of that year. The HiTec Marketing Director surpassed himself and persuaded the players, who had just returned from pre-season training, to come and join in all the fun. They were so impressed by the playing ability of two young boys that they arranged for them to have trials for the Club. The FA Cup was also present so it was a fitting finale to the first Essex Police / HiTec Junior Schools Football and Netball Tournament.

Even though I was a senior detective I did not lose the knowledge that all police officers had to be close to their public to know what they want and perform their duty balanced in accord with the demands. Shutting themselves off behind desks, steering wheels, computers and telephones does not give you any chance of giving a first class service.

A police officer has got to get out and in with the public to give himself / herself any chance of achieving success. Unfortunately too many officers had the "us and them" attitude and did not have the ability to bridge the gap between the Police Service and the public they were on oath to help.

Mixing with the community and charity people outside of the job helped me to keep my feet on the ground and keep a sense of proportion with the violence and problems we, in the Police Service, saw every day. A balanced view of life as a whole confirmed that the world was not a place of total thuggery and crime, the majority are honest, kind and just want to live a normal peaceful life.

Too many officers get cloned with the wrong attitude. As one officer put it, "Let's get out amongst the opposition!" This same officer considered that the charity and community work that others and I were doing, was only a ruse to get promoted. As he did not participate in either, work for others or promotion exams, it is not worthy of further comment.

Even so twenty-three years policing and public spiritedness saw me at last accepted in the rank of Inspector. My "Yes" came with a sigh of relief from all my family, close friends and mates in the job that would cringe after every time I was given a "No" in the past. My best mate, and I downed many a bottle of Scotch after he had heard that I had failed again, and we cursed the "tossers" who had got the okay for promotion as we drank the lot.

This time it was champagne that he brought round. All could breath a sigh of relief and would be greeted with a broad smile instead of a grunt from my poker face. At the eleventh time of trying I had been promoted.

Normally you had to wait for a vacancy to be given my "pips" but the National Criminal Intelligence Service, the NCIS, was being formed and applications were invited for all ranks including Detective Inspector.

This was exactly what I was waiting for, the opportunity to use all the years experience I had gained on the Regional Crime Squad, Major Investigation Units and the CID. I just knew that I stood a chance!

Arriving early, I had time to walk the two miles or so from Fenchurch Street Station, along the Embankment, through Westminster and into New Scotland Yard where the interviews were to take place.

The determination I showed in my stride alone was enough to make that job mine. The interview went like a dream and I was accepted as the first Detective Inspector, or Regional Intelligence Coordinator, to take command of the South East Region of the National Criminal Intelligence Service.

The Christmas of 1991 provided me with many presents, passing the promotion selection board and being accepted for NCIS. The Annual Christmas CID bash was one I will always remember, as during the course of the day I went up in the Force Helicopter no less than eight times.

I had been managing an investigation with our HQ Major Investigation Team into a number of thefts of lorries with high value loads. The lead up to Christmas every year saw revelry "jump ups" where booze, cigarettes, even chocolates and other cargoes were hijacked. In some the lorry drivers were kidnapped and held until the goods were hidden out of sight.

The villains we suspected of doing these jobs carried anti-surveillance tactics in and around our counties narrow country lanes and were therefore very difficult to catch with the stolen goods. Our team were able to follow on major roads but the small roads belonged to the helicopter. It was not possible for the chopper to hover indefinitely so he parked near to our Christmas party venue. WE had reached a crucial stage in the job and I had to be available to navigate and command the operation from above. Selfishly I wanted to enjoy both parties.

All was reasonably quiet when I filled my first plate of food from the festive buffet. I had eaten most of my roast turkey and vegetables when I was called to the chopper. The first time up was not so bad. Cold but bright and sunny we hurtled northwards for ten miles but had to return as the targets stopped.

Another bit of roast and up again we went. This time the stomach gave a little flutter but soon calmed down as another stop occurred. The team crackled on the radio, " Looks as if they're doing the shopping!"

Another five times we went up then down, between each one I managed to get through all courses of the buffet and was on the cheese board when the eighth one took us to a large farm complex and three huge barns. Christmas had come early!

In the coming dusk the arrest and search teams could drift in without being seen. The helicopter pilot suggested that we do a victory roll as the arrests were made but I declined the offer, knowing full well that he would not be happy with the Christmas Fayre contents of my stomach decorating all walls of his machine.

The barns were bursting with the proceeds of five lorry loads, Scotch whisky, wine, cigarettes, designer clothing, leather coats and Levi jeans. It was to be a brilliant Christmas!

The new-year brought on the fresh look only marred by a telephone call in the middle of the night from an American law enforcement agent. Groggy and half asleep but in automatic I answered the call just the same as all others you got used to receiving, calling you out to the scene of a murder, rape or other serious crime. Dorothy and I had got used to it.

The deep-south voice said, "Sorry Bob. But I had to call. We've lost the blip!" His unit had been tracking a ship, laden we believe with cocaine. Since the big fraud that we investigated when I was on the RCS, several agencies had been following the large amount of money that had not been recovered, around the world from bank to bank, continent to continent. It had now, they suspected manifested into a whole cargo shipload of cocaine.

He continued, "Do you know anything your end?" Eighteen months ago I stood a chance of locating RCS senior officers who might help, but now they had all moved to different locations and departments. I apologised and said I would try. He thanked me and I went into the toilet as normally would after being startled in the middle of the night.

Sitting on the loo contemplating that operation, the telephone rang again. Dorothy answered it and then shouted, "It's your American mate. He said that it has definitely been sunk!"

I couldn't get to the phone quick enough. "What was that?" I garbled. Cool and calmly my mate said, "We reckon that the ship has been sunk!"

I said, "How? I mean, why?" He replied, "I don't know but you know what we can do and see with our equipment. (I knew that they could track using satellites as we had even received photographs of suspects' car number plates from them in the past)

He continued as I regained my thoughts, "It was complete daylight, no storms, slight swell but nothing to worry about. She was chugging along quite nicely when suddenly she was gone! That size ship would not go down that quick unless it was blown out of

349

the water. We've spent over a year watching this lot and it just went up in smoke!"

I was just about to say, "Don't you mean down?" but held myself back when he continued, "Our people are asking questions all round. I just thought you might be able to find something out on the QT?"

"I'll do my best mate", I replied, knowing that I probably stood next to no chance of doing so.

Over the next few days I called or met every conceivable old contact I could in then hope that someone would have answers, some speculation was offered and others, who I suspected knew more, just shrugged shoulders.

Could they really sink a whole ship, just like that? Would I ever know?

Perhaps on NCIS I might be party to such knowledge?

Chapter Fifteen
THE NCIS – THE UK FBI

Set up, in 1992, by the Conservative Government as the flagship of its' manifesto for the next elections the NCIS was labelled as the UK's answer to the FBI. The only problem was, that it had neither been given the specific mandate nor the necessary power and authority in law to dictate procedure or regulate the other law enforcement agencies in the Country.

It was only yet another tier of law enforcement destined to confuse and create discord amongst the agencies dedicated to locking villains up.

Having now at last been promoted to a substantive Detective Inspector I was determined to carry out my responsibilities as one of the two Regional Intelligence Coordinators for the south-east of England.

Here was my chance to put into operation the essentially collective approach that was needed to combat the modern criminal. For too long we had spent more time battling against each other, mostly to boost ego and nearly as much for personal advancement, accolade, promotion and sometimes sheer bloody mindedness, than actually investigating organised crime.

A sense of competition was healthy to boost the will to spend long, uncomfortable, boring, family destroying hours waiting and watching the villains to accumulate enough positive evidence to gain anything like the possibility of a conviction. But not so much that it stifled effective action.

In most incidents this attitude had bordered on the line of obstructive and other occasions the over zealous use of "keeping our cards close to our chest" had proved to be counter-productive.

As Intelligence Co-ordinator of the north section of the South East Region of NCIS my area covered the counties of Oxfordshire, Buckinghamshire, Berkshire, Bedfordshire, Hertfordshire, Cambridgeshire, Norfolk, Suffolk, Essex, all of the Metropolitan Police areas north of the river Thames and the whole of the City of London.

To cover this huge area and mass of population I had a team of five Detective Sergeants, twelve Detective Constables, two Customs and Excise Officers and one Detective Constable from the British Transport Police.

We wanted to make changes for the better and started with high morale, individual intentions focused and a future holding nothing but excitement and anticipated satisfaction.

Our up-beat enthusiasm for the concept of the new organisation helped us sail through the adverse conditions of having no offices, no desks, no cars and no radios. The 1st of April being April Fools' Day and the inaugural day of the NCIS seemed appropriate but we got on with the job.

At one of our many office meetings that were held to try and construct an effective force in crime detection, the Head of our Region, a Detective Superintendent from the MET, said, "You are the cream of the police forces in our Region and you will be expected to work in extremely difficult situations but I know that you are all professional enough to pull through!"

On the way out he turned to me, putting his arm around my shoulders and said, "What does it feel like to be one of the top ten DI's in the country?" I smiled politely, but even then in those first few days, I could identify that this man, although brimming with confidence and vast experience in intelligence gathering, had to come to terms with a concept fraught with problems and impossible targets for success.

Fine words and aspirations he had, but nothing to back them up with when trying to convince our parent Police Forces, what our role was.

My chiefs in Essex were convinced that we were going to sort out the prolific problems we had with gypsies and lorry thieves. The MET did not want us at all and in their usual bulldozer way just looked upon us as another "constabulary", pushing us aside while they carried on with the real policing.

For years they had been given the role of both the national and international response to UK policing. Anything that required investigation or protection outside of the gambit of local responsibility was carried out by the MET. The NCIS was a threat to their credibility as the "UK's finest" and they were not going to let go of that very easily.

One of the main construed aims of the NCIS was to encourage law enforcement units to focus on specific main targets and nominate those criminals who were considered by them to be the top public enemies. The idea being that the NCIS would develop intelligence on these persons to a certain point when the case file would be passed onto the investigation units, for them to secure evidential material to prosecute.

In the past the UK the major law enforcement agencies had nominated their own targets in the thousands. With no limits and no governing body the system was in chaos. Some individual units had ownership of over five hundred targets. It was a practical impossibility for any one unit to work on so many people at the same time and as no other agency could target these individuals, such flawed practices log jammed other operations.

Part of my responsibility was to visit these agencies and persuade them to curtail such methods and cut their targets down to a maximum of ten at any one time and inform them that if they did not conform then the NCIS would dictate what persons they could have as targets.

Right or wrong, legal or not, this caused calm compliance in most, but a furore in some offices, especially those who had greedily abused the system, by targeting too many suspects.

In the MET unit, that had over 500 targets alone, I was politely asked to leave. At first I refused saying we had to sort this problem out but was then bodily thrown out by the DCI who, as he did so, said, "We do not take any truck from the Constabularies. Fuck off!"

Another, a Customs and Excise Investigation Team, were working on targets that, a Regional Crime Squad branch had nominated months previously. They were more subtle than the MET and invited me to lunch with the C & E officer who was on my team. After the "pie and pint" convivial meeting in the local pub and pleasantry conversation we were taken to the offices of the C & E Solicitors department to meet their legal representative.

In a wonderfully impressive building, with huge golden façade on the south bank of the River Thames we were greeted by poker faced security guards. Even though introduced as bona fide visitors by the C & E Team members we were subjected to complete body searches for bugs and guns. With other visitors being allowed access with minimal checks it was obvious to me, and not surprisingly to my own C & E officer, that a point was being made.

The purpose of all the meetings I had with these agencies was, with friendly persuasion; try to convince them that working together was better than operating in conflict and disregard for each other. It was not only dangerous, particularly as firearms were carried with regularity but completely counterproductive.

We considered ourselves to be more like referees than anything else. This was not the way the C & E Solicitor looked upon us. When we eventually entered his office, this short "Danny Devito" figure launched into a tirade of preposterous accusations of corruption, collusion with the enemy and lining our own pockets.

It was such an amazing stage show, that I sat back in my chair quietly allowing this blast of abuse and crap shoot straight over the top of my head. It would have been so easy to enter into the contest of pointing fingers and desk thumping but I could see no sense in it. After all I was here to appease and Improve relationships.

The anger subsided and the little man sat down, sweat beading his forehead and I saw my chance to say something. I explained the NCIS position of promoting good practice and wanting to assist to ensure the best results but this held no water with the man.

He went off into another finger waving assault and this time threatened to have us arrested and charged with obstructing justice and conspiracy to pervert the course of justice if we interfered with his teams operation.

NO AUTHORITY

We at NCIS felt that such intransigence was in itself obstructing justice however there was little that we could do about it without specific legal authority.

Clear and concise terms of reference and clear instructions underwritten by legislation had yet to define the role of the NCIS or any other tier of law enforcement if we were to be an effective force against crime.

The Service had been set up in haste by a government desperate for votes in a bid to prove that they were the party that considered the fight against organised crime to be the highest of priorities.

Short of funding and operational goals and objectives, inexperience at Home Office level, the task of making the NCIS effective was always going to be up hill.

Well meaning and founded with a strong desire to succeed, we set about the task of bringing together all the law enforcement agencies, with a common purpose of locking up villains who for too long had profited, because of those very agencies' inability to work to compliment each others effort.

Along the way we did have some success and passed to the agencies intelligence files that were worthy of their efforts. With some reluctance they took on the work. For my own teams part we gained credit for some excellent results taking gangs out for major frauds and drugs importations. During this time I paid out the largest sum of money, £15,000, to one of my snouts, for information that he gave me that crucial lead to clear up some armed robberies.

WHO SUNK OUR BOAT?

I even met my mate, Hank, the guy who had lost the ship. We met at a US Embassy party and over several margaritas we moaned the night away about the bastards who had torpedoed his shipload of cocaine.

He reckoned it was one of the renegade countries in Europe that took an executive decision to sink it "as it would not be in their national interest to have a floating cocaine warehouse off their coast".

I was sure that he knew who the country was but even the excessive alcohol did not allow him to say. He did admit that they had blipped a sub in the area but did not elucidate further. Together we complained that too many agencies struggled with the necessity of entente cordiale and he spoke of, "the swine would not scratch his back after everything, he had done for them, and was not worth a fucking cent!"

The margaritas kept coming and I told him that it was a pity that so much time and effort had been wasted by all of us just to see the ship go down and the main targets get away, Scot-free, to carry on another day. I reflected on the thoughts I had two years previous when we covered a meeting, in a Madrid hotel, between the high-ranking villains who were planning the shipment.

They were all there, the Russians, a Cypriot, two Columbians, a Yank and three Brits, all under one roof and with a complete entourage of heavies and money-men. It did cross my mind, "Wouldn't it be wonderful if we just blew the lot up in one go! Take them out. Using the cover of the terrorists, ETA, we could blast them to kingdom come and save our continent so much pain and misery!" Shame, we had to play by the Queensbury rules!

One of his colleagues joined us and we continued to spin the dissatisfaction of the present law enforcement efforts. A good moan and criticism of others actions was the in vogue conversation amongst investigators. Very rarely were there congratulations for work well done but almost always, jealous disdain of success and glee at another's demise. It was a common trait amongst investigators.

We continued our droning; nodding in agreement that there was still no real valuable and sustainable exchange of information and intelligence between services. Too few spoke to each other, we did not cooperate, we duplicated on operations, looking at the same guys and there was too much unhealthy competition.

Hank exclaimed, " You know your NCIS is just going to be another unit competing against the others. Little good would come from it. Just like us. We are always tripping over each other. We don't talk to one another. There is no central control because of the "Big Brother" fear!"

The alcohol had taken its toll and all three of us felt compelled to move to the comfort of the large lounge suite. Procrastinating further, we sank back into the huge cushions, almost putting a formalised Press Release type statement together as a conclusion to our deliberations, "We wasted millions, in resources and opportunities, and any impact against international criminals was severely diminished because of these inadequacies. As a result we only scratched the surface. Our public deserved better."

The drink won as we nodded into silent agreement.

I spent a great deal of time giving presentations to senior officers, police authorities and Customs trying to spread the word of working together and the innovations and ideals of the NCIS.

Promoting the facts that the villains were only concerned in making money and it did not matter to them whether it is fraud, slave trade or drugs. They chose the work, calculated the crime and had no parameters. We specialised too much and were perhaps blinkered in our practices. The NCIS would fill that void and concentrate on the individual targets, monitoring the whole picture of their activities, bringing the specialist investigation teams into the operation at the time when intelligence required the verification of actual evidence.

The same applied to terrorists, they would like their followers to believe they were politically motivated but committed criminal acts to fund their cause, Extortion, drugs, prostitution was known to support them. Today's freedom fighter was invariably yesterdays criminal and vice versa. All terrorists and criminals overlapped in their activities.

This brought the Secret Service and Special Branch into the fore as yet another tier of law enforcement, further complicating the task of formulating joint strategies in the fight against crime.

Exchange and interchange of intelligence and information on major criminals had to be centrally controlled and analysed for the best value and results but the NCIS was not equipped for the task.

NOT A WINNING COMBINATION

It was my job, as best I could, to bring all other agencies together to interact as one unit. To not do so would be playing into the villains' hands.

I tried to impress the Chief Officers of Police Forces by telling them about our current operations. Encouraging them to put some thought to the fact that we were losing ground against the criminal.

They looked at me in disbelief when I said we had intercepted a suitcase containing over £1 million in used notes on its' way to the Balkans. We suspected that it was money raised from prostitution and drugs supplies; we had bugged it and were hopeful of success in bringing the criminals who were responsible to justice.

With the collapse of the Soviet Union our liaison with the eastern block law agencies had improved but with the barriers of the iron curtain being removed, the freedom it provided caused an alarming rise in criminal traffic.

I stated at these presentations that, " the Bobby on the beat, under their command, was just as important a cog in the wheel at either end of the trade route but the logistical nightmare it created needed to be sorted out by Governments, if we were to catch up and succeed. We had to get used to this new dimension for national and international crime and break down both the internal and international barriers."

"Villains' take no notice of borders or boundaries and there was a new terrifying level and tidal wave of violence and contempt for life, and we were lagging behind."

"We had to rid ourselves of political infighting, egoistic advantage and prestige building if we were to beat this attack on our society."

I am sure that these forays into the regions had no affect whatsoever and were treated with disdain and ridicule. NCIS was in its' infancy and had to put its' own house in order before it could wag the big stick at the other agencies.

My team were working well in being ambassadors for the cause and intentions of the NCIS, but were having the same problems at the lower levels, as I did with the bosses. The NCIS identity had not been set in stone by the legislation and therefore it was difficult specifically to put this across to others.

Morale started to ebb low and frustrations edged in from top boss to low administrator. Even moving to our new plush offices in Vauxhall hadn't turned the enthusiasm up to any degree.

We needed a "pick me up" so it was decided to organise some functions where we could meet on a social basis as a team, a Christmas party was suggested and I volunteered to arrange it.

I used my experience to set up the Welfare and Social Club for the South East Region and formulated a Constitution with its Officers of the Club, the committee, its aims and objectives and methods of democratic policy to ensure it achieved the social demands of the employees and staff of the Service.

We held the party at a restaurant in Chelsea and had a great time, I dressed up as a fairy complete with tiara, lace dress, white tights and magic wand. More like one of the ugly sisters, I took my team through a rendition of the twelve days of Christmas with the wording altered, by me, to take the piss out of some of the bosses and other characters in the group. I think it went well and know that it pulled my team together even more.

THE ROT SETS IN

My efforts were stymied by feelings I was starting to have. I had felt unwell during a flight to Luxembourg, a muzzy head and stomach cramps had turned to sickness and diarrhoea by the time I had landed in the small principality.

It was not an unusual task, nor likely to be dangerous, and something I had done a hundred times before, looking into bank accounts with the police and judiciary of the area, in the hope of finding patterns and evidence.

I had worked with the Foreign Office and was taken through the necessary legal authorities by a Luxembourg Police Officer. If I had not been doing things by the book and skating on thin ice I would have understood the tension I felt inside as my stomach cramped up and I bent double over the sink in my hotel room. I went dizzy as I spewed up for the up-teenth time and then manoeuvred to place my bum on the loo to release my bowels. I passed out on the bathroom floor at one stage coming round a short while later.

By the time it came to do the bank enquiries and meet the judiciary, to carry out my investigations, I was so weak I could hardly speak. My sweat soaked shirt and handkerchief held up to my foul-breathed mouth told its' own story.

Convinced, I had eaten something that upset me or caught some virus, with the help of the officer, I ploughed through what was required. I am sure that the officer clapped his hands with glee when he put me on the plane home.

Shortly after this trip I completed a management course for Inspectors at the Hertfordshire Police Training School. A welcome break from the humdrum of NCIS, but the course did not stop me from feeling strangely distant and muffle headed. I could not put my finger on the cause of this, as it happened at varying times of the day and night.

In the informal classroom setting, amongst the other students, the sounds would suddenly be muted and the atmosphere dimmed in the room. I went to have my ears syringed at the Doctors thinking that would sort it out. But it had little affect.

I went back to NCIS, not giving these feelings any second thoughts, but got very concerned when I had what I can only describe as, blackouts.

The first of these occurred after I had been sent to a Joint Regions Crime Seminar at Lincolnshire Headquarters on the outskirts of the city of Lincoln.

I had driven to Norwich, 200 miles there and back, the previous day and was hopeful that I would be allowed to stay in a hotel over night in that area, then drive, refreshed, onto the seminar that started at 10.00am the following morning. My Regional Commander would not sanction this, due to cost cutting. Having got back home from London at about 11 pm I had to get up at 4.00am the following day to drive to Lincoln. I was knackered!

The seminar was attended by, Chief Officers (Assistant Chief Constables) from all Police Forces bordering Lincolnshire, Regional Crime Squad Coordinators (Detective Chief Superintendents) again from all RCS areas and Intelligence Officers from those Forces. A gathering of some very important and influential people and the type that it was so essential to impress. The presentation I was to give had to be tip-top to crucially gain support for our cause.

Although I was tired, I managed to get to the venue on time and the seminar went well. I even received some compliments for the presentation.

I left the headquarters in plenty of time for a leisurely drive back to Essex via the A1 road, A14 and M11. A journey I had done on many occasions.

BLACKOUTS

I remember leaving the ring road around the city then nothing. I came out of a haze to the sound of car horns and shouted abuse. I realised I was stationary at a set of traffic lights. The engine had stalled and cars were manoeuvring either side of me to get passed. I couldn't gather my thoughts for a few seconds and looked to see where I was.

I then saw a sign post with "Town Centre" thereon and the towns of Ely and Cambridge in different directions. Another road sign stated,

"Welcome to Kings Lynn". This was nowhere on my route and I was about 50 miles away from where I should have been!

"What the… How the fuck did I get here?" I muttered to myself. I checked the clock in the car. I had lost one and half-hours. I checked my watch. Yes, that said the same time but I could not remember anything about the last ninety minutes or how I had got to Kings Lynn.

A little shocked but thinking this was only that sort of time when you lose track of time. I drove back through the fens to Cambridge and onto the M11 and my usual route.

Apart from a mild sweat and a little diarrhoea, which I put down to the minestrone soup at lunch, I felt no after effects from the experience. It must be fatigue!

Until, that is, two days later, when I was driving home from the Regional Office of the Crime Squad at Police Headquarters Welwyn Garden City Hertfordshire. I drove out of the complex and then onto the A1 towards the M25. Once again a route that, over the twelve years I had been in the RCS and NCIS, I had done numerous times before.

I remember turning clockwise onto the M25 and then nothing until I heard this lady's voice saying, "Are you alright dear?" I felt a light hand on my shoulder, gently shaking me, and again, the voice saying, "Alright dear?"

I was in the main terminal of Stansted Airport. I went cold and hot as I struggled to understand how I had got there. Holidaymakers and business travellers were scurrying around with suitcases. It took me some time to come to some sense. I was shaking uncontrollably as I tried to piece together why I had come here.

My team often used the Police Station at the airport for meetings so it was a usual venue to go to, but why now? I should be driving in the opposite direction not be 30 miles away and here. The shock took its toll as I got up from the seat helped by the lady. "I think you should go to the first aid people", she said.

Panic set in as I remembered my car and ran outside to find it. I had case files of operations, mobile phone and my jacket with all my own papers, credit cards and money inside. I felt in my trouser pockets. I did not even have my car keys. I ran blindly into the subway that led to the car parks. People moved out of my way as I hurtled out onto the car park area.

The impossible sight of thousands of cars did not help to curb my anguish. I ran to the left and scoured the lines of vehicles. It was amazing how many cars were identical to my Volvo. I doubled back passed the subway entrance and through to the other car parks. Still no sign!

I was in despair, sweating profusely and still dazed by the situation. How? Why? What had happened to cause me to be like this? Was my car on the motorway somewhere? Had I been in a crash and knocked out? How did I get here?

I rubbed my hands over myself looking for signs of injury or crash dirt. I was as clean as a whistle!

I caught sight of a Policeman's helmet across the top of the car roofs and resigned myself to the embarrassment of relating to him my story. As I walked between the cars to him I realised he was standing beside a green Volvo the same as mine. Parked in the centre of the car park lane, blocking the road, drivers' door wide open stood my abandoned car.

"Are you DI Bob Craven?" the officer asked. "Yes", I reluctantly replied. "Sorry sir. But you have got to move your car. I appreciate you may have a job on to leave it like this but people can't get by!" he ordered politely. I nodded and apologised and he added, "Can I say that it would be more secure for your brief case and phone, to have locked it!" I was so grateful that I could have kissed him but I just apologised again.

The keys were in the ignition! I drove off in exhilarating relief. I needed time to get my wind back and try to put some sense to this. I drove to the tranquillity of Hatfield Forest nearby and parked up. I fell asleep, drained, exhausted and sapped of all energy, not knowing or finding out, what had gone wrong inside my mind. How had I driven all those tens of miles without remembering anything?

An elderly cousin lived in the lovely village of Hatfield Heath at the back of the forest. I had looked after her over the years but this time it was her company and tea that I needed to bring me back to reality.

I still have no idea why or what caused these terrifying situations.

On the following Sunday, my family and four carloads of friends and relatives drove to Leonardslee Gardens in Sussex. In May, the wonderfully scented azaleas and brilliantly coloured rhododendrons set out on spacious grounds with walks and peaceful areas to picnic, where we could while the day away. It is one of our favourite places.

In the stroll round I had separated from the group and sat on a large stone in the beautiful rockery area. My mind drifted and then hurtled into a chasm, the people in the garden were still there going about as normal but part of me was tumbling into space. I started to spin and whirl downwards and I could feel beads of sweat on my forehead and my neck burst with heat.

I grabbed hold of the rock to steady myself as my daughter, one of my friends said, "Are you all right, Bob?" I mumbled something and shot off in the direction of the toilet as I felt my bum twitch. I sat in the cubicle for what seemed ages, nothing came out, although the whole of my insides was turning over like a cauldron.

Eventually coming out to the applause of my crowd of friends and some jovial remarks, I settled down as best as I could, weakened by the experience and worried that something serious was wrong with me. I just could not figure out what was going on inside me.

The next day I went to work at the NCIS Offices as normal.

Chapter Sixteen
WHAT THE HELL'S GOING ON

The day after Leonardslee was quite normal, The Monday morning meeting, or "prayers" as it was nicknamed, of us senior ranks followed by lunch and then onto a MET Organised Crime Unit office to discuss a crossover of operations. My DCI accompanied me. There were the common problems of sorting out amicable courses of action with the unit but nothing hot tempered or confrontational.

The previous days episode still played on my mind but this day was nothing out of the ordinary. For some inexplicable reason I felt nervous, lethargic, shaky, my head spun and I bit my nails incessantly. This was not unusual as I had always been a nail nibbler but recently this habit had grown far worse. I had destroyed my fingers until they resembled stumps of skin.

The DCI was a chain smoker and I commented on this, being bad for his health, when we went to a pub for a post meeting debrief. He retorted, "At least I don't bite my nails!"

We talked through the meeting and then about my teams operations, for a while, and then I left him to go home.

BOB CRAVEN

THE MISERY LINE

The train journey from Fenchurch Street to Leigh on Sea was very strange.

I had the peculiar sensation that I sat inside a box looking out onto this scene of people on a train, a television set in reverse! All sounds were muffled, like listening to someone talking in another room.

Clare and Karen worked in the City and I looked forward to the laughing and giggling with their friends as we travelled home together. I enjoyed the banter we had on those journeys, on the "Misery Line." This rail line was renowned for regular delays, breakdowns, disputes and the brunt of ridicule but the warmth of my company more than compensated for the old, draughty, bone shaking carriages.

It was a delight to be with my own daughters and their friends. I was the old softie, target of their comments and loved the attention and mickey taking.

This time, though, something was happening to me that terrified me. I tensed up inside but tried to settle back into my seat and calm down. I slipped into a doze as many commuters did to overcome the boredom of the trip. I woke up suddenly, could not control my breathing, my throat closed up and I could not get my breath. Startled and panicking I opened my eyes. I was still in this box. I could move as normal but my chest tightened even more as I fought to breath normally. I started to feel sick and felt my bowels move strongly.

I could not see at what stage we were on the journey and looked up and down the carriage for the toilet. A working operational clean toilet was a rarity on such trains so I knew that this was going to be difficult. I looked at the girls and I knew they sensed something was wrong. They both frowned and Karen mouthed are you all right and Clare nodded the same.

We reached Leigh in the nick of time; I burst out of the carriage and ran for the gent's toilet, a fair few yards away on the London bound platform.

In desperation, I made it, just in time, to vomit into the urinal. My false teeth came out with the force of it and they hit the floor. My whole stomach felt as if it was coming through my body and throat. I was expecting pools of blood and everything else that could come out with it.

I was drained of all strength and dragged myself back along the platform and up to the concourse and out onto the roadway where Clare was waiting for me in her car.

Karen was in the back seat and both looked at me tensely. I reassured them that I was okay and we drove home. Dinner was a bit of a blur, whereas it was usually full of laughter, with the girls telling us the latest gossip at work and Dorothy telling us tales of wisdom and what she had been doing in her day.

My mind was going wild. I could here my heart beating and thought it would bounce out of my chest. I could not control my breathing and my chest was tightening up even further. I remember telephoning the Doctor and then one of our friends. I thought I was on the verge of dying with a heart attack. I had had these feelings and pains before and heart problems were discounted but this time it was worse. Dorothy took me to the Doctors Surgery where I broke down in total anguish. He checked me over but could find nothing wrong with me. I was astounded. The pain was there, bad as ever. I had been violently sick and could feel diarrhoea coming on. He put little stickers all over my chest and checked me on his portable heart monitor and it came up healthy.

I was so confused. Feeling the way I did and it not showing on the tests or monitor. I could not take it in.

By the time we had got back home, other friends had arrived. They had obviously been in touch with each other and had come round to give what support they could. I went into the lounge and sat down.

My head was swimming. I could not get any air again and ran out into the kitchen. I broke down, weeping and sobbing. One of our friends came rushing out after me and said, "Come on mate. Hold it together. This is not like you. This is not happening to you".

That night was the most frightening period I had ever spent. I kept going in and out of a state of mind-blowing experiences. One minute

I would be laying in bed the next I was hurtling through a continuous stream of thoughts and pictures. The alarming speed and rate of knots the pictures were passing me or me passing them, sent my mind whirling, making my stomach churn and head swim. My mind was being tossed around like a cork. I had no control and nothing to grab onto. I buried my head in the pillow in a vain attempt to get some respite but this was useless.

The confusion this caused during my normal time out of this helter-skelter was immense. I could not bring myself to understand what was happening. Had someone slipped me some LSD? Was there a conspiracy against me from within the job? After all I was leading a team against major criminals who were capable of such a thing?

The diarrhoea I had was worse than any caused by the foul curries I had whilst on CID courses in the Midlands. Did I have a contagious incurable disease that was sending me writhing in a delirious sweat just like you see in the films?

So the thoughts went on until once again I would hurtle into another down time. Thoughts flashing by, thumping my head, my chest started to feel like it was caving in. I was losing consciousness. I had no breath. I could not breath in or out. I was dying from within.

I would wake again crying. My whole body felt drained of every piece of energy, sapped of strength and any will power. My chest ached and my heart pumped so hard I visualised it rising from my chest.

I was terrified of what was happening to me. I had always been a black and white person and very dubious of anyone experiencing the inexplicable. Ghosts were and are for the weak and the paranormal is for the nutcases. But this was something else.

Dorothy did her wonderful best to help and comfort me. The pained expression she had on her face told me how confused she was and her frustrating inability to identify what was wrong with me.

The following days and weeks still remain very hazy. The down times drifted away only to return again.

My closest of friends visited regularly, and together with Dorothy, Clare, Karen and their boyfriends supported me as best they could.

It was like sitting in a television set watching what was going on around me and having no control over actions, movements or volume. My mind and thoughts seemed to be encased in a cotton wool box, muffling sound and restricting my hearing.

A visit to my GP and taking the prescribed drug Prozac only put me into a zombie state, mumbling with slurred speech. The Doctor was very sympathetic and reassured me that I was physically fit, having no heart or circulatory problems or diseases to worry about. He stated that my problem appeared to be anxiety and depression but he could not determine what might be the cause.

A friend suggested that the Police Occupational Therapy Unit might be able to help.

DESPERATE NUTCASE

My immediate reaction to this suggestion was " I am no nutter", "That is where the no hopers go" and so on. The ignominy, shame and fear of the possible truth by accepting the help of the Occupational Therapy Unit seemed too much. But some gentle persuasion from everyone around me, and the thought of some salvation from this pit I was into, was enough to get me there.

The nursing staff at the Unit were sympathetic and very kind, although not giving any immediate answers to the millions of questions I wanted to ask, were able to reassure me that help was at hand.

A very understanding Force Welfare Officer came to see me soon after. We talked for ages, he listening intently as I described the incredible feelings I was suffering.

I felt confident that official support was in hand in addition to the help given me by my closest friends and family, all intent in getting me out of this mess.

This gave me the self-determination to identify what was happening to me and find a route out to full recovery.

The pills I was taking seemed to make me very dozy to the extent that my thoughts and speech were very slow at times and I spent long periods asleep or spaced out. I decided to take the chance and stop taking the pills. I wanted to get back in control of my mind and body.

My nights were strewn with shivering and sweating. Dorothy did not complain once at having to wash the soaked sheets every morning and was there, every time I woke up shaking and sobbing uncontrollably.

I seemed to go in and out of normality but mostly be in my box looking out. An evening concert trip to Leeds Castle was a nightmare. In the dark and out of sight I coped well but in the light I had great difficulty in keeping things in my mind together. Dorothy needed a break from her ordeal. I should have stayed at home and paid the price pushing myself back into my box even further.

Shortly after I suffered from panic attacks which amounted to a number of very different experiences.

I could not bring myself to go out of our house or my very enclosed garden, content to stay safe and secure inside.

A car exhaust backfired and I ducked behind the settee in our lounge, terrified and bursting into sweat and shakes. I emerged, dripping wet, embarrassed and feeling very stupid and confused some minutes afterwards. Why had I been so frightened?

My sheltered cocoon was a garden seat at the back of the garden round my fishpond. A small area with colour, peace and quiet with just the fish, frogs, birds, flowers, insects and me.

There seemed to be an invisible barrier stopping me from going any further than the front doorstep. On one occasion one of Dorothy's friends crashed into a wall in her car outside our house. I instinctively ran out to help. I got to the middle of the road and suddenly felt I was sinking through the concrete road surface as if it had turned to liquid. I blindly ran back into my little cocoon in the back garden.

I stayed there for the rest of the day, sweating, heart pumping, chest aching, dazed and deep in those dreadful helter-skelter thoughts. When I came out on the other side of these I suddenly realised that I had actually gone out onto the road and I had survived. I was elated and the next day I went to the front door.

I opened the internal door to the porch and then the front door. I stood opposite the door and placed my foot against the wall and pushed myself off and through the doorway onto the front path of the house.

Our front path is only about 18 inches wide and separated from the public footpath by a small garden containing lavender bushes. Even standing with my back immediately to the wall a passer by could touch me. Fearful of this I flattened myself against the wall and edged along it towards the front of the house just like we were taught in firearms training. Only this time it was more serious!

I made it to the front garden and stood on the small lawn for quite sometime heart pounding and sweating. Suddenly the worst happened a neighbour walking his dog confronted me "Hello mate how are you now. You are looking well. Heard you were poorly. Nice to see you about". He walked off down the road.

My immediate thoughts were that he said I had looked well. I had lost a lot of weight during the first two weeks of my problem. Not exactly the best way to get fitter but he had said I looked well. He could not see what was going on inside my head. That was important, as although I felt rough I was also fearful of people thinking I was a nutcase and seeing the signs on me. This gave me a tremendous boost.

As the days progressed I managed to get out onto the footpath and further into wider spaces. Dorothy drove to the sea front and other places gradually widening the horizons. It must have been strange to her to have me sometimes screaming to take me home or seeing me cowering somewhere.

The Leigh Fair held in the Library Gardens was a nightmare. As harmful as any charity event could be the stalls formed an alleyway, down which I just could not walk. The prospect of me going through such an enclosed tunnel of stacked stalls, flags, bunting, stall holders shouting, kids screaming and bands playing was just too much to contemplate. Dorothy was told to go on ahead. I eventually managed to penetrate the outer fringes of the tunnel. Having found the experience not as oppressive as I first imagined I managed to get out the other side with only minor sweats and a fuzzy cotton wool head.

Shops and supermarkets could be the same, the lights, the tall enclosing shelving, and low ceiling, noise. All of these could have an effect on me that would creep up, linger inexplicably and then suddenly switch off like an electric light. Upon doing so the feeling I would get of elation at being back to normal was fantastic.

I must say that at times when this happened Dorothy must have felt I was showing my usual dislike of the shops. There were many other places where I suffered this, areas that I liked and felt comfortable in, so I was let off the hook on that one.

During the months that followed I received treatment from a psychiatrist designated by my own Essex Police Force. The thought of me of all people having to see a psychiatrist still gives me the shivers but the relief of being able to speak to someone, to drain my thoughts and nightmares onto her was tremendous.

To say I was desperate would be an understatement. Dorothy, the girls, my friends, we all needed to know, to find out and identify what was wrong with me. I wanted to get my mind back, be in control and get back to normality. I just needed to be shown the way!

Everything was a mystery and the long consultations with the Dr, productive. We would talk through my life and experiences in a way that rinsed through my thoughts and feelings. I would be drained and exhausted after each consultation but the process had a refreshing and cleansing effect that made it well worthwhile.

The psychiatrist showed great concern for my black out experiences and the times I had been assaulted. I was referred to a neurologist for tests to check that there was no brain damage. I had blood tests, eye tests and goodness knows whatever tests but all happily were negative, nothing untoward found.

In some way I was pleased but it did not help my situation, I needed tangible answers.

WHAT THE HELL IS PTSD?

The psychiatrist mentioned for the first time, post traumatic stress disorder or PTSD. I had not got a clue what she was talking about and my first reaction to this was to look intelligent and nod. Although I would clutch at anything to get some explanation as to what I was going through, the very word "stress" was abhorrent to me. I had no time for stressful weaklings!

She explained further about other stress trauma sufferers. The people from all different professions and walks of life inexplicably hit by nightmares, panic attacks, depression and anxiety after a frightening experience, incident or tragedy.

Although desperately wanting reasons and explanations of my predicament I still had some foreboding and suspicion that the truth was still being kept from me but I played along with the situation. There must be some more tangible reason other than stress?

Counselling was recommended as therapy to put me on the road to recovery. I was warned, though, that sometimes, PTSD could be a permanent disability, but one, fortunately, that could be lived with.

I grabbed hold of any opportunity to get me out of this mess. At times I would just burst out crying, weeping and blubbering like an uncontrollable child. My sensible side would despair as to why I was doing this. I had no worries. I was financially sound, had a happy marriage, wonderful wife, family and friends and the committed support of the Job. There was no simple explanation. It was happening and I had to contend with it and counselling at the nutty farm it had to be.

The sessions started in earnest with a group of six to seven people. It seemed to me that their individual problems that ranged from bereavement, child birth and work were far greater than I had suffered and some showed such extreme signs of suffering that I felt somewhat of a fraud actually being there.

The exercises and tests we carried out collectively gave me time to reassess my feelings and reason with what had happened to me and actually identify a path for the future. The despair very slowly diminished and some light at the end of the tunnel started to show.

The sessions had their lighter moments when we found ourselves laughing at adversity and finding some humour in what was happening to ourselves. I can only hope that the other patients have found a better life for themselves.

Relaxation and learning to control my breathing to either bring my pumping heart, down or up, to a balanced level was also recommended and to do this I attended a local doctors surgery where a group of experts, in relaxation, held sessions.

The problem was that these were always held on a Thursday evening; the very day we usually had a curry or chilli con carne. It was rather unfortunate for the other people attending, that the relaxation was so successful to my body that loud flatulence or snoring emitted from my orifices, in response to the soothing music and therapy received. This caused a few silent ripples from the horizontal bodies as they lay upon the floor of the surgery and there was only the odd wry smile or knowing nod in my direction from the polite people attending as they left. So kind and so thoughtful!

My feelings on the first visit to the therapy unit for counselling were a mixture of fear, embarrassment and hope.

The hospital being so near to Police HQ and the people I knew. What if I bumped into someone from work? How would I explain? How would I cope? What would they think of me going to the mad house?

These questions were never really answered, as the days that followed were just full of the kind of help, understanding and guidance for recovery that I had so longed for. Through subtle and cleverly thought-out group sessions I was able to look into the depths of my own mind and life identifying what I was about, how I ticked, my past experiences and how I felt about them and what others had done around me during the incidents.

It gave me the opportunity perhaps for the first time in my life to look at myself, give myself time and space, spoiling myself in ways I had not been able to do before.

I gradually started to get out cycling and walking for miles. My team mates from the NCIS heard about this and bought me my own beautiful mountain bike as I was wearing my daughters out.

I would ride off for hours along the country lanes and paths, once getting a telling off from a farmer for cycling on a footpath. This was the first crossword I had heard since my breakdown so it was quite traumatic. There I was cycling along the sea wall between South Fambridge and Wallasea beside the River Crouch, no one for miles either side of me when up pops this farmer from his field wagging his finger at me.

The effect was quite severe at the time sending me into thought tumbles, loss of breath, sweating and dizziness. I could not ride any further and spent the next hour sitting and eventually sleeping on the long grassed bank until I had sufficiently calmed down to continue. I walked the next mile and then rode back home convincing myself that the situation was nothing to worry about and hoping that the farmer had not called the Police who would be waiting for me when I returned.

I still found that crowds were a problem for me, the rushing of people going past me and the noise and clatter and the feeling of being enveloped by the confusion of it all. I would feel my mind drifting into a whirlpool, which gradually grew tighter, and tighter drawing me down until I tumbled completely into its centre and plummeted down into the black abyss. Complete and total exhaustion would follow.

On one such occasion we had a dinner party for six of our friends, the main meal was finished and the liqueurs were being served, quite a bit of wine had been consumed. I felt extremely happy and contented. Conversation was being carried out over, around and above me on all sorts of topics. The voices grew louder as each friend competed to be heard. I found difficulty in focusing on any one conversation and started to hop from one to the other catching only fractions of the content. My head started to swim and throb with extremely loud voices that got louder and louder. I felt the whirlpool coming on and my throat tightening. I was fighting for breath and felt like I was travelling at a death defying speed on a roller coaster.

I convinced myself that it was only a flash back and tried to shrug it off and continue with the evening. After all I was amongst friends, cosy, safe and happy. The absolute exhaustion created by this experience was unrelenting and eventually I had to concede and do no more but retire to bed for a restless uneasy sleep.

I tried to put specific reasons for these occurrences. Was it alcohol, over doing things, worry about the future or something logical and understandable not only for me but those around me and of course those at work who by now, I felt, were becoming a little restless with my absence.

It was ridiculous to think but I selfishly wished that my affliction could be one, like cancer, or other serious physical injury or a heart condition that would have been easier to accept!

COULD SUICIDE BE THE ANSWER?

In the early days of my first discovering my problem I received many messages of support, comfort and understanding from friends, colleagues and relations.

Without such I am sure that I would not be in such a reasonable shape now. There are people that do suffer, have nobody and must be in such terrible despair. A counsellor warned us that suicide is an option that we may have to confront and deal with and added strongly that anyone who should do so must be firm and make contact with a relative or the therapy unit emergency line.

I knew what he was referring to and on two occasions telephoned the line as a last resort to unburden my twisted mind. This would not be the last time that suicide sprung up as a solution.

Amongst all the good luck messages I received I was surprised to hear from a number of officers who had suffered from a variety of stress problems. Some I had not met before, others I had known and would never had dreamed that they could have suffered in such a way.

The message from them was clear, " Hang on in there. I have been there. It will go away eventually. Do not worry! "

Some even gave me hours of their time to talk through what they experienced which so closely linked with mine.

I look back on their visits as the nearest I can get to a turning point in my situation and of paramount importance to the road to the recovery I so desperately wanted.

I was so dazed with my situation, whilst still appreciative of my need to get back to work, and became disassociated with time. I seemed to drift from doctor to therapy and back again. My progress was painfully slow and my impatience showed with mood swings and tantrums especially directed at my closest and dearest, wife and daughters. There were times now I look back where they would have had every right to pack up and leave me.

During some days my life was in small pieces, just sitting looking into space, crying and weeping, being angry with frustration, the sitting in a box and looking out continued, smashing light switches with my fist in sheer annoyance of not knowing what was going on, being intolerant of Dorothy and the girls and mopping up sick and sitting on the toilet for what seemed like ages.

My mind is in turmoil. The help I have received is well intentioned. But there are so many questions that I wanted answered and all the wonderful, patient people that have helped me through the recent months of despair and anguish could not give me, that extra leg up, to understand what my world has come to. I did not know how to deal with that?

Since the blackouts and going off on sick leave my real friends had rallied round Dorothy and I, to give us what support they could give. Some of these were high ranking police officers who, although not entirely understanding my problem, knew me sufficiently enough to realise something out of the norm, and not in my character, was happening to me. Their support and friendship was a crucial factor to my building a life after it's untimely destruction.

None of our friends asked questions of me, although I knew they were asking it of Dorothy and our daughters, Clare and Karen who were living at home then. They did not doubt me, even though neither I, nor anybody including the doctors I was consulting, could say exactly what I was suffering.

377

The trust that these people showed in me was, and still is, nothing short of magnificent and gives me the confidence to say what I feel, no matter how bizarre, to try and explain what is happening to me.

The most crucial helping hand I received to establish what was happening to me was the visits to see the psychiatrist and the counselling. Demeaning as it first appeared, it turned out to be the best that could be done.

The meticulous analysis of my personal police file / records, incidents that had occurred and a précis of my medical record showed a pattern of events that pointed toward the resulting PTSD.

Discounting football injuries, they noted that I had been seriously assaulted on five separate occasions and that the cause of the feelings I suffered was the brain recounting these incidents again. She explained that the mind never forgets a shock or trauma, that it retains the thoughts and fears of the situation but in time pushes them further back into the memory. Sometimes the traumas reappear and push the mind and body through the same processes again, manifesting in the type of feelings, emotions and bodily functions that I have been suffering.

SNIVELLING WRECK TO POWERHOUSE

I went for consultation and counselling every week for ten weeks and during that period went through methods that could help pull me out of the mire.

None of my counselling group had been the victim of assault but the approaches to dealing with the differing causes were very similar. The one area that did differ significantly was that although I experienced huge strength and massive thrusts of positive energised thinking, almost to the extent of beyond control.

At one time I would be a snivelling wreck and another a powerhouse out of control. The complete opposites were a strange concept and difficult to understand, crying one minute and being able to take on the whole world in another.

Dealing with the snivelling wreck was hard but somewhat easier than the powerhouse. Looking at life's trails and saying to yourself, "At the end of the day. Does it really matter?" A catch phrase that had a lot of common sense in the unit but in the harsh wider world of reality could not be taken too far or too literally.

Bringing myself up, changing my thoughts, or "picture" as the counsellor would say, from the doldrums of sadness and despair, to the memories of happier, comforting, friendly time was simple compared to the latter.

On a high, hurtling along at 30 thousand feet, adrenalin pumping, focused, positive, multi-tasked, exhausted but exhilarated and achieving, I had no reason to dream of being anywhere else, until I hit that brick wall. The aftermath of the mental tumble that happened at this point was always the worst. The vomiting, diarrhoea followed by the sweating and cotton wool head. I went from extrovert to introvert at the drop of a hat so often but it did not dawn on me that these opposites were to be a significant part of my problem and one that I would extreme difficulty in recognising.

At the same time the consultations were, in a way, like an investigation as I felt the Job were getting this psychiatrist to test me out as a genuine case or catch me out as a malingerer. The dirty words of working the system were always never far away from me as I detested the many officers I had heard of using this ploy to retire from the force early on a nice fat pay off.

I did not care about this, if I got better, it did not matter to me what other people thought. I wanted to be cured of whatever was wrong with me, and get back to work at NCIS, my dream job.

More tests followed checking my heart, brain, nervous system, theories were discussed investigated and shelved.

WHO STOLE MY BRAIN?

My one and only goal was to identify the problem, deal with it, get my stolen brain and common sense back, get us out of this mess and get back to work and normality. Such concentrated efforts did not seem to be working and I would get so frustrated and angry.

Positive, structured, concentration and hard work, to me, always, produced results, but nothing seemed to be working. Following the advice and self-counselling methods pushed me forward but only a short distance, not far enough for me to, even convince myself, that I was anywhere ready to return to work

I was bitterly disappointed and bewildered when the psychiatrist sadly said, "I believe you are definitely suffering from post traumatic stress disorder. It may well be a permanent problem that can only be dealt with, effectively, from outside of the Police Service".

I was stunned and struggled to come to terms with what she said. Did she mean a cushy job somewhere? No! She said, "Outside of the job!" My first reaction was, "No way!" I did not want this. She is talking about taking away my life, my ambitions, everything I have lived for, my career and all that has occupied my life since I can remember. I don't want this.

She explained further that I had done tremendously well in pulling myself up from a massive mental and physical collapse, a total breakdown, but there was a limit to what I could achieve and dealing with the effects beyond that limit would be difficult whilst I continued to serve in the Force.

I had to balance my life differently to cope with the demands of PTSD and carrying on as a Police Officer could have serious implications for me, and the Job.

Although deeply upset and disappointed I had to agree but how was I going to cope. Okay the Job were getting rid of me, their problem was taken care of, but how was I going to get on outside of the Police world.

Chapter Seventeen
GETTING A NORMAL LIFE

The different theories given to me by the medical professionals and the welfare officers gave me real sense of the proportions and problems I would face in the future. PTSD, at that time, was a mystery to the authorities and an even greater one to someone who is diagnosed as suffering from it.

Both plucked at straws hoping that they had a cure or answer for it, firstly to help those afflicted and close second, to cut down the cost of expensive pensions and time lost through sickness.

KICK UP THE ARSE OR LOVE

Speculation of what caused it and how to deal with it emitted from many individuals and authorities. They ranged from, " Everyone suffers from stress! Give them a good kick up the arse", to, "loving them to bits and pandering to their every needs."

How I would have appreciated either of these if they had any likelihood of getting me back at work.

The former was an easy option for those bosses who lived in the Stone Age, whose answer to man management was to rule by fear and wagging the big stick.

I slapped myself around the face, deliberately cut my hand with a Stanley knife and hit my leg with a hammer hopeful of forcing my mind away from the pit I was in. A friend played "devils advocate" and threw a few "fucks" into me in an avalanche of abuse to coerce me into action. None made any difference!

Ladies used the "Mumsie" approach and showered me with warmth, comforting cuddles and soothing, soft, persuasion and "there there's! Everything will be all right, Bob. We are all here to help you".

This was insipid and over the top, I wanted understanding and support but I did not want to be smothered like a little boy squashed to the bosom of his maiden aunt.

I asked my GP for his thoughts on my condition, he confirmed that too much speculation and wild guesses existed in medical profession and not enough was known about PTSD for him to give a concise opinion but he had complete and absolute confidence in the expertise of the consultant psychiatrist. As a suspicious bastard, his approval gave me confidence that the psychiatrist was not the Essex Police senior officers' lackey doing their dirty work to get rid of me.

My GP also told me of the theory that PTSD could be associated with adrenalin levels in the body. Comparing it with the "flight and fight" instincts in us all he questioned if my "highs" of enormous energy and "lows" of exhaustion could be put down to an imbalance of adrenalin, "After all", he continued, "PTSD is purported to be physical condition. It may be that your brain has lost its ability to control your adrenalin. Hence the massive difference in your strength and weakness. The blackouts you suffered maybe a result of this imbalance but it is not possible to measure it."

I obviously showed signs of some agreement and he added, "But do not take this as a correct diagnosis. I am not the expert. This was just a theory in a medical journal."

I needed to hear something other than wild guesses and this theory fitted my hopes of finding a solution. I would grab hold of any theory and put it to the test and this was perhaps the most tangible answer to my conundrum. I thought that the relaxation breathing I used to meditate could be put to balancing my adrenalin.

At the same time I had just read a book describing the phenomena of panic attacks, another problem I had no knowledge of. Mostly suffered by women, panic attacks were accepted and dealt with as a normal part of life. Men, with the risk that the macho image would be dented, were less likely to recognise the symptoms of panic attacks. Admitting them would be a weakness just as it was considered that any form of stress was detrimental to their standing as the stronger of the sexes.

I shied away from any form of medical books; in the light that one could create more problems if they have too much unskilled, inexperienced knowledge. This book did, however, help me understand an aspect of these panic attacks that may have appertained to me.

GETTING BACK IN CONTROL

Getting back in control of your mind and body was the key aspect of the book and fell into the right area for me. I wanted to get my mind back but needed to be given a route. The breathing exercises I learned at relaxation classes were a very simple way back.

Lying on my back comfortably on the floor in a warm room with feet and legs outstretched and arms beside me, I would breath in deeply through my nose, filling my lungs then hold my breath for the count of ten. I then breathed out, emptying my lungs and held my breath for the count of ten, then breath in again and so on.

Every time I felt a down time coming on I would do the exercise and likewise when I envisaged an "up" I would do the same. Difficult to keep the concentration but it worked well with me usually falling to sleep, put down probably to the fact that I was feeding large quantities of carbon dioxide into my system.

This was a breakthrough for me, and something practical, and "in your face", that I could do, to get me on the right road. It was slow, time consuming and needed constant concentration but I patiently perfected the task until I could virtually do it automatically, anywhere, without, even, lying down.

At times I did get complacent and forgot to relax before the appropriate time and found myself taking a tumble again. It was not the perfect answer but the nearest I had got to sort myself out. I still had a long way to go.

FORCED RETIREMENT

It came as no surprise when Dorothy and I were asked to go to Police HQ to see the Chief Superintendent (Personnel) after being about six months off duty. I had gradually been coming to terms with the inevitability of having to retire so it was not such a shock when this was mentioned.

I broke down! Why should this be? I was young. I had the best job I had ever wanted. I missed being with the lads. I still had so much to prove, to do and achieve! I was not ready for the scrap heap and I certainly had not made my mark in Society.

Dorothy was crying. I could not ask what was going through her mind! The fear and uncertainty of our future and the affect it would have on her and the girls must have been dreadful.

In a peculiar way I was the lucky one. It was my head that was doing this and only me that could deal with it. She had the girls, the house, the finances and me, needing constant attention to cope with. It had been hard for her in the last six months and she knew that it was going to get harder.

She realised that there was no choice in this and, deep down I knew that there was something about my problem that was going to take a long time to go away, if it ever did. I was torn between the two situations - go back to work and gamble on what the job threw at me or retire and concentrate on repairing my mind and forging a new future.

I had no option I had to be honest with myself, Dorothy, our girls and the future, retirement it had to be. We were destroyed, the promise of a pension, topped up with an "Injury on duty pension", did not compensate for the heartache and feeling of devastation and bewilderment.

A year ago I was riding high on the crest of wave doing the work of the ultimate detective, now I am cast aside, a statistic for the records, a pebble thrown in the pond only remembered as long as the water ripples.

I was apprehensive with the prospect of a future outside of the job but in reality it was the only course I could take to find some kind of respite. That day will go down as one of the blackest in our lives.

We had to be quick to tell the family and friends. Although there was little danger of "rumour out of control" doing its usual thing we did not want to leave anything to chance.

We arranged to meet our very closest friends in the job at our local favourite pub, The Crooked Billet at Old Leigh. An emotional scene followed after the announcement with all of us having a good old cry and the latter part of the evening tinged with "What the hell" to "You lucky bastard I wish I could get out".

DOES IT REALLY MATTER

A saying that I had been taught during counselling sessions was, "At the end of the day does it really matter?" and "There is always someone worse off than you." Sweeping they may be but such an outlook does help to adjust and balance your life when all the chips are down and so much is against you.

The concept of a normal life can never be ruled or altered drastically by this approach but in bouts of depression and deep gloom and doom these sayings have quite often brought me back to appreciating what I have got and not what I haven't.

The reality of forced retirement hit us like an express train. The letters and cards we received were wonderfully kind, helpful and considerate but our deepest worry, our future financial position, was never satisfactorily outlined to either Dorothy or me.

I was not in a very high state mentally to deal or understand the ramifications of early retirement let alone work out the complicated formula that would show what pension I would be entitled to.

Personnel, Welfare and colleagues had said that I was being cast on a disabled pension but nobody explained how this was worked out, what my entitlement would be or how much I would receive.

ISOLATED AND OUTCAST

The Police Federation, Welfare Department and the Force Pay Office gave me three different figures that I could expect and I received a letter stating that I was judged to be 30% disabled and would receive a disability pension to that degree.

We were on our own and left to get on with it. Letters asking questions for clarification were unanswered and received no replies after leaving messages.

We felt isolated and virtually outcast.

Coping with the disability took all my time and the papers I received from the Police Service went over the top of my head. Dorothy and I tried to sort them out but eventually had to trust the Force to look after us. Just like they had always done!

We concentrated on getting me back together and desperately sought some light at the end of this long tunnel. All around us encouraged a positive attitude towards the future and pointed out the good things. It was still very difficult coming to terms with the disaster falling about us and the strain of it all was a huge drain on our strength.

Everyday we had friends, family and colleagues ringing us, popping round for a cuppa and a chat, geeing us up and giving us support and enthusiastic hopes for the times to come. With people like these how could we fail?

Essex Police paid for me to attend a "Pre-Retirement Course". These were provided to assist officers to resettle into a new vocation and give advice on financial matters and benefits that may be available.

Well-intentioned and well meaning I went on the course too soon and rarely got to grips with what was being said. I wrestled to focus my concentration and spent most of the time dealing with my inner thoughts and feelings over what was about to happen and missed a lot of the details.

I needed a longer time to get to deal with forced, unplanned retirement and its' complexities and never got that individual care that my brain needed.

I envied others on the course and tried to listen to the aspirations of moneymaking projects and pleasurable, relaxing pastimes they could now enjoy. Muzzy headed and way out of my mental depth of understanding, I dearly wished that this could be the same for me.

FINANCIAL DESTRUCTION

My first pay cheque in retirement arrived a few days after I had officially left the job. My total income, including both pensions, had now been cut by two thirds. With no allowances and of course no overtime that was what we were left with.

Our outgoings were very high with several loans and an extremely high mortgage.

I had not considered retiring at all. It was not something you did at the young age of 46. In the Police Service you did not look at that, until you were fifty and even then I would have wanted to continue until I was at least 55 or older, if fit enough and still enjoying myself. All our finances were geared for a long and happy police service and then retirement. Put it down to bad planning, whatever, but who would have guessed that being cast early through injury would happen to me!

Drastic action had to be taken. We managed, just about paid off the debts, with the exception of the mortgage, which was too high. The only way that we could do this was to move a smaller home and cut down our mortgage payments. It was a mess but as they say, "There is always someone worse off!" Very true but little comfort when it is thrust upon you and you are not mentally capable to take it all in. The worry of being able to survive was distressing and caused as much mental strife as the trauma.

The situation would have been far different if I had been able to plan for retirement as I had expected to.

ANNIE IS AN ANSWER

Throughout my demise and the time it had taken me to recover Dorothy was always at my side doing everything she could to help me. I wanted to surprise her with something that would show her my appreciation for all the life long love she had given me. She always wanted a veteran car and had seen one in a garage at the lovely Essex village of Great Bardfield whilst on a country drive.

I secretly, with the help of a few friends, I bought the car for her birthday that was a few days before I retired. Our friends took us for the same country drive and we went for a casual look in the garage. There with the biggest bow round its body and a birthday cake on the bonnet was her 1934 Lanchester six light with resplendent chromed bumpers, front grill and hub caps, gleaming highly polished black paintwork and bees waxed leather seats. This was probably the only time that I have ever totally surprised her being one of these persons who likes surprises but only if she knows about them before.

Our first drive with our friends from the garage to the picturesque Finchingfield was one of those rare magic moments never to be forgotten. "Annie", the name Dorothy gave her car, purred through the clear winding country lanes. Clear because the unfortunate drivers behind could not get passed a car whose maximum speed was 35 mph on the straight downhill.

Respectful overtaking motorists were always given a thank you blast from her deep-throated horn.

Over lunch we could not keep our eyes off Annie being inspected by so many people while she was parked outside. "Perhaps that could be what you could do", said one of our friends. "What?" we said. "Well you, Dorothy, are good at flowers. You could do weddings with the old car. It would be relaxing. No pressure", they replied. That could be the answer!

THE LEAVING DO

It is customary to have a leaving do and with so many friends to say goodbye to, it was only appropriate to celebrate having such a great time in the job and hold it at Southend Police Station, where it all started. I was very dubious not knowing how I would cope and dreading the possibility of making a fool of myself.

Over 150 family, friends and colleagues attended. Some travelling great distances and needing overnight accommodation, some who I had not seen for many years, particularly wanting to wish me well. I had sent invitations out to everyone I could think of, who I had served with during the last 26 years but I was so pleased to see many others who I had missed and did not realise held me in such high regard. You may loose a few friends in these circumstances but these are far outweighed by those who care.

The warmth from such friends was one of the many thoughts that crossed my mind when I felt so bad that suicide was strong option to get away from my feelings. On such occasions I would prepare for death and think through how I would do it without too much upset for others. Every time I would be pulled back by the thought, "Yes okay for you. It will solve your problem completely but you will let all those, who love you, down". The level of genuine love and warmth from all was so essential for the push forward.

The send off I was given reinforced the tremendous bond that existed between us.

Speeches by colleagues, praising my dedication and commitment to the job, were both kind and embarrassing, for me, and a huge boost for the Dorothy and the family. Tales of professionalism, skill and madness impressed them, especially my Dad, who said after, "Well done mate. Typical of you though, fall into a bucket of shit and come up smelling of violets!" The cards, gifts, speeches and warmth shown to us on that night gave us strength and determination to create a new life and focused future.

At the do I read a poem that I think was appropriate for the occasion and the support I had received from everyone during my illness. This was about friendship standing the test of time. It was my way of saying, "Thank you for years of trust and friendship and for being there with us, when I needed it most."

The sincere wishes were such a tremendous support for us and never forgotten.

THE IGNORANT

There was the other side of the coin when, the "friends" I thought I had crossed to the other side of the road rather than speak to you. Not the type that could not cope with speaking to someone after bereavement, but a deliberate act to avoid you. It was the course that the most unlikely ex-colleagues would take. I never know if it was through embarrassment or because they thought I had "worked my ticket" to retire early on a cushy sick pension.

The Police magazines were full of articles questioning the system of illness retirements and the ease with which officers, mostly those who were in the shit, found they could retire and escape discipline charges. I abhorred this and sure that I had not retired in that way made my feelings known in a letter to the publishers. If they had really known what it was like to be forced to retire when you did not want to and the financial crisis that it caused. It was something I had to do for both, Dorothy's sake and mine.

This type of nudge, nudge, wink, wink mentality manifest itself later when I went to a friends' wedding where I saw an ex-Met DCI. He introduced me to his daughter and son in law by saying, "This is Bob Craven. He was a DI in Essex and successfully used the system to retire early!" The wink, smile and nudge he gave his son in law as he said this sickened me so much that I just had to leave them without reply.

Another "friend" made a great play by saying to me, "You've done well mate. You're well out of this lot. Nice big fat pension. You must be laughing all the way to the bank. You lucky bastard!"

"I am bloody lucky. I am earning one third of what I was one month ago and I have probably got to sell my house to get by. Sometimes I don't know what day it is, I sit in a daze exhausted from spewing my guts up and crapping for hours. It is so bad that suicide is a common option. Yes I am fucking lucky!" I retorted and walked off shaking with fury, leaving him making futile attempts to apologise.

This was the first of many such occasions when friends and relatives showed their lack of knowledge about post trauma stress disorder. Like me six months earlier they were in the dark. I had to tell them to put them straight but at the same time in doing so I felt that I was justifying my position when in fact I did not have to.

A lot of the time I was quite normal and no one would know that I was suffering. On the outside I looked okay, suntanned and healthy looking, but inside I was in turmoil, head in a spin and throbbing and stomach churning.

People seem to relate and understand a physical disability. I had to come to realise that in our world a disability that can actually be seen is far more acceptable than one that is inside your head. Oh! How I wished sometimes that I were a cripple and not a nutcase!

THE SWANSONG

We had always looked forward to a swansong holiday as everyone hopes to when your working life is over so we allowed ourselves the luxury of a holiday in Canada, whale watching and touring the Rockies.

"You and Dorothy deserve it!" said friends and colleagues were eager to point out, "You have paid for it in more ways than one. After the beatings that you had many would have given up well before you did. And you have paid 11% of your salary for your pension for all those years. So nobody is giving you anything for nothing.

BOB CRAVEN

Take it and get on with your life. You have earned it in blood and dedication".

With the help of Air Miles coupons from the supermarket, Sainsbury's and the copy of the National Geographic on British Columbia we flew off to Vancouver.

It had been twenty years ago that Dorothy had been looking at a Golfing Magazine belonging to one of our friends, when she saw a photograph of a golfer standing in the beautiful green riverside valley of Banff, with a backdrop of snow capped mountains. Pointing at the guy as he took his swing, she said, " One day I would love to be standing right there."

We promised ourselves that we would do this when I retired. That was happening now, ten or so years before I ever anticipated to leave work, As it was unlikely that we would ever have the opportunity again for such a trip of a lifetime we took the bull by the horns and decided to go.

The girls took us to Heathrow and tearfully saw us onto the plane. I was apprehensive and in a low period, it was almost as if it was a last farewell and I would never seeing them again. Excited for then prospects of a good time but unsure how I was going to be but resolute that Dorothy would have her dream of "being there" fulfilled.

It was the least I could do for the suffering she had had to endure in coping and looking after me.

I suppose I was foolish to think that a magic wand would be waved during the trip and I would be healed but the PTSD tagged along. Several meals and visits to places of interest were spoilt by the frightening and terrifying mind tumbling, sweating and vomiting.

The beauty of the Chateau Hotel at Lake Louise was put to the test when I had a bad turn in the reception area and had to get to our room quickly. I just made it to the toilet in time as my world closed in. The nightmare night ended in sweat soaked sheets that were kindly changed by the hotel staff.

Even in Banff, the place of our dream, I descended into a pit as we walked through the town. On both occasions I used the breathing technique to get my mind together but frustratingly reminded of this demon in the back of my head.

Even on the holiday of a lifetime, the happiest occasion one could ever wish for, I lost control of my own body and mind. In spite of these set backs, we had a great time, but as ever, on these occasions under normal circumstances, an anticlimax ensued when we arrived home.

Where do we go from here, what do we do, how do we get the money in.

DOORS SLAM SHUT

It is not until you leave an institution like the police that you realise how lucky you were inside than out. A huge door slammed tight behind you, no more welfare visits (they had too much to do with serving officers), no protection supplied by the Police Federation, our Police Union (two letters written to them – one did not get a reply and the other typed at 2.00am in the morning while I was going through a bad flashback replied, basically, "What do you think I could do about it!"

I continued to have major problems and mental set backs and needed to consult the psychiatrist again. We naturally paid her fees ourselves but when asked, the Essex Police Finance Office refused to pay the consultation fee.

We could not afford for private health insurance on pensioners money, but, in any event, they would not provide funds for treatment of PTSD, as it was a mental health problem. I tried to argue that the experts considered it to be a physical disability but they would not budge.

An additional problem surfaced when I went for my first annual assessment with the Police Surgeon. I had no idea what it was or what was involved. He was very friendly and by coincidence was the same Police Surgeon who, foolishly, had his car and valuable medical contents stolen, the same stolen car that had smashed me, and a uniform PC, off the road, a few years previously. I had known him for nigh on 30 years. He took my blood pressure and temperature, tested my reflexes made a note, talked about the weather and sent me away.

I had been with him for no more than twenty minutes. Two months later I was told that I was now less disabled and my pension was cut by a third. I was in despair, ex-colleagues were so angry and supported me in an appeal. The whole business put me back almost to where I was two years ago. I am told that from that date forward, only qualified doctors, experienced in the field of the appropriate disability, carried out these assessments.

It was just as important to me to have the right assessment from the point of view of honesty and confidence. I wanted honest answers from qualified people to give me confidence and help me. In addition, I wanted to be assured that serving officers were being given the degree of expertise that would help them to avoid the problems I experienced. They would effectively gain from my pain.

I had nothing to hide and expected the Police Service to reciprocate with fact based expert assessments.

TRYING TO HELP OTHERS

I put together my own account of what had happened to me, based on the notes I had made during the therapy sessions, calling it "Bob's Story." I have used this in this book, taking me a long time with a failing ability to concentrate for very long, I typed it out and sent it to the Chief Officers of Essex Police in an attempt to prevent more officers suffering like me and destroying themselves, save the loss of good officers and their skills to the Job and avert the huge losses incurred in pension payouts.

I went to lunch with the two Assistant Chiefs, they are friends and were very conciliatory but I am sure they did not know what to make of my story. Showing concerns that such a publication would have a detrimental affect on me, if I tried to help, they did not pursue it further.

A small presentation, I did do, for budding counsellors in the force underlined their concerns. I ended up exhausted, drained and very emotional having to be helped home by a best mate. It was not a good idea!

Only one comment emanated from the official police side and that was from a Welfare Officer who thought the story was theatrical, not the most helpful of criticisms but coming from an ex-police officer and starched report writing background it was excused. Bob's Story and perhaps this book may be construed as theatrical or even drab and starched but I am not doing it for some prize as a literary masterpiece. If it makes just one person, sit up and think then it has succeeded.

OLD ZEST RETURNS IN PATCHES

Friends and old colleagues gathered round and set me on a path for some normality. I joined the National Association of Retired Police Officers (NARPO). I thought I was the youngest, but not by a long way, I had forgotten that any ex-officer, whatever years of service, was able to join. Messages of support and sympathy for my problem poured in and gave me new heart to make the most of life.

Ex-colleagues, who more business like, formed the Ex-Essex Police Business Association (EEPBA), whose aims were to assist officers in the difficult transition from the cocooned Police Service to the rigours of business management.

Both these organisations were just what I needed to get my life back in gear.

Yes! One huge door had shut but others had opened slightly.

I used the normality time I had to set about planning and balancing our new life.

I still had a passion and enthusiasm for being involved with charitable events. Nobody around me would stop me or hold me back although Dorothy would question if I should be doing anything.

BOB CRAVEN

I helped a local hospice to set up a Fun Day at a large park in Southend. The event was a success but unfortunately I was still in the early stages of learning to deal with my disability and the work involved was a step too far and took its toll on me. I had to be careful and balancing life was going to be more difficult than I realised.

The problem was still that I burned red hot with enthusiasm, not appreciating that the flame would be snuffed out at any time and anywhere. I could not control that. Yet!

One of the issues I have to continue to appreciate is starting something that I cannot keep up and therefore letting people down midstream.

Chapter Eighteen
REAL LIFE ON THE OUTSIDE

A huge determination to prove that I was not some nutcase, as I was affectionately referred to by some friends, and the need to earn much needed cash to make up for the huge loss in earnings we had suffered, made me throw everything I had into any work that I was capable of carrying out.

Making that transition in the face of the problems of PTSD, and its' unpredictable flashbacks and everything else that went with it, was going to be more difficult than I could ever have imagined.

WHAT ARE FLASHBACKS

People, who have some knowledge of the disorder, frequently refer to, "flashbacks", but I have my doubts that they really know what it is like to experience one.

I can only describe my own experience but this may differ immensely from those of others suffer from. For me, they are not like that portrayed by actors in films and on TV, when the nasty experience manifests itself vividly in sleep and the character relives that moment so dramatically usually waking up screaming and soaked in sweat.

Although suffering very similar, I have never actually experienced my traumatic incidents in such clear and concise pictures, so as to recognize where I was, or when it was happening. My mind and body is taken over by waves of feelings that I cannot stop coming and have to deal with them as best I can at the time.

It is learning how to deal with it, that is so important and this is very much down to the knowledge and understanding of them, not only by myself, but also of the people around me. Those who do not have such tremendous support will find it much harder and at times, impossible to overcome.

I have never been able to identify any specific triggers that would cause these flashbacks or feelings. They appear to come from inside me and are not influenced by anything outside.

Since the disorder had been diagnosed both Dorothy and I used to keep a note of what I had experienced just prior to a flashback and I also kept a diary of my every thought. We recorded anything and everything I had done prior to the attack.

What I eaten, who had spoken to me, what had been said, how it had been said, what I was wearing, what the weather was like, what I had read, what I had watched, where we had been, noises I heard, smells around me and so on and so on. The list was endless.

Family and friends would be walking on a tight rope afraid to make some move or word that would trigger me off.

Eventually, we had to admit that there was no pattern and therefore no reasoning behind, where or how the feelings were triggered. Although flashbacks occurred more at night, they just came and went when they did, no matter where I was, whom I was with or what had happened previously.

It is this unpredictability that is perhaps the hardest to come to terms with. Not knowing when I am going to melt down from a normal healthy person into an uncontrollable mess.

The best way I can describe it is like this: -

If you could ever imagine being stuck on a railway line in the middle of the track and you can see a train heading towards you, slowly but surely, and there is absolutely no chance or possibility of you doing anything about it. You cannot move, you cannot stop the train, it's coming down the track. It's going to hit you! The sky darkens and envelops you but you know the train is still coming. It's still going to hit you.

Your mind is totally saturated with the extreme unimaginable pain you are about to go through, the frustration and despair of not being able to do anything, the thoughts of family, friends, future hopes that you are no longer going to see, the panic and strength of tearing at the invisible bonds that hold you on the track, the rush of the train as it hits you and pours through your body drawing out all your strength and dragging the emotions of fear, panic and despair with it and then the elation of all elations, as you suddenly realize that the train has gone right through you and is now passed down the track.

You are completely exhausted and on the brink of unconscious but your bonds are gone. You are free. The sky is blue. The sun is warm. You have a huge strength pulsating your whole body into areas of such power and force that nothing can stop you. You are not just clicking your heals with satisfaction. You are reaching out for new heights, never before attained and sticking a "v" sign up to the rest of the world.

These feelings can last for days or just minutes but each time the knock out affect is the same.

Throughout this whole rush of an experience I sweat profusely until my clothing is soaking, my stomach churns painfully causing wind of extraordinary velocity, I vomit irrespective of what I have eaten and sit on the toilet for ages with endless diarrhoea. I can usually overcome these feelings and control what happens with the breathing and meditation but is very hard, exceptionally so, on the more serious times.

The depression that it causes can be overcome but the despair of trying to understand why it is happening when I have such a perfect life in all other respects sometimes makes it that much more upsetting.

When my mind and body is low with depression, it is far easier to bring myself up as I realise that am feeling bad, my stomach is going through its crazy cycle of shits and sickness. I feel so weak and lethargic, fall to sleep or sit in a daze staring into space. This is just not normal and does not feel that way. It does not take a brain surgeon to come to that conclusion. It is hard to bring yourself out of this mode. The discipline and concentration to meditate and carry out the breathing exercises is still difficult but eventually I can get myself out of the mire and back on an even keel.

Sometimes my mind will react to it normally and give myself an automatic, kick up the arse and back into gear, just as anyone not suffering from PTSD would do. After all we are all prone to a bout of depression at some time. Life is full of peaks and troughs but my experience is that there is a huge difference in the depth and height of mine.

My GP had explained to me that my body may have lost its ability to control my adrenalin. It was a situation of opposites, none was supplied, when I most needed it, to bring myself out of the depths of depression and at other times, when I was in orbit I had uncontrollable amounts. At these times I had such power and drive that my brain was in danger of overload.

He theorised that my blackouts could be caused by massive amounts of adrenalin hitting my brain and that reacting and closing down, naturally saying, "I've had enough of this". Whether this was right or wrong it did help me to put things in a kind of perspective and identify that at low times I had to bring myself up and up times I had to bring myself down. Recently I have been told that it is some kind of traumatic amnesia.

As I said, the low times were easier to get out of than the high. When you feel bad you want to get yourself better. It was almost impossible for me to recognise that something was wrong when I was motoring at 200 mph, feeling terrific, the strength of ten men and a mind so focused and motivated that I could change the world single handed.

Dorothy would be the first to bear the brunt of the problems. She would know, looking from the outside that I was "off on some trip" and friends have said recently that I often would not "do things by halves" during my regular crusades.

FRUSTRATION, ANGER AND DESPAIR

Some of these times would take me to points beyond reason, and any attempt by outsiders to stop me, slow me down or even give friendly advise, would be considered as an attack on me personally and result in a violent exchange of words. At slightly more controlled times I would try to figure out why "people did not understand me or my quest". My frustration would eventually identify "lack of communication" as a reason for them not comprehending or getting to grips with my ideas or innovations.

Frustration would turn to despair as I failed to get them to understand and I would become violent, mostly verbally, usually towards Dorothy, my faithful punch-bag.

Having unsuccessfully vented my feelings onto her, it is not unusual to for me to take it out on a wall or anything else that could be punched, kicked or head-butted.

My temper and inability to control it, when I thought I was such a cool and collected person was terrifying. After this mayhem exhaustion would follow and in that period my mind would regain some sanity for me to reflect back on what had happened.

If I pondered too much I would go down the spiral again to deep depression and this is when the thoughts of ending my life would come. To feel that you cannot control your mind, and that you are as crazy as some of the many nutters, you have taken to mental institutions, is very hard to come to terms with. The only hope you have of controlling it is to breath exercise, or meditate and is very hard to come to terms with, when you are a "feet on the ground person", as I thought I was.

It is even more unbelievable that the condition would take me to the point of thinking that the only way out from this mess was to remove myself from everything. I was the problem. Everyone else was coping with life. Getting on with the every day trials and tribulations.

I was the odd one out, the only one with a problem. So remove me and the situation is resolved.

THAT OLD SUICIDE AGAIN

Throwing myself threw a third floor window in a store in Norwich was an option, once when I was out with Dorothy. Just walking out to sea off the shore at Southend and waiting for the tide to come in and take me out. Making sure of the job by tying myself to a buoy chain to hold me down and get my body recovered. Hanging and wrist cutting was not possible, as I always thought that this was gruesome for the copper who had to deal with it and so traumatic for the relative or friend who found me.

Shooting myself? Well I would need a gun and again too messy. Sleeping pills and polythene bag over my head seemed a good idea. Peaceful, dignified, dressed in my best suit ready for the funeral. Dorothy and the girls would be so upset, I could not say goodbye, they might want to stop me, how could I hurt them so much by doing this, what would my grandchildren think when they're Mums' told them how I left this world as a coward, taking the easy way out, releasing myself but causing so much anguish to them.

So the thoughts would go on until I regained my wits and sanity and washed the feelings away. Always coming round to thinking about my girls and Dorothy and the good things we had and the positive aspects but wary of tipping myself over the edge once again.

Constant concentration, to keep the balance at the correct level and this is something that requires a 24 hour 7 day a week focus.

In the past my mind has been awash and even totally immersed in a current crusade that leaves no room for anything else. My thoughts would be unabated towards achieving the objective.

Any other matters were unimportant and trivial compared to the particular project in hand.

A crusade to work would kick-in good thoughts, positive thinking, taking me away from the nightmares of the incidents, and the depression and anxiety that the flashbacks were causing.

GOOD HARD WORK IS THE ANSWER

Throwing myself into work would shroud over the bad and give myself the opportunity to push them into my subconscious.

I searched in all directions. With anyone and everyone I could think of who might be able to give or help me find a job. Taking some desperate measures and calling friends I had not seen for years. Most were very sympathetic and understanding but as soon as I mentioned that word "stress" you could hear their mind go into overdrive. With some I felt obliged to explain that "my stress" was not "that dirty word" but caused by specific incidents. You could feel that my explanation did not count for anything and there was still a great suspicion in their minds.

FIRST HOPES TO EARN

The ideas our friends had to use our old car, Annie, for weddings and Dorothy to do the flowers was brilliant.

She did all the technical work with me being the general runabout and also the chauffeur, complete with 1930's attire, of the elegant 1934 Lanchester Car, "Annie".

SEE PICTURES – DRESSED FOR THE OCCASION

This little business was a boom. We were part of the family joy and happiness of a once in a lifetime event and a major part of the wedding arrangements. Together put so much effort into making the day one to remember for the bride, groom and all concerned.

Dorothy would, meticulously, guide the bride through the vast array of flowers that would make up the bouquet she had always dreamed of for her special day. Hours would be spent going through the library of flower arranging books and catalogues that Dorothy had armed herself with.

Colours would be so important to compliment "The Dress" and colour scheme of the whole wedding. Size of bouquet and type of flowers so essentially combined to balance with the hairstyle and stature of the bride to provide that gasp of approval from the guests.

Table decorations of the right height, colour and arranged to both excite and relax those seated at the wedding breakfast. The groom, the first to be seen by the guests, and his attendants resplendent with matching buttonholed flowers that set the scene for a perfect day.

While Dorothy and her friends busied away at their ultra important task I would be sent on errands of paramount importance to relieve them of the mundane work and spend hours during the two days leading up to the wedding checking "Annie" over to make sure she would pass the testing time of getting the bride and proud father to the ceremony on time and thereon the bridal couple to the reception.

Checking oil, water, tyres, sweeping the remnants of the last wedding confetti from off the plush carpet and removing it from the most unlikely places and crevices inside the spacious interior, bees waxing the leather upholstery to give it that so comforting aroma of clean country air, polishing the anthracite black paintwork body and gleaming once again the mirror chrome bumpers and wheel domes and painstakingly using a toothbrush to remove all traces of dirt from between the spokes on "Annie's" delicate slender wheels.

Very much treated like an elegant elderly lady "Annie" only faltered once out of all the many weddings we used her. Her small sewing machine engine would chug away taking any distance and incline at her own pace. Sometimes very slowly to the annoyance of the stream of vehicles she always had following her. With a clear road in front on all occasions except when being overtaken by her impatient followers, who rarely failed to show the respect that such a graceful old lady deserved. I am sure that she knew her right to the road and strutted her stuff accordingly, to show she was still about, demanding attention and showing off.

She was not really to blame on the one occasion she faltered. Just like many old dears, she just did not like excessively hot days. It was over 30 degrees centigrade and a clear blue cloudless sky. Perfect conditions for a wedding but not the air-cooled engine of an old girl with a carburettor, only inches from the searing heat of the exhaust manifold. Fuel in the carburettor was evaporating so quickly after a lengthy run and it was only a matter of time when all power in her was to fade.

In heavy traffic at a stoplight, she halted within three hundred yards of the church. The beautiful bride seeing the funny side with an uneasy smile and her father trying to hide his anger so as not to spoil his lovely daughters day. This was not a time for indecision and any delay could create a further inconvenience of mild humour turning to full blooded fury. Of course we always joked that the bride had the right to be late in any event and Annie may want that to happen. It was however a joke and never supposed to happen.

We had our contingency plan to save the day. Our friend, who was transporting the bridesmaids in his Rolls Royce, had pulled up behind us to offer his assistance. The bridesmaids were rushed off to the church and dropped off and he came back to collect the bride with minutes to spare for the ceremony. One stage resolved another to settle.

Dorothy produced the ice packs from our freezer box in our own car that we used as an escort / support vehicle for such emergencies. Like a woman hit between the legs during a hot flush Annie seemed to moan slightly and settle on her axles as the cooling packs were held against the carburettor.

As if smelling salts had been applied the old girl perked up and after an acceptable lull for her to get her breath back she started first time and triumphantly we turned the corner to the church. Unfortunately the wedding party were in the church so a finish line greeting was not there, but we could now, confidentially, wait to take the bride and groom to the reception.

The quite understandable comments followed as they alighted Annie for the short journey that followed. The finale to the embarrassment was the photograph of the groom making out that he was pushing Annie to the church whilst the bride drove her. A great photo especially, as Annie, politely and respectfully, hid all her feelings of indignation.

Hot days were the norm for the weddings and one particular wedding couple were very pale and frustrated after their photographer had taken an extraordinary long time of one and half hours to take those all important pictures. Realising nerves were at low ebb I suggested that we took a longer route to the reception venue, just to take some time out and relax.

They eagerly agreed as long as it was not too long and we trundled off to take a circular route via the seafront and the famous Rossi's Ice Cream Parlour. To the astonishment of the staff and the walkers on the seafront, there we sat eating the most delicious ice cream cornets, with the doors open to the soft sea breeze, the bride, in beautiful gown, sitting on the wide armchair seats and the groom on the running board below her, licking huge cornets of cooling ice cream.

Refreshed we drove the now relaxed happy couple were driven to the reception. Some hilarity, mixed with relief followed as the guests, cancelled search parties and applauded when told what had happened.

Ice cream was not the only refreshment that we supplied for the occasion. Celebration was the purpose of the day and what better way to celebrate than to toast each other with champagne after the ceremony, in the peace and quiet of your own armchair on wheels.

After the photographs were taken we would take the couple to the rear of the car where on the boot box we would have a neat little basket holding two glasses and a half bottle of the best-chilled champagne.

Surrounded by flowers, perfectly arranged on the box by Dorothy and sporting a heart shaped "Just Married" sign it made an excellent moment for the happy couple to toast each other and receive some "oohs" and "ahhs" from the guests and the Mums to get the hankies out.

Sometimes the champagne had a greater affect on the couple than one would have wanted. Never causing a major problem but a certain amount of fun verging on near disaster. One couple had been hitting the alcohol before the wedding ceremony and the champagne had been the straw that broke the camels back.

I had to stop suddenly for the groom to spew up in the middle of the local high street. Not a problem for me but the bride did say that she hoped nobody had a camera and how bad it would be if the ensuing photograph were produced as a memento of their big day.

On another time it was the bride that could hardly stand up after the champagne. On a very cold February day the Register Office was running late with the ceremonies and the only alternative, was for the happy couple and their maid of honour to wait in the comfort of Annie's soft interior.

Her comforts were only basic and in the winter quite Spartan therefore we supplied thick woollen blankets and flasks of hot coffee to keep everyone warm, cosy and happy. Unfortunately the bride did not realise the amount of whisky, I put into the coffee and by the time she had drunk the champagne after the ceremony she had very wobbly legs and rolling eyes. With a distinct concentration to organise her slightly slurred speech, she kept repeating to herself saying that she was so very, very happy. All ended well, so I was told in their letter of appreciation that we received soon, after they returned from honeymoon.

Being the personal chauffeur to a bride and groom is an extremely honourable and prestigious position to be, in particularly, straight after the romance of a wedding ceremony. The happy couple would be expected to engage themselves in amorous clinches and emotions.

Out of respect I would not look into the wide angled interior mirror as I drove from church to reception. However, when driving along the open lovely country lanes of north Essex I could not help but notice the liveliness of Annie's springs. Her soft bouncy suspension was unusually active and causing some heavy movement in the rear of the car.

Thinking that we may have a puncture, I glanced in the mirror in preparation to pull over, when I saw the brides lacy garter flash across my view, followed shortly after by the back of her head. Laying shock aside I braked gently to a halt and got out of the car. I made out I was inspecting the wheels while the couple adjusted their positions and straightened clothing. After a convenient pause I got back into the driver seat and having thought about the possibility of unwanted marks on the leather seating said, "Sir, Madam you must appreciate that I am in a very unique position and the master of discretion, which I assure you is sacrosanct, but I do not think it is appropriate or fair that I am present when the marriage is consummated". The coy look on their faces soon changed as my stern face turned to a broad smile and the bride said, "I am terribly sorry Mr Craven. We did get carried away a bit. This is so great!" She then buried her lips onto those of her groom and, as far as I know, stayed that way, without coming for air, until we reached the reception venue some 15 minutes later.

The work as florist and chauffeur was a beautiful job. We were always part of the happiest day of the couples' lives and made to be so welcome. Never an angry word or a sad situation, some tears of course as their loved ones start a new chapter in their lives.

It was so complete to be away from the violence and turmoil of police life. I thought that we had really found our niche in life again. We called our little firm "Perfect Partners" with stationary and business cards showing our Annie surrounding by garlands of roses. We were getting back to normal!

IT WAS NOT TO LAST

It was not to last even though our popularity increased and business was booming. The meticulous efforts Dorothy and I made to provide a good service upped our order books and nearly every weekend during the summer months.

I had continued to suffer the PTSD problems and the clothes saturated by sweat were perhaps the only visible sign anyone would have noticed as I drove around. Diarrhoea and sickness was a worry and I had a couple of narrow escapes, only just making it to the venues in the nick of time, before having to burst my way to the toilet.

Near misses were getting more frequent and total loss of breath and dizziness went onto fainting and collapsing feelings. I started to get so bad that, I was concerned my embarrassment would turn a couple's one wonderful day into a disaster. After a vomiting session behind Annie as the happy couple sat waiting I decided, I could not allow that to happen so I stopped the venture.

This was to be the start of our ideal balanced life but was not to be.

It was a sad day but the right decision to take. We enjoyed the pleasures of Annie's quaint charm and sold her, a few years later, to a couple that needed a partner for another equally beautiful 1930's Lanchester six light. When the new owners drove her away I am sure she gave a little cough and splutter of a farewell tear as she chugged out of sight.

I still needed to find something to occupy my mind and "change the picture", as described in the counselling, to take my thoughts away from the adrenalin rushing moments that caused the mental sickness. I continued to seek that right balance to keep me busy, sane and as normal as possible.

On one of the many walking jaunts, I used, to try and "find myself" I went into a local employment agency to fish for that perfect combination of enjoyable, stress free employment.

The young ladies dressed in the smart uniform of the national company were very helpful. I did not tell them of my disability. I was not asked, assuming that it may have something to do with prejudice or discrimination if they did, and filled out the numerous forms describing my experience and capabilities. The basic requirement of computer literacy was to be tested, and I sheepishly sat at their PC that would assess my level of expertise.

The tongue in cheek answer to the young personnel clerk, that I had vast experience from my police days was about to be severely put to the test. To my complete amazement I passed, not with flying colours I am sure but sufficient for the agency to consider me for a number of positions.

I was concerned that they would be after the commission they get from the companies, rather than my personal aptitude, and carefully went through the job descriptions of the work offered for interview. I could not afford to cock this opportunity up.

Satisfied that the work did not show areas of concern and was confident that I could do the tasks involved with little worry of causing me further mental damage, I went for an interview at a large bank in the town.

I was taken on and put in charge of income application forms for loans and credit cards. Taking them out of envelopes and scanning them onto computers for checking and vetting by staff elsewhere in the company. The money was nothing to speak about but it seemed I was now back in society after such a long time away. I could ride my bike down to the bank buildings easily and feel that I was of some use again.

No pressure, no stress and friendly, chatty people to work with. It lasted a week with me spending most of my time in the toilet doing my usual business or soaking my clothes with sweat, head swimming and despairing with the frustration of not knowing why I was feeling this way.

I could not continue, in fairness to the company and myself. Deeply embarrassed I wrote to the agency apologising for my condition but did not expect to receive any further offers.

The peaks of hope and troughs of deep disappointment were situations both Dorothy and I had to come to terms with.

Undaunted my enthusiasm to succeed and get my life back was still very high!

ARMCHAIR I.T. AND GARDENING

Offers of working for solicitors were frequent and something I thought would be too oppressive and more likely to cause me harm but I had to consider anything that would provide income.

My first opportunity to get back into the legal fraternity was given to me by our daughter, Karen who worked for a large legal company in the affluent London Lincolns-Inn area, the centre of civil litigants in the UK.

Her bosses invited me to lunch. He already knew my circumstances but I felt compelled to say to him that I was not, particularly, after work that would be unsuitable for me. He replied, "You may not be, but your expertise is rare in my field and it maybe, that I want you to work for me". His response gave me a lift of confidence that had been lacking in my life since being forced to leave the Job.

I agreed to carry out work for him tracing people and assets but being selective what work I took on. Concerned that I would take a tumble I limited the work and avoided contracts where any potential confrontation was likely. Simple investigations and analysis of documents, at my own pace and from within my own home were ideal for the disability. When I felt bad, I could retreat and use the better times to do the work outside. I knew I had found the right combination.

As my skills became known, other firms and solicitors requested my expertise. I joined E.P.I.C, the Ex-Police in Industry and Commerce, a national business, networking organisation of retired police officers.

I also became a Member of the Institute of Professional Investigators and was entitled to have the letters M.I.P.I. after my name on correspondence.

Offers of contracts came in regularly as my skills were advertised and marketed in the circulars and lists of members sent out by these organisations. The analytical investigation experience I had gained in the NCIS and RCS was a new innovation in the business and commerce fraternity.

As my popularity increased I was made even more aware of the need to balance out my work with the disability of PTSD and make sure that I did not dive into my pit once again.

Manufacturing Companies, Financial Institutions, Banks, Insurance Companies and Civil Litigants contracted me to carry out complicated investigations that required an analytical approach. I could sit in the comfort of my own home, measuring out my day in the balanced order I needed. I set a timetable for the work to accord with my mental state and if I found that unseen pressure was looming, I would use a clause written into my contract to either sub-contract or terminate the work.

As a result, using the Associations network, I gave away many lucrative contracts to other ex-officers or enlisted help to fulfil the work that I could not capably and satisfactorily carry out. The system worked so well that Dorothy and then Clare and Karen joined in helping out with the admin, insurance and legal advice, with two other friends doing the office work.

They were also keeping an eye on me!

I needed to be reminded by them often, mostly at times when my enthusiasm would be so great that I lost sight of the PTSD problems. I would be deeply immersed at the task in hand working, quite often, through the night concentrating all my efforts and completely taken over by the thrill and satisfaction of being normal, not taking any notice of the frequent visits to the toilet or my inability to relax and take some time away from my project.

Dorothy would show her concern and try and persuade me to slow down and I would snap, producing an angry tirade of violent abuse almost spitting blood at the audacious suggestion that I might be harming myself. Incensed that such a suggestion should be made I foolishly continued at manic pace until collapsing completely, totally exhausted and unable to put one foot in front of the other.

I soon found myself tumbling into the mind spiralling, stomach churning, throat closing, chest tightening, heart thumping, sweat streaming and loss of control. If I had not gone too far into oblivion I used the breathing techniques to get myself back. This could take a few hours or in the worst times two or three days. I could never be certain how long it would take.

A lull in the work enabled to me take stock on the life I found myself leading. I took up gardening. Several friends had suggested, that such a relaxing pastime, one that I loved and was good at, would be "just up my street." It would give me a small income, not be over powering and doing something that gave me a great deal of satisfaction and enjoyment.

The popularity of my work quickly got round in a very short space in time and I had a steady stream of gardens to look after. The pleasurable parts of the job covered over the hard graft that I had to do in some.

Friends had just bought an old 15th century farm, buildings and land near to us. It sat in the centre of a beautiful river valley, full of wild life and destined to become a country park. The peace and solitude of the farm and surrounding land was amazing. Besotted by the natural beauty and enveloped by the quiet and stillness, I threw myself into clearing the overgrown flower beds, starting up allotments and bringing the gardens back its' previous splendour.

I was in heaven! It did not stop my problems but when I did suffer my friendly owners would tell me to, "take time out, go lay in the barn or your favourite spot in the wild flower field!" They understood and were ideal bosses for my situation.

I lay with closed eyes listening to the songs of the skylarks, the rustle of the wind through the long grass and taking in the sweet smells of the wild flower meadow. Losing track of time I would return conscience-stricken for them to say kind and understanding words of comfort and offer me a cup of tea.

Even in this idyllic setting I insisted on throwing myself at a conservation project. Not satisfied with just simple gardening I jumped on a bandwagon and hurtled into helping to turn the area around the farm into wild flower pastures. Consulting the local council, attending meetings with wild life specialists and giving presentations on the prospect of a much-needed natural haven in the area. I was motoring at 200 mph again and Dorothy would implore, "Why don't you be just an ordinary gardener? Why have you got to be on a continuous crusade?"

I pushed the suggestion aside.

However natural consequences of my friends having to move back to the north and the farm being sold stopped the project.

This coincided with further offers of work with solicitors and financial institutions and a completely different world.

THE OPPOSITION

I had received offers to work for defence lawyers or "the opposition", as ex-police colleagues would call them. Even though described, by those in it, as a "honourable trade", I thought that this might be step in the wrong direction.

However, I would not know unless I tried it! My curiosity would never have been satisfied and the rewards were tempting so I took up contracts with legal firms in the London Area.

It was unlikely that clients would know of my background therefore confrontation was minimised. The solicitors knew of my disability and were aware of the need for a balance.

Realistically it was always a risk and luckily somewhat amusing when a clients' father recognised me.

I had to clarify some parts of the evidence on a fraud case I was analysing and met the client at the defence solicitors' office.

The client sat in the interview room beside an older man, who recognised immediately. He was an old East London villain who I had locked up years ago for armed robbery. Much older and fatter with shaved baldhead he scrutinised me with a screwed up face.

I sat opposite them at the desk and the older man said, "Fucking hell! It is you! When the boy here told me it was a Mr Craven he had to meet, I wondered if it might be you."

The hair stood up on the back of my neck as I waited for the violence. His trial had been a dirty one with accusations of corruption and he being "fitted up". I expected the worst!

To my astonishment the father looked at his son and continued, "Don't worry mate. What better than to have the ex-old bill defending you! They don't get much better than this bloke."

I couldn't disagree! He was wrong though because the evidence was so strong against his boy that he got four years in prison. Even so, after the trial, he shook my hand and thanked me for doing my best.

After that scare I turned other offers down, until an old friend asked me to help out, an old acquaintance of his. The case was a large drugs conspiracy trial. I reluctantly took up the challenge, in the face of some frowning from those close to me. This was more to do with the size of the case and my disability than the dangers of the client knowing me.

A rough look at the evidence against the client showed that there was no case against him but the prosecution persisted and the trial went ahead.

I took no pride in the success but gained a slice of fame when the client was the only one of twelve to be found non-guilty. The remainder received sentences of 12 years imprisonment. The analytical methods I used to expose the prosecution case and cast doubt on the evidence against our client created a deep interest among the other defence teams.

I received the appropriate pat on the back from the solicitors but during the trial, PTSD had taken its' toll. Part way through the trial I had to sub-contract work on the case to other ex-officers in the Business Association. Falling sick and exhausted I had to be honest with myself, by balancing of work with the disability. I had to prioritise my professional responsibilities against my personal health.

For the first time I was directly involved with the accountancy of the defence case files and astounded, by the complicated system that small defence lawyers had to cope with, to gain payment from the Legal Aid Board, now Legal Services Commission.

No wonder so many good honest solicitors were retiring or "going to the wall" into bankruptcy. They needed to hire accountants to deal with the paperwork involved and this took precedent over the primary task of defending their client.

Although inspected regularly the paper mountain was impossible to check thoroughly for cost effecting, and could easily overrun a small firm with disastrous consequences.

Open to abuse and so complicated as to be unmanageable and uncontrollable by the Legal Services Commission itself, unscrupulous firms were able to earn millions of pounds in fees unhindered and unchecked.

On a huge fraud case that required a team of over thirty of my sub-contracted analysts it became obvious even at the early stages there was no evidence to link the client with any illegal behaviour.

An independent pre-trial revue of the prosecution evidence and the defence case would have concurred that it was a waste of public money. When I floated this idea with the defence lawyer he angrily disagreed as he, "was likely to earn over £3 million out the case." Five years later a Crown Court Judge kicked the trial out, stating that it should never have been brought to Court. It had cost the taxpayer in excess of £25 million. What a waste!

Glaringly obvious, the only way to be able to appropriately and fairly defend an accused at a cost effective level would be to have a Crown Defence Service. Funded by Government and over seen by the Legal Services Commission this would help to achieve justice for the defendant at a price that is compatible with the Prosecution Service and providing a high level of service that could be monitored and audited appropriately.

More successes led to demands to analyse evidence in many more very large fraud cases. Analysis of complicated defence cases flooded in and we were inundated with lorry loads of case files.

It was not possible for me to do this work alone, and my worsening disability made matters even more difficult. The excitement of approaching success and acceptance as normal was a huge incentive and pushed other priorities to the background, even my common sense.

To enable us to do this work we enlisted 35 other analysts, mostly ex-police officers to chart this work in smaller pieces and send the results to me for final analysis. A perfect situation, so I thought, with no pressure and the comforts of working from home with understanding client solicitors

I worked flat out on the days when I had the power of a hundred men, analysing data from 4 o'clock in the morning to dusk that night. With such strength I could make up for the other days when I plummeted into the mental whirling pit and then deeper to the stomach churning and ending in total exhaustion. My resilience to this topsy-turvy world of complete opposites was rewarded by the achievement of a normal wage earning life and the feeling of importance when we received payment for or work and sent the cheques out to the sub-contractors who had helped me.

Concentrated analytical tasks require intricate and complete concentration and under such pressures mistakes were inevitable. A few minor mistakes in my analysis caused even more difficulties and soured the whole business when a solicitor breached our contract and refused to pay for work we had carried out.

The errors were trivial and a ruse by him to delay payment. At the Civil Court, where I eventually went to retrieve my losses, I was told that solicitors were the most common users of this ploy to save expenses. Other contractors to the legal profession confirmed being owed huge sums by lawyers using this delaying tactic.

We, eventually, were paid but it left a bad taste in my mouth and turned down all further requests from the legal profession.

BALANCED CHANGES

I continued to suffer the major PTSD problems and changed the emphasis on the work. I carefully selected the type of work to accord with the disorder looking to recreate the balance I desperately needed to keep my feet on the ground.

I gave away so many lucrative contracts to keep the balance right. Working from home in the peace and quiet, where I was in control and not open to being side swiped by problems was the best option. I was safe and secure and much fitter and capable of building myself up with planning, for a big moment like a meeting or seminar of carefully selected friends.

This ranged from helping a major national company who were losing stocks of steel, estimated at £1 million worth a month, between there manufacturing plant in the north of England and their distribution depots in the south and south west.

They had found great difficulty in getting a Police Force or Squad to investigate the matter, as they could not specify the area where the steel went missing. There being no FBI in the UK such crimes were of little interest to cash strapped Police Forces trying to perform their duties to the demands of their local communities.

I took on the task with two other ex-officers, analysed thousands of delivery notes, lorry tachographs, worksheets and other data. We isolated the common denominators within the company and identified the persons responsible. We produced a prosecution file with statements of evidence from numerous witnesses and documentation, photographs and charts supporting a prime facie case against five employees and three handlers of stolen steel.

The problem then came to get a Force to take on the task of arresting and interviewing and charging the persons responsible.

We eventually after some persuasion got a CID officer in the Metropolitan Police to take it on. He explained that he was retiring in three months time and had nothing to lose if his bosses came down on him but he would do his best to get the job done. We never heard another word from him and subsequent requests for an update with his office fell on deaf ears.

In frustration the company dismissed the employees involved to rid themselves of the problems and the losses stopped.

CORRUPTION, TANTRUMS AND THE SACK

Our unique style of investigation produced other contracts with various companies, banks and financial institutions in the City of London. In this Financial Capital of the world, the emphasis was in profit and as long as that was not compromised then moral issues came close second. Coming from the disciplined, credited and strictly monitored calling of a police officer, it was a cultural shock to enter the intrigue and profit manoeuvring world of the city business fraternity.

A friend after thirty odd years in the square mile warned, "Don't get too confused! Remember a City businessman makes money in whatever way he can. Honesty is not always the right policy to make money. Corruption and double-dealing is a way of life here. You must accept that to get on."

I was contracted to carry out security surveys and set up an investigations division in a large bank. At the end of the term the Head of Security asked me to stay for an extra year at a substantially improved contract.

The work was intriguing but my PTSD problems hampered me personally. I pushed myself to travel into the City every day, with the understanding of the immediate bosses and colleagues I could balance the tasks with the exhaustion and sickness. The bank had twenty buildings within the space of the "square mile" therefore a toilet or bolthole was never far away.

There was a vibrant buzz atmosphere in the City, the like of which I had not been able to experience since being kicked out of the Police Service. Alive with being wanted and needed I overcome my difficulties for the best part of the time and threw myself into the job.

I set up the investigation department, created a good working relationship with the local police and accepted the tantrums of the rich money market workers who had their toy cars or favourite pen stolen from their desk. Even when the top executives had all their laptop computers stolen I managed to hold back a rye smile.

FILLED PANTS AT LIVERPOOL STREET

Regular visits to the loo or the parks nearby to hold my head in my hands and regain my brain from a tumble and apologising to the cleaner at Liverpool Station for the vomit on her shining bright tiled floor did not stop me from motoring along, enjoying myself and fulfilling my life once again.

The Liverpool Street problem taught me that my disability was never far away but I had the confidence to deal with it just as every other disabled person deals with their day to day encumbrances. Going down the escalator, taking a short cut through the station concourse, to one of the many office blocks my company covered was normal and a common route.

Nothing traumatic was going on as the dizziness and fainting feeling took over my mind and body. I managed to keep my balance until I got to the bottom of the escalator but eventually collapsed to my knees against an advertising hoarding nearby. I vomited my breakfast up and over the pristine tiled floor as my bowels opened up producing a warm sensation in my pants. Trying to hold my hands simultaneously over both my mouth and bottom and tucking my briefcase under my arm at the same time, I ran for the refuge of the toilets.

Leaping several steps at a time, down to the lower level, my panic increased as I hit the turnstiles and had to fumble for 20p to get inside. Releasing my hand only to feel my bowels empty even further and the pungent smell filled the air, I forwent the 20p and jumped over the turnstile. Hitting the door of the nearest cubicle I dropped my trousers just before my stomach completely emptied onto the floor and my dangling clothes.

I sat exhausted on the loo and could only wait in despair to regain both composure and some degree of cleanliness. My only hope of cleaning myself up was to remove all my lower garments and wash them at the sinks in the area open to all the men who used the conveniences. It was embarrassing to stand there with a bare lower half but I had no alternative. Head down not wanting to make eye contact with anyone, I hurriedly managed to wash out the mess sufficiently, to be able to put my trousers, although wet and clinging, back on.

My socks were also stained and dampened. I discarded them and my underpants in the waste bin and replaced my shoes, making sure that they did not contain anything nasty. I noticed that they had holes in the soles and amused myself of the thought that the runny crap had just poured straight through. Keeping my raincoat wrapped close around me to hide the wet trousers and slipping along in my sock-less shoes, I made my way as quick as I could to the nearest menswear store.

Marks & Spencer was my oasis. I dived into the trouser racks, 29" leg and 36" waist was not a popular size but luck was with me.

One grey flannel pair of trousers, a pack of underpants, pair of black socks and pair of leather shoes disappeared with me into the changing cubicle.

My haste had obviously alerted the male shop assistant to the possibility of a shoplifter and he called to me, if he could be of any assistance. I shouted to him, "No mate. I have just crapped myself and need a complete change of clothes. I'll be all right!" I do not think he got a whiff of anything but he muttered something unintelligible and retreated back to his cash till. He did give a dubious look as he scanned the bar coded labels, that had been separated from the clothing that I was now wearing, and gingerly handed me bags to put my wet items into. He used a piece of scrap paper to pick up the credit card slip, I had just signed so as not to make physical contact with my unwashed hands and then watched me intensely until I had passed through the exit doors and onto the street outside.

When I got back to my office there was a bit of banter about my new shoes and trousers. I made the excuse that a bus had blasted through a large puddle and drenched me. This was the closest I had got to being found out about my problems. Other times I managed to survive by disappearing out of sight.

WICKED WORLD AND THE SACK

I did not feel inhibited and continued with my job with confidence that I had the strength to carry on as normal. Attending meetings, seminars and advisory groups, I stood up in front of discerning bank staff explaining the reasoning behind the security arrangements we had throughout the company buildings and the need for a constant awareness to keep vigil on their surroundings. I concentrated on the fact that it did not matter what security device was in place, if it was made by humans it could be shagged by them.

Using this approach and telling them that it was a "wicked world out there", I was incensed when a senior executive from the engineering department sneered and scoffed at the presentation completely scuppering the intentions of creating a watchful and security conscious staff by saying, "Well I am in deed frightened now that I live in a wicked world. How I am ever going to sleep at night!"

A month later the disaster and tragedy of 11 September in New York when all values, reasoning and understanding were destroyed, the wicked world I had tried to portray had hit us straight between the eyes in a way that even I had never thought possible. I hope that executive reflects on his attitude in a less cynical way and deals with security more responsibly.

My work on the RCS and NCIS had been closely linked with the banks and financial institutions as the top villains had to use these to stash their millions away somewhere. The tin dug in at the bottom of the garden could not hold the vast sums of money they were gained from the illicit trades so smoke screen companies and bogus front men were used to gain the credibility from commerce.

The City of London is considered to be the soft centre of the financial world and now that so many foreign banks had taken hold there it was that much easier. Banks and Institutions from outside the UK are less committed to the British society and therefore unconcerned with the affect that illegal trading can have on the population. Together with the fact that their concentration is primarily on profit, they pay their staff bonuses regularly exceeding £1 million, makes the incentive of identifying crooks amongst their clients less likely.

Even with the draconian legislation of the Criminal Profits Confiscation Acts the banks only pay token efforts towards identifying criminal clients. In my contracted bank, with 20,000 staff employed, in the City alone, there were only two officials dedicated solely to investigating criminal profits.

Plenty of staff concentrated on possible harm to the bank but only these two looked outside.

When I received information from some old friends in the security service that two of our senior executives were suspected of associating with the Mafia, I took it to the Global Head of Security. These guys trusted me with the intelligence they had and wanted the banks cooperation to nail the villains.

I flew to our head office in Europe and asked for his authority to help. I also informed him that I did not want to be "piggy in the middle" on this issue as I suffered from PTSD. I had already been sick twice in the plane coming over and then again in the arrival lounge much to the annoyance of the airport security staff who thought I was drunk. I did not think that the tenuous situation had been responsible for triggering off my problems as I had them regularly under normal circumstances. I was caught, by my passion for catching villains, between my loyalty to law enforcement and company.

Being caught and pulled between the conflicting priorities was never going to be a good position for me.

I reiterated that this information was implicitly trusted by me. Whether it was so unbelievable or the man was in danger of losing his job I do not know but he did not believe me.

Two days later they, "had to let me go" as the company "could not be held responsible for any problems I may suffer whilst on their premises". I had told him that PTSD disabled me and he had decided to use it to "shoot the messenger."

Was my lucrative contract terminated because I was, too loyal, honest or just stupid?

Friends said I should have sued the company for discrimination but, in a way, losing the contract was a relief. I did not have to keep looking over my shoulder all of the time.

The incident showed me once again the frailties of our society and its' incapacity to work together to defeat crime.

ENTHUSIASM NEVER WANES

I still had this massive urge and enthusiasm to use the skills and expertise I had been so successful with. The contracts with the business fraternity had shown me that there was a total lack of co-ordination between the police and commerce in using intelligence and information that all possessed to clear up crime effectively.

Differing agendas and priorities on both sides meant that the villain could coast through the middle without fear of being detected because those that were looking at him had isolated each other from the process and lost out on crucial joint information that could amount to real evidence against the villain.

Speaking to present members of the Police and Intelligence agencies there had been little positive progress to achieve and effective deterrent in this direction since 1994 when I retired. There was no common denominator that could deal with this situation apart from certain anti-fraud and haulage companies initiatives.

Working into the night hours after early rising to start again I put together a discussion document to look into the setting up of a joint initiative to fill this gap in criminal investigation by all agencies and businesses.

Not knowing where I would be able to fit in or in fact earn anything from the venture. I was spurred on by my own desire to work at effective investigation and close in on the villains in whatever way I could.

The concept was to set up an agency that would feed information on suspected criminals from business to the Police on a national basis. Companies were less likely to pass on information that did not appertain to their type of business as it had little affect on them.

However so often a company would have intelligence on suspected criminal activity and have no means or in fact encouragement to pass this onto the Police.

It either fell outside their business interests and / or the Police did not have an appropriate department to deal with it.

A massive hole of wasted opportunity existed in the system of intelligence gathering. It could be that important catalyst bringing together all types of businesses, security associations and law enforcement to fight the entrepreneurial criminals who do not confine themselves to one type of crime.

My concept would fill this gap and produce a viable effective solution but the nuts and bolts of how it could be formed had to be thrashed out. Mad, but for the sake of one meeting I thought it was worth a go!

Friends and family gave me all the support as usual but some, more discerning would be questioning me, "What exactly will you get out of it or where do you fit into such an organisation?" was the usual query. "I don't know", would be my reply, but I would use the positive approach that I would not loose.

No income from the venture but satisfaction that villains could be nicked and put away by people putting their heads together in a common approach never used before.

As a first step I arranged to hire the local Police Sports and Social Club Room. The venue of the meetings for our Ex-Essex Police Business Association (EEPBA) and the type of location used by the Ex-Police in Industry and Commerce (EPIC) also an equivalent non-profit making national organisation.

Invitations to send a representative and a synopsis of the initiative, labelled "The Business Crime Intelligence Service", was sent out to all Chief Constables in the south east and to business and commercial concerns including most major financial institutions.

Of the 250 sent out, all at my own personal expense, I received 153 replies from the business side, three nice apologies from Chief Constables that neither they nor a representative from their force would be able to attend and a rather indignant telephone conversation from a Chief Superintendent in London, "Not to disturb his Chief Constable with any such crap!"

It would appear that the business side of the security industry were eager to attend to brainstorm the concept but the Police had no ambitions to even discuss the possibility.

A form of coup de gras followed with the Secretary of the Club telephoned to ask me if the Room I wanted to hire was being used for a business venture. I explained to him the concept of the initiative and that the venue was to be used to discuss and brainstorm the idea as a possible runner and referred him to the website I had set up.

He came back to me a short while later and said that I could not hire the room if I was not a member of the Club. I thought that was strange as I thought had been a member throughout the last five years of police service and that this had continued after retirement.

I had hired the Club on numerous occasions for functions and thought I was a member.

He said I was not a member and cancelled my booking. I was stunned and shocked to be treated in such a way.

I had been trying to form an initiative to fight crime and had been struck in the face by the very friends in the Police that I was attempting to help.

All voluntarily and with no prospect of reward I still cannot come to terms with being treated in such a diabolical way!

Throughout this drive, as normal, I had coped with the ramifications of the PTSD problems, even having to take two days out after the rude and abusive telephone call. Even though I was working from within my "box" I found the feed back from the business community, both positive and open for discussion but from the Police, absolute nil.

My Home Office contacts were deeply disappointed but politically had to stay neutral as observers when I cancelled all the arrangements for the seminar.

The businesses were dumbfounded with disbelief when I cancelled the seminar!

WHY BOTHER

After the dust had settled and I had time to reflect on the past few months of madness I questioned myself, "Why am I running myself into the ground for a job that has discarded me and does not care a less what I think or believe in?" Perhaps it was time to leave my passion for crime busting and lifetimes' work behind!

Was I now a dinosaur trying to relive or continue my ill lost career or was I genuinely but foolishly trying to implement the impossible.

The idea of a national partnership between the Police and the Business Community may have been sadly beyond the realms of understanding and experience of senior officers. But I cannot help but think that someday in the future one of these officers may have a magnificent and sudden brainwave that such a partnership would be possible and get a knighthood for the original and innovative idea!

I needed to fill the vacuum and get employment, setting about applying for work that would balance with my disability and applying for over a hundred positions. Going on three interviews always being devastated by rejection and suspicious that any knowledge of my PTSD would be the reason for the knock back.

UTOPIA AT LAST

Things were to change with the elation of being accepted as Deputy Assistant Registrar / Clerical Assistant at Southend Civic Centre Register Office for the grand sum of £6.50 per hour.

Dorothy and I were over the moon with excitement and so happy that I had found an employer that entrusted me with work. We were back in society again, out of no mans' land and back in the fold of a working environment and the pay would help to give us a normal life.

The work had no pressure and involved dealing with customers at an enquiry desk, researching records for birth, marriage and death certificates and assisting the Superintendent Registrar at wedding ceremonies. It gave me the wonderful opportunity of using my skill at handwriting certificates and signing my name as an important official.

I had found the right blend of work, pleasure and satisfaction. The bonus was the very nice understanding people that I worked with. It made the job of dealing with my PTSD that more easy and relaxed but I was suffering very badly. I seemed to be spending more time cowering in the toilets and getting the flash backs, the vomiting was not so bad but weeping, diarrhoea and exhaustion crippled me.

One Saturday, after a morning of weddings I went into a serious mind tumble. My brain went wild after I could not calculate the loss of £3.50 in the Registrars' expense account book. The Superintendent quickly sorted out the ridiculous situation but I could not stop my mind, then body whirling round and round.

The usual follow on effects sent me down and out and even by the next Monday drained and exhausted by the aftermath I had difficulty in maintaining normality. I telephoned Dorothy to pick me up. I dissolved into another nightmare; my second breakdown and you know the rest.

The visit to the doctor followed. Did it have to end like this?

Chapter Nineteen
SO WAS IT ALL WORTH IT?

So where do I go from here? What do I do now? I refuse to allow myself to be a zombie, do nothing, looking at four walls. This book has filled the time, given me some closure, been a bit of an emotional roller coaster and helped to put behind me the things I wish to forget or push them back further into the depths of this ridiculous brain that I am now stuck with.

I have given up all those pressures that have the slightest possibility of causing me problems. Turned into a recluse by choosing to avoid places that might have the some debilitating affect.

I owed so much to Dorothy, Clare and Karen but did not need their insistence to give up all my activities. I knew I had to do it and stop gambling with my sanity.

I resigned from the posts of the Southend Branch secretary of NARPO, the National Association of Retired Police Officers and the assistant secretary of the EEPBA, the ex-Essex Police Business Association so there's no chance of them causing me difficulties.

My frustrations and anger continue to blast away inside me. I am still young enough to do something, but wiser, now more than ever and realistic, that although life goes on, it must be at a far slower pace than any other time in my life.

I longed to still be able to spring out of bed in the mornings, get shaved, shampooed, showered and dressed ready for action in smart suit, shirt, complete with cuff links and tie ready for a "normal day" doing a job that I could enjoy and work with a normal people.

I have to accept my mind and concentration going completely haywire, even though I could, often do numerous tasks in workaholic mode, my mind would, inevitably, blow and a zombie took over me in the exhaustion that followed.

All at a time when I should have been clicking my heels in the air!

Would I recommend the job to my daughters? Of course, the thin blue line it may be, spat at one minute, praised and thanked another, there is not a day that I would have missed. I would do it all over again!

One police pensioner asked me, "What do you think you achieved in the Job?"

He continued before I could answer, "I thought when I joined, it was my opportunity to do something for the community. I would make a difference, lock up criminals and solve the troubles of so many. Now I look back after 30 years service, I can honestly say. No matter how hard I worked. I did not make one iota of difference. The blokes we locked up have now got families who are committing the crime. The public are scared to go out of their homes. What do you think?"

Slightly irritated somewhat I paused and said, " I don't think it was a waste of time. If we hadn't have been there what would the world be like. I fulfilled my dream of being a detective on the CID, the RCS and the NCIS.

Sadly my time was cut short, forced to retire before I had completed the job, left a vacuum with no defining moment where I could accept that I could do no more. Even so I would do it all over again, every minute of it and would recommend anyone to give it a go. It is the best job in the world!

WHERE'S THE BLAME

His obvious disappointment in not making the impact, he set out to do, sparked off my thoughts. The world of Policing and Law Enforcement is not just down to the Bobby on the beat.

It is well known that there are individuals in the various think tanks, within the government departments, who feel that the public are well able to self police their own society, and that there could be a case to argue, that we do not need a police force.

In the opposite are those that think that the best course for order and stability is a total police state.

Both have reasonable principles to argue their cause but common sense dictates. Both are too extreme and would lead to anarchy in one direction and dictatorship in the other. Either option is completely unacceptable.

With that knowledge in mind each and every government, who has been in power, has tried to coast through the middle of these options by carrying out a balancing act to ensure that we do not venture too far either way.

Their efforts help to provide a stability that allows a level of criminal activity that is just about acceptable to the majority of society. It is quite true to say that the vast majority of us still do not suffer from crime and as long as the situation stays that way then respective governments will continue to follow that path.

The Police however are left to pick up the pieces when the balance does not accord with public feeling and bear the brunt of any backlash when it all goes wrong.

It is quite right that the Police have this duty and bear the responsibility to enforce the law as our democracy dictates.

However questions must be asked of the other parts of society, who must also, bear a responsibility when the legal system fails to perpetrate the law to its full extent, as it was intended, when first enacted by our elected parliament.

Although huge sums of money are paid out there is little affect on crime figures. Millions of pounds are spent on the Police, The Crown

Prosecution Service, the Courts, the Judiciary, the Bar, Defence Case Lawyers, Probation Service and the defendant whose rights are also upheld to the finest degree to detect, adjudicate and rehabilitate but no significant improvements are noticed.

It is appalling that so many earn so much out of the system yet so little financial or compensatory attention is paid to the fine members of the society who attend court as witnesses to do their "public duty" or the actual aggrieved parties.

They have to rely on the benevolence of the local charitable Victim Support Scheme or the meagre support of the Criminal Injuries Compensation Board.

All too often whole lives are destroyed and even in the best of cases when persons are convicted of the crime the aggrieved has come to terms with the Judiciary sentencing the defendant to a beating with a feather duster.

Money is poured into rehabilitating criminals but the aggrieved victims have to rely on charities to deal with their needs even though their trauma and loss is far deeper than anyone else can ever imagine.

It is not right that victims of crime should be treated in such a disdainful way, and not given the professional support to recover from their ordeal that is so freely given to the criminals.

Victims have to overcome their own injuries and pain. Little support is given to their plight and that of those close to them. The strain on families and dependents is horrendous. Dorothy will vouch for that!

My own mother was recently the victim of crime when her handbag was stolen. At 80 years of age it is no surprise that she was severely shocked by the incident. A couple of visits from the overworked and very kind volunteer from the Victim Support Service were all the official help she got. Knowing their workload, the Investigating Police Officers did what they could. Mum was left to deal with her ordeal and trauma herself, and her family and get support through her GP, whose progressive surgery had the services of a Stress Counsellor.

This support should be available as a right from a Victim Support Service funded totally by Government. The victim of crime is the result of deficiency in our society caused by the lack of positive action by Government. The victim is the only person left in the legal process that does not receive officially funded support, having to rely on charity. That is not morally right!

It is a sad reflection of the time we live in, that most good causes and charities rely on the help of volunteers and the odd handout from the National Lottery whereas the bad causes are swamped with bottomless social support assistance from Government Departments.

It is an indictment on our society that a criminal is more accepted as being in need, than someone who is a victim, seriously assaulted, victimised, disabled, elderly, honest or mistreated as a child.

WHAT ABOUT THE KIDS?

The deficiencies in our social responsibilities have not changed in the last thirty years since I first became a police officer. There is still a lack of communication between the police, social services, education authorities and the court services. Early signs are seen by any one or all of these groups, but no significant joint system or forum is set in place to effectively head off, and prevent children from becoming victims of or as the result of crime.

Dedicated Head Teachers and their staff, probably the first carers to identify problems, complain of inactivity and lack of communication with and by Social Services. All the hard work that Social Services carry out barely scratches the surface and they, in turn, complain of under funding and staffing. The Police do the same, but also hide behind the misinterpreted shield of Data Protection legislation, that stops them from exchanging information. All this "shrugging of shoulders" and "passing the buck" results in so many children becoming victims.

It is not just the victimised children who have been attacked or assaulted who are victims of crime. The children in criminal families suffer from the indirect results of their relatives' actions and lifestyles. They are even more vulnerable and therefore more likely to become criminals and create more victims. Apparently 25% of persons serving terms of imprisonment come from broken homes and inadequate family units.

The simple event of holding joint meetings to discuss the social welfare of a child in danger and talking to each other would be of such tremendous benefit. Too many children are let down by the terrible system.

A service of intensive caring of children and their families by a concentrated effort from all agencies would prevent so much suffering. If caught at the earliest recognition of problems, age should not be a bar, then the better the chance. Even expectant parents of lower moral, financial and educational standards should be considered for care and guidance to ensure that their child has the best possible start in life.

The Local Authority, health groups, social carers and playgroups, primary and junior schools should be the major monitoring posts to identify those most in need. All too often we are dealing with the problems after it is past the time of prevention, the crime has been committed and we have to mop up the debris.

In all these areas early warning signs such as poor parenting, moral standards, bad language, neglect, low self-esteem, poor role models, poor attendance and truancy, bullying and disaffection are signals that a child is vulnerable and in need of intensive care and dedicated attention.

All agencies working pro-actively, attacking the problems and talking to each other, would save so many lives from destruction.

I hear the argument for more police officers on the beat to prevent crime but what is the point if the tide of criminals is still being forced out of an inadequate social system during the early years of our children. High quality social values have to be firmly entrenched at the first earliest age and opportunity. This is not being achieved at present.

The Education Welfare Service, dealing with truancy and aligning problems, is a step in the right direction, but responsible agencies are still in danger of carrying out too deeply specific responsibilities in parallel to each other and not linking in to solve the overlapping problems.

A child of four, on her first day in the school playground, was over heard telling her friends that her Mum had stolen the lovely pair of new shoes she was wearing. At such an early age she is in danger of believing that dishonesty and stealing is normal. Who is told? Not a social services problem is it? Not a school problem, nothing to do with education is it? A police problem, maybe, but where will that end? So nothing is done and the child knows no better. A joint approach by these agencies would at least stand a chance of improving that girls' outlook on life.

When the parents have problems like drug addiction, alcoholism, inadequate behaviour, poor housing, disability and poverty who; co-ordinates a response to the cry for help? So many times it goes unnoticed, and if recognised, who heads a team focused on resolving the situation for them and their children? None of the above agencies are able, or resourced enough to be able to meet, and effectively deal with the situations.

As a result a tide of criminal and anti-social behaviour is pumped continuously into society and is never likely to be stemmed unless positive action is taken. Concentrated efforts on families and children of junior school age and below must be a priority to help slow down this flow. It will never stop it but it will significantly change the lives of more children, teaching them the rudiments of right and wrong at the earliest age and supporting families at the most difficult of times.

A pro-active approach to social problems rather than a, fire brigade, re-active response would make a serious and crucial impact.

Our troubled housing estates have been the same for years with little sign of improvement. Whether you live in London, Manchester or locally in Southend and Basildon our present welfare system does not give encouragement or pride to the residents.

People living in a deprived areas just mete out an existence and are given no hopes or aspirations for the future. This produces apathy and at its' worst anger. Agencies that show they care, and can work together to improve the lives of a community in need, would have wonderful results.

I have now seen four generations of criminal families grow up in deprived housing estates with the same problems repeated over and over again.

Standing in the playground of one school waiting for my grandchildren I met an old villain I had locked away some years previous. He was there with his granddaughter, a girl in her late teens, and waiting for his great grandchild to come out of class.

The granddaughter had a little boy of about three with her. He was getting impatient and shouting at his Mum. She turned to him and shouted, " Come here you fucking little shit, before I knock the fuck out of you!"

The ex-con looked at me in despair with eyes welled up and apologised, "I'm sorry mate. What chance do they stand? I know I've been stupid and wasted my life, it's bloody useless over there. Look at it. It hasn't changed in 25 years since you nicked me. I know people think we are shit, but it gets so ingrained in some, it takes a lot to get it out." The school bell rang, the kids came running out to their parents and we parted company.

The school asked me to be Father Christmas at their Fair and during the class parties. Not a bad undertaking normally but I had to give it some hard consideration before accepting the task. The one thing I did not want to happen was to have one of my PTSD wobblies so I talked it through with my daughter, Clare who was on the PTA Committee. She explained that the Head Teacher would accompany me and all I had to do was sit and give presents out to the children, including my own grandchildren.

It was one of the most magical experiences that I could ever have imagined. 280 children filed through my grotto; assisted by three elves from the junior school I handed out the presents. The Head call out the names so I would know whom to say.

Sweating buckets under the heavy hooded red suit and snowy beard I managed to disguise my voice so my grandkids would not recognise me. Although my granddaughter did comment that, "Father Christmas had a voice, just like Granddads." Her Mum explained that all Father Christmases sound like Granddads because they were so good.

The procession of kids varied from the suspicious to the lovable. Some eyed me up and down, trying to look behind the beard to see if I was real and four gave me colourful letters asking for presents. It was quite an emotional experience but for all the right reasons and, more importantly, not because of some mental flashback.

The ex-cons' great grandkids came through. The smart uniforms ensured that they looked no different than the others from well off homes. They were all so young, so innocent, so new to life, I couldn't help thinking and wondering how many of these children would be a victim of our inadequate social system in the future.

Their school is superb with dedicated caring staff often awarded for educational excellence, but they and the other agencies need more resources to get as many of the children as possible onto the right rails for a brighter future.

If funding is not available then priority should be directed to this preventative approach in preference to the rehabilitation of the lost causes from the prison system.

Rather than prison, many more minor offenders should be sentenced to a tougher system of forcing them to pay back something to society. Meaningful visually based community projects, like improving conditions in run-down estates, would impress the public more and save the huge expense of prisons.

STATISTICS AND CHEATS

Crime Statistics are manipulated or interpreted to suit the Police Commanders or Government Departments prestigious or political ends. They can never be relied upon to give a true picture of what is really happening out at ground level.

Factual and true figures are impossible to record. The general public are fed only the information that is designed to send a message of calm. It is considered to be professional suicide to give a true picture.

So we are left with the only source of coverage by the media who are so obsessed with their need to sell papers that speculation and irresponsible sensationalism is rife.

The community is then left with making their own mind up and their perception is dictated by news headlines rather than specific facts. A nasty murder in Huddersfield will cause all the elderly ladies in Southend to be frightened of going out, a paedophile on the loose in Reading will create panic in Newcastle as all mothers insist on picking their kids up from school.

These are natural reactions and I would not deter anyone from taking the same course. Years ago when we did not have 24 hour TV news coverage and local radio and TV, ten national papers and local papers delivered to your door every day we thought the streets were safe to walk in at whatever time. Although we did used to pick and choose the areas and locations carefully, particularly when the streetlights went out at midnight.

Whatever way you look at it you be hard pushed to see a news headline, "Police fail to detect 65% of crime!" The most common is a fanfare type headline heralding the latest police crack down or Major Operation. But experience dictates that all the hard work carried out by the law enforcement agencies will only scrape the surface of criminal activity and in my time the maximum detection rate has only ever reached 35% of actual recorded crime.

With many crimes not being reported by victims through apathy with the system and so many villains getting away with it who says crime does not pay?

We have even got so called honest villains now appearing on television helping the public, on security issues, to foil would be burglars and probably earning a good living out of it. Of course they have paid their debt to society, as far as the our form of justice states, but I wonder if they ever fully compensated their victims by paying them back in full for the pain, loss and suffering they caused.

Both in prosecution and defence I have seen so many villains who have been the unluckiest defendant in the world and been caught for their very first offence ever! At subsequent court proceedings a pro-forma script can be written for most by their solicitors that their client is "starting a job on Monday" and "their girlfriend is expecting their first child at anytime".

A solicitor quite openly laughed with other defence colleagues that he had used this "instruction" from the same client over six occasions in the last year to get him out on bail. On three occasions it was in front of the same Magistrates who did not have a clue that he was having them over. It was a game to him although he would say he was only carrying out his clients' instructions. Every one of us, including solicitors, should have a moral respect for the victim and be perpetrators of the truth in Court.

The Courts should be the venue where the investigation of the truth is the paramount concern of the Judge, Jury and Advocates. All too often the villain is allowed through the immoral deviance of his defence team to escape conviction.

My experience working for numerous defence solicitors consistently proved that moral conscience and truth is secondary to financial reward.

The destruction of a victim of a crime is never fully taken account of when a sentenced is passed. Yes, a Judge has to do his duty in the light of all the facts set out before him and leaves sentiment behind to a degree to be fair. But the fairness is too weighted in favour of the accused.

Police Officers and other professions see first hand the devastation that crime can cause to a victim. In many occasions the victim does not want retribution or revenge but recognition of what has happened to them and how deep the incident has penetrated into their lives.

In my case I have no real thoughts either way against the men who assaulted me. Three of the skinheads have been involved in committing crime all their lives and are now serving sentences for armed robbery and firearms offences. They did not learn anything from the ordeal of three months in a detention centre. They probably received further education whilst at the school for "up-and-coming-villains", in how to have the system over further and the rudiments of being a successful thief and law-breaker.

One of the guys, who hit me in the loaf of bread incident, has turned into a fine family man and showed sincere regret when we met later. He said he would be forever sorry about what he did to me. After he was ordered to pay me compensation by the court, for months I received the irregular princely sum of £1 or £1.50p dependant on what he had paid in. It was a paltry sum and unnecessary as his apologies meant more.

Another bloke, the tough guy from the same incident who gave the Inspector and PC such a rough time, helped me out late one night when I was flaked out with exhaustion. I had been sick and bad. He was the driver of the bus that picked me up from Leigh Railway Station and probably thought I was drunk. When I could not get off at my designated stop, he left his bus and passengers and virtually carried me the 100 yards from the bus stop to my front door. He said that he hoped I would forgive him one day, very noble in comparison to the Inspector who has never apologised to me for getting me into that mess.

The driver of the stolen car, who gave me the ride on his bonnet, looked me up after he had completed his sentence. He apologised profusely for his actions and reiterated that he was in total panic as the bullets hit his car. Strange that I should receive his condolences but the Metropolitan Police never gave me such courtesy.

My treatment is nothing compared to that of a victim from outside the Police Force. Even though I have suffered and still am, I was better equipped for the prospect of being a victim than a person outside could ever be.

I was more prepared because of the camaraderie, the natural support, working closely together, laughing at adversity, coming to terms to the horrors of murder, rape and other tragic scenes of crime by making light of the sights we saw, and even making macabre fun as we hardened to the reality of what was happening.

I can vividly remember my incidents, blow for blow, kick by kick and word for word because they are played back to me in a too often clarity and also in major physically unspecific terms so frequently it is very hard to put them the memories away. I am fortunate though not to have suffered rape or been closely related to a murder victim. I could never imagine how it must feel to have a life obliterated and savaged.

The distraught faces of the parents of a recently married lovely young couple, murdered in the home, they had scrimped and saved for and set up for such a beautiful future life together. The contrast in that ransacked room, where their mutilated bodies lay stabbed by a burglar who killed for the sake of two rings worth only a few hundred pounds. A wedding photographs of the happy and proud family and the bride and groom lying smashed on the floor with spatters of blood whipped across the faces.

These parents not only had their children taken away but their future hopes of family days, Mum shopping with daughter, Dad playing golf or visit to the pub with son. No grandchildren to play with, to adore and spoil.

I look at my family and grandchildren and see in them everything that these parents have missed and look at the burglar who was released after serving ten years of a life sentence. He is now back behind bars for a further aggravated burglary, another victim and another devastated life.

Everyone else involved in criminal cases gets paid, rewarded for their work. Police Officers, solicitors, barristers, judges, court staff, prison staff and so on, all earn a pretty penny out of it.

We were the only ones to benefit out the incidents. The villain is okay. He is still walking this earth, creating his form of havoc and destruction, and given aftercare by the state so that his every need is secured.

What about the poor victims, if they were lucky, they could get counselling, if they could afford to pay for it, but it is only a short-term cushion for a life sentence of their own.

Society is letting these people down. Nobody can bring back their loved ones or turn the clock back to restore their lives but we should be respecting their wishes as to sentencing and give them the opportunity and support to help them achieve some closure on the incident in an attempt to achieve some reparation of the past.

When sentencing criminals, more consideration of the victims' feelings would help. Their trauma is massively affected by the lack of thought for their feelings about the crime committed against them. Some would wish to forgive, even in the most abominable cases, but others may wish more extreme punishment.

Above all sentences must be realistic and calculated to be a real deterrent with more emphasis being placed on reparation for the victims of crime. This way the victim will stand the best chance of achieving closure and move on with their lives.

THE UNEDUCATED

Articles in Police publications remind me, that there are still very few people who understand what PTSD is like or the benefits of seeking counselling before the disabling effects go too deep.

It is not helpful and still makes me angry when ex-police officers extol and wallow in their experience of having been given numerous black eyes, dragged dead bodies off the beach and attended numerous murder scenes without any ill effects. One heading of "Stress is for Wimps" criticising those that need counselling and throwing jibes is demeaning and bordering on the line of discrimination but still the Editors allow it to be put into print.

Staid and blinkered claims of, "It didn't happen to me so why should it happen to anyone else" are out of date and the fly in the face of the research and findings of the many eminent psychologists and medical experts who have studied post-traumatic stress disorder.

I overheard a conversation between two ex-officers, the pleasures of retirement were being discussed but the officer nudged the other and said, "Course, I didn't retire with stress like so many of those bastards do!" The listener appeared uncomfortable with what had been said but it did not stop me from feeling hatred, contempt and then dissolve into depression and want to crawl away.

There is no doubt that it has been the uneducated attitude of fellow officers and the disgust that they have shown that has probably sent me into being reclusive.

Close friends accepted me for what I am but I felt I wanted to tell them as best as I could what was wrong with me. It was very difficult to explain without churning myself up inside without going into a tumble.

They gave me time, space and support when I needed it most.

Some mates, still serving, would tell me the senior officers were still not doing anything about it and most were still "the boot up the backside brigade" or came out with comments like, "If they don't like the heat then get out of the kitchen", or worse, "they should just be fucking kicked out. Useless bastards!"

I am not so naïve to think that this book is going to change such deeply entrenched attitudes but it might.

RECOGNITION OF PTSD

My Dad and I talked about my problems. For the first time in his whole life we spoke about the Second World War. I had been telling him, how I valued the mates that had stood by me and helped me through my ordeal and said, "You must have found that in the horrors you experienced with your mates." I held a photo of him with a group of his mates, taken when he was on leave in Cairo.

He said, "They were never around long enough, Bob." I looked surprised as he took the photo from me and said, "These are all dead! All killed during the next two months after the photo was taken."

I said, "What during a big push or something?" He said, "No, we were snipers. We used to be sent to shoot an officer or commander or someone important. We went behind the lines. They never came back."

I said, "You always joked about being the latrine orderly." He replied, "Could you think of a more crap job than killing someone?"

I nodded in agreement as he stroked the photo with his fingers deep in thought. After a moment or two he said, "I know exactly what you are going through. I saw lots of blokes in the same state during the war but nobody took any bloody notice. They shot some them. They were worn out, that was all. You take it easy and take what help you can get. Some of them would still be here if they had got the help."

He was hurting so we changed the subject only to go back to it as he said, "I've never told anyone else. It is not something to be proud of but I had to do it!"

I said, "It was war Dad, you had little option." I felt an empathy with him but I could never compare my situation with his terrible experience and memories.

A month later my Dad passed away. I wondered if he had wanted to off load that memory for some considerable time and for reasons only best known to himself decided to tell me.

Although, deeply proud to have been told, if only he had been able to tell someone else years ago. Unlike me, he had not been given the help to talk and off load the bad memories that were holed up in his mind. The counselling had shown me how I could tell the world about my problem and have no fear for the consequences. Although I knew to do so too often could have an adverse affect.

Perhaps it was this realisation and my speaking to him about my problem that helped him to release his thoughts. I did not want to pursue the subject further unless he wanted to and he died before I could find the opportunity.

The conversation with Dad gave me, even more, determination to carry on pushing myself to work and still continues to provide that energy to prove my worth in society.

I would have massive amounts of power and energy to put together the most outlandish of projects. Pushing myself, and everyone else around me, to extremes. The Business Intelligence Service was such, I had no idea, what or how it was going to work or even be viable. Besotted and totally immersed in the concept I worked day and night heading into oblivion and failure.

Dorothy would patiently allow me to go head over heels into my dreams and bear the brunt of the fall out when it fell about my feet.

Supporting me in my disappointment and standing the financial pain when it cost us money. Two charity events that I tried to put together failed by lack of support and cost us hundreds of pounds.

My determination has also been my downfall in completing this book, propelling me into getting it done even though describing my problems has the danger of churning up all my PTSD problems and creating both anger and despair.

But still I had this indescribable urge to achieve and prove myself. A red mist would descend over me throwing me blindly into something without any regard for the wider consequences.

On duty and off it did not matter.

Scaling three floors up the outside balcony of a block of flats to arrest a madman without ropes, ladders or other safety devices, taking on scores of Chelsea football supporters on my own in Southend High Street with my puny truncheon, the Chelmsford Club fiasco, throwing crack cocaine, that I had found in a pub, down a toilet in front of the angry druggie, volunteering for the impossible and many more times when I would take on the impossible or do something stupid without a thought for those around me.

Then I would have the down times of deep despair. The saying, "losing your mind" has always been taken for granted but when you are experiencing something inside your head and are conscious of what is going on but have no power to do, or change what is happening, that saying becomes all the more clearer.

Sitting watching your body go into freefall and not being able to do anything about it is horrendously frustrating and brings on an anger that you could never imagine.

I could be anywhere but more than often it would be during the night when I experienced a flashback. I have got to recognise the lead up of the strange anticipation of something closing in on me, my heart increasing its' pace, my breathing quickening and chest tightening. A lot of the time I can calm myself down and do breathing exercises and take control but at night and other weakened times I am more vulnerable and the full force of the feelings takes me over completely. I am hurtled into oblivion.

Dorothy is there at all times, clinging onto me and settling me down as best she could. I know she feels helpless and despairing but she is there helping me hold onto my sanity as I am swept along. The tumult subsides and the downtime goes on.

You are crying and sobbing for no reason, dribbling with saliva into your loved ones arms, you are with friends but cannot stand the noise and everything is closing in upon you, smothering you, closing your airwaves, choking you, you smell the strangest things that have no bearing on where you are, you are shaking uncontrollably, your heart is pounding, your chest is tightening up and collapsing inwards, you sweat until your clothes are soaked, you are in the most wonderful places and with the most loving and caring people but you feel like shit, you are hurtling down in a helter-skelter of mind tumbling thoughts, your stomach churns and you can feel the contents reaching for your mouth and bowels sometimes actually reaching them and discharging out, your mind goes blank and all energy is sapped from every single part of your body, everything is pointless, you want to get off this world and just curl up and die and then a switch is thrown somewhere in your sub-conscious.

You are elated and relieved it has passed and subsided but then you are angry and annoyed that you cannot control yourself. You are a grown mature man behaving like a child or elderly incontinent, for Christ sake! The anger reduces to mild frustration and then normality until the next time, but when and where?

In bed tonight, in the quiet and peace of my lovely garden, on the lovely cliffs above Lyme Regis in my favourite county of Dorset with the commanding views of the Cobb and Golden Cap, in beautiful Scotland below Ben Nevis with my family, on Christmas Day with my lovely family and gorgeous grandchildren, amongst the bushes next to my grandsons' football pitch, there is no place that can offer me a haven of respite.

I have to cope with the feelings every day and there are no triggers that can be said to cause the problem. Anything minutely traumatic that I am unprepared for or sudden can throw me out of sync and send me into a tumble. It could be something as simple and minor as a comment by someone, news article or TV programme. Obvious experiences such as a recent car accident can send me into prolonged times of disorder and disruption.

All tablets and forms of treatment and therapy so far have been temporary and always ended in the pure and simple fact that I have to live with PTSD and deal with it myself. A quieter, balanced, settled and controlled life is required with a stability carefully monitored.

This leads to a lifestyle, unusual for me, of wanting to be alone and being in the company of trusted friends and family. A reclusive existence that is alien to me and unfair on Dorothy.

I have to accept that the depth of the disorder in me is as permanent as they told 11 years ago and that is unlikely I will ever lose it. The Police Service are dealing with the situation of trauma better than ever, but have a long way to go where retired officers are concerned. After care is just as important as in service care but is sorely neglected.

Their main course of any action is pension related and what level of disability you have to accord with your pension benefit. Each year I have to go for an assessment to tell them that I am still the same nutcase that they told me I was ten years ago. There is no other communication between us officially, unofficially I do talk to member of staff in the Occupational Health Dept who counsels me from time to time, usually after I have sent her an email containing a complaint in gobble-de-gook.

I am sure that if I had known the symptoms of PTSD all those 25 years ago when I had the incidents and counselled at a very early stage and would now be in a far better position mentally, physically and financially.

With that awareness and recognition, The Police Service would be saving time, money and efficiency, and affected serving officers and their families would be able to live a normal life.

By recognising the symptoms early and gaining professional help and support this terrible disorder can be prevented or at least toned down to an acceptable, liveable level.

AWARENESS ESSENTIAL

Awareness of the condition is so important for the individual and the Service and it falls upon each, to take all steps necessary, to prepare themselves for the probability of this affecting them. Not to do so devastates lives, careers and devalues the Service that I so wanted to perform. I do not think I failed in my life's work but know that it was so tragically cut short at a time when I had so much still to offer.

In many ways I hope that this book goes some distance to counteract that and also helps the uninformed, what is the real meaning of post-traumatic stress disorder and how it affects the lives of those suffering it.

Writing this book has been elating, funny and brought back for me many happy memories of my life and the job that I so dearly loved. It has been upsetting and distressful sometimes throwing me backwards into tumult. The time has come when I want to put all my experiences behind me and push them deeper into my sub-conscious and hopefully away for good. Only time will tell?

Words will never be able to express how so thankful and grateful I am at having Dorothy by my side. I could not have coped or survived without her. PTSD not only destroyed our lives, it took away from us all hopes of having a normal life.

I am worried about Dorothy's health now and the affect that caring for me has had on her.

It has got to the stage where my mind is so blown that I only have short windows of common sense and some normality, so my daughters, Clare and Karen have had to take over a lot.

Without my family and friends I am sure that my situation would be more serious so in a way I am luckier than some other sufferers. They have been there when I needed them most.

I hope this book gives some help and understanding and prevents other lives from being destroyed.

I trust that anyone who reads this can take out of it what affects them most and deal with their lives accordingly to avoid the suffering that post traumatic stress disorder causes.

I WAS LUCKY

I was lucky, as without knowing it I had balanced my life and career in the Police Service, the "Snowdrops" and tiptoed through the PTSD problems that were festering inside me.

Without realising it my loving family and friends had given me the security and care when I needed it most. My passion for the Job and zest for life masked the extreme opposite times when I went into deep depression and then catapulted myself beyond the point of normality when I went off on some crusade, more often than not trying to achieve the impossible and pumped up to such a degree that blinded common sense.

If I had realised in the 1970's that the emotions of crying for no reason and the extremes of my lifestyle were the first signs of PTSD then I am sure my life would be far different now.

Nowadays experts from Occupational Health are hopeful that preventative counselling after incidents, and when the very first signs of PTSD appear, can stop it in its tracks.

It is 11 years since being diagnosed with PTSD and 30 years since suffering the first of the incidents that brought about the destruction of my life. Specialist psychiatrists tell me that my disorder is so firmly entrenched that it is permanent and will never go away and assess me as 80% disabled and unable to live a normal existence. To make matters even worse emotional trauma has brought about asthma that further exasperates my problems, particularly when I am trying to control my breathing. Doctors warn that the stress, strain and imbalance of body chemistry in me could cause more serious problems if it is not controlled.

With the continued help and support of my family and friends I get through the times when my mind disintegrates into a mire of confusion, shaking uncontrollably dipping and diving in and out of sensible consciousness and sobbing and crying with frustration and anger. Dorothy will cling onto me as my chest seizes up, my lungs fight for breath and my stomach does its' own thing as all my senses are obliterated and cloud over.

After a few days or sometimes several weeks I eventually recover and brilliant, lovely days of normality return when I can appreciate what I have, but I never know when the horrible will return.

Yes, I am lucky! I could be one of those unfortunate people who have used the final solution of suicide to rid themselves of the problem. At the worst times I can quite empathise with their reasoning.

Anyone involved in a trauma related incident could suffer, in the future, the way that I do. PTSD is not fussy whom it destroys! At the first signs professional, qualified help and advice must be sought to stave off permanent disability.

If this book prevents one more person from suffering PTSD – then my very effort and emotional overhaul was completely and utterly justified and worthwhile.

GLOSSARY OF TERMS

A

BH	-	Actual bodily harm
B & B	-	Bed and Breakfast
Bagman	-	Assistant to senior officer
Banter	-	Jovial conversation
Blue Serge	-	Uniform Cloth
Boob	-	Breasts
Booze	-	Alcohol
BTP	-	British Transport Police
Bubble and squeak	-	Fried mashed potato and cabbage
C & E	-	Customs and Excise
Cats Whiskers	-	Full of pride
CID	-	Criminal Investigation Department
Cock up	-	A mistaken action
Conchie	-	Conscientious Objector to War
DCI	-	Detective Chief Inspector

DCS	-	Detective Chief Superintendent
DI	-	Detective Inspector
Drill Pig	-	Sergeant in charge of Marching
Dripping	-	Fat from joint of meat
DS	-	Detective Sergeant
EEPBA	-	Ex-Essex Police Business Association
EPIC	-	Ex-Police in Industry and Commerce
FBI	-	Federal Bureau of Investigation
GB	-	Great Britain
GBH	-	Grievous bodily harm
Gliff	-	Incident suffered
GP	-	General Practitioner – Local Doctor
Guards	-	Army Regiment
IRA	-	Irish Republican Army
Jankers	-	Punishment fatigues
Judges Rules	-	Set procedures for dealing with accused persons
Knackered	-	Exhausted
Lodge	-	Freemasons meeting place
Loo	-	Toilet
MET	-	Metropolitan Police
MIPI	-	Member of the Institute of Professional Investigators
Mods	-	Fashion conscious youths
NARPO	-	National Association of Retired Police Officers

NCIS	-	National Criminal Intelligence Service
Nick him	-	Arrest him
Oxford bags	-	Baggy trousers
Panda Cars	-	Small police patrol car
PE	-	Physical Education
Pratt	-	Idiot
Probationer	-	Raw recruit police officer
PTSD	-	Post Traumatic Stress Disorder
RCS	-	Regional Crime Squad
Ringing Cars	-	Alter the appearance and identity
Rockers	-	Leather jacketed youths
SGT	-	Sergeant
Skinheads	-	Shaven headed youths
Sprats	-	Small fish
TK	-	Telephone Box
Tramp	-	Hobo – homeless person
Tripper	-	Holidaymaker
Truncheon	-	Wooden Stave or stick
UK	-	United Kingdom
Up the creek	-	Hopeless task
Wally	-	Pickled Cucumber
Wank	-	Masturbate
Weeble	-	Egg Shaped Toy Figure
WPC	-	Woman Police Constable

ABOUT THE AUTHOR

Born in Southend, England in 1947 he joined the Southend on Sea Constabulary in 1967.

He progressed from Police Constable to Detective in the elite undercover Regional Crime Squad.

With 12 commendations for bravery and excellent police work and an expert crime analyst he was promoted to Detective Inspector and appointed to the National Criminal Intelligence Service, the UK FBI.

During his career he suffered five serious assaults and in 1994, chronically disabled by Post Traumatic Stress Disorder, was forced into premature retirement.

Struggling with PTSD and financial destruction he attempted to carry out various types of work until a third mental breakdown totally disabled him in 2001.

Cared for by his wife and family Bob still lives in Southend.

Lightning Source UK Ltd.
Milton Keynes UK
171449UK00001B/185/A